Total
Cash
Management

A Company-Wide System for Forecasting, Managing, and Improving Cash Flow

Alfred M. King

McGraw-Hill, Inc.

New York   San Francisco   Washington, D.C.   Auckland   Bogotá
Caracas   Lisbon   London   Madrid   Mexico City   Milan
Montreal   New Delhi   San Juan   Singapore
Sydney   Tokyo   Toronto

10553837

Library of Congress Cataloging-in-Publication Data

King, Alfred M.
    Total cash management : a company-wide system for forecasting,
managing, and improving cash flow / Alfred M. King.
       p.   cm.
    Includes index.
    ISBN 0-07-034604-6
    1. Cash management. I. Title.
HG4028.C45K55   1994
658.15′244—dc20   93-49531
                                              CIP

Copyright © 1994 by Alfred M. King. All rights reserved. Printed in the
United States of America. Except as permitted under the United States
Copyright Act of 1976, no part of this publication may be reproduced or
distributed in any form or by any means, or stored in a data base or retrieval
system, without the prior written permission of the publisher.

1 2 3 4 5 6 7 8 9 0 DOC/DOC 9 0 9 8 7 6 5 4

ISBN 0-07-034604-6

*The sponsoring editor for this book was Caroline Carney, the editing
supervisor was Fred Dahl, and the production supervisor was Pamela
A. Pelton. It was set in Baskerville by Inkwell Publishing Services.*

Printed and bound by R. R. Donnelley & Sons Company.

This book is printed on recycled, acid-free paper containing a
minimum of 50 percent recycled de-inked fiber.

This publication is designed to provide accurate and authoritative
information in regard to the subject matter covered. It is sold with the
understanding that the publisher is not engaged in rendering legal,
accounting, or other professional service. If legal advice or other expert
assistance is required, the services of a competent professional person
should be sought.

    *—From the declaration of principles jointly adopted by a committee of the
American Bar Association and a committee of publishers*

To my wife,
Mary Jane,
thanks for holding my feet to the fire.
Without your push, this book
would never have been finished.

Contents

134439
0553837

Preface

Every decision made in business involves *cash*. Those companies facing a short-term "turnaround" situation inevitably focus 100 percent of management effort on cash management. Even more sensitive to the importance of cash are firms which are in bankruptcy. Financial officers of well-run and well-financed organizations implicitly understand that cash is a fact of business life. What is usually lacking in basically profitable firms—those not necessarily growing quickly—is an appropriate understanding by *non-financial* managers of the true importance of cash.

Growth in sales volume and profitability requires *cash*; often lots of cash, particularly in competitive environments. As we will see in this book, when two or more firms are fighting it out for growth and market share, the one with greater cash resources is bound to win. Winning *requires* cash. The good news is that winning also *provides* cash for subsequent growth.

Thus this book is founded on two key precepts:

1. Cash on hand, or access to cash, is required for every aspect of growth.
2. Every employee can affect the availability of cash through the application of simple rules on a day-to-day basis.

What is needed, but so often missing, is an *awareness* of the importance of cash by every employee. Most employees take it for granted that their paycheck will be delivered Friday morning, and that vendors will be paid on time after supplies or raw material have been ordered or delivered. Few employees worry about customers paying their bills for merchandise shipped last month or for services performed. "They" take care of such mundane details and, in this case, the "they" are the company's financial staff and accountants.

What is needed is Total Cash Management (TCM). Just as Total Quality Management (TQM) requires 100 percent involvement, so too does TCM. Decisions on granting credit to customers are often made by marketing, while manufacturing determines inventory levels. Both decisions affect cash. Investing in new product development is treated as a *period expense* for accounting purposes, but really represents a long-term cash commitment by a firm's engineering and research departments. Capital expenditures which will reduce operating expense, or provide capacity for new production also demand cash up front, with the benefits to be felt in the future.

It is safe to say that every company and every organization will benefit from the availability of cash in amounts sufficient to fund all reasonable growth plans. The question then becomes, how do we obtain that cash? There are basically only two sources of cash for a firm. The first is *profitable* sales to customers which are turned into cash when the customer pays. The second is access to cash from banks and other lenders, such as lessors and finance companies, with banks being the primary source for most firms. How to structure a company's operations so that banks are willing to extend a significant line of credit is an all-important aspect of Total Cash Management.

The first step in adopting a TCM approach to profitable growth is to instill what we call *cash sensitivity* in all managers and employees. Most readers have worked within budgets and implicitly understand that the availability of cash affects the ability of an organization to implement plans. What is less common is the corollary. Their own operating decisions, day in and day out, impact the amount and timing of both cash inflows and cash outflows. Relying on the financial and accounting staff to worry about cash simply is not enough.

Everyone must be involved. What this book recommends, and then shows how to implement, is a *systems* approach. The Total Cash Management system is applicable to large as well as small firms and to not-for-profit as well as for-profit organizations. Service companies, manufacturing companies, retailers, and wholesalers can all benefit. Owner-managed firms, true "small businesses," will receive particular help from this book since they are traditionally short of capital (i.e., cash).

In one sense Total Cash Management (TCM) is an outgrowth of Total Quality Management (TQM). Just as many U.S. businesses have successfully adopted TQM, with often startling results, so now companies must reach for the next plateau—profitable growth. But as the book shows, any kind of growth strategy requires access to *cash*. Cash is the lifeblood of every business. With it, all things are possible. Without cash, companies face Chapter 11 bankruptcy.

One of the primary lessons learned from the Quality movement is that all levels of management and employees *must* be involved. It does no good for a company to rely on inspectors at the end of the line to check each item. By that time, it is too late. We have certainly learned that quality can not be "inspected in" to a product or a process. The only way for an organization to achieve consistent levels of quality, much less to attain the ultimate goal of "continuous improvement," is for *everyone* to participate and believe in meeting customer needs.

Focusing on perceived customer satisfaction—one of the major definitions of quality—has accomplished all sorts of good things, such as shorter lead times, lower inventory levels, as well as reduced scrap and warranty expense. Finally, some firms achieved increased profits resulting from sales growth and increased market share.

However, not every firm that has attempted to adopt Total Quality Management as a company goal has succeeded. The business press is full of stories about organizations that have become discouraged and given up on TQM, leading employees to treat the experiment as another "flavor of the month" brought to you by management. Why TQM fails so often might be the subject of a very good book, but it is obvious that at least one key component of future growth is often lost sight of. The real purpose of TQM is increased volume and increased profits. But it is impossible to "save" your way to success, even by eliminating so-called nonvalue-added activities.

Total Cash Management, as a system, is simple in concept and easier to install. Most nonfinancial managers have a fear of numbers—a belief that accounting and finance is best left to specialists. While they may have taken an accounting course at one time, they now view accountants as "bean counters." Or they never studied accounting at all, hire an accountant to do their (personal) taxes, and just don't ever consider cash as a subject for polite discussion.

When we deal with cash we are not talking brain surgery or rocket science. We are really just speaking the language of business. The purpose of this book, then, is to help readers translate cash (the language of business), into the day-to-day vocabulary of every employee whose actions impact cash. If, as the author believes, *every* employee has an influence on cash, the book should attain wide readership.

The author has a background in Accounting and was a Controller and Chief Financial Officer of both private and publicly held firms. But this book is written primarily for *Operating Managers*, not accountants. In fact, there are a number of accounting and financial reporting conventions that positively obscure the role of cash.

A major thesis of the book is that, given a choice between maximizing reported income (as accountants calculate it) and maximizing cash flows, the choice should always be for the latter. Yet most company performance measurement systems and bonus calculations focus on reported income, not cash flow. This is why privately held firms often have a big advantage over publicly traded companies. The successful owner of his own company by definition invariably understands cash, or the business would not have succeeded. An employee of a publicly traded conglomerate, however, hardly ever thinks about cash, since "someone else" always seems to pay the bills.

Many executives, particularly from large firms which have had to downsize, think they can start a new career by running their own business. The one aspect of running a business they lack, no matter how good they are at selling, or manufacturing, or engineering, is to understand and control cash. Accounting conventions say that a dollar spent on a desk is entirely different (because it is capitalized) from a dollar spent on advertising or salaries (because these are charged to expense). Readers of this book will learn the fallacy of trying to distinguish between *capital* and *expense*. The truth is a dollar is a dollar, and when you write a check it makes no difference to what account your accountant charges it.

Those same executives who want to start their own business are often surprised to find that their friendly local bank is not at all eager to lend money to help fund the new venture. Just what do banks want and what does it take to obtain a line of credit? Surprisingly, particularly to those who may have been turned down for a loan, banks positively want to lend money to customers because that is how they make a profit. What they do not want is to be the lender of last resort. Calling up a bank on Wednesday to borrow money to meet Friday's payroll is *not* the way to get the banker on your side. Making your banker part of the team is a critical element of Total Cash Management and some constructive ideas are presented here.

Finally, the contents of this book are presented exclusively from the perspective of the user. Practice is emphasized over theory. Since every business decision affects cash, every responsible manager should see what he or she can and should be doing to participate in Total Cash Management. Every company, every executive has to make a choice. Manage your cash or it will manage you. Companies which adopt TCM as a goal and actively pursue its objectives, will be the winners in the run up to the Millennium, the year 2000.

A phrase popularly attributed to Donald Trump is that "cash is king." In fact, that was the tentative title of the book until Total Cash Management was adopted. Regardless of the title, cash *is* king, and the only way to get enough of it is to adopt the principles of Total Cash Management.

Good luck in applying those principles.

Alfred M. King

1

Total Cash Management Will Increase Profits!

IBM changed its normally ultraconservative
accounting policies so that it could treat some
of its new leases as sales, counting all the
revenue and profit up front rather than a bit
at a time as the money actually came in.

PAUL CARROLL
Big Blues: The Unmaking of IBM [p. 59]

What Is Total Cash Management?

Cash is the lifeblood of every organization. Without cash you cease functioning. An overall coordinated program—(1) to maximize the availability of cash and (2) to make sure that available cash is used optimally—will give any organization a strong competitive advantage. *Total Cash Management* (TCM) represents an extension of the concepts of Total Quality Management (TQM). Whether managers are aware of it or not, *every* decision they make affects cash. Every decision made by anyone in a company affects cash. Any time you decide to buy goods or services, you are committing to cash outflows. Every employee on the payroll must be paid in cash. Every sale to a customer, as well as a decision to advertise to that customer, involves cash. The long-term

1

test for the success of *any* organization is its ability to have a positive cash flow. Cash receipts *must* exceed cash disbursements.

A company should strive to develop Total Cash Management *before* any of its competitors. After all, Deming and Juran were from the United States, but they were heeded only in Japan for many years. We had the opportunity and blew it. Now we have a second chance. If we can provide optimum cash management, or what we refer to as *TCM,* American firms will dramatically improve their own productivity.

Today the total importance of cash is truly recognized—by *every* employee—in only one environment. When a company is near death, when the "turnaround" specialists are called in to revive the organization, cash suddenly becomes King. Every single decision is measured by its impact on cash. That approach to management makes sense because the life or death of the company (or any nonprofit organization for that matter) truly rides on the ability of the turnaround specialist to help the organization achieve a positive cash flow. Forget about accounting reports, forget about net income, forget about the distinction between an asset (inventory) and an expense (payroll).

Cash isn't everything, it is the *only* thing, to paraphrase the late great Vince Lombardi, the famous Green Bay Packers coach. Why wait until a company is staring Chapter 11 in the face? Just as Mr. Lombardi focused on the basics of blocking and tackling, day in and day out, so *should* all managers focus on the basics of managing cash, day in and day out.

What most managers miss is the fact that each and every decision they make directly affects cash flow. *Most* profitable firms run on the basis that, as long as something was in the budget, it's OK to do it. As long as the company (or my division, or my plant, or my product line) is "profitable," cash is not a problem. Someone up there in "corporate" will pay the bills. They always have; so why worry about cash.

Total Quality Management, or TQM as it is often referred to, has truly become part of American business culture. Unlike many other new "insights" that became popular for a while, were tried, and then faded fast, Quality has become a way of life for most successful organizations. The focus on customers, an understanding that there is always room for improvement, the knowledge that most business *processes* involve managers and workers from several functional disciplines have all become ingrained. It is unfortunate that it took a "near-death" experience for the U.S. economy to change the way we do business and adopt Quality. However, we seem to have learned from the Japanese, and then built on their experience. So, if the ultimate success of our economy depends on meeting them and then beating them on Quality, we will succeed.

Two key aspects of Quality carry over to Total Cash Management.

First, we have learned from the gurus of Quality (Deming, Juran, and Crosby) that every department and every individual has a role to play if the term *total* is to be applied to an organization's products and services. It is not up to an Inspection Department to provide quality assurance as items flow from the assembly line to outside customers. In fact, in the ideal TQM environment, there would be no Quality or Inspection Department because all employees are focusing on improving the quality of their operations, no matter where within the organization they are located. In short, *everyone* is involved in Quality with a capital *Q and* with a small *q*. We will see that, for cash, the same holds true. *Everyone* is involved.

The second lesson to be taken from the Quality movement is that almost every improvement involves more than one functional discipline. Quality teams are important *within* a department, but they are even more important *between* departments. Quality teaches that every work unit has both suppliers and customers. To improve the output for *customers* may well require changes not only in the way *we* do things, but in the way our *supplier* (whether internal or external) does things for us. Since suppliers are usually in another department and have their own agenda, any process improvement invariably requires cooperation, along with an understanding of the *tradeoffs* necessary to provide for the ultimate customer, the person or organization that pays us cash for our output. In this respect, cash is similar to Quality: We are dealing with suppliers and customers, inflows and outflows of cash.

But there is one big distinction. *Internal* customers and internal suppliers do not involve cash flows. The budget statements may contain allocations "charging" your department for its use of EDP or chargebacks for telephone service. But internal charges from an internal supplier are always one step removed from where the cash transaction took place.

The trouble with using the term *customer* in two ways, both for the outside person who really pays us cash and for the internal user, is that it is too easy to get them confused. When one word has two meanings, difficulties in communication are bound to surface. In the final analysis, *whoever pays us cash is our only real customer. Whoever we pay cash out to is our only real supplier.*

In terms of paying vendor invoices, a typical organization might have the Purchasing Department send the approved invoice to the Accounts Payable Department, who would enter the information in the computer so that Data Processing can issue a check. Accounts Payable in this process is the "customer" of the Purchasing Department, and Data Processing is the "customer" of Accounts Payable, and so forth. A mistake or slowdown in Purchasing can cause rework in Data Processing. The concept of supplier and customer makes sense for performance measurement and for identifying opportunities for quality improvement. But it confuses the issue when we deal with cash.

Using the term *customer* to refer to *internal* users is detrimental because it takes attention away from cash. If cash is the lifeblood of an organization, then bankruptcy is simply a lack of blood. Any organization that does not have cash to pay its bills, and cannot get any more, is out of business.

Where does cash come from? After the initial capital infusion, and the availability of borrowing which is always limited, cash can come from only one source. Customers who pay their bills, who are paying us for the goods and services we provide, are the real source of cash. You cannot—and do not—transfer cash *within* an organization.

Most employees never stop to think where they get their paycheck. It just shows up every Friday; they cash it and then enjoy the weekend. This can go on as long as the inflow of cash exceeds the outflow. Stop the inflow, however, and suddenly everyone's attention becomes focused. Ford has made a permanent addition to the U.S. business vocabulary with "Quality is Job 1." We would maintain that "*Cash* is Job 1."

The list of firms that have been reorganized in the bankruptcy courts is lengthy, and in almost every case they went into Chapter 11 because of a shortage of cash. Customers were paying less than employees and suppliers were taking out. In addition to those firms who actually filed for bankruptcy, a very large number of companies have gone through "restructuring" and "downsizing," to use just two of the popular euphemisms. Without exception, every time there is such a downsizing, either there is a negative cash flow or a well justified fear that negative cash projections will be realized unless changes are made.

Look at Ford. This giant instituted its new Quality policy only after experiencing extraordinary cash losses because of reduced sales (the reduction in sales perhaps attributable to customer perceptions about the quality of previous Ford cars). Change was essential. Ford chose to regain a positive cash flow through increased sales; their only problem was that customers did not want to buy the existing product, which had to be improved to be salable. Ford's emphasis on quality was logical, and it worked, but the real *motivation* was the need to turn around cash.

No organization can exist for long with a negative cash flow, with but one exception. If you can print your own cash, you can keep on going as long as people are willing to accept your paper. The U.S. government has run deficits just about forever, because it has a total monopoly on printing money, and it will undoubtedly continue for quite a while. The rest of us—state and local governments, nonprofit organizations, or for-profit businesses must all have positive cash flows or we die. It is that simple.

Unfortunately, in most organizations today very few individuals are concerned with, or even alert to, cash flows. As long as creditors are paid and the salary payroll met, no one thinks about cash. Emphasis in business is almost always placed on *income* or *profits,* never on cash.

It is true that in the very long run *cash flow* and *profits* tend to follow each other. A very profitable company almost always will have good cash flow. However, companies that are experiencing the opposite phenomenon (running at a loss) can do so for quite some time before they run out of cash. It is very easy for a firm to show modest profits in its P&L statements to shareholders and creditors, and yet be financially strapped.

Accounting is thought of by most business people as a rather exact science, heavily mathematical in nature. The fact that even billion-dollar firms show financial statements to the penny misleads the public into thinking that every one of those tens of billions of pennies has been accounted for. A recent report by the General Accounting Office (GAO), Congress' audit arm, is instructive. Reviewing the financial reports of the U.S. Customs Service, GAO reported:

> The Customs Forfeiture Fund's fiscal year 1991 financial statements showed that the Fund had $6.4 million more in cash than what was recorded in the Fund's accounting records and that Customs could not determine the reasons for this difference.... Customs had arbitrarily added a $10.6 million item, labeled as a "miscellaneous net increase to cash," in order to balance its statement of cash flows and Customs could not explain what the amount represented.... These unexplained amounts could have been due to incorrect entries in the accounting records, misappropriation of funds, theft, or a combination of these factors. [GAO/AFMD-93-55, pp. 2, 4]

To put this in perspective, the Customs fund's net cash provided by operating activities was $70 million and total revenues were only $238 million. So a $17 million discrepancy is "material" by any standard. The government, with all its resources, could not keep its books, in this department, accurate to the nearest $17 million. This Customs fund represents approximately 1/5000th of the total U.S. budget. It would be totally unfair to extrapolate and say that the government's cash position is out of balance by $75 billion. Or would it be? The truth is, we don't know.

What is true for the federal government is equally true for the private sector. Neither General Motors nor AT&T nor any other multibillion-dollar organization can account for every penny, every dollar, or even every million dollars. There are a tremendous number of estimates in any set of financial statements.

Profit, which is a residual figure (left after subtracting all expenses from all revenues), is subject to wide variation, depending on who is doing the accounting. Most accountants would feel they were doing well if they got the total revenues accurate within 1 percent, while a 2-percent range on total expenses would get most accountants a passing grade. But this means there could be up to a 3-percent range in profits. Since most companies have net income of 3 percent or 4 percent of revenues, a company's "true" income could be doubled or erased depending on who was preparing the statements. The Securities and Exchange Commission *should* require a warning on *all* financial statements:

> Warning: The Securities and Exchange Commission has determined that financial statements are not exact. Overreliance on the accuracy of these statements may be injurious to your financial well-being.

If financial statements and the reported profit are potentially inaccurate—and they are—we *can* still rely on one anchor. It is hard to argue with cash. Cash is easy to measure. Just look at your bank balance. Some people would add short-term marketable securities, which can be sold immediately, to cash in the bank. Others would subtract any current bank borrowing to arrive at a *net* cash position. In reality, cash is more than today's bank balance. It also consists of the cash you have *available* from borrowing. For purposes of measuring progress over time, a broader definition is needed—that is, cash in bank, plus marketable securities, *plus available lines of credit* minus current short-term bank borrowing.

For purposes of knowing whether enough cash resources are available to meet next week's payroll or to keep current with important suppliers, the amount of current borrowing is less important, and the amount of unused available borrowing power is more important.

The major point of this book is this:

> Sales can *always* be expanded and operating costs can *always* be reduced by the proper investment of cash. Most firms have far more profit opportunities (sales minus operating costs) than they have cash; so wise choices are important. Each manager and each employee affects cash with every decision. Total Cash Management, therefore, involves the efforts of *everyone* in an organization to use cash, a scarce and valuable resource, in the most profitable way. Because future needs are always going to be uncertain, Total Cash Management also requires financial flexibility, the availability of cash reserves to take advantage of unexpected opportunities.

Benefits of TCM

Total Cash Management, like TQM, involves everyone. In an ideal world every employee would think about the cash consequences of his or her actions. A sensitivity can be developed that hiring and purchasing decisions, that new product and capital expenditure decisions, and that advertising and marketing decisions must all be tested against the measure of available and future cash resources.

It is ironic that very sophisticated techniques have been developed over the last 40 years for estimating and analyzing the cash flow consequences of investments in capital assets. Internal controls are set up to prevent managers from making unauthorized capital expenditures of even $5000. Yet if a sales manager hires an additional clerk to speed up the processing of sales orders, justified on customer quality grounds, no thought is given to the $20,000 annual cost.

The basic assumption is that somehow the $5000 spent on a personal computer (PC) is different from hiring the clerk. *Wrong!* Cash is cash. The clerk's salary and benefits will have cost $5000 at the end of three months, and will have been charged to expense on the P&L, while the $5000 spent on the PC will have been capitalized and will show on the balance sheet as an asset. Does the bank account look any different at the end of three months whether the payment was to Computerland or to Ms. Jones? No, in either case there is $5000 less.

If we develop a new customer relationship by granting 90 days to pay for the initial merchandise order, instead of our normal 30-day terms, at best we will have to wait an additional 60 days to get our cash. This is not to say it is a bad decision. It may be a very sound one. But there is a cost to the company in having to wait 90 days to be paid. In fact, there is a cost of having to wait 30 days, but 30-day terms are so ingrained that we seldom stop to think about it. Suppose we could get all our customers to pay their bills 10 days earlier, on average, than they do now. What would that be worth? Whether we should try to accomplish this or not is susceptible to analysis, and an emphasis on Total Cash Management would focus attention on this issue.

The two scarcest resources in any organization are cash and management time. Good management, with sufficient cash resources, can accomplish almost anything. The federal government has unlimited cash, but not necessarily good management. Many companies have the management but not the cash. The purpose of TCM is to put the maximum available cash in the hands of management, and to provide guidelines in evaluating the inevitable tradeoffs.

The Conflict Between Cash and Profits

Most companies manage to maximize profits, or at least report a satisfactory level of profits. You cannot pay people with profits, only with cash. While *profits* is not a dirty word and is in fact a very desirable objective, profits are not the same as cash. Profits are a construct of accountants, a theoretical measure based on artificial rules and regulations. For example, a company in the United Kingdom will report very different profits from an identical company in the United States, even disregarding such "minor" details as taxes and exchange rates. If a U.K. firm buys a U.S. company for cash, at a price in excess of the value of the tangible assets, the resulting excess is called "goodwill" and is written off at once against net worth. If a U.S. firm pays the same amount for the same acquiree, the excess amount of goodwill must go on the balance sheet as an asset and be written off as a charge to profit over the next 40 years. Given identical cash flows, the U.K. firm will have higher reported profits, but essentially the same cash flow. If a German firm has a good year, it can reduce reported profits by setting up hidden reserves, which will smooth out changes in reported profit in subsequent years. A U.S. firm, on the contrary, is at least theoretically precluded from smoothing out profit and has to report to its shareholders far greater fluctuations due to short-term economic conditions. Again, the cash flows will be the same, but what shareholders and creditors see may be markedly different.

Sometimes companies face a choice between reported earnings and cash flows. The action they take—how they structure a transaction—will raise profits and lower cash, or vice versa. For example a provision in the income tax law allows companies to pay less taxes if they calculate their inventory values on a last-in/first-out (LIFO) basis, but the law also states that companies must report the same way to their shareholders and creditors. Without going into the details, LIFO reduces reported income in a period of rising prices, but also reduces taxes, which increases cash flow. Some companies have not been willing to take the "hit" to earnings to obtain the cash flow benefits of LIFO. Other examples could be cited, but the principle is important.

For some companies, usually publicly held, maximizing reported earnings is paramount, while many private firms do everything to maximize cash flow and do not worry about reported earnings. A debate on the efficient market has been carried on for years, and people today either believe in it or they don't. Those who believe in the efficient market say, in essence, that reported earnings, irrespective of accounting adjustments, are less important to investors than knowing what is going to happen to cash flows in the future. Disbelievers focus more of their attention on reported earnings, assuming that cash flows in the future are directly related to current earnings.

The point is that, for significant periods of time, cash flows and earnings can diverge. Because investors sometimes appear to focus more on earnings than on cash flows, many management groups put greater weight on reported earnings than cash flow. This is a mistake.

Growth in a company can only come from cash or from the availability of cash. One could argue that more cash will be available from creditors if earnings are higher, but most lending officers, whether at banks, insurance companies, finance companies, or lessors, focus like a laser beam on cash flow, because they know that is the only way they will ever be paid back. If professional lenders use this approach, it behooves management to adopt the same strategy. In the long run is it better to please the stock market or to please the credit market? Since most firms only rarely seek funds in the equity market and most still rely on credit from one source or another for their growth plans, the answer is pretty straightforward. *Cash is King.*

Marketing Looks at TCM

The phrase *Cash is King* is not only catchy; it is also undoubtedly true. How, then, should we honor those responsible for bringing in the cash? Without doubt the salespeople of any organization deserve recognition in any book on cash. Without sales there would be no cash inflow. You could have the best budgeting system in the world and your finance staff would feel proud of themselves. A world-class Research and Development operation could generate brand new products at a terrific pace. State-of-the-art production facilities could draw in admirers from around the world. And so on. But if the customers don't buy, and then pay for, your products, everything else is useless.

Now some skeptic is going to say, "Yes, but if we couldn't *make* the product at an acceptable cost, marketing would have nothing to sell, therefore production is most important." This, of course, demonstrates the seamless nature of modern industry. It is true that all functional areas are totally interdependent. Nevertheless marketing and sales have to be considered "first among equals" just because they bring in the cash.

As a broad generalization, sales representatives—those who get customers to say yes and bring back signed orders—are better paid than others. Sometimes the author has heard highly qualified managers in other areas complain that people in sales are overpaid. The response always has been, "OK, if you think sales reps earn too much [the complainers are really saying they are underpaid where they are] why don't *you* go do their job and then you will be paid as well as they are." The point is that pay and responsibility tend to go together, and most organizations recognize the importance of sales and the marketing function through their compensation systems.

In terms of Total Cash Management, however, the importance of marketing is often lost to sight. Most businesspeople think of cash management as the Treasurer's responsibility, as a series of techniques designed to conserve cash, to prevent existing cash resources from being spent. (A corollary is the attempt to squeeze out the last bit of interest income by investing surplus cash.)

Total Cash Management is far broader. It emphasizes the importance of *maximizing* cash resources, not just spending existing cash efficiently. The basic premise is that cash provides a competitive advantage. The company with the most cash can outspend competitors, increase market share, *and* simultaneously reduce operating expenses. TCM therefore affects marketing in two ways. It puts a burden on them to increase sales, which turns into cash when customers pay their bills, and to *use* cash effectively to increase sales volume.

In Chap. 3 we discuss how cash resources can be utilized to increase sales. Credit terms can be a powerful competitive weapon because prospective buyers know that a longer period to pay for purchases is equivalent to a lower price. Yet granting longer terms is not as likely to draw a competitive response as a straighforward price cut. In a different vein, selling to customers whose credit rating is marginal may be a very effective way of increasing sales volume and profits. This requires an understanding of the cash costs of production compared to cash receipts, after allowing for possible credit losses.

The whole area of collections on outstanding receivables is covered in Chap. 7. Cash can be used to increase sales, but this does not mean giving away the product. Once sales terms have been agreed upon by both parties, it is totally reasonable to expect that customers pay on time. There is no difference between giving 30-day terms, and actually being paid in 45 days, and allowing 45-day terms and insisting that customers then pay in 45 days. What is not acceptable is granting 45-day terms and then passively accepting actual payments in 55 or 60 days.

Production Looks at TCM

There are two areas in which production managers should consider cash as an asset capable of making them perform better. Every factory supervisor has at least a dozen ideas for improving productivity. Some may involve simple rearrangement of the work flow or acquisition of inexpensive material handling equipment. More often than not, improvements to reduce costs, both direct labor and overhead such as set-up, require the acquisition of capital assets. As we have seen, it makes little difference, with regard to cash flows, whether the accountants make us capitalize a purchase or charge it to expense. Given how companies do their budgeting, with greater controls on capital assets than on expense, it may actually be easier to buy needed equipment if it can be charged to expense.

The point is that the new assets and equipment will help managers perform existing operations at lower cost and, perhaps more importantly, start to produce new products. Sometimes investments will be made to produce internally that which is now purchased from outside vendors. In other cases brand new products will be made available for sale by the Marketing Department.

There are twin pressures on every production executive: cost and volume. First, competitors have adopted the concept of *continuous improvement*, which means their production and operating costs are being constantly reduced. You must spend cash today to remain cost competitive. Second, high-volume products require increased capacity, and new products demand capabilities probably not present.

In every manufacturing operation there are far more good ideas on how to spend cash, if it were available, than there is cash being devoted to lowering costs and raising capacity. In most cases this is because the future cash flow benefits of today's potential investments have not been properly identified. Too many firms have unrealistically high capital budget hurdle rates, which then restrict managers from doing what is really in the firm's best interest.

Only occasionally is the real constraint recognized. Cash is *not* the limiting factor. The availability of *management time* is, in reality, the true constraint on expenditures for productivity and capacity. Too often the critical resource of management time is spent in wasted efforts to convince others, such as financial analysts who know little about the in's and out's of manufacturing, that cash should be made available. When that time is spent internally, rather than in implementing sound plans, you can identify a company that is running well below its potential.

The whole subject of inventories—as well as the cash investment tied up in raw materials, work in progress and finished goods—is usually misunderstood. It is true that cash is tied up in inventories and that a reduction in inventories will free up cash and make it available for other purposes. What is often lost is that inventories perform a valuable function. Put directly, in most cases business could not function without inventories. Operating expenses would rise and customer service levels be degraded, if firms tried to eliminate inventories.

Instead of carrying zero raw steel inventory, which could be done by buying it from a warehouse every day, it is far more economical to order once a month from a mill. The cost of carrying, on average, two weeks' worth of raw steel inventory is less than the premium paid to a warehouse. Instead of setting up and tearing down machines every day, it is less expensive to have longer runs and carry some work in process. Finished goods inventories could be kept in a centralized warehouse for customer shipments, and quick deliveries made by Federal Express. Alternatively many companies have found it more economical to have decentralized warehouse locations, which incurs excess finished goods inventory levels, but speeds up most deliveries and reduces freight and express charges.

Inventory levels, requiring cash investment, must be made in the context of a firm's overall business strategy. Inventories represent a necessary cost of doing business. Arbitrary edicts to "cut inventories 10 percent in the next four months" usually are counterproductive. Any benefits to cash are likely to be more than offset by the impact of higher operating expenses and reduced customer service. By the way, have you ever wondered why edicts like that are always, "cut by *10 percent*"? You never hear of a demand for a 9-percent or an 11-percent cut! This shows that the usual thought process is arbitrary and fails to focus on the realities of cash.

Engineering, Research, and Development Look at TCM

Part of what is usually classified in financial statements as overhead, or Selling, General, and Administrative (SG&A) expense, is R&D and engineering. These are usually treated differently from production and marketing. Sales quotas on the one hand and production goals on the other make it easy to quantify these important areas. It is much harder for, say, a pharmaceutical firm to specify in advance the exact output of their new product development function. Management knows what it *wants* to accomplish, but more often than not successful accomplishment of those goals is outside the control of the firm, such as in the hands of the Food and Drug Administration.

It is easy to measure the *inputs* to R&D, the discretionary levels of cash resources to be devoted in this or next year's budget. It is relatively easy to measure the benefits of the desired *outputs*. Unfortunately all too often there is absolutely no connection between the level of input and the usable output. To borrow a term from the petroleum industry, many dry holes in R&D have to be drilled before oil is struck. Nobody knowingly starts a research project that will fail, just as nobody knowingly drills a dry hole. It's just that the odds for success are always less than 100 percent. When you are dealing with risky outcomes, but where one winner can easily pay for 10, 20, or even 30 losers, ordinary financial analysis is not at its best. When creativity is more important than brute force, cash is necessary but not sufficient.

As a generalization, there is significant positive correlation between total R&D efforts and beneficial output. So the more cash resources you devote to the area, the greater are your overall chances for success. Certainly the opposite is true. Spend nothing on new product development, and few manufacturing or service firms will survive for long. Only companies with a positive cash flow can afford to support investments today that we know will not pay off until some time in the future, if at all. Because of the lack of *direct* connection between cash resources invested in R&D and possible outputs, we will not cover R&D in this book. Without positive cash flow, however, which is created by TCM, R&D would be impossible. Any engineering and R&D managers reading this book should cheer on their colleagues so that cash resources *will* be available.

Human Resources Looks at TCM

If the Human Resources (HR) Department, what some used to call Personnel, has overall responsibility for the staff of an organization, employee morale level, and employee productivity, then Total Cash Management is vital. Without cash you cannot pay employees. As will be discussed, *every* manager must assume some responsibility. Ordinarily a Human Resources Department would not be concerned about cash, assuming that someone else, perhaps Finance, worries about it.

There can be no bigger boost to morale than to see a company expanding, with employment growing. Conversely, downsizing (or, to use the latest euphemism, rightsizing) probably is the greatest single detriment to morale. Whether morale, *per se*, correlates all that closely with productivity is an open question. In fact you could make an argument that, when employees see others being laid off, they may work harder and at a minimum will give the *appearance* of working harder.

No writer on management issues, to the best of our knowledge, has ever asserted that poor morale is desirable. Common sense suggests that a financially healthy, growing organization is going to be a better place to work. Employees should be able to see that what they are doing as individuals is contributing to meeting the goals of the organization. Thus if Total Cash Management is adopted as a management strategy, and reinforced by HR in employee communications, the author suggests that employees will respond favorably. A "virtuous cycle" can be set up, as good behavior leads to positive cash flow, and positive cash flow leads to growth.

Thus, in our opinion, while a Human Resources Department cannot take the lead in any TCM approach, it should play a strongly supportive role. However, HR responsibilities and cash flow intersect in one area, and that is in the actual processing of payrolls and periodic payments to employees. Should employees be paid by check or by deposit directly to their checking account? The cash consequences (discussed in detail in Chap. 5) are surprisingly large.

The major reason that HR managers should be familiar with the contents of this book is that almost every cash decision affects more than one department. Total Cash Management effectively involves tradeoffs; for example, cutting finished goods inventory, the responsibility of a Materials Department manager, may impact sales. Until all levels of management in all functional areas really understand the benefits of TCM, and can look at the "Big Picture," avoiding "suboptimization," there are bound to be conflicts. In the final analysis, decisions involving specific tradeoffs will have to be made by line managers at a high level. But HR can and should understand that going to a TCM environment, while beneficial overall to the organization, may pit one functional department against the other in the short run. Knowing that these conflicts may occur will then provide HR with the opportunity to provide the necessary training in advance.

Finance and Accounting Look at TCM

Despite his background in financial management and his training as an accountant, the author has carefully focused on *all* functional areas, not just on finance and accounting. The first thought anyone has, when dealing with cash, is that it is the responsibility of the "numbers guys." In the same way, when the Total Quality Movement was getting started, most managers really thought it was the responsibility of the Inspection Department or Quality Department, if that function had recently been given a new name.

One factor distinguishes organizations that have adopted Total Cash Management from the way most companies are run. The role of the accountant is changed. The most common perception of Controllers is that they are the ones who go out on the battlefield after the fighting has stopped and shoot the wounded. They say no to most proposals. They look backwards. And so on. In a company that has adopted TCM, the financial managers are the ones who prevent the fights from starting. They say yes to most proposals. They look forward. They point out the *benefits* of additional investments.

TCM is practiced in a number of organizations, although probably not under that name. There are a number of organizations where financial managers are an active part of the management team. It is interesting that in many firms Controllers ask their peers in *other* concerns, "How do I get to play on the management team like you do? I know I have a lot to offer, but ..." Why don't they ask their compatriots in their own firm? The author confesses he does not have the answer. But, as an old financial type, he recognizes that, for TCM to work, the financial staff has to act as coaches, not as auditors.

Too many accountants were originally trained as auditors. And every auditor's secret dream is to find the "Big One," the big embezzlement or the big fraud. To do this, he or she must always look for things that have gone wrong, never to look for what is working. A good sales manager will take the tips and techniques from the best salesperson and try to instill them in others. An auditor will try to find what is wrong with one sales rep's expense account, and then go look for the same fault in every other representative's time and expense reports!

With behavior like this, is it any wonder that Sales, Marketing, Production, or HR managers don't look for opportunities to have lunch with their

Finance colleagues? Would you like to eat lunch two or three times a week with the IRS auditor reviewing your tax returns?

This is not the place to tell finance and accounting executives how to manage their careers. Communication, however, is always a two-way street. Someone has to take the initiative to open the dialog, so it might as well be you. If you really see how the availability of additional cash resources could help you do your job for the company better, why not ask two questions.

1. If I make this investment in my area (or in someone else's for that matter) will the company really be better off, as I suspect it will?

2. Where can we get the funds to make this investment?

It is surprising how often just asking for help, in this case from a finance manager, will get him or her involved in helping you solve your problems. In most organizations, other than the CEO and the COO, Finance managers are usually the only members of management who have access to the Big Picture. The process of putting together a budget and periodic forecasts, as well as responding to financial analysts, bankers, and auditors, means they have to have a pretty thorough understanding of the business and of the dynamic interactions among various parts of the organization. At lower levels, a plant or a division, the local Controller is used to being asked why or what.

More often than not, financial managers answer questions defensively, possibly with the attitude that they are going to be blamed if things go wrong. *Every* financial statistic can be made to look bad, although the converse is not always true. Any level of profit, for example, no matter how high, is going to be less than last year, or less than budget, or less than forecast, or less than expected given the increase in sales volume. Even if expenses are less than forecast, someone can ask, "Why didn't you spend the money and get the results that that investment would have made?" More examples could be given but the point is clear. Financial reporting, other than to shareholders where the bright side is always stressed, tends to be negative. Top management seemingly always wants more.

Because of the flexibility in accounting, for a brief period accountants *can* make a bad period *look* good, even if it isn't. With a management that wants more, accountants always like to keep something in reserve for when it is "really" needed. This kind of gamesmanship ultimately breeds cynicism and a negative attitude, both on the part of the accountants and on the users of statements.

This brief analysis of the financial reporting process is not a complaint, merely an attempt to explain why too many Controllers are *not* part of the management team. All too often they are perceived as an outside score-keeper. No baseball manager has ever gone to the scorekeeper to ask for advice on strategy or to handle an important player trade.

Who should, or even can, take the initiative in changing this state of affairs is hard to say. Few things are so ingrained as company culture. Changing a culture is difficult, except in times of crisis. Since the thesis of this book is that you do not have to be in a crisis situation to install Total Cash Management, it is obviously going to be harder if the financial staff is on the outside, looking in.

Who Is Responsible for TCM?

There is a significant difference between responsibility and who ends up shouldering the day-to-day work load. Very few things get done without top management approval. Usually it takes top management initiative before any kind of significant change takes place.

The number of things that a CEO is supposed to do is amazing. Almost every writer on a specialized topic admits that, without a CEO's involvement, progress will be slow or nonexistent. This is true whether it is gaining productivity improvements from computers, encouraging employee involvement in Quality, or minimizing legal expenses, just to pick three disparate elements. Everyone wants the boss's attention. So when we say that top management must be involved in the installation of Total Cash Management, it may sound like that familiar old song once again.

If cash is truly a scarce but valuable resource, and ways can be found to improve its productivity, there will *not* have to be much push from the top down. Individual employees and managers are generally motivated to take actions that they think are in the organization's best interest. As already mentioned and as discussed throughout the book, Total Cash Management involves tradeoffs. It involves being willing to show an accounting "loss" to increase cash, a willingness to spend money today to obtain benefits tomorrow. In short, the major change really is the *focus* on cash as the primary criterion in making decisions.

If a company is truly going to be run to maximize cash inflows and to determine optimum levels of cash expenditures, then there has to be a single message that *cash*, not accounting income, is the basis of measuring performance. Today's *internal* accounting and reporting ties into *external* reporting for shareholders and creditors. For the last 60 years American business has been judged by outsiders on the basis of reported income. Generally Accepted Accounting Principles (GAAP) have been developed and refined, some people think, to excess. All this effort has been devoted to relating revenues and expenditures on an accrual basis. Accrual accounting (that is, disregarding the timing of specific cash receipts and disbursements) attempts to calculate income based on when the economic transaction took place. There is an implicit assumption in GAAP that the cash flows will take care of themselves and that, while the cash may come in sooner or later, in the long run income and cash will equalize. (The great economist, Lord Keynes, in discussing some aspect of economics that relied on the long run for things to work out, is reported to have responded, "Yes, but in the long run we are all dead.")

Cash flows are not incompatible with GAAP income. In the long run whether an item is capitalized as an asset or expensed immediately makes *no* difference in cumulative income. That long run, however, can stretch for 15 or 20 years, depending on the assumptions made by the accountants.

> A prospective purchaser was performing "due diligence" on a small appraisal company prior to an acquisition. Since appraisal companies, as one of their services, help clients develop and maintain fixed asset records a question was asked, "Could we see *your* firm's own fixed asset records."
>
> One of the principles of fixed asset records is not to try and keep track of assets with minimal value. Many companies today have a policy of charging off to expense any item costing less than $500 or even $1000 or more, simply to reduce the expense and effort of maintaining records that provide little in the way of property control. Don't spend $100 to keep track of $25 is the theory.
>
> Imagine the surprise when the appraisal company's own records showed assets such as $3 ashtrays and $8 wastebaskets. Asked why these items were capitalized and maintained on the books, the bookkeeper somewhat sheepishly responded, "Well, you see, the employees each have a few shares of stock and the company determines the dividends per share based on the reported income. By capitalizing the ashtrays, wastebaskets, etc. we raised the company's income, and therefore increased our dividends."

This vignette, which is true, has several lessons. First, capitalizing items to increase reported income only works for a short period. Pretty soon the annual depreciation charges on what was set up as an asset in previous years starts to equal the amount of new purchases, particularly in the area of office furniture and fixtures.

The second lesson is that even professionals, in this case an appraisal company dealing with its own assets, do not do everything properly. Of course, examples of lawyers acting as their own attorney or physicians who don't treat curable symptoms could also be brought forward. The point is that management has to make things happen. In the absence of positive direction and supervision, individuals will sometimes do things that appear to them to be in their own interest, even if the greater good would demand something else. This is sometimes referred to as *suboptimization*. Total Cash Management explicitly tries to eliminate such actions, with the goal always being to maximize cash flow on an enterprise-wide basis.

Finally, the vignette should show the conflict between cash flow and reported income. By capitalizing the small dollar value assets, the company lost the benefit of an immediate tax deduction. Most companies treat assets the same for both books and taxes. If a profitable firm chooses to capitalize something that could be written off to expense, you can be sure that your friendly IRS agent is *not* going to call this to your attention. In this instance, although the amounts might have been small, the appraisal company had the dubious distinction of paying unnecessary taxes to Uncle Sam. This is *not* what TCM is about!

The responsibility for *implementing* Total Cash Management belongs to every person who is making decisions regarding purchases, sales, and hiring. The responsibility for *administering* TCM, for making the analyses involving tradeoffs, probably belongs to the Accounting and Finance Departments. The responsibility for *setting policy*, saying that cash will be the organization's primary motivation, obviously has to come from the very top, either the CEO or the principals who own the business if it is privately held. Interestingly enough, closely held firms are usually very sensitive on the issue of minimizing taxes. They often go out of their way to do so; these same firms do not usually put equal emphasis on the other aspects of TCM.

2

How Operating and Budget Decisions Impact Cash Flow

If you have trouble understanding a
complicated financial transaction, just follow
the cash.

AUTHOR UNKNOWN

"You cannot trace cash flows in a business" is a truism among accountants and auditors. You may borrow money from a bank to invest in a new machine tool. The specific $100,000 loan proceeds, however, very quickly lose their identity. Every business is receiving cash and disbursing cash on a daily basis. Unless one sets up separate bank accounts for each type of transaction—and this in itself would be a wasteful use of a scarce resource—there is no practical way to identify where any specific balance came from or where it should go to. In short, to use a term popular in the grain business, cash is *fungible*. Whether you have one thousand dollars or $1 million, every single dollar requires the same effort, has the same purchasing power, and is worth no more or no less than any other dollar.

Why state what is seemingly so obvious? Specific cash cannot be traced because individual dollars lose their identity. But this is not the same thing as disregarding cash and cash flows. As the quote above implies, cash and cash flows follow from, and are directly involved in, every business transaction. Just because cash, whether currency or bank deposits, is so prevalent and is used every day, we often take it for granted. Except for financial managers responsible for the so-called Treasury function, most operating managers in business never give a moment's thought as to *how* a bill will be paid or the next payroll met. Since it has happened effortlessly and without fail as long as they have been with the company, why worry about something that is working?

Of course, at home, where most families are on a budget and savings for particular goals are necessary, cash seems far more important. This is not a book on personal finance, but most readers undoubtedly have experienced differences of opinion within the family as to how a limited income can accommodate an almost unending list of spending desires. Coordination of spending decisions and allocating the limited resources are absolutely necessary. Somebody has to take responsibility for seeing that cash commitments for mortgages, car payments, credit card charges, and spending money do not exceed cash coming in. No family member can spend money, or run up bills, without being aware of the impact of those actions.

Cash management, whether for a family or a business, involves matching inflows and outflows. The bankruptcy courts are full of individuals and families, as well as companies, who either neglected this simple arithmetic equation, or believed it did not really apply to them.

In business, responsibility for seeing that there is enough cash is *usually* placed with only one individual, the Treasurer. It is his or her responsibility to pay the bills and meet the payroll. This is wrong. Because they feel that cash management is a specialty, most line and staff managers do not worry consciously about the company's cash. They really do *not* think, day to day, that their own business actions and decisions affect the company's cash balances, impacting the job the Treasurer has to do. In point of fact, they do. Yet, as discussed, all cash is fungible. *Every* dollar that is spent or committed has the *same* impact on the firm.

A business, however, is not a family in several ways. A profitable business has several sources of cash. With the exception of meeting the payroll and paying Uncle Sam what has been withheld in taxes, a company has significant flexibility as to *when* it disburses its cash. Companies often have several sources *where* they can obtain cash. Because cash is indeed fungible, a smoothly running corporate cash operation is possible, as long as supply (cash available) equals or exceeds demand (cash requirements).

A family can get into trouble, can have a recurring series of fights between husband and wife, if one partner spends money without communicating that fact to the other partner. A wife cannot without warning go out and buy a car at the same time the husband signs up for a surprise anniversary present, such as a 10-day cruise.

There has to be some mechanism for reconciling income and expenses. In most businesses, and in some families, this mechanism is a budget. Without a budget a company would find itself, like certain families, making uncoordinated commitments that can lead to disaster.

Controlling Cash with Budgets

How can a business coordinate the flow of cash through a budget? Just what is a budget and how does it work? Entire books have been written and MBA courses presented on budgets and budgeting. Organizations like Institute of Management Accountants and American Management Association continuously offer professional development sessions on this important topic. In this chapter we can only cover what a budget *should* do, while leaving the specifics to later chapters.

A *budget* is a financial representation of the future operating plans for an organization. It displays, in monetary terms, what management hopes to accomplish and what resources will be required. There are widely varying philosophies about budgeting. Some people think the budget for next year should be easy to accomplish, so that employees will feel good about their performance. At the other end of the spectrum, some CEOs put out a budget that represents a stretch. The belief is that, in striving to meet a tight budget, employees will perform better than otherwise. A third common approach to budgeting is to forecast, as accurately as possible, what will happen, whether or not it represents an improvement from current levels. Later we will discuss the impact on cash of each of these budgetary approaches.

What is important to remember is that:

Budgets affect performance.   Budgets affect cash.

Corporate budgets are invariably put together in financial accounting terms comparable with monthly, quarterly, and annual financial statements. This means adopting the conventions inherent in Generally Accepted Accounting Principles (GAAP). A second important point to remember is that:

GAAP financial statements are not cash.

Assuming most readers are not accountants, this statement requires some explanation. Accountants, and others familiar with the difference between accrual accounting and cash, may want to skip to page 28.

Accrual Accounting
and Cash Flows

At first thought it might seem that financial statements of businesses should deal directly with cash flows. Sales represent cash inflows, and expenses represent cash outflows. We measure and report sales revenue as the top line of a Profit and Loss (P&L) Statement, while all the remaining lines represent the cost of the goods sold or services provided (what financial analysts refer to as Selling, General, and Administrative (SG&A) expenses). Aren't these all directly related to cash? Surprisingly, the simple answer is no.

Sales do not tie directly to cash inflows. Cost of goods sold may be based on production paid for in cash disbursed months ago. SG&A consists both of expenses not yet paid for in terms of cash outflows, offset in part by charges for items that were paid for years ago. This sounds confusing, but it need not be.

Start with sales. If we reported sales revenue in the financial statements based on cash receipts from customers, we would not recognize that we have shipped goods, or provided services, for which our customers owe us money. When is profit generated? Is it when we ship the goods or when we collect the cash? Since there may well be 45 or even 60 days between a sale and receipt of the cash, this distinction does make a difference in *when* we tell ourselves and others that we earned a profit. Accountants, financial managers, and ultimately corporate management all came to the conclusion that it was easier to measure "real" sales performance by looking at shipments, not cash receipts. For GAAP reporting, sales revenue is recognized—and profit measured—when customers first have a legal obligation to pay, not when they do pay.

The ramifications flowing from this admittedly somewhat arbitrary decision affect cash in several ways. First, sending out an invoice upon delivery of the product does not guarantee that our customer agrees with us that he received what he ordered at the time and place desired. Later we discuss how some retail chains are notorious in not paying their bills by claiming there was some "error" in shipment. Cash is available to meet payroll and to pay your bills only when your customer agrees with your invoice and makes a conscious decision to honor the debt.

Of course, in a continuing relationship, if a customer does not pay promptly, you may cease further shipments; so there is usually leverage on both sides. Nevertheless, as any credit manager will tell you, an invoice and cash are two distinct concepts.

The second effect of recognizing sales revenue before cash is received is something that accountants call receivables. *Accounts receivable* are the amounts presently owed us by our customers for goods shipped and services performed for which we have not yet been paid. With the exception of some small percentage, say 1 or 2 percent for anticipated bad debts, receivables can be considered as future cash flows, the exact timing of which may be somewhat uncertain, but the ultimate collectibility of which is not in doubt.

The final impact of having sales revenue based on shipments, not on cash collected, is that an opportunity cost is associated with the funds tied up in receivables. Although we have shown the revenue and related profit when we billed the customer, we have to meet our payroll right now. No employee can be paid with receivables! You and I need true cash to pay our bills.

The State of California recently had budget problems and paid their bills and their employees with IOUs. Obviously an IOU is *not* cash. What saved the situation was that the commercial banks in California were willing to treat the State's IOUs as cash for their depositors, giving them credit in their bank accounts. In turn, however, these very IOUs were *not* cash to the banks, and had to be treated for what they were, interest-bearing debt. The fact that the State of California was willing to pay holders of the IOUs 5-percent interest, tax-free, took some of the sting out of the banks' decision to honor the IOUs. Only a sovereign government, such as the United States, which prints money, can pay its bills with debt. Everyone else has to pay cash.

From the perspective of a company and its cash management, the longer customers take to pay us what they owe, the more interest cost we incur. Take, for example, one big sale to one customer, who then takes 60 days to send us a check. We must continue to meet our payroll with up-front cash. Companies can, and do, go to their bank and borrow, telling the bank that they will be repaid as soon as their customer pays them. The bank, in the business of lending money, provides cash to meet the payroll and charges interest.

Are we in the business of lending money to our customers but not charging them interest? The time value of money, the fact that a dollar 60 days from now is worth less than a dollar today, is a vital part of Total Cash Management.

A second area in which GAAP financial statements depart from a direct reflection of cash flows is in how inventories are handled. Disregarding for the moment factory overhead, look only at the labor and material cost of building widgets. We buy raw materials from one of our suppliers, we pay our employees to manufacture the widgets on equipment that we own, and then put the finished widgets in the warehouse, waiting for customers to order them. Since very few companies can produce goods only after getting customer orders (customers demand faster turnaround), inventories are an essential element of almost all manufacturers and certainly of every wholesaler and retailer. "You can't sell from an empty wagon" is a phrase particularly appropriate to understanding cash flows.

In preparing financial statements, should we show as Cost of Goods Sold the current period's cash disbursements for raw materials and direct labor, or in the case of a retailer the amount of this month's purchases from its sources? At first you might be tempted to say, "Yes, why not?" Technically this could be done. But the *meaning* of such statements is questionable. We would be offsetting cash receipts from previous sales with cash disbursements being made now for future sales. We would be comparing apples and oranges.

Go back to the term, Cost of Goods *Sold*, which is a key line in the Profit and Loss Statement. Taken literally, this phrase means that we want the cost of the items we reported as sales, not the disbursements of current production made in anticipation of future sales. We want to measure the *profitability* of what we accomplished this month or this quarter, not necessarily the cash flow impact of today's production decisions.

The answer is simple. Accountants decided to recognize the cost of the goods produced, but not yet sold as an asset. By definition an *asset* is something of value that can be turned into cash at a later date. In practice, the accounting entries are straightforward. The cash costs of producing goods for future sales (inventories are no more than items held for future sale) are accumulated and shown as an asset on the balance sheet. They are removed from the balance sheet, and called Cost of Goods Sold in the month the items are physically shipped.

Thus the dollars shown as inventory on the Balance Sheet are exactly matched by the physical assets still on the warehouse shelves. In the same way, the amounts shown as Accounts Receivable on the Balance Sheet are exactly matched by the file of invoices not yet paid by our customers. We can look at a Balance Sheet and in most cases find the corresponding items, either as a legal financial obligation or as tangible property.

Expenses and Cash Disbursements in GAAP Statements

Just as there is a difference between Sales and cash receipts, or Cost of Sales and cash disbursements for current production, so accountants distinguish between "expenses" for financial reporting and actual cash outlays. As already mentioned, cash can be paid out—a check written— either before or after the amounts are actually reflected in the P&L. While this makes good sense when properly explained, readers should be aware that a certain amount of judgment is involved in deciding how much to charge currently. Three accountants, approaching the same situation, will probably arrive at three different answers, and, if pressed, each could provide a rationale for his or her decision. The accounting *rules* are clear. They are just hard to apply in practice.

Let's take a simple purchase of a computer, such as the one this book was written on. Say in 1994 it cost $5000, including the printer and the software. Should the entire $5000 be charged off as an expense the month, quarter, or year it was purchased? Despite rapid technological progress in PCs, three-year-old machines still do the job they were purchased for. If a personal computer can be expected to last five years (for our purposes this can be considered a reasonable assumption), then you want to charge only $1000 to expense each year for five years.

This charge, called *depreciation*, recognizes that the value of an asset diminishes over time. Even though a ten-year-old computer might physically be here, it really has little economic value today. Should a computer's cost be written off, then, over five years or ten or something in between? Right now, five years is our best guess, but at some point in the future we may find out that we were wrong in 1994.

Accountants recognize that some estimate of useful life is necessary. Barring truly major changes in economics or technology, once they start with a given life, accountants continue with the original estimate. This means that some items ultimately will be written off totally while they are still in use and have value, while others will be worthless but still carried on the books at a dollar amount representing depreciation expense to be taken in future years. Setting these lives, possibly adjusting them in the future, is one of many reasons that three accountants can come up with at least three answers.

Getting back to cash, what is the relation between depreciation expense and cash flow? This is one of the simplest problems in TCM, although one that causes more confusion than anything else. Students are often taught that you measure cash flow by adding back depreciation expense to net income. As an algebraic equation this concept possibly is workable. In terms of paying your debts, it is as hard to pay with depreciation as it is with receivables or IOUs.

Even if nothing else from this chapter stays in your mind, remember these four words:

Depreciation is not cash!

Go back to the fundamentals. Five thousand dollars of cash were paid out when the computer was bought. Period. We may choose for accounting purposes—in fact, are required by GAAP—not to reflect this as an expense in the period we bought the asset. But accounting conventions differ from cash disbursements. Recognizing as an expense only one-fifth the purchase price each year for five years, one-third for three years, or even one-tenth for ten years does not change our bank balance—which went down on day one.

When you focus on cash, this explanation about depreciation is so simple that many readers will think, "Of course that is the way things are."

The author would wager, however, that most managers in business tend to look at the expense line on their own department's budget report—or on the firm's overall P&L—and think that the amounts shown are *really* what the department or company spent. Unfortunately, financial statements often take on a life of their own. Most nonfinancial managers think that what the accountants (with their own esoteric rules) have prepared *must* be right. Expenses, however, are not cash outflows, just as sales are not cash inflows.

Things get even more confusing. Items like depreciation are expenses but not cash flow, because the cash has already been spent. But there is another category of expense where cash disbursements have not yet been made. Accountants refer to these items as *accrued expenses*. Two examples will demonstrate the difference between current expense and current cash outflow. (1) Warranty expenses, which will be incurred by a manufacturer on sales of today's production, may not be paid out to customers for at least the next five years. (2) The amount of vacation time taken by an employee this summer probably was earned last calendar year, based on the employee's length of service.

Warranties. An automobile manufacturer may warrant that the power train will not suffer any defects for five years. Obviously if every single car were built perfectly (the ultimate but unattainable goal of Total Quality Management), there would be no warranty expense within the next five years—and no need to provide today for that event. In the real world, some (small?) percentage of power trains will fail within the five-year warranty period. In the interest of matching revenues and expenses, so that true profit can be determined, most readers would agree that it is fair to charge this year's P&L with an estimated amount to cover anticipated costs associated with fixing the power trains that go bad. In fact accountants are *required* by GAAP to accrue such expenses. GAAP, however, does not tell you how much to accrue or even how to estimate the amount.

The estimation of future warranty expense for items produced and sold this year ultimately requires judgment. If a company is having a good year, very conservative estimates may be made, reducing reported profits and providing a "cushion" for future years. Conversely, in a year of poor earnings, the controller may be under pressure by management to assume all is well, the products really were well built, and very little future warranty expense will be incurred. This boosts this year's reported profits.

Notice that, no matter whether the optimistic or conservative viewpoint is adopted, the amount accrued today does not affect the actual amount to be spent over the next five years. Customers who buy the cars and claim a warranty adjustment on the power train, paid in cash in, say, three years, do not care in the slightest whether the company has or has not accrued anything. The company is liable—period. The accounting entries of three years ago do not affect by one cent the cash outflow this year to fix someone's transmission. Cash goes out when the transmission breaks down.

Assuming the conservative estimate of warranty expense made three years ago was accurate, the manufacturer will pay out the cash, but the charge will be to the warranty reserve, not to current year's expense. In a perfect world at the end of five years, the warranty reserve would just have been worked down to zero, and no further entries to profit or loss would have been required. If the original estimate were off, the optimistic view turned out in error, additional charges to expense would be required. Those entries would hit the P&L of a year subsequent to when the product was shipped. The errors of the past must be made up. You cannot go back and reopen the financial statements from three years ago.

Again, it must be repeated that whether the original estimate of future warranty expense was accurate has no impact on the timing or amount of cash outflows. In terms of Total Cash Management there is no difference between the world's best accountant who makes a perfect estimate of warranty expense and the world's worst accountant who missed by 300 percent. One accountant may be promoted, and the other lose her job. There is still no difference in the cash.

Future Vacations.   Matching revenues and expenses requires that this year's P&L be charged for all vacation earned by employees, whether or not it has yet been taken. For most organizations, vacations can be taken only after they have been earned, based on a policy that usually provides more vacation time for employees with greater length of service. For vacations (and cumulative sick pay, which is handled the same way) that are earned this year but that will be taken in following years, accountants have to estimate at the end of the current year how much vacation time has been earned but not taken. If employees are allowed to carry forward unused vacation time for several years, but lose it after, say, three years, the recordkeeping and analysis can become complex. Often Human Resource Management will be involved in the administration and calculation of accrued vacation time. In all events, an estimate is made and a charge shown on this year's P&L for Accrued Vacation Liability.

Then an employee takes his or her vacation. Rather than charge the payroll expense to current production or to cost of goods sold, since vacation time is considered not to be productive, the current outlay (the actual gross pay for the time on vacation) is charged to the previously set-up reserve or allowance.

The Generally Accepted Accounting Principle that accrued but unused vacation time be charged as an expense of the current year, even though the cash will be paid out in subsequent years, was accepted quite recently. If a salaried employee takes two weeks vacation every July, and another two weeks the following January, does it make any difference in which year the vacation time had been earned? If the employee is not replaced while on vacation, no incremental expense is incurred to hire a replacement. The actual cash outlay to the organization for someone making $52,000 a year is just that week's salary, $1000. For the first year on the job, the company will charge $56,000 to expense, to provide for the four weeks' vacation. Assuming no change in the rate of pay, cash outlays will then continue to be $1000 a week, for 52 weeks each year whether the employee is in the office or at the beach.

Only in the last year the employee is on the payroll will the vacation accrual reverse. That year, the last four weeks of vacation taken will be charged to the reserve. It probably is safe to say that, for an employee going off the payroll, the final vacation time is truly nonproductive from the firm's perspective. For all the intervening years a lot of calculations had to be made, particularly if salary rates changed and the number of weeks of earned but unused vacation fluctuated. From the perspective of understanding cash flows, the old system, known as *pay as you go*, was closer to economic reality. Accounting for accrued vacation time on the P&L may make good accounting sense. Unwittingly, however, it caused reported income to deviate farther from cash flows.

In summary, notice that once again charges to expense and the related cash outflows do not match up. Is one correct and the other wrong? No. The P&L, reporting revenues, expenses, and profits are simply constructed on a set of accounting conventions that implicitly assume that the timing of cash flows is irrelevant. A P&L is not currently designed to be, nor is it, a statement of cash flows.

The purpose of this section is not to bash accounting. Today's P&L does an excellent job of meeting the objectives of *matching* revenues and expenses. Profit is the one minus the other. If we want to understand profitability, the work of accountants is helpful. If we want to understand cash flows, however, the Surgeon General's warning should be modified:

> Using the P&L to understand cash flows may be dangerous to your financial health.

How Budgets Affect Cash

Most day-to-day and month-to-month business decisions have usually been preapproved in the annual budget. Thus decisions made in the course of preparing an organization's budget will have far-reaching consequences in terms of Total Cash Management.

Budgets usually present an optimistic picture for the forthcoming year. No CEO likes to be accused of pessimism or, worse, an inability to overcome adverse circumstances—turning such challenges into what is often euphemistically called opportunities. How many budgets are prepared forecasting a *reduction* in sales, cutbacks in expenses, and reduced profits? A conservative budget, prepared during a recessionary period, might at worst show that operations next year were expected to be level with this year. But, horror of all horrors, never an absolute reduction.

Thus we start out with the premise that most budgets are positive in outlook, assuming that good things will happen to good people. Sales managers *always* predict sales growth. Isn't this the American way? Who wants to be the wet blanket and say that sales will not increase? That really is un-American! As we will see, a multitude of cash consequences, most of them bad, follow directly from the optimism inherent in almost all budgets.

One of the basic principles of budgeting is that a business plan should be internally consistent. The parts must all fit together logically. If sales are expected to rise by 7 percent from last year, then production also must increase more or less proportionately. This may mean overtime in the factory, some new hiring, and possibly some significant capital expenditures for increased capacity. Further, if sales are to rise, it will probably require more sales and marketing staff, not to mention increased staff support in areas like order entry, accounting, and human resources.

Suppose a budget is put together with an optimistic sales increase. But other line managers, those in the categories often referred to as Selling, General, and Administrative (SG&A), say, "We don't believe sales are really going to go up by more than 1 or 2 percent and *we* will budget accordingly." At this point the overall corporate budget would be out of phase and would show far too much operating profit.

Why? The Cost of Goods Sold would have to match the sales volume, and the gross profit would be up by at least 7 percent in absolute dollars. But operating expenses, up by perhaps only 2 percent (because the other executives figured that a 7 percent sales increase was unrealistic) means that operating profit dollars and operating profit as a percentage of sales would rise more than proportionately. You might argue that this is the way things *should* be. SG&A expenses are often considered fixed, that is, they are not *supposed* to vary with volume. As sales volume goes up, the fixed expenses should remain level, and the forecasted profit *should* increase more than proportionately.

Two things are wrong with this picture. First, remember that the proposed budgets for the SG&A departments were predicated on the managers' own estimate of a 2 percent change. What would have been the expenses, and the resulting profit impact if they had budgeted for a full 7 percent increase in volume? Obviously they would have budgeted more. Human nature says that, when things are going up, don't miss the opportunity to get on board.

134439

If sales go up and you did not request enough staff in the budget, how are you going to get the work done? No manager wants to go back in July, and say, "Gee, sales really did go up by the budgeted amount, but I guess I underestimated how I was going to get the work done." As a manager, would you rather say, "Gee, sales did go up by the budgeted amount, but my staff [less modest managers would say "I"] is able to do the work with one less employee than we forecast!" It does not take a Ph.D. in psychology to determine which statement is going to be more acceptable to top management.

The second reason why a 7 percent sales increase should not be accompanied by only a 2 percent expense rise is actual experience. Relatively few companies, whatever the reason, have ever been able to keep the growth in SG&A expenses much lower than the rate of increase in sales.

Be very suspicious of expense budgets that are disproportionate to sales.

These comments are not meant to imply that, once sales are determined for a budget, everything else is determined mechanically, as a simple arithmetic formula to be applied to all other expenses. On the contrary, the thesis of this book is that each department should determine its proposed budget most carefully. It requires a full knowledge of all specific factors affecting performance—and of the resulting resources required—to meet the objectives of all "customers." Blindly following last year is as bad as gamesmanship to provide a cushion.

Why Sales Are Hard To Forecast And Cash Inflows Uncertain. In determining a budget, an organization first has to project revenues, and all other categories of expense *should* follow more or less proportionately. Let's look more closely at the differences between sales and all other items affecting cash flow. Sales volumes depend on decisions from people *outside* our organization. All other disbursement decisions are made by people *inside* our organization. Which of these are under our control?

A sales forecast is obviously not the same thing as a sale. No cash has changed hands until the sale is closed. We can *hope* that existing customers will continue to buy, that price increases will stick, that last year's advertising campaign will bring in new customers this year, and that engineering's latest product will be accepted by the market. Further, we can believe that GNP growth will accelerate and economic conditions improve, that our major competitor will be tied up in the merger announcement recently made, and that the proposed new EPA requirements will open up a new market for one of our existing product lines.

Every one of these assumptions affecting next year's sales is important. Depending on how many actually come to pass, and to what degree, will determine the actual sales totals 12 months from now. Trying to forecast the future today, to predict those sales, has always been difficult if not impossible. But because it is difficult does not stop us from trying. We make a sales forecast and secretly hope that some of the unanticipated negative factors will be offset by good things that we did not forecast. In other words, we know we will never be absolutely right in our sales projections, but experience suggests that all the errors won't go in one direction.

The important thing about this discussion is that almost everything affecting sales is *external* to our organization. You may or may not be able to forecast accurately whether the dollar will go up or down against the yen, which would affect competitors' imports and our exports. But even if we can forecast foreign exchange rates, we cannot *control* them. Whatever they turn out to be, whether we forecast them accurately or not, our sales will be impacted by myriad economic and competitive forces. All those forces are impacting us. We can only respond, not mold them to suit our requirements.

In terms of TCM, then, it really is very hard to get a handle on anticipated cash inflows. We know what we hope will happen, and past experience can provide some overall parameters. That is, despite all the uncertainties we can be pretty sure sales will not go down, say, 40 percent. But by the same token, history suggests that only rarely does everything positive work out at the same time.

In summary, if we budgeted an optimistic 7 percent sales increase, there is a high probability that sales will be somewhere between +10 percent and −15 percent. This is, in absolute terms, quite a wide range. It may even be the difference between profit and loss. It is not, however, as though we were looking at either winning the Irish Sweepstakes on one hand or facing Chapter 11 on the other.

Cash forecasts dependent on sales are bound to be uncertain. We will discuss later in the book how companies can adapt to this uncertainty. But in terms of the impact of business decisions on cash flow, the key point is that inflows inherently are both hard to forecast and somewhat uncertain in amount and timing. Those who uncritically accept a sales forecast as the basis of making decisions impacting cash flows are only fooling themselves.

A sales forecast can be developed in a couple of ways. From the bottom up, you can poll sales representatives, who in turn contact customers. From the top down, a Sales VP might say, "Sales *will be* up 10 percent." Or you might use the most "scientific" market research techniques known to Madison Avenue. *All* these approaches are inherently subject to a wide margin of error.

Now perhaps the real problems of budgeting can become a little clearer. We have already stated that every budget must start with a sales forecast and that everything else flows from that. You cannot budget for next year, forecasting future cash flows, without an idea of your revenue stream. But, shades of *Catch 22*, we can never get a good reliable sales forecast. Should we give up budgeting? Hardly.

What is needed is very simple indeed. Prepare the sales forecast just as it always has been—whether top down, bottom up, or with outside experts. Just do the best you can, and remember:

Every sales forecast is going to be wrong.

The single biggest mistake companies make is not that they forecast sales incorrectly, not even that they usually respond too slowly to changes in market conditions. Where people and companies go wrong is in *believing* their own sales forecasts. It is fine to present an optimistic face to the world. But when you start believing your own propaganda—and acting on it—you are headed for trouble.

Companies may forecast a 7 percent sales increase and then adjust, in totally appropriate ways, all supporting operations and increasing fixed expenses, as we will see in the next section. What is rarely asked is, "What if sales don't increase 7 percent? What if they don't go up at all? What if, heaven forbid, they go down 3 percent?" Merely asking these questions will go a long way in preventing budget myopia.

Budget Myopia: Why Expenses Always Are Close to Budget

Believing your own propaganda—acting on your sales forecast as though the projection itself were reality—may be the principal reason companies get into trouble. All knowledgeable managers, with the best will in the world, try to provide their departments with a cushion. There is always a feeling that budgeting next year's expenses "realistically" will make the job easier. Even more persuasive is the belief that this really is in the company's best interests. To paraphrase a well-known phrase, "What's good for my department is good for the company." This very commonly held idea has some overall consequences for TCM that are not usually understood.

An approved expense budget is essentially authorization from management to commit the resources necessary to provide the capacity required to meet the stated objectives. As is usually the case, the primary objective is to meet customer needs at some level above the current year, say a 7-percent increase. If every department has planned appropriately, and if the sales increase occurs, total expenses will be in line and the predetermined profit objectives will be met. As they say in high school geometry, QED.

As we have seen, however, a funny thing often happens on the way to our goal. Our customers forget to do their part. They do not buy as much as we expected, or they buy the wrong mix, or the seasonal purchasing pattern changes unexpectedly. Whatever the cause, sales do not meet budget targets. And if the targets were deliberately set high, to encourage performance from the sales staff, the shortfall can be significant.

Meanwhile, what about all the support departments, including Production? At this point in our discussion it will come as no surprise to find out that almost every department is close to targeted expenses. If expense and production targets were themselves an increase from last year, new hires would have been made, inventories built up, commitments made for new distribution, and so forth. You might suppose that expense increases would not actually be consummated until the corresponding sales increases were truly visible, not just a gleam in the eye of the sales managers.

Reflect for a moment. It takes substantial lead time to gear up for increased volume. New hires have to be identified, recruited, and trained before they can be productive. Most budgets are developed for the following year on a monthly basis; that is, the final approved budget shows projected sales revenue and all categories of expense for each of the 12 months. Working backwards from projected sales, Production and other support departments have to be in sync.

Inevitably a significant part of any planned increase in overhead will have been accomplished, or certainly committed to, prior to the antici-pated sales ever being realized. In the best of circumstances expense commitments *must* lead sales. That is why every start-up venture (whether a new business or an expansion of an existing operation) loses money at first. Cash goes out to provide the capability of meeting customer needs. Then, if and when they buy, cash flows back in. This is the famous working capital or cash cycle taught in every college business, accounting, and economics text.

You must make the investment before you see the return. From the perspective of TCM, a budgeted sales increase, with its corresponding increases in production and expense commitments, inevitably will cause cash to be disbursed first. So far this may seem like common sense, just restating the obvious.

What happens, though, if the sales increase projected in the budget does not occur as anticipated? The higher expense level will be matched against last year's lower sales, resulting in lower cash inflows than anticipated. But more often than not, any corrective action on expenses will be delayed. There is a natural reluctance to cut back immediately after having ex-panded. Firing or laying off newly hired employees is bad public relations.

Contributing also to the lingering of higher expense levels is the expectation—some would call it a wish—that, "Sales *will* pick up." This is when the wise ones nod their head about how hard it is to predict sales, the fickleness of customers, unanticipated competition, and delays in new product introduction. These are rationalizations, perhaps, but on the other hand quite possibly a realistic analysis.

The real issue is when, if ever, the budgeted sales increase will actually take place. Nobody likes to cut back. Laying off employees may well be the toughest job any manager has; so, if nothing else, this encourages a feeling of, "Let's wait." From a TCM perspective, every day of waiting causes cash outflows to be higher. Assume that sales are level with last year, but expenses are at the substantially higher budgeted levels. Is it any wonder that raising profits at a faster rate than actual sales increases is a difficult achievement? More often than not, sales are *less* than forecast. Sales managers may or may not be blamed. Ultimately the CEO has to shoulder the responsibility, since he or she (and the board) approved the budget.

Meanwhile, the individual department managers look good. Expenses, including the all-important salary and wage account, are on or even favorable to budget. It is only at the top level, on the P&L of the operating unit, that the mismatch between sales and expenses shows up. Take the Order Entry Department as an example. Assume a 7-percent sales increase requires an extra clerical employee. If that person had been hired on schedule and was now on board, the department's monthly expense report would show actual expenses right on budget. The Order Entry manager is not considered responsible for the fact that sales are below plan. In fact, the manager did her job and is now ready to handle the expected higher volume.

Going up the chain of command, performance is almost always measured in terms of how close a manager is to budget. Being worse than budget is obviously bad. Showing expenses at or below budget levels is considered good, irrespective of whether the total organization is meeting overall targets.

The conclusion is that today's budget system has a built-in bias toward encouraging optimistic sales projections, expense levels that rise to meet the new "needs," and an individual incentive to provide a budget cushion in each department. All three of these biases are totally contrary to the philosophy of Total Cash Management.

Budget Decisions, Expense Commitments, and Cash Flow

As we have seen, budget decisions on expense levels assume a life of their own. The forecast soon becomes the reality. An upward ratcheting of commitments is built into organizations with a growth orientation. In terms of Total Cash Management, a new consciousness must develop.

Every time an individual is added to the payroll, fixed cash outlays increase. Very few managers perceive that *they* have a responsibility for cash inflows. Someone else has always taken care of meeting the payroll. Understanding is generally lacking of the very real relationship between specific growth actions, taken in good faith, and the future increase in cash requirements needed to pay for those commitments.

If cash is truly a scarce resource, then decisions involving cash must be made on the basis of "the greatest good for the greatest number." Very real tradeoffs should be made on the basis of rational decision making, not on who shouts the loudest at budget meetings. Let's look at some of these tradeoffs. Following are six possible actions that could be proposed by department managers for next year's budget. Each of them directly or indirectly involves cash commitments:

1. Open a new warehouse to serve the Southeast. Speeding up delivery will increase sales next year.

2. Develop a dating program for customers to encourage them to order early. This will help smooth out production during otherwise slow periods and reduce overtime during peak periods.

3. Purchase a new numerically controlled machine tool. It will reduce production costs as well as shorten lead times, thus speeding up deliveries to customers. There is over a year lead time required to get the machine installed, tooled up, and running.

4. Start a new R&D program to follow up on a recent discovery. This is a three-year project. If it is successful, we will have a strong competitive advantage.

5. For an older product line, which still appears to have some life in it, implement a major new advertising and marketing program.

6. Install a new 401(k) savings program for employees, with the company matching 25 percent of employee contributions.

Coincidentally, each of these budget proposals has the same $400,000 price tag, at least as first measured by the manager proposing it. Let's look first at how these would be considered in the normal budget process, and then look at them in terms of cash flow.

1. Open a Warehouse. There would be little dispute that speeding up deliveries to customers will increase sales. Fast response time is becoming an ever more important competitive weapon. There are tradeoffs involved between a number of geographically dispersed warehouse locations and one giant centralized distribution center. Even the most ardent advocate of centralization admits that, for items with significant bulk or weight, delivery times are going to be reduced if the warehouse is near the customer.

Opening the new warehouse is estimated to cost $400,000 for the rent plus the personnel costs for the manager and five staff. The sales manager estimates that $10 million of product will be shipped from the new facility, with the company enjoying its 40-percent gross profit margin on those sales.

2. Dating Program. One of the company's product lines is highly seasonal. The Production manager wants to spread out anticipated production into the slow period. One way to do so is to encourage customers to order early, ship the product to them, but not expect payment until much later in the season. Working with the controller, the sales manager calculates that $1 million of additional receivables will be outstanding for four months or an average of $334,000 for the year.

The factory manager is enthusiastic. Operating costs, primarily the need for temporary help plus overtime, will be dramatically reduced, saving some $175,000 in production costs at anticipated production levels.

3. Purchase Machine Tool. No company can afford to fall behind competition in terms of higher production costs. One of the factors that has encouraged shifting production to countries like Mexico is a desire to reduce labor costs. There are, in practice, only three basic ways to reduce production costs: (1) Change the product design. (2) Reduce labor rates by moving to low cost areas. (3) Substitute capital for labor. Purchasing a $400,000 machine, which one man can operate and which will eliminate two hourly workers, seems like a good investment. The savings of a net $100,000 a year factors in savings in overhead based on a 100-percent overhead rate. It does not calculate any cash benefits from much quicker set-up. This, in turn, would reduce lead time and speed up delivery. These are intangibles, perhaps, but nonetheless strong competitive tools.

4. Initiate New R&D Program. Many, if not most, firms plan for new products and services and have to make investments up front to discover and develop these new ideas. While charged to current expense, as required by GAAP, most R&D programs are thought of as "investments" by company management. In this case $400,000 a year for three years will have to be spent to develop a new blockbuster widget. The payoff, while somewhat uncertain, could be a product with annual sales of $50 million.

5. Advertising and Marketing Program. The term *cash cows* entered the business vocabulary several years ago and referred to long-time products, with little growth potential but a substantial existing customer base. The profits from such cash cows could be harvested and used to invest in new "growth stars." The assumption was that customers would continue to buy these cash cows without a requirement that the seller commit significant additional marketing effort.

Experience has shown that even for the most well established products, continued marketing effort is required. Competitors are not dumb. They can spot our cash cows and go after those customers. In this case the Marketing VP and the Sales Manager agree that a $400,000 advertising and marketing program is necessary, or we will lose $5 million of sales with a $2 million gross profit margin. With the program we will fight off the competition and keep the sales.

6. Install a 401(k) Savings Program for Employees. In terms of budgeting, is any employee going to stand up and say this is not a great idea? Added to individual self-interest is the undeniable fact that any company must be competitive in its benefit programs if it is to attract good new employees as well as retain existing ones. Disregarding any costs to set up or administer the plan, it will still cost $400,000 for the employer to match 25 percent of anticipated employee contributions.

The Board of Directors Looks at the Budget

Let's look at each of these budget proposals from the topmost perspective of the Board of Directors. Company management has already bought into each of these terrific ideas. Should we approve this proposal? The usual thought process would go something like this.

1. Warehouse. It is unrealistic to assume that all $10 million of shipments will be *new* or incremental volume. Some estimate is needed as to how much extra sales will be generated by virtue of speedier delivery. For sake of discussion let's say 85 percent will be sales of existing product to present customers, now to be shipped from this location instead of another warehouse location. This still leaves $1.5 million of true new sales, and, with a 40-percent gross profit margin, the company will be better off by $600,000. Subtracting the $400,000 of new operating expense leaves a net gain of $200,000 of additional operating profit. All in favor, vote yes.

2. Dating Program. The immediate P&L effect is a net gain in operating profit of $175,000 from reduced manufacturing costs, with no net outlay for equipment or other capital expenditures. Regardless of how you calculate the cost of capital (what cash is *really* worth to the firm), the return on an investment of $1 million of additional receivables for four months appears more than satisfactory. All in favor, vote yes.

3. Purchase Machine Tool. Assuming that a 25-percent ROI ($100,000 savings related to $400,000 purchase cost) meets the organization's objectives, this seemingly needs little analysis, except perhaps to assure that the product line(s) made on the equipment have good sales prospects. We do not want to reduce the production costs of buggy whips or hula hoops. All in favor, vote yes.

4. Initiate New R&D Program. This is a tough one. The one thing that is certain is that we will spend $400,000 a year, probably for at least the three years called for in the proposal. But, if the program is successful, getting a competitive head start on a $50-million product makes this a much better bet than a lottery ticket. If we are having a good year now, and budget projections show satisfactory increases for next year, most companies would follow the adage, "You've got to spend money to make money." In the absence of any better R&D proposals, this looks like a pretty good bet. All in favor, vote yes.

5. Advertising and Marketing Program. The choice presented is pretty clear. Spend $400,000 and save $5 million of sales. Or do not spend it and see competitors capture that volume. All in favor, vote yes.

6. Install a 401(k) Savings Plan for Employees. Here is at least a potential conflict of interest, because the people proposing it are those who will benefit from it. Thus the Board should be the ones to decide, not line managers. How do you measure the benefits of spending $400,000 next year and for every year thereafter? Reduced employee turnover and making the organization appear to be a progressive employer for prospective new hires are both certainly desirable goals. All in favor, vote yes.

Understanding the Real Cash Flow Impact

What we have described and discussed in these minicase examples are typical decisions made in the budget process. Employees are encouraged, at least once a year, to stand back, look at the overall business or at least their segment, and propose what they think is needed. With pressure to improve the bottom line, to keep sales volume growing, and to increase profits, many proposals are floated. The usual review process winnows these down, with the best ones included in the final budget package. When the budget is approved, a green light has flashed to move forward.

Somehow, in the real world, things never work out quite the way they are supposed to. Managers sometimes try to go back and ask, "Why *didn't* we get the savings we anticipated?" Part of the problem is that, as discussed, cash is fungible and you really cannot trace dollars. The other reason is that nobody asked the tough questions up front. Nobody flashed a red light and said, "Stop! Before you invest $400,000, what else will happen?"

Proponents of any proposal are always enthusiastic. The finest manager in the world, trying to be as objective as possible, still *wants* things to get better. Since there are only so many good ideas out there, and presumably we have already discarded all undesirable ones, what remains *must* be good. Unless everyone in the organization is totally cash conscious, who really is going to ask those tough questions?

This is what TCM is all about. The *right* questions will be asked. Each of the six budget proposals will now be analyzed in terms of *total* cash impact. There is no guarantee that *understanding* the total impact will actually make things any better. It will, however, eliminate a lot of unpleasant surprises.

1. Open a Warehouse.   Opening a new warehouse involves a lot of different functional departments. It is not going to happen by itself. Just as a few examples, someone is going to have to choose the specific location (state and city) and then identify the best parcel of land. Contracts must be arranged with both architects and builders, and the actual construction monitored. New staff has to be recruited and trained. Communications facilities (telephone, computer, and fax) must be established. Arrangements have to be established, possibly after some trial and error, with new carriers.

Depending on the size of the organization, all of these tasks will have to be done by one or two individuals who may have had little experience in each of those functions. In a small organization the many hats that one person has to wear, a lack of specialization, may have a corresponding advantage. Whoever is doing the expansion work undoubtedly is knowledgeable about the company's business, knows what the firm wants to accomplish, and can make decisions quickly. In a larger business, specialists from the Real Estate Department would select several sites, and a committee would choose the finalists, with the ultimate decision reflecting lots of viewpoints. An Engineering or Construction Department would get bids on the building and select the contractor. The Personnel Department would send someone to recruit the new staff. Perhaps the MIS Department would have responsibility for computers and communications. And so forth.

For the larger firm there could be serious delays, while each department performed its specialized task. Who would coordinate the work? If it is a Project Manager, how much real authority would he have to set the priorities of employees who worked for managers in other departments? The point is that it is easy to *decide* to build a warehouse. But, as we all know, "The Devil is in the details." All of the details, however, *must* be attended to before the first shipment can leave the loading dock of the new warehouse.

Now let's look at the impact on cash just of the activities needed to get the warehouse up and running. As discussed, either one or two key managers (in a small business) or a number of functional specialists from different areas (in a larger organization) will have to spend time and effort arranging all the administrative details. (Some people refer to this kind of activity as "administrivia" —unfortunately all too accurately.)

A cash cost is associated with the salary and travel expense of those involved, but this is the tip of the iceberg. What about the tasks these people would have been doing in the absence of the warehouse project? Either they will not be done—with a consequent adverse effect on the business—or additional staff resources will have to be hired, either full- or part-time (the latter often are referred to as consultants). Either there is an opportunity cost for what is not done to get the warehouse designed and built, or extra cash outlays are made to provide additional resources.

But there's more. Look at a brief, but usually painful, aspect of every change: the change itself. Opening a new warehouse to provide faster service to existing customers and to be competitive to attract new ones will involve establishing relationships with new truck lines. Your shipping clerks, or your customers, have determined the best routing from your old shipping point. Quality problems have either been ironed out, or customers have learned to live with existing schedules, whatever they are.

Now, suddenly, old patterns are going to be thrown out and new relationships established. Inevitably there are going to be late deliveries, incorrect routings, and in the final analysis some trial and error until good reliable suppliers can be identified and trained in your way of doing business. Meanwhile there will have to be expediting, duplicate shipments, and returns. The result will be unhappy customers for at least a brief period.

All the effort during the "shakedown" will require extra time, effort, and cost. The chances are that these types of cash consequences are rarely, if ever, anticipated in the financial projections. When they do occur, they seem so natural nobody questions them. It is only when the monthly or quarterly financial statements come out behind budget that the explanation of the shakedown is dredged up. They could, and should, have been anticipated. All start-up costs are just that—costs—and all have cash consequences.

Finally, cash is going to be needed to stock the new facility with inventory. If a company has three warehouses and now opens a fourth, the chances are very high that total finished goods inventories are going to rise by one-third. There is no reason to anticipate any economies of scale. If anything, given the somewhat random nature of customer orders, there are likely to be individual stock outages at the new facility, requiring interwarehouse shipments. In theory, the more locations a company has, the higher will be the required finished goods inventory.

Look at it another way. If all customer shipments were from one centralized warehouse, total inventory requirements would be at a minimum. This would be accomplished at the cost of higher shipping costs to customers and slower delivery times. It has to be both faster and cheaper to ship to Jacksonville from Atlanta than from Minneapolis. It is also going to be faster and cheaper to ship to San Francisco from Salt Lake City than from Minneapolis. These reductions can be achieved only, however, by having all the same items, the same SKUs (stock keeping units), at each location. Taking the total inventory from one centralized warehouse and splitting it in, say, thirds will not work.

Minimum safety stocks at each of three locations must be greater than one-third of the previous total to avoid an unacceptable reduction in timely shipments. Backorders are costly. Interwarehouse shipments are equally costly, truly nonvalue-added. Having reasonable inventory levels to provide the required levels of customer service from each location will inevitably increase total cash tied up in inventories. For a wholesaler who buys all inventory from suppliers, the cash consequences are easiest to see. Opening a new warehouse in Atlanta will require significant cash outlays. These must be factored into any operating decisions and into any budget projections.

The proper way to budget for the new warehouse, then, would be to list *all* cash outlays required:

1. Staff time planning and implementing	$ 50,000
2. Start-up or shakedown costs	100,000
3. Annual costs for interwarehouse shipments	35,000
Subtotal: Cash outlays charged to expense	$185,000
4. Initial Inventory requirement	350,000
	$535,000

As you can see, there are three types of disbursements, each of which should be treated differently in the budget.

First is the initial inventory requirement, which will appear as an asset in the balance sheet and is never charged to expense. This really is, in conceptual terms, part of the capital cost of the project.

The second type of cash outlay is the $150,000 representing the staff time for planning and implementing, plus the start-up costs. These will never be charged as such, and thus will not appear directly on the P&L or budget reports of any specific department—other than perhaps the out-of-pocket travel costs, which quickly lose their identity anyhow. But even though these opportunity costs will never show up directly on a single line of an accounting report, they still exist. It is exactly this type of activity—unanticipated work effort with no incremental revenue impact—that causes profit centers to miss their planned target, leaving people to scratch their head and wonder, "What went wrong?"

There is nothing wrong in incurring these costs. They are natural and should be expected. If a manager really thinks through the process of opening a new distribution facility, all these items make sense. In one way or another the organization will be giving up something else to get the warehouse up and running; once the first shipment is made, there are bound to be glitches and false starts while systems are worked out and refined. If there is one lesson that Total Cash Management should teach, it is:

Every activity has a cash cost.

Thus, whether or not the $150,000 can ever be separately identified or even analyzed after the fact, the cash consequences *will* appear. These cash consequences *can* be anticipated. The cash consequences *must* be built into the original planning.

The final type of cash cost is the $35,000 annual cost for interwarehouse shipments. Unlike the one-time start-up costs, which are perhaps hard to pin down, this is easy to identify and budget for. Just as the promise was made of higher sales revenue and gross profit from the new facility, so should an understanding be made that the company will continue to incur these incremental operating expenses year after year. The fact that they are related solely to the addition of another distribution point is simply a financial offset to the future gains otherwise anticipated.

2. Dating Program.   Let's assume that the production costs to be saved are real; that is, out-of-pocket cash payments for overtime and temporary part-time help will be eliminated. Is there any downside? Many firms with seasonal product lines, such as toys or skis, already offer dating terms to encourage retail customers to order early and to accept delivery early. In effect, the retailer customers accept the physical inventory and the costs of storage in exchange for a price discount. This price discount can be either a reduced purchase price, extended credit terms, or both.

The real issue boils down to whether the sales to be generated are, in total, going to be greater than they were before. Or will customers simply rearrange the timing of the *same* number of products. If incremental sales are to be generated and production costs reduced, this is a win/win situation, and everyone gains.

If, however, customers order only the same amount as before, but simply take delivery earlier, the question becomes just what will the new payment pattern be? Retailers and wholesalers, as a group, are as cash-conscious as any part of American industry. If you are selling toys and right now are delivering in September, with payment due in December, what will really happen if you deliver in June with payment terms set for November? You had been offering 90-day terms, and now you are offering 120-day terms. But will retailers really pay in November, when they have not started to get cash in from sales to *their* customers?

Suppose, despite terms calling for payment in November, that your customers do not send in their checks in November. What will you do? You can make all the phone calls in the world, but you probably will still not get cash until January. So shipping in June instead of September will add an additional three months to receivable balances, and all that will be accomplished is the fact that customers will store the product in their warehouse, rather than you storing it in yours. This may or may not be a good idea. What if your customer goes into Chapter 11 over the six months he is holding your goods?

Reducing production costs by smoothing out or leveling production is a good idea any time, as long as the production will be sold this year. Placing it at your customer's disposal may or may not be a wise decision.

3. Purchase Machine Tool. As in the warehouse example, acquiring a new machine tool entails other costs, in addition to direct out-of-pocket cash charges, with potentially far-reaching consequences. Things such as disruption to production schedules while the new equipment is installed may be small in comparison with the costs incurred in debugging the new machine. Very few things work perfectly from day one. Usually a lot of trial and error is involved to ensure that equipment is running at full rated capacity. During that trial and error period, additional scrap will be generated, idle time will be increased, and so forth. This does not mean installing new up-to-date equipment is a bad idea, just that it should be fully thought-out to avoid unpleasant surprises.

The real caveat in this proposal should be the overhead savings. Reducing two direct labor employees, at $25,000 each, is a real cash savings of $50,000. But the remaining savings are calculated because there is a dollar of overhead for each dollar of direct labor, and it is assumed that if one is cut so will the other. *Wrong.* There is no necessary correlation between the two. In fact, putting in a new N/C machine may raise overhead; such things as programming and maintenance may actually increase.

Calculating savings based on an assumed correlation between a direct labor base and overhead has brought disaster to many firms. The real question to be asked is, "In addition to the savings from two less direct workers, where else in the factory will cash savings be generated, and how will they show up?" Only measurable savings should be cranked into a cash analysis.

Offsetting this, at least conceptually, is the *benefit* obtained from speedier set-up and reduced customer lead time. It may be hard to quantify any sales increase or competitive advantage, but many firms in different industries are attempting to differentiate themselves by promising, and then delivering, quick turnaround to customer demands.

4. Initiate an R&D Project. Would a decision to invest $400,000 in R&D be any easier if the amount were capitalized as an asset, rather than charged to expense as incurred each month? As we saw, the impact on cash is identical. Whatever the purpose, writing a check in January for $33,333 (one-twelfth of $400,000) reduces the bank balance, irrespective of how accountants treat this in the financial statements. Theoretically the decision should be made as to whether to invest in a research project by management's evaluation as to the possibilities of ultimate success. As we saw, only one out of ten projects may actually pay off. How do we make the decision?

> A businessman with a difficult brain tumor was referred to a prominent neurosurgeon. He asked the doctor, "What are the odds of success?" The surgeon responded, "I've got bad news and good news. The odds of success are 100 to 1 against you. But stop worrying, my last 99 patients died!"

The truth of the matter is that not every decision can be made on the basis of cash. Total Cash Management cannot and will not solve all business problems. American business is run by people, not computers, because judgment will always be required. How much to spend on R&D, and which projects to support, ultimately is a matter of management judgment, tempered by the availability of cash.

The argument of the pharmaceutical companies that they need profits to support their research efforts is absolutely correct. If they *knew* which project would be the winner and could drop all the losers, their R&D budget could be slashed, thus allowing lower selling prices on the existing product line. But the history of breakthrough drugs suggests that anticipating and thus backing *only* the known winners is impossible.

5. Advertising and Marketing Program. That there is some correlation between advertising today and sales tomorrow is beyond question. But how do we decide whether it should be $400,000? Maybe only $300,000 will do the job, or it may take $500,000. And there are other ways, besides advertising, to spend money in marketing and promoting a product line, some of which will be discussed in Chap. 3. As with the R&D issue, any decision on investing in an advertising or marketing campaign must be made by experienced managers, looking at a variety of alternatives. Selecting the one best strategy is ultimately a matter of faith. Certainly the number of new product failures that consumer goods firms have made, and continue to make, suggests that spreading your bets may be a good idea. The more cash you have available, the more bets you can make. If you were down to your last $400,000, would you put it all on this one product line? The key point, however, is that the amount spent on advertising is going to *retain* existing sales links, not generate additional sales. Therefore cash outflows will be $400,000 higher next year to support the *same* $5 million of sales this year.

6. 401(k) Savings Plan. This type of decision is driven partly by tax considerations, partly by political beliefs (should individuals, or their employer, or the government provide for retirement income), and partly by competitive pressures. In short, intangible factors may be as important as the direct cash consequences.

If the company feels that its total compensation package is, or may become, uncompetitive and that $400,000 is available, then the issue becomes what will get the best return? Should it be salary and wage increases, cash that can be spent today by employees? Should it be in the form of tax-favored benefits, such as additional insurance? Or should it be to help employees finance their retirement years?

In terms of Total Cash Management, the only real issue is the cost to administer the plan. The budget proposal included the comment, "disregarding any costs to set up or administer the plan...." But TCM suggests that one cannot disregard such costs. People complain about overhead always going up, and how it is "fixed" when cutbacks have to be made. Well, overhead is simply the sum of thousands of small commitments, including the administration of benefit plans. (There *is* no free lunch.)

If the $400,000 is added to today's compensation directly, as an across-the-board 4-percent increase, there will be no increase in administrative overhead. There will be a corresponding increase in the company's share of Social Security, unemployment tax, and other programs, which are directly related to gross payroll dollars. But setting up a new *type* of program very definitely will add to administrative costs. Consultants, actuaries, lawyers, accountants, and investment managers will all get into the act. Many firms have found that employee investment choices can cause problems. Buying a common stock fund is great, as long as the market goes up, but when the market goes down, the company is likely to get blamed. Meetings have to be held with employees to explain the plan, and so forth. In short, as with so many other great ideas put forth at budget time, more often than not there are hidden costs, which *must* be ferreted out.

Recommendations

The essence of Total Cash Management is that virtually every business decision is affected by, or itself impacts, cash. The more cash an organization has, the greater is its flexibility, and the more options it can pursue.

One of the biggest mistakes people in organizations make is to disregard the direct cash consequences of the specific plan under discussion. Even more dangerous is to disregard the *indirect* impact of any decision. Sometimes these indirect consequences may turn out to have even greater effects on cash flows and cash balances.

Because budgets are the tool that many organizations use to make strategic choices, it is imperative that those responsible for preparing budget recommendations fully analyze both the direct and indirect cash consequences of each project. Those with the responsibility for *approving* a budget have an equal task in reviewing the presentations and asking their own questions.

It is easy to decide to spend cash, particularly if seemingly plenty of it is available. But, as a firm like IBM found out, this can change quickly. One year they had so much cash available that the best alternative was to go out in the stock market and buy back literally billions of dollars of their own stock. Just a few years later, after severe losses, they had to replenish their cash by selling securities, but by then their credit rating was down and the cost of borrowing was up.

Forecasting cash requirements is tough, whether you are IBM or any one else. The lesson should be, therefore, to test the cash consequences of *every* business decision.

3

TCM for Marketing

Increase Sales Through
Total Cash Management

*Price wars are nothing new in the
computer-disk drive market.... The price wars
have already landed some companies in
serious trouble.... When will the slashing
end? No company wants to back down because
drives must be sold fast or they become dated
and lose even more value.... The likely result,
most analysts figure, is that stronger
companies will start eating weaker ones. The
three largest drive makers have plenty of
cash–$1.5 billion combined–to go shopping.
And the next three biggest companies would
make juicy prey.*
> *Business Week,* July 12, 1993 [p. 31]

In both tennis and boxing, there is a saying "A good *big* man will beat a good *small* man every time." If everything else is equal, size counts. This is true in business as well: A cash-rich firm will beat a cash-poor firm every time–if the well financed firm takes advantage of its resources. Good management and a sharply focused strategy, however, can overcome sheer financial muscle. Just a look at the personal computer business should suffice. First Apple, then Compaq, and finally Dell, in hardware, and then Microsoft in software, all took on IBM and ran rings around one of America's wealthiest firms–wealthy at least in the early and mid-1980s.

But if that is not persuasive, contrast Ford and GM with the Japanese upstarts who priced their initial offerings below the umbrella offered by the Big 3.

Customers, whether individuals or companies, pay attention to price. To be able to offer lower prices means either having lower operating and production costs or accepting lower margins, combined with the financial strength of sufficient cash to keep the business going. It is easy today to look at the competitive advantages Wal-Mart has, but few people are aware of the high-risk strategy involved at the start. Once the formula works, and the growth becomes self-sustaining, it is easy. Getting to that point, however, requires a total understanding of every facet of the business, including how it impacts the demands on and the supply of cash.

If you can afford to undercut your competitors' prices, you will increase your market share. Increased market share, in turn, provides the volume base over which to spread fixed costs. The questions therefore become (1) can we afford to cut prices, and, if so (2) should we? This is not to say that all companies should try to be price leaders; by definition only one firm can have lower prices. Some businesses do very well having higher prices, higher margins, and lower volume. But on balance the more aggressive companies, striving for growth, are the ones that usually win the race.

Volume vs. Margins

Many years ago it was a common sight to see three or even four service stations at an intersection. Prices, while not advertised boldly were often identical. Brand loyalty was high. A Shell customer would hardly think of buying at a Standard Oil station, and vice versa. Each station had relatively low volume, and reasonable gross profit margins.

Today, there are far fewer stations, brand loyalty has decreased dramatically, and a lot of gasoline is sold on price alone. In fact the term *service* station is dropping from common usage in this era of self-service. But there are still many locations where more than one station survives, and it is interesting to compare prices and pricing strategy. Some stations consistently are price leaders, always striving to be lower than their competitors, while others seemingly are willing to forgo volume in favor of higher margins. If you were to predict which station will be here five years from now, the odds would have to be on the high-volume/low-price firm. Years ago 20,000 gallons a month was a large station, but now some are doing 100,000 gallons a month or more.

Think about the economics. The land cost is the same irrespective of volume. The capital investment in underground tanks, pumps, and office/convenience store is the same. The high-volume station, however, has to be open longer hours, and in the final analysis is going to be run by hired managers and a lot of minimum wage employees who need supervision. The lower-volume station, often owner-operated, may end up today with the same net profit, because a 3- to 5-cent difference in selling price translates to a substantial difference in gross margin. Put another way, the volume station can be cutting its gross margin by 25 percent or more; thus, just to break even, it has to sell 35 percent more gallons. Over time, however, if consumers become more price-oriented and less brand-motivated, the volume approach is the way to survive.

Now let's look at the cash requirements for a low-price/high-volume strategy. These break down into (1) operating expenses and (2) inventory investment, and (3) receivables in industries selling on credit.

Operating Expenses.   These tend to rise as volume increases and salaries (including benefits) must generally be paid quickly, that is, weekly or every two weeks at the latest. Since payroll costs tend to remain constant, irrespective of short-term changes in volume, cash resources must be sufficient to carry a firm for a period of time if volume is less than anticipated. Thus using low selling prices as a marketing strategy, hoping that the lower *margin rate* plus the increased level of expenses will more than be offset by higher volume, is a gamble. The gamble can pay off, but, as with participants in a poker game, inevitably there will be a string of bad luck and you want to be able to stay in the game financially until things turn around. The stronger your balance sheet, or the greater your access to credit, the greater the likelihood this approach will pay off.

Inventory Investment.   This tends to go up as volume increases. Distinguish between the turnover *rate* and the absolute dollars of investment. All other things being equal, higher volumes improve turnover ratios. But since the purchase of inventories has to be paid for before you receive cash, expanding the product mix or enlarging the inventory level has cash consequences. It is interesting to peruse the catalogs of successful mail order firms. Invariably they get started with a product or product line that sells well. The analysis then goes, "Well, our biggest cost is the catalog printing and mailing postage. So it won't cost much more to add another product or product line." What is forgotten is that more inventory also has to be added. Further, as discussed in Chap. 4, to maintain an order fulfillment rate becomes progressively harder the greater the breadth of products sold.

If you are selling only fresh pears by mail, your inventory management policy is limited to estimating total sales for the year, assuming the fruit keeps well in storage. Irrespective of whether people order boxes of 5 pieces or boxes of 30, the packaging can be done at the last minute. If you are selling a variety of fruits, some of which you grow and some of which you purchase (for example, if you expand your catalog from pears to fruits), you now have to have a substantially bigger starting inventory. Further, keeping the inventory in balance is progressively more difficult. What if you overestimated the demand for apples, but are running out of oranges? The point is that having a volume approach to business, trying to spread the fixed costs (in this case catalog printing and postage) over greater total sales, involves investments that may not be anticipated, on one side, or to lower sales leading to markdowns or losses.

Receivable Balances. Accounts receivable certainly go up in absolute amount as sales volume increases. Receivables will likely increase more than proportionately if a company pursues a high-volume strategy. Sales will be made to less creditworthy customers on the one hand, and on the other existing resources devoted to collection efforts will be spread over a larger base, making it less likely that any one customer will be followed up closely.

As we saw earlier, an increase in receivables does not impact reported profit, but directly affects cash flows. Financial statements showing substantial profits may provide a false sense of security to management. To restate the obvious, you cannot meet your financial obligations with receivables; liabilities such as payroll must be paid in cash. Therefore a volume strategy, if it is going to be successful, requires an understanding that there will be a strain on working capital. The availability of cash must be assured in advance.

Strangely enough, a company that recently suffered a decrease in sales is likely to have good cash balances, while a company whose sales expanded faster than expected will likely find itself running out of cash just as reported profits are at an all-time high! This is because, as sales increase, the days sales outstanding tied up in receivables is going to be in the order of 50 days or so. In practical terms this means that no cash will be coming in for sales generated during the two previous months.

But as volume increases, payroll and purchases from vendors go up proportionately. Payroll will have to be met in two weeks, causing an immediate cash drain. Vendors, seeing their own volume increasing, may be willing to grant extra credit. Experience suggests that keeping vendors happy during an expansion phase is important, and prompt payment of payables requires cash outflows faster than the inflows from your own customers.

So a market-share volume strategy, while desirable in the long run, can be pulled off only with Total Cash Management in mind right from the beginning. Put a different way, company managers should view implementation of Total Cash Management as a necessary first condition in order to be *able* to undertake a serious growth strategy.

Competitive Response

If a firm adopts a growth/volume strategy, and has the cash resources available to finance this approach, one danger is still often overlooked. The world is not static. Your actions are going to have a direct and immediate impact on your competitors. If you cut your price to win a particularly attractive piece of business, one that your major competitor thought she had sewn up, you must ask yourself, "What is she going to do in response?"

This is not to say that bold action is unwise because of fear that competitors will react. It is to say that *not* taking such reactions into account in planning can lead to unpleasant surprises. A good analogy in Washington is seen in the way Congress evaluates proposed tax law changes. If an increase in, say, capital gains taxes is proposed, the revenue impact is measured by applying the proposed new rate to the current volume of realized capital gains. The system explicitly assumes that taxpayer behavior will not change just because of the higher rates. In practice people make individual economic decisions based on their understanding of the consequences. This is why, more often than not, predictions of the increase in tax revenues, based on a static assumption of behavior, are wrong. People pay attention to the world around them.

In business, exactly the same behavior response syndrome exists. Going back to our gasoline station example, one station on a corner with four competitors would obtain 50 percent of total volume if he cut his price today and nobody responded. It is the knowledge that competitors *will* react that prevents totally destructive competitive behavior, although the recent history of the airline industry suggests that not everyone has learned this lesson.

There is nothing wrong with changing your behavior, getting more aggressive, and going after volume, as long as you do not fool yourself into thinking there is some sort of free lunch. If you want to increase your market share and are willing to pay the price, go ahead. Cut prices, for example, but just don't be surprised if others follow.

However, this may not be the worst thing in the world. If competitors cut their prices to match yours, they are going to experience the same impact on their cash. Their receivables will go up, maybe their inventory investment will have to rise, and their margins will shrink. In other words, by declaring war, cutting prices to obtain increased market share, there are going to be casualties on both sides. Once again we get back to the position that the competitor with greater financial strength is likely to win, *if he is willing to take the losses to be incurred during the struggle.*

The point here is a subtle one. Your major competitor may be a division or a subsidiary of a very large parent company, one with virtually unlimited total financial resources. But having the resources and using those resources to compete with you are *not* the same. Large Fortune 100 or even Fortune 500 firms for the most part have substantial cash resources, or can borrow them at very low incremental cost. But at the same time each of those firms has a number of separate product lines, customer categories, or geographical areas in which it is competing.

If you as a smaller firm are going up against a small unit of a giant multinational firm, it is hard to forecast what will happen. If your competitor's division manager has a lot of clout at headquarters, asks for help, and receives it, it may be that you are a lightweight going into the ring against the World Champion heavyweight. The prognosis is not good. But equally likely, if not more so, the central financial staff of a large multinational firm may not respond to the entreaties of a division manager out in the field. She may be told she is on her own. Or the division manager herself may choose not to respond directly to your competitive thrust because of an unwillingness to take a short-term hit to her reported earnings.

Remember that, in large companies, relatively few individuals (other than those who have taken this book to heart!) focus on cash. The emphasis invariably is to meet budget commitments for reported profit. In large firms, the impact of specific business actions on cash is accounted for only by a charge on the internal P&L. The real measure of performance in such large organizations is a comparison of actual to budget. Thus if you adopt an aggressive posture, the management of the division that is your competitor may be unwilling to cut prices, not because of the impact on cash, which they don't even think about, much less worry about. What they are trying to protect is reported profit.

To the extent that they match your new aggressive pricing policy, they are going to *immediately* affect their profits. Under accrual accounting, profits are measured at the time of sale. Cutting prices next week, on the next big order, will have an instant impact on this month's financial statements, irrespective of when that customer pays, whether there are future sales volume gains to be obtained, and so on.

This may explain why so many privately held firms, not under any pressure to report earnings quarterly and often managed to maximize cash flows, not taxable income, can remain competitive and even grow at the expense of larger, better financed publicly traded competitors. If two organizations start out the race absolutely even on day one, the firm that measures its performance on total cash flows is going to win the race. The firm that worries about each quarter's reported earnings is going to fall behind.

One small example will suffice. Publicly traded firms, reporting to security analysts, are severely penalized by the market if they do not live up to earnings expectations. Most favored of all are firms that promise and then deliver steady quarter-to-quarter and year-to-year growth. Unfortunately, the world does not usually work that way. There are ups and downs. So how do you report an up quarter, expected by the analysts, or continue the required 10-year tradition of constant growth, when things are not so good?

If the public had access to the internal shipment or delivery records of most publicly held manufacturing firms, a strange phenomenon would become apparent. If daily shipments were plotted on a graph, perhaps 50 percent would occur in the last week of the month and, of that, a large percentage on the last one or two business days. At the end of each fiscal quarter, the pressure for deliveries, which can be reported as sales, increases exponentially.

How are those last-minute items produced and shipped? Overtime, on the one hand, and expediting of missing parts on the other go together to permit a plant manager to meet his month's quota. But at what price? The overtime and expediting are truly nonvalue-added costs. Even worse, for the first week of the following month the plant is recovering from the adverse impact of the expediting, which often consisted of borrowing parts from other almost completed assemblies. And workers, who at first welcomed the additional overtime pay, now have become accustomed to extra income at the end of each month; so the impact on productivity is obvious.

In total, then, the efforts of a publicly traded firm to meet budget quotas, month by month and quarter to quarter, add real costs. Does the ultimate customer really care whether the shipment was made on June 29 or July 1? If you are not managing for reported income, or if your fiscal year ends on July 15, you do not care either. But the tyranny of the calendar continues, combined with the rigid definition of sales imposed by accountants. (Sales can *only* be reported and profit measured if the item actually left the shipping dock.) This leads inevitably to counterintuitive actions if efficiency and cash flow are the real criteria for success.

This ability to forget the constraints of the calendar, to concentrate energies on only those actions that enhance cash flows (keeping expenses to a minimum while maximizing cash collections from sales) is the secret weapon that enables smaller firms to take on successfully their larger and better financed competitors. Put another way, large firms, more often than not, are unable fully to use their strengths because of the artificial restraints caused by their internal budgets, as well as the rigidities of external financial reporting.

Going back to our analogy at the beginning of the chapter, a good big firm with lots of cash resources can always beat a good small firm with limited cash resources. Focusing those limited resources, however, on a relatively narrow market, one "too small" for the larger firm to *really* care about, will provide a winning strategy.

Longer Terms Equal a Lower Price

Another strategy that utilizes cash as a competitive weapon is how you grant terms to your customers. Suppose as a buyer, you have two offers from otherwise identical prospective vendors; one requires cash with the order and the other will grant you "normal" 30-day terms. Which will you choose to do business with? This hypothetical choice is not realistic. It is extremely unlikely, if your credit is good, that a new vendor would insist on immediate payment. Nevertheless, just thinking about it makes the point. Longer terms are equivalent to a lower price.

If you as a buyer would make that choice, then what are the implications for you as a seller? Could you increase market share by granting longer terms? Almost certainly the answer is yes. The beauty of this technique is that it can be tailored to very specific marketing objectives. We are not talking about a general across-the-board price change. If industry standard terms are net 30, going to a net 45 for all customers will have unpleasant consequences. Your receivable balances will go up approximately 50 percent. Your market share will most likely increase only slightly, because your competitors will *have* to follow or lose so much business that they effectively would cede the total market to you.

Competitor response, therefore, is absolutely critical, unless you want to make a preemptive strike and "up the ante" so much that weaker competitors drop out of the market. There is a problem with this strategy. Suppose it *is* designed to drive out competitors; that is, you change terms back to net 30 when some of the smaller firms have indeed dropped by the wayside. You probably are going to be accused of predatory pricing. Some court will certainly equate the longer terms with a reduced price, and there are laws against predatory pricing. There is no need to become involved in legal problems.

Selective Use of Extended Terms.   Compared with price cuts, this is a very powerful tool, one that can be used with the precision of a surgeon's scalpel. Whether it is a brief promotion, designed to boost volume near the end of a quarter, or it is aimed at a single competitor in a particular geographical area, offering extended terms is equivalent to a price cut but without the difficulty of subsequently raising prices. A formal price cut can be difficult to rescind. A temporary price cut, announced in advance as such, has a different problem. The trade will find out about it almost at once and all customers will want it, even if the purpose is to boost sales in a local area. Further, a temporary price cut invites competitors to match the price cut, negating any short-term advantage.

Offering 60-day terms, when 30 is normal in the industry, can be controlled much more easily. It can be given just to one or to a group of customers. It can be withheld from accounts that do not have a good payment record. Finally, it can be withdrawn much more easily than a formal price announcement. In cash terms, extending terms by 30 days (from net 30 to net 60) is probably equivalent to a 1-percent price reduction, assuming the cost of capital is 12 percent on an annual basis. Having sufficient financial strength to be able to offer longer terms, which from the seller's point of view means slower cash inflows, is a powerful competitive weapon.

Consignment of Merchandise. The ultimate extension of terms is to any payment defer until the merchandise is sold. For a cash-short retailer, being able to obtain inventory with no cash commitment may seem like the ultimate. In some industries, such as art dealers, this is the way things are done. An artist will let a gallery hang her pictures and is glad to get the exposure. The gallery assumes the operating costs of rent and sales help. When a customer pays cash, the gallery in turn pays the artist. Nobody is financing anyone else. However, discrete works of art, which are easy to identify and keep track of, may be the exception.

If a store has items on consignment from several sources, it has very real inventory and accounting problems. Sales must be recorded very carefully, so that proper credit can be given each seller. Who absorbs shoplifting losses? How often are settlements made with consignors? Stores, such as second-hand clothing outlets, which operate on a consignment basis, find that there truly is no free lunch as a result of not paying for their own inventory.

Many manufacturers, by financing dealer inventory at low or even zero interest cost, are effectively providing goods on consignment. In the farm equipment and construction equipment industry, which relies in large part on small locally owned dealers, 100-percent financing is common. Even in the automobile industry, where manufacturers typically charge interest on so-called wholesale receivables, the dealers are essentially receiving a $20,000 asset (the new car) with only a promise to pay when the car is sold.

From the dealer's perspective, low-interest or no-interest financing of inventory may literally be the only way he can stay in business. An inventory of 100 cars represents a $1- to $2-million investment. The bigger the dealer, the larger the inventory that must be kept. Public opinion to the contrary, selling new cars in the 1990s can be far from lucrative, as shown by the steady decline in the number of dealers. So the economics of the industry suggest that a multibillion dollar manufacturer can and should help finance the dealers' stock in trade until it is sold.

If every dealer remitted immediately upon sale the $20,000 for each car sold, or the $50,000 for each tractor sold, the system would be ideal. It would be a perfect example of a win-win situation. The manufacturer, who made the basic product and pricing decisions, gets his cash as soon as a retail customer makes a buying decision. The dealer, in practical terms, has none of her own money invested in the inventory and earns a gross profit from each sale.

There is one small flaw in this otherwise ideal scenario. What if the dealer is facing a cash shortage, perhaps because she has to make payments on rent, payroll, and taxes, and chooses to take the $50,000 cash inflow from the sale of the tractor and pay other bills? Cash, as we saw in Chap. 2, is fungible, coming into a business and going out of the business. The salesperson does not try to trace the source of his paycheck and does not even care. Neither does the IRS or the landlord. The only person with a vested interest in the specific proceeds of the tractor sale is the manufacturer. It was his tractor that got sold, and he wants his money right away.

Without going into the legal niceties, it is safe to say that, while on paper the manufacturer is well protected, in practice it may be hard for him to keep track of all the items a dealer is *supposed* to have. Manufacturers typically send auditors, or expect the local sales representative, to monitor sales by the dealer. Printouts are provided to check off, by serial number, the assets that the dealer has not reported as sold and that therefore should still be on hand. Guess what? Sometimes the dealer's physical inventory does not tie up with the manufacturer's records!

Discrepancies can be caused by any number of circumstances, but they fall into three categories. (1) The tractor is not sold, but is on loan to a farmer as a demonstrator. That's OK. (2) There is a mistake in the paperwork, either at the manufacturer or at the dealer (say two dealers legitimately swapped tractors), and it is a matter of getting the records straightened out. (3) The dealer diverted the cash from the sale, sometimes referred to as *SOT* (sold out of trust) and neglected to pay the manufacturer, either deliberately or accidentally.

Sales on consignment, in short, lend themselves to abuse. In turn this requires extra recordkeeping, monitoring, auditing, and ultimately confrontations between the parties, which must be resolved. There is always tension between a manufacturer and a dealer or distributor. Manufacturers think the dealer is not working hard enough; dealers complain about everything from the product itself, to pricing, to field support. This tension is only aggravated by disputes over consigned inventory.

There may not be a better way to do business. In terms of cash flows and cash requirements, consignment of inventory may be the best solution. But it does require a lot of effort to make the system work. In effect, the almost unlimited extension of credit represented by the consigned inventory is a giant collection problem for the manufacturer. There may be a false sense of security, because in theory the assets are supposed to cover the real debt. Legally the manufacturer sold the assets, and has a security interest until a retail customer is found. In practice, it is really the manufacturer's own inventory, but under the physical control of a possibly undercapitalized business owner. The potential for trouble is never far away, and there are really no good solutions.

Granting Credit to Poorer Credit Risks

There is a saying, "You get what you measure." If a credit manager is measured on the amount of bad debts that have to be written off, what is a likely result? She is going to work hard to collect outstanding receivables, certainly. But even more to the point, she is not going to want to take chances on potentially poor credit risks. For a credit manager it is easier not to sell to someone in the first place than to work hard at collecting a past due account four months later.

As we will see in Chap. 4, the out-of-pocket costs associated with additional production are low. Put another way, the incremental profits from additional sales at the margin often can be substantial. The best way to analyze the situation and to arrive at reasonable credit decision rules is to look at real cash flows.

First, determine the present level of bad debts. This includes only accounts written down or written off because of the customer's inability to pay. Sales adjustments because of disputes, shipment errors, and quality problems may show in the financial statements as bad debts because they were uncollectible. But not all uncollectible receivables are bad debts, at least as defined here. What we need to know is the percentage of sales that we would not have shipped in the first place, had we known originally that the customer could not pay for them. Nobody deliberately ships merchandise or provides services knowing they will not be paid. Obviously, each of today's true bad debts represents an error in credit analysis at the time of sale.

Having determined the true level of bad debts with today's credit policies in effect—and it is likely to be relatively low, such as 1–2 percent of sales—the next step is to estimate the cash contribution from incremental sales if they are collected. Essentially this is the sales price less variable production costs, costs of warehousing and shipping, and any sales commissions. Some people use the term *avoidable costs*, which, while imprecise, is as good as anything.

Subtracting avoidable costs from sales gives a margin, and for most companies this is going to range anywhere from 40 to 60 percent. Note that at some point all fixed and overhead costs must be covered, but we are talking right now about decisions at the margin. Should we or should we not accept this particular order? If we do not take it, what of our fixed expenses is going to go away? The answer is that, for this decision, the 40- to 60-percent figure is relevant.

However, to be totally fair, if we grant credit to a marginal customer, we should expect, and therefore allow for, longer collection time and additional resources required to monitor the account and follow up on payment promises. Since this is a rough approximation at best, let's be generous and subtract 10 percent of sales for the extra costs associated with doing business with marginal customers. On a worst case scenario we would still be ahead by 30 percent of the sales dollar if we sold or delivered to a marginal customer, one who our normal credit screening would reject, and the customer did in fact pay us for the goods or services.

This is so important that it is worth putting a different way. If we absolutely know that someone is never going to pay us, the decision is easy. Don't sell! But if there is a reasonable chance that, with some hand holding perhaps, the prospect will ultimately pay, then it is a matter of evaluating the probabilities.

Of our present customer base, 98 percent pays. If only 75 percent of the prospective marginal customers pay, we will still be better off with the volume than without it. We can, in short, afford a 25 percent bad debt write-off on this class of sales and still bring in more cash.

To avoid putting the Credit manager in a bad light, according to today's rules of thumb, we should set up a collection reserve of 25 percent of these marginal sales right from the start, the day of shipment. This means identifying each marginal customer, one who would ordinarily be turned down, as part of a new sales classification. It is vital that these incremental sales maintain their identity in both the accounting and sales records. At the end of one year—and it will take at least that long to evaluate fairly the experiment—a review of sales volume and actual bad debt experience will reveal the true benefits. The Credit manager will get credit for the incremental sales, not blame for the higher level of write-offs.

The real economics of most businesses are hidden by the accounting and financial reports. All overhead expenses are usually spread over all sales, which makes it look like profit margins are uniformly low and the cost of bad debts very high. More often than not, it is a very profitable exercise to give the marginal customers a second chance for credit approval, add their sales volume as truly incremental, and then measure them separately, without an allocation for expenses that would go on with them or without them.

A word of warning, however. This approach presupposes that credit decisions are made by someone other than the sales representative. If the sales rep, in practice, decides credit limits and is paid on a commission based on sales or deliveries, this approach will not work. What we are recommending is a measured lowering of credit standards in order to increase sales incrementally. Higher bad debts will occur, and it will take several months to show up.

The solution is not to pay any commissions on these identified marginal sales until the cash is received from the customer. If commissions are earned based on cash received, then the sales reps should be empowered. They should be given the authority to extend credit to prospective customers that don't pass the normal screen, but who in their judgment represent reasonable risks. Giving each sales rep a budget for such credit risks, and not penalizing them if some ultimately do not pay, will in practice expand sales and directly impact cash flow in a favorable way.

One question has not been answered. How do we identify which of the customers we should accept, prospects who ordinarily would have been turned down? As with the famous dictum about obscenity, "I cannot define it, I just know it when I see it," there is no substitute for human judgment. It may be impossible to write rigid rules or program a computer to make these decisions for us. What we are looking for are small, newly established companies with good growth prospects. If we go the extra mile with them now, then, if they are successful, they will remember the help we gave them at the start. If they have a bad credit history today but convince us that things have really changed, the chance we take now is probably reasonable.

There is such a thing as loyalty in business. We prefer to do business with our friends. Remember, every large successful company today started out at some point as a small enterprise, seeming risky at the time. It is unreasonable to expect any Credit manager or salesperson to bat 1000 or even 800 in picking possible winners from known losers. But as we just saw, if you can maintain a 750 batting average—and good judgment and common sense will accomplish this—your cash flow will be aided. Just do not let obsolete accounting and financial reporting conventions lead to bad decision making.

Using Dating to Even Out Production

One of the major benefits of Total Cash Management is that it integrates all business decisions. The impact of production levels on inventories has an effect on cash. Increasing sales volume raises receivables but reduces inventories. Spending cash resources on new product development or on a marketing program draws down cash right now, with benefits expected in the future. One of the principal messages of TCM is that every business decision should be made in terms of cash impact, not in terms of how it shows up in a departmental budget report or in the next quarterly 10-K report to the SEC.

A perfect example of utilizing cash in a marketing program to help production, with an ultimate benefit for each functional area and for the business as a whole, arises in firms with seasonal demand or seasonal production. If you make toys, retail sales are concentrated in November and December, while if you produce boats, demand is greatest in the spring. If you are involved in the canning of beans, corn, or other vegetables, your production is totally controlled by the growing season.

Taking the seasonal demand situation first, let's look at how pricing and sales terms to customers can help reduce operating costs. A manufacturer of sailboats requires a significant amount of space if he is to store finished goods output prior to shipping the boats to his customers, boat dealers. Further, the manufacturing process for boats made of wood is rather lengthy and requires highly skilled labor. These characteristics are diametrically the opposite of those required for a just-in-time production system.

It is simply not realistic for boat manufacturers to wait until they receive orders from dealers in the spring or for dealers to order only after they make a retail sale in April. With the best production system conceivable, you as a boat buyer are not going to order a boat in April and then wait for the factory to process your order. Delivery, if made to order, would not be before August, and, as someone put it, the boat then isn't three months late, it's nine months early. For certain types of luxury goods, unless orders can be delivered quickly, the sale will be lost. It may take us six months to make up our minds to buy a new car, but once we place the order we would like the car right away. That is human nature.

The implications of this are that, somewhere in the distribution channel, an inventory of finished goods must be available. For sailboats this inventory can be in any of three places: the boat builder's production facility, at a warehouse location, or at the dealer. If it is not in one of those three places, retail customers are not going to wait for production.

With regard to the first alternative, if retail sales are concentrated in the spring, this means that most of a year's production has to have been built by January or February. For a manufacturer to attempt to store eight to ten months' production at his own facility has two problems. He probably does not have the physical space, and the cash requirements (the funds tied up in inventory) are going to put a real strain on both working capital and borrowing capacity.

Second, moving the finished goods inventory out to geographically dispersed warehouse locations throughout the country is going to solve the physical space problem at the factory. But then it adds the cost of shipment into and out of the warehouse, plus complexity problems if a dealer on the east coast wants a particular model of boat located only in an Oregon warehouse. There is more flexibility if the entire finished goods inventory is in one place. Disbursing a finished goods inventory of boats in warehouses is probably not cost-effective.

The third alternative is to let the boats be at the dealers' places of business. This is ideal, because dealers will order the models they think their customers will want. Delivery to the retail customer can be almost instantaneous. From the manufacturer's perspective, this will help smooth out production during the year, if the boat can be shipped to a dealer upon completion, irrespective of the season.

With the last alternative, what we have described is a win-win-win situation for the manufacturer, dealer, and retail customer. If production is carried out smoothly throughout the year, the dealers will order what they think will sell and have it on hand, in inventory. When the selling season arrives, customers gain by being able to see exactly what they are buying. Manufacturing costs will be minimized and sales will be maximized.

This terrific scenario has one minor flaw. Most dealers are undercapitalized and cannot pay for inventory ten, eight, or even six months before a retail sale is made. The obvious solution is for the manufacturer to extend very long terms to the dealer for early ordering and delivery. And this is what happens. For an order placed by a dealer in August, for November delivery, the manufacturer may well offer *both* a seasonal price discount and delayed payment until spring.

The cash consequences go both ways. A significant price discount, perhaps 10 percent, will come right out of finally realized cash receipts and ultimately out of profits. Extending payment for up to six months has the direct impact of delaying all cash receipts for that period. In other words you as a manufacturer cannot expect either the retail customer or the dealer to lay out cash before the product is useful or usable. But the seasonal discount in November will allow dealers to offer a price reduction to retail buyers if they make a buying commitment prior to the normal buying season. And the delayed payment terms provided by the manufacturer allows the dealer to offer comparable terms to the retail buyer.

The big win for the manufacturer comes in spreading manufacturing activities throughout the year. A smaller, highly trained work force and reduced physical manufacturing facilities are needed if 30 boats are made each month for 12 months, compared to trying to build 90 a month for four months and then laying off the workers. It does not take an MBA in finance to figure out the cash savings from smoothing out production, never mind the benefits in improved quality from a trained work force.

How big should the price discount be? And how long should delayed payment terms be? No all-purpose formula can be developed. The variables are the gross profit from increased sales (since a certain number of sales would never be made if inventory on hand was not available), reduced hiring and training costs (including reduced unemployment benefits), and much smaller investment required in physical facilities. These are offset by the interest cost on the outstanding receivables and the price discount.

The greeting card industry for years has offered to delay payments from dealers for seasonal cards if orders are placed early and shipments accepted prior to the selling season. A company like Hallmark figures, rightly, if a dealer has a basement full of Christmas cards in August, even if they do not have to be paid for until December, that dealer will set up his display earlier and ultimately sell more cards than if the system was cranked up only from November 15 on. Interestingly, to encourage large orders, which in turn may boost total sales, the card manufacturer may offer partial credit for unsold Christmas cards, if the dealer keeps them until next year. If the dealer needs the cash or does not have the space, then the traditional post-Christmas "50 percent off" sale is held. Since there is a 50-percent gross profit in greeting cards, the dealer breaks even (not including overhead) on all cards converted into cash after the holiday season.

Finally, let's look at agricultural products, which have a finite growing season. A vegetable canner cannot buy fresh vegetables from farmers in Wisconsin except in July through early October. But farmers can sell the crop only when it is ripe. By definition, then, all production and sale by the farmers are going to be concentrated in a very short time frame, no matter the desires of either the farmer or the vegetable canner. The cash problem for canners is that they have to pay the farmer immediately upon delivery, but receive payment from supermarket customers only when they ship later throughout the year.

The unfortunate circumstance for the canner is that, just when the supply is greatest, say September, retail demand is at its lowest since many people prefer to buy fresh, locally grown produce rather than canned vegetables. Reducing the price of a can of peas or corn or tomatoes is not going to switch consumers to the canned product. Here the only solution is for the manufacturer to hold the inventory and hope that prices rise throughout the next ten months. The cash requirements to be in the canning business are substantial, and that is basically why the business is concentrated with a relatively few large well financed firms. Total Cash Management is powerful in many ways, but the laws of nature, such as the timing of the normal growing season, simply cannot be overcome no matter how good the financial strategy.

Cash Requirements for New Product Introductions

All the published statistics show that the failure rate for new consumer products is absurdly high. Despite spending, in some cases, millions of dollars, large sophisticated firms seemingly are unable to predict what will and what will not strike consumers' fancy. Failure of a new product launch has multiple consequences, including the write-off of all the investment spent getting the product to market. Perhaps even more serious is the loss of time and momentum, since the earlier decision to go forward with product A inherently meant that possible product B was not pursued. So when A is a failure, and a decision is made to revisit B, valuable time has been lost.

This discussion of Total Cash Management cannot help select winners from losers (if we could, such a book would be a guaranteed best-seller). TCM can provide tools to increase the odds in favor of a successful new product launch.

Retailers (of consumer goods) and distributors (of industrial products) are not, all other things being equal, looking to add items to their inventory. They too know about the failure rate for new products. Sophisticated distributors also know that, every time they add something to their line, significant costs are associated with the move. Not only is there an investment in inventory dollars, but the logistics system bears an additional burden. Space is required on shelves, transportation has to be arranged, more paperwork will be processed (from purchasing, through receiving to payables), and in the final analysis employees have to cope with more complexity. Therefore there is a natural reluctance to change, which in practice means it is easier to say no when your sales force wants them to try a new item.

The solution is to make it economically attractive for your customer to buy. One of the most effective ways is to use cash resources creatively. How can you provide a higher-than-normal gross profit for your customers, to help them offset the increased costs they will bear? There are a number of ways.

Price Discounts and Delayed Payments. These are both going to be attractive to customers. Raising your customers' gross profit through price discounts will, of course, adversely affect your gross margins and have the further disadvantage that nobody likes to see, a subsequent price increase. So a low introductory price has to be used cautiously; you do not want to train customers to expect a continuing low selling price. But certainly being willing to sacrifice some gross margin early in the new product cycle may be a sound investment, one requiring a willingness (and ability) to withstand a temporary reduction in cash inflows. On the other hand, pulling an unsuccessful new product idea off the market has even more catastrophic consequences. A continuing "investment" in low margins in the initial stages not only makes sound business sense, it may be the only way to persuade your customers (retailers and distributors) to add your new product. Related to initial price discounts is the opportunity to delay payment. If 30-day terms are normal, then offering 60 or even 90 days for a new product means that the customers' cash requirements will be reduced. They will still have all the costs associated with adding an SKU to their line, but fortunately that analysis is not carried out quite so frequently. The argument is potent: "There is no investment required, because you will be able to sell the item and collect from *your* customer before you have to pay us."

In terms of Total Cash Management, is there any difference between a temporary price discount and a temporary lengthening of credit terms? The answer is no. In one case we get our normal cash receipts, say, 60 days late, and in the other we get less cash in on normal schedule. Since a cost is associated with the investment in 60 additional days receivable balances or with reduced gross profit, it is a matter of how you choose to allocate your resources. Of course, offering both a lower price and delayed terms might be irresistible to your customer—if you can afford it. Making this kind of decision is what marketing people, and sales representatives with a good feel for the market, get paid to do. What is important is that they truly understand the concepts of TCM—the cash consequences of alternative marketing investments. Assuring the success of a new product offering, even at the cost of providing price discounts and longer terms, may be preferable to seeing a good product idea go down in flames because of customer unwillingness in the short term to try it. Using cash resources to encourage customer purchasing decisions can be a very sound strategy, assuming you have those resources available in the first place.

Buying Shelf Space. This recent development in the grocery business is sometimes referred to as a "slotting allowance." It boils down to a recognition by large retailers that shelf space is their most valuable asset. With a finite amount of space in any store and an almost infinite number of prospective products that could be carried, store management is turning this asset into a cash generator. Manufacturers who want A&P, Safeway, or Kroger to stock their item are told that an up-front cash payment is necessary. That payment simply provides the manufacturer with the right or privilege of selling items to the store, at normal terms. Put the other way, if the slotting allowance is not paid for, a competitor's products will be displayed in the space.

This approach started out with frozen goods, where there truly was a limited volume of space in freezers. The addition of a "new" product meant either substituting it for an existing line or buying more deep freeze capacity. The store chain faced a significant cash commitment if additional frozen foods were to be added. So it made sense in effect to ask suppliers to share in the incremental costs when both parties would benefit.

Now, this same concept is being applied to everything from spices to beans. It is not a matter of additional capital outlays or additional cash operating expenses. The limiting factor is the size of the store itself, and in effect the store owners are in a monopoly position, able to charge "rent."

The next logical step, therefore, was to charge the rent in the form of a slotting allowance. Once again, suppliers with strong cash resources were in a position to muscle out less well-financed competitors. To some, the stores' behavior may not seem ethical, but if there is greater demand than supply for a limited resource, in this case shelf space, the market economy has solved the issue through the price mechanism—cash.

Financing Your Customer. A good example of this form of using cash as a marketing tool is the jet engine manufacturer. The industry has only three suppliers of essentially comparable products, products with relatively few potential customers and a very high unit selling price. Jet engines also have the characteristic of requiring vast up-front engineering expense, as well as high corporate and factory overhead and support. Winning or losing a single order can have a material impact on profitability, cash flow, and ultimately the survival of the engine manufacturer.

It is no wonder that, assuming the products are priced the same and have the same performance specifications, competition among the three became centered on who could provide the greatest resources to the ultimate customer for the jet engine, the individual airline. Airlines have for years been financially troubled because of ongoing operating losses, and it is logical that they would specify a particular jet engine if they received large low-cost loans. Perhaps GE, the best capitalized of the three suppliers, would have an advantage here because of its captive finance company. On the other hand if the finance company has to stand on its own and show shareholders a separate profit, then a Pratt & Whitney or Rolls Royce could have an advantage.

On a much smaller scale, the automobile companies—GMAC as an example—finance not only their dealers who are their immediate customers, but also the ultimate retail buyer. One way to stimulate car sales has been to provide below-market interest rates to retail buyers. Again, a use of cash as a marketing tool, one that is equivalent to a price reduction, but with the advantage of much greater flexibility. Special financing terms can be offered on certain models only or in a specific geographic region without going through the trouble of having first a general price reduction and then a price increase when the marketing objectives have been accomplished.

Coupons. This type of nonprice discount still has cash consequences. The concept underlying coupons is that consumer demand will pull the item off store shelves. Meanwhile retailers have an incentive to stock the item because, as sales increase because consumers use the coupons, the store will receive its normal margin. The manufacturer absorbs the total cost of the coupon, which is the consumer's temporary price cut. In addition, the store is reimbursed, say, 7 cents for the administrative and clerical costs of processing the coupons. Because of economies of scale, most manufacturers rely on third-party firms, some of them located in low-wage Mexico, to handle the store reimbursement procedure. In addition, because of the potential for abuse, strict audit procedures must be set up and maintained.

Coupons, therefore, represent a fairly expensive way to get consumers to try a new product or switch from a long-time competitor. But it works, or none of the large sophisticated consumer product firms would continue the practice. What coupons require is deep pockets—plenty of financial and cash resources. Once again, if two competitors, otherwise equally matched, choose to fight it out in the marketing arena, the one with greater firepower, cash in this case, will win. This may explain why today there are only three large soap manufacturers or three large breakfast cereal suppliers. The cost of entry to the marketing battle, in terms of cash resources, is formidable.

Advertising. This is the grand-daddy of all marketing tools. It is only necessary to point out that, unlike coupons, advertising can be bought in exceedingly small increments. True, few can afford $800,000 for a 30-second Super Bowl TV commercial. But almost every retail business can advertise locally in newspapers, while industrial products can be promoted inexpensively in trade publications. The old saying is undoubtedly true: "I know that half of all my advertising is wasted, it's just that I do not know which half." But if you really can't make perfect buying decisions, at least neither can your competitors.

Perhaps the key point, in terms of Total Cash Management, is the role of advertising and advertising commitments in a period of economic difficulty. Advertising professionals, quite logically, argue that in tough times advertising should be *increased*, not cut back. If advertising really causes sales to be made, why cut back just when you need the sales the most. On the other side of the argument is the Corporate Controller, who argues that there is no hard evidence regarding the short-term impact of advertising on sales. The benefits from past expenditures can be expected to continue for a while.

Finally, while advertising is truly an investment in every sense of the word—an expenditure today to obtain a benefit in the future—the accounting profession has chosen to deny economic reality. Under Generally Accepted Accounting Principles (at least generally accepted by accountants, if not marketers!), all advertising must be charged off to expense as incurred. This means that, even if you have sufficient cash resources to continue your advertising campaigns in recessionary times, your P&L will be hit immediately.

Since earnings are going to be down anyhow, there is often pressure to prevent them from falling further by reducing advertising. Here is a perfect example of the perversity of accounting rules. Rational executives of publicly traded firms should and do respond to the stock market. The market seemingly wants steady earnings, not cash flows. If sales are off and advertising does not provide an *immediate* boost, it is hard to argue for continuing the ads, with the consequent impact on short-term earnings, no matter how smart a business decision it might be.

Here is another example of the advantage of a closely-held private firm. It can weigh the long-term costs and benefits of advertising, without pressure for maintaining quarter-to-quarter reported earnings. Thus in some ways a period of economic difficulty can give a cash-rich private firm a terrific economic advantage over its public competitors. All you need is the cash.

Research and Development.   R&D is very similar to advertising in terms of Total Cash Management. There is no certainty that any particular expenditure will have a positive payback. There is bound to be a delay between today's R&D disbursements and any future revenues. There is an accounting requirement that all R&D expenditures be written off as expense immediately. The fact that R&D meets almost every test of what is an investment carried no weight with the gurus of accounting. Because some, if not many, projects end up as "dry holes," with no future economic value, the accountants said, "Let's write off *all* R&D, just to be sure we don't carry a particular loser as an asset, an asset without any value."

Nobody ever argued that failed R&D projects should be capitalized as assets. Because auditors and accountants were uncomfortable trying to determine *which* projects were winners and which were losers, it was *easier* to write them all off. Easier, but not better. Management, responsible for continuing or terminating particular projects, presumably feels capable of evaluating each project on a go or no-go basis. Why can't the accountants?

The final bottom-line impact of immediately charging off all R&D to expense is that large, well financed firms have a huge competitive advantage, while smaller privately held companies, which may have to rely on outside sources of finance, are terribly disadvantaged. In point of fact the U.S. Department of Commerce, with its interest in helping the country develop leading edge technology, has shown concern about this phenomenon. Until the accounting rules change and bankers are not scared off by reported short-term losses, small firms are going to be unable to sustain R&D. If bankers and other creditors look askance at losses, losses caused in part by the mandatory expensing of all R&D, what is the impact on the U.S. economy? Everyone agrees that small businesses tend to be more entrepreneurial, more likely to come up with new technologies and new products. To accomplish this requires current outlays today, for R&D, in the hope of hitting it big tomorrow. Penalizing reported earnings for today's R&D expenditures, which in practice then impacts the availability of cash resources, is poor public policy.

(Don't believe for a minute that accounting rules are of interest only to accountants. Look at the impact on postretirement health care. Once the FASB said that companies had to account today for those future expenses, many firms reevaluated their plans and almost without exception reduced the promises of future benefits and in many cases changed the level of today's benefits.)

Volume Discounts

Over the years there has been great social concern that large companies, as buyers, have a competitive advantage over smaller firms. If they could buy cheaper, then they could sell cheaper. And if they sold cheaper, they would drive their smaller competitors out of business. This dispute has been well covered in academic dissertations, as well as textbooks. While this book is not the appropriate place to argue the pros and cons, what is important is the idea that large buyers have an advantage. How that advantage should be handled and what is the socially most desirable outcome—since the interests of consumers may not coincide with those of smaller suppliers—are ultimately political issues.

From the TCM point of view, the understanding is that there is going to be a relationship between the volume of sales and the price paid. Obviously the more you buy, the lower your unit costs should be. As a seller, you will receive less, but may have lower operating and selling costs. Understanding the cost/volume and the volume/price relationships is important to both parties. Buyers can perhaps extract lower selling prices in exchange for the higher volumes, or, put another way, the loyalty shown by repeated purchases should be rewarded. (Using leverage as a large buyer to reduce purchasing prices is covered in Chap. 4.)

For the seller, a true understanding of the benefits of dealing with established customers can justify lower selling price. Another way to look at it is to evaluate the profitability of doing business with the relatively few largest customers as contrasted with the real costs of numerous smaller customers. Perhaps aggressive pricing, which involves cash flows, can convert presently small customers into long-term large buyers. If you think about it, the best of all worlds, from the perspective of cash flows, would be a few large customer accounts. They would have relatively low selling expense and an assurance that payments would be made at agreed-upon due dates. It is likely that total profits and cash flows would be greater than dealing with a much larger and constantly changing group of smaller customers.

Unfortunately today's accounting systems tend not to highlight the profit disparities among customers. Almost all overhead costs tend to be spread evenly over sales volumes. This means that such things as engineering and customer service costs at the front end, and warehousing and distribution costs at the other end are *allocated* in accounting reports. This method of accounting and cost analysis was once described as the "peanut butter" method, since almost all costs are taken in total and then spread smoothly across the board. When looked at closely and analyzed in detail, most firms find that certain customers, or classes of customers, require more than their share of engineering and customer service resources. Warehousing and distribution costs may vary not so much with total volume, but rather with the number of customers or number of shipping destinations. This approach to cost analysis is usually referred to as *activity-based costing* (ABC). The whole purpose of ABC and its tremendous benefit in the marketing arena is that for the first time we can truly know which customers are carrying their weight and which may be losers.

It is hard to generalize that all large customers are profitable and that all smaller buyers are losers. In fact, companies often find that one or two large customers are so demanding and receive so many special services that they are part of the problem, not part of the solution. But by and large an examination of all costs incurred in meeting customer requirements—starting with product design, and going through manufacturing and distribution to selling and customer service—will disclose that a *lot* of costs are being incurred because of the large number of small accounts.

This does *not* mean get rid of them. You undoubtedly would be worse off without the business volume of small customers than with it. What it does suggest is that *keeping existing customers and expanding their volume* should be a high priority. Lots of overhead costs, now spread across all sales, are caused by the *number of customers*, not by the dollar volume of sales. This would include much of the accounting and credit functions and the out-of-pocket costs of maintaining a sales staff. The cost per sales call (travel and living expenses) is the same, whether the customer buys nothing, $1000, or $50,000. The cost of maintaining information on shipping requirements, ordering trucks, following up on lost shipments, and other activities is customer-driven, not volume-driven.

In many cases it will pay to undertake this exact kind of cost analysis, using activity-based costing. Accountants have tended to resist adoption of ABC, but the information is so valuable that marketing management should insist on it.

Assuming that the profitability is as forecast (that large customers tend to provide a more than proportional share of overall cash flow and profits), then it logically follows that pricing should recognize this phenomenon. Discounts based on volume come directly out of profits. But that is not the issue. What is important is to understand that losing a large customer, because a competitor offers lower prices, can be very costly. Of course, price is not the only variable in a buyer/seller relationship, as the TQM movement has demonstrated. But if all *other* factors are equal, buying decisions will be made on price.

The lesson is that rewarding good customers with lower prices than those offered to occasional buyers is plain good business. Providing customers with an incentive to concentrate their business with you will have long-term favorable benefits. Just because the typical accounting report does not necessarily show this in the manner described should not be an excuse for inaction. Get the facts and act accordingly.

In the long run selling prices tend to follow costs quite closely. If, in fact, you have significantly lower costs in doing business with large customers—whether or not those costs are revealed in your accounting reports—the buyer will expect to capture a significant share of the savings. Alternatively, competitors understand that their costs undercut yours, you will lose the business anyhow, and your cash flow will be affected adversely. Finally, by keeping selling prices in line with real costs, you will be assured of full compliance with antitrust laws regarding discriminatory pricing.

Cash Discounts for Prompt Payment

In many industries this is a relatively easy decision, because every one offers customers standard terms. While the actual range of terms is relatively wide, for this discussion, let's look at "2/10 n 30." As every finance student knows, this means that customers who pay within ten days can deduct 2 percent off the invoice price. If they do not take the discount, the amount is due "net" at the end of 30 days. So far, so good.

The economics, to both the buyer and seller, are the same. If taken on day ten, a 2-percent discount is equivalent to a 36-percent annual rate of interest, *assuming* the invoice will otherwise be paid on day 30. These assumptions are interesting and must be carefully evaluated. How do we explain the fact that any number of well run and well financed firms do *not* pay within ten days? Very few companies can earn 36 percent in any other investment!

Given the quality of mail service offered by the U.S. Postal Service, it is almost an impossibility for an invoice to be mailed, the item received by the customer, a check to be cut, and mailed back to be *received* by the sender in ten business days, much less ten calendar days. Therefore the terms "2/10" have to be defined, in order to be operational. Is the ten-day period counted from the postmark on the return envelope? Is it the date on the check? Or is it really *15* days, again with the same problem in definition?

This may appear to be a nit-picking discussion, but keep in mind that most billings, disbursements, and cash applications have been automated and are handled either by computer or by low-paid clerks. *You* are not deciding whether an unearned discount should be allowed or charged back. Neither the computer nor your clerks know good customers from marginal ones. Unfortunately, in this age of automation, rules must be developed that can be written down and programmed for a computer. Compounding this particular problem is that most payments are sent to a bank lock-box (discussed in Chap. 5), and you may not even have the envelope or maybe even a copy of the check to verify dates.

But if you do not have rules about when cash discounts will be allowed, and when they will be charged back as unearned, it is a sure bet that your customers will soon discover the absence of any discipline on your part and some of them will start to exploit this anomaly. Pretty soon they will be paying in 30 days and still taking the discount. Then where are you? The prompt payment aspect has been lost, and you have just provided *some* of your customers, not necessarily the ones you would have chosen, a 2-percent price discount. Now you have the worst of both worlds, an unanticipated price cut, plus no improvement in cash receipts.

Monitoring Cash Discounts. Monitoring is an absolute necessity. This means that decision rules have to be established and that those rules have to be followed religiously. Because payments are mailed to your bank's lockbox or processed by entry-level clerical help, the rules must be understandable, such that good customers will not become upset. In practice this means that a 2-percent discount for prompt payment cannot be in ten days, no matter how ancient the tradition of such terms.

A suggested approach would be to program your computer to show, in a prominent location on the invoice, that a 2-percent discount, an amount of *x* dollars, will be allowed if payment is *received* by you on or before a specific calendar date. "A 2-percent discount of $835.65 will be allowed if payment is received by us on October 31, 19XX." The only question is how much leeway should be provided. Given the flexibility of computers, it would be feasible actually to have different elapsed time schedules for specific customers. The point is that realistic timetables should be set up and then adhered to. If a good customer misses the schedule consistently by one or two days, it is relatively easy to reprogram for that circumstance. But for routine day-to-day transactions, a firm policy of charging back unearned discounts must be adhered to.

We need not repeat here what to do with customers who choose not to avail themselves of the discount period, and also do not pay within the stated 30-day period for net. At this point the offering of a cash discount is no longer a marketing tool. (Collecting past-due receivables is covered in Chap. 7.)

No law of nature says that cash discounts have to be 2 percent. Some firms have found that a 1-percent or even $\frac{1}{2}$-percent discount can be effective. Many firms have set up instructions in their accounts payable systems to pay *all* invoices offering a discount on the discount date, so as to take the discount. In other words, any cash discount not taken represents a black mark for the Accounts Payable supervisor. Under such circumstances the customer's computer does not distinguish between 2 percent and $\frac{1}{2}$ percent. They are both cash discounts and the same decision rules apply. Before jumping into this approach, however, be advised that some companies do distinguish between the two and program their computers, depending on current interest rates, to accept some discounts and disregard all smaller ones. As interest rates go up, a small cash discount becomes less meaningful, while in a period of low interest rates a 2-percent discount can be quite meaningful.

This leads to an alternative strategy, *raising* the discount rate for prompt payment. For example, a manufacturer of seasonal farm equipment offered a 4-percent discount on purchases paid for within a short period. This accomplished three things.

First, it allowed the salespeople to promote this as a price reduction. For dealers able to pay promptly, the net cash purchase price of the manufacturer's products just went down. That was very well received.

Second, the company enforced the discount terms strictly, having told the dealers this would be done. The result was that cash receipts were truly speeded up. Average days sales outstanding went down. Customers who formerly chose to forgo the smaller cash discount, and then did not pay promptly on the remaining net terms, now had no choice but to take the higher discount, because it represented an unparalleled profit opportunity. If you are operating as a dealer on a 20-percent gross margin, an additional 4 percent is meaningful.

Finally, management examined extra carefully the credit status of the relatively few dealers who did *not* take the 4 percent. Only a dealer with real cash flow problems was forced to forgo the opportunity. But if such a customer could not take advantage of the opportunity to increase his profit margin, it meant that the entire business was shaky. In short, this became a superb early warning system to detect future credit problems.

The only downside to this policy was that the manufacturer gave up 2 percentage points of his own gross profit. Given the economics of his business, relatively high fixed costs, the extra volume this policy generated ended up increasing profits. But even if there were a small diminution in absolute dollars, it might be a sound strategy. The speed-up in collections and the drop in total receivables freed up significant cash resources, thus improving ROI, although on a smaller base. Credit losses were reduced, administrative time and resources freed up, and the company used the lower price reflected in the 4-percent discount as a marketing benefit offered its customers. The secret, if there was one, was to make the cash discount so attractive that customers *had* to take it.

Using Inventory Levels as a Competitive Marketing Tool

As a consumer, trying to buy something at retail, what do you look for in selecting a store? Convenience, low prices, good service, and a good selection of merchandise in stock are all important, but in the final analysis it is the merchandise itself that separates one store from another. Inventory levels make a difference. Having the right goods at the right place at the right time is the ultimate secret of success. Customers may even pay a premium, if they can be sure of finding what they are looking for.

Over the last few years innumerable books, articles, and speeches by consultants have focused on reducing inventories. The advent of computerized inventory control systems have allowed inventories to be reduced, in large part because the whole manufacturing and distribution system has become more efficient. This has led to much shorter lead times, and the ultimate expression is JIT, just in time.

It is important to understand that the thrust of JIT and of all inventory reduction programs is still to make sure that customers, the ultimate users, have what they need when they need it. It does *not* mean reducing service levels because items are temporarily not available. JIT does not mean reducing the breadth of selection offered a customer. It does mean eliminating unnecessary safety stocks, inventory held because of an uncertainty as to whether replacement merchandise will arrive before present levels are gone.

At the manufacturing level, wholesale distribution level or retail level, customers do not want to pay suppliers for inefficiencies in the system. Competition, if nothing else, will force suppliers to become efficient, to be able to deliver quickly. This means either having the desired items on hand, in the case of retailers, or very readily available with certain and quick delivery farther up the distribution chain.

JIT is an *approach* to running a manufacturing or wholesale business. From the customer's perspective the test is not the supplier's inventory level, but the certainty that orders will be filled. Ideally this can come from quick set-ups and small lot sizes, with the ultimate being production to customer order and no inventories. Whether or not this goal will ever truly be realized is immaterial in a discussion on the use of cash to aid marketing.

Assuming your customers do not care how you run your business and are only interested in results, results are measured using two tests. The first is the percentage of orders filled on time. When you order a shirt from L.L. Bean and they promise next day shipment in their catalog, you care only that this happens. You do not want a back order, regardless of the cause.

The second test of inventory levels—and some would put this first—is whether the supplier or store stocks the item(s) you are looking for. Nothing is more frustrating than chasing from store to store, or making phone call after phone call, trying to find out where to buy something. All other things being equal, a broad line is a powerful competitive tool. Maintenance of a large number of SKUs (stock keeping units) has two kinds of costs associated with it. First is the sheer dollar value of the inventory, although for this purpose, ten items of one part have the same cost as one each of ten different parts. The difference is in the expenses associated with having a part number in the inventory control system. Warehouse space, cost accounting records, and purchase (or make) records must be maintained. Costs tend to go up exponentially, not just proportionately, as more items are added to an inventory.

Those who buy by mail notice that mail order catalogs start out as specialized purveyors, say of vitamin pills, but then the company starts adding health and beauty items and maybe even furniture. A 20-page catalog becomes a 60-page book. Now consumers have to look through more pages to find something, and the company has to increase its sources of supply, its shipping methods, and the demographic characteristics of its customer base. Pretty soon this constant addition of lines becomes self-defeating. The only question was why it took Sears so long to get out of the mail order business, after their catalog regularly exceeded 1000 pages. The control and pricing problems became greater than the profit on the incremental sales.

Within reason, however, customers like a broader line. The firm that can afford both the direct and indirect costs of more inventory items, with only a minimum of stock-outs of the items carried, will invariably increase market share. The secret of the continued survival of the local hardware store is its broad line; you can be pretty sure of finding what you want there, and will even pay a premium over the price at a Home Depot for the convenience and service. The cash tied up in slow moving inventory at the store is paid for by the relatively high profit margin.

The fact that some businesses thrive on large inventory, slow turnover, and high margin, while others focus on high turnover and lower margins with a narrower line, indicates there is no one best way to serve the market. But to do either approach right takes cash tied up in inventory, and the better financed competitor has an almost unbeatable advantage. Going into a store with bare shelves does not invite repeat business.

Meeting the Cash Requirements
of Total Quality Management

Total Quality Management (TQM) is the current buzzword for giving customers what they want and is identical to Marshall Field's dictum from 100 years ago that, "The customer is always right." Let's couple that with another old saying: "The more things change, the more they are the same." The other thing that has not changed is that, with the exception of true professional or personal services, cash resources must be invested to provide maximum levels of service. The so-called marketing mix is just that, a combination of attributes required to meet customers' needs. Inventory levels, pricing, credit terms, discounts, coupons, and all other tools and techniques involve decisions that consume cash now, in the hope that they will provide more cash when the sale is made.

One of the key corollaries of TQM is that one should not provide *more* than is necessary to meet customer expectations. Nobody expects to buy a Cadillac for the price of a Chevrolet. If GM were to provide Chevrolet buyers a car that is the equivalent to a Cadillac at a Chevrolet price, this would not be within the terms of reference of TQM. Chevrolet buyers expect a certain level of performance, comfort, and power, while Cadillac buyers have different expectations.

What is important is that each class of customers receive what it wants. Prompt delivery of the car, the availability of parts when needed, a competitive price, and credit terms at market rates are all aspects of the total product perception. A Lexus does not compete with a Camry; the customer expectations are different. Within those separate markets, however, Toyota has used its resources well to provide Lexus buyers with the very best luxury car and Camry buyers with the very best midsized car.

All aspects of the marketing mix must work together, because overspending in one area will not offset deficiencies in another. Optimum spending of available cash is required. Should limited resources be invested in designing a new model or in building a new warehouse for spare parts? This is a management decision. No company has unlimited resources. Choices must be made. But the more cash that is available, the easier are the decisions, and the fewer sacrifices required.

This is why maximizing the availability of cash is so important, why Total Cash Management can pay off. As we said at the beginning of the chapter, a good big man will always beat a good small man. A company with bigger cash balances can always beat a competitor with fewer chips at the gaming table of business.

4

Squeeze Inventories for Cash Savings

What lies ahead? The future's not ours to see.
Che sera, sera. What will be, will be.
                    FROM THE POPULAR SONG

There is no free lunch.   POPULAR SAYING

An astute observer once commented that almost anyone can become an instant "expert" on the subject of inventories—even start a new career in management consulting. All one has to do is to go into any work place, factory, warehouse, or retail establishment, look around with a serious demeanor, and state with firm conviction, "You have too much inventory here." Nine times out of ten the observer will be right. And on the tenth there is a better than even chance listeners will still agree!

As with the weather, *everybody* in business complains about inventory. Unlike the weather, however, inventories *can* be managed. Managing inventories properly, balancing the cash investment required with the benefits that inventories provide, is a never-ending task. One of the recent tools recommended by the management gurus is "continuous improvement." For inventories, unfortunately, this is not possible. Inventories cannot improve with age, with the possible exception of fine wine and whiskey. Without constant managerial attention, inventories invariably deteriorate.

What Do Inventories Accomplish?

One of the most fundamental questions, yet one that is rarely asked, is, "Why do we have inventories?" As will be shown later, inventories involve an out-of-pocket investment in cash, are subject to spoilage, deterioration, and obsolescence, and cost money to keep, in terms of insurance, taxes, storage, and handling costs. At first blush, these are all negatives.

But "The future's not ours to see." We can never tell what will happen, whether it is the timing and amount of sales to customers, meeting a specific production schedule, or receiving purchased goods when they are due. Only if we had absolute assurances on purchases, production, and orders could we achieve the ideal of *no inventories*. Only if orders from customers arrived just in time to produce, and our production process were fast enough to meet customer orders, could we do without raw material and finished goods inventories. Work in process (WIP) would be minimal and limited by the cycle time of production. But in the real world this does not happen and inventories are needed to balance sales and production.

As an example, a general contractor who builds custom houses to order is in the ideal situation. As a home buyer, you provide the lot and put up cash for the contractor to order materials as needed throughout the construction cycle. The contractor receives final payment upon completion of construction. There is no raw materials inventory, no finished goods inventory, and only minor WIP if he orders and pays for shingles or sheetrock before receiving cash from you the owner.

But very few other manufacturers or producers can stay in business without inventories; they cannot see the future. As we will see in Chap. 11 on budgeting, it is necessary to *forecast* sales, to guess what customers will order and when they will order. Since customers in most businesses don't tell you exactly what they will order or when they will order it, and in most cases don't themselves know this, you as a supplier must have finished goods on hand to meet unexpected or unanticipated demand. For items with a relatively short production cycle—not aircraft or ships with a production time of years—most manufacturers sell enough types of items that it simply is not feasible to produce to order. Even if you try to produce to order, everything cannot be produced at once, and customers may well order multiple items from one vendor for delivery at the same time.

In short, to stay in business you must have finished goods on hand. Almost by definition you cannot know exactly *what* will be ordered. The only solution is finished goods inventories. But by the same definition, some of your guesses will be wrong; some of what you produced in anticipation of sales will not be ordered when you thought it would.

Carried on for a period of time, this phenomenon leads to a gradual build-up of finished goods inventory, much of it with a slow turnover.

Why we have to have raw materials inventories, then, is equally logical. We cannot count on our suppliers being able to ship everything we need on the day we need it. Few production processes run so smoothly that every production schedule is met 100 percent of the time. Further, once a production sequence gets out of phase, the problems seem to compound. If we then had to wait for our vendors to deliver to a fluctuating production schedule, we would rapidly be even further behind.

The only solution, then, is to order materials based on our anticipated production schedule, knowing full well that some of what we order and receive will not be needed immediately. That excess is called "inventory."

It is our inability to see the future, no matter how hard we try, that both requires inventories and causes them to get out of balance. It is inherent in our imperfect world.

Another factor causes us to hold inventory. We are required to buy minimum economical order quantities. That is what separates wholesalers from retailers. You go into a store as a consumer and buy one vase for Mother's Day. You cannot buy, and a wholesaler would not sell, just one vase. The retailer has to buy a minimum of one case, say 12 vases. No matter how "hot" the item, they are not all going to sell on day one. Hence the retailer's inventory. The gross profit earned by a retailer is in part a return on the investment she must make to have the inventory on hand, ready to sell one item at a time.

The wholesaler, in turn, had to buy from the manufacturer in lots of 12 cases. No glass manufacturer can have hundreds of glasses, vases, decanters, bowls, and other items in a line and make them one or even 12 at a time. An economical production run may be 100 cases of each SKU (stock keeping unit). Again, no one wholesaler is going to order in this quantity. So the manufacturer has a finished goods inventory irrespective of his ability to forecast sales. A perfect forecast still would not get every wholesaler to order on the exact day or even in the week the items were produced. Yet the production cost would be totally uneconomical if one tried to manufacture in very small lots.

Finally, because manufacturers find it economical to produce in relatively large lot sizes, it makes sense to price the product accordingly. A carpet manufacturer will charge less per yard if a retailer orders a full roll, as opposed to a single order for one living room of just 20 yards. Ordering in larger quantities means lower purchase costs.

This means that an engine manufacturer, dealing with hundreds of vendors, almost all of whom have either minimum order quantities or volume discounts or both, will have to have substantial raw material or purchased parts inventories, both for physical and financial reasons. The more you go toward a "lean production" approach (discussed later in the chapter), the more critical is either absolute assurance of getting delivery on schedule or of having sufficient items on hand and immediately available.

Put a different way, inventories, despite their cost, actually are a critical ingredient in keeping production costs down. Look at what happens when arbitrary orders come down from the top to "cut inventories 15 percent by the end of next month." This may not have happened in your firm, but it is a well known phenomenon in many otherwise well run organizations. The logic is excellent. If we cut inventories and free up the cash, our ROI will go up, and the cash can be used elsewhere in the business. Just what we have been arguing for throughout the book!

Reducing Inventories: How Do We Maintain Customer Service?

Companies that try to reduce inventories within a very short time frame quickly run into trouble. Unless you change the way you do business, the levels of inventories you need will stay the same. As an example, you may have ten strategically placed warehouses throughout the country, located to provide no more than one-day delivery to any customer. To provide at least a 95-percent fill rate at each warehouse, there is located $1 million of inventory. With ten warehouses, $10 million worth of finished goods is being carried, day in and day out.

If an edict comes through to cut inventories by 15 percent across the board, cutting each warehouse's inventory by 15 percent will be a disaster. Customer service at every location will plummet. There is really only one practical way to reduce inventories 15 percent. You have to close one or more warehouses, not reduce inventory levels at each of the locations. Closing one warehouse will free up $1 million in inventory, which can be sold quickly from the other locations. The remaining nine locations can probably continue to function with the same stock levels. If do-able, this closing would mean that inventory turnover is indeed speeded up, since the same level of sales to customers would now be supported by 10 percent less inventory. Two thirds of the president's goal would have been achieved, and the remaining $500,000 reduction could probably come from a 5-percent improvement in recordkeeping and other efficiencies in the remaining nine locations.

What is wrong with this picture? Implicit in this scenario is the assumption that closing down a warehouse is not going to affect sales. Is this realistic? Unless new and faster means of transportation are found, such as substituting Federal Express for UPS ground service, some customers are going to notice a deterioration of service levels. If there was a good reason in the first place for opening the warehouse, now closed, what has changed? Was the original decision wrong? If the original decision was correct, then there are bound to be adverse consequences from reversing that decision, unless customer demographics have changed. If in fact sales levels from the closed warehouse had never achieved the desired levels, then the question is, "Why did it take a top management edict to force a decision? Who has been minding the store?"

The point is that, as business conditions change, responsible managers should *continuously* be reviewing operating decisions in terms of the impact on cash flows. If a particular strategy is not working, the cash consequences of alternate plans of action should constantly be reviewed. Inertia is both common and comfortable. A lack of a push from the top, however, is not a good reason for inaction. As will be discussed, if one properly charges for the cost of carrying inventories and does not treat them as a free resource, this kind of continuous review will be a lot easier.

Inactive Inventories Are Inevitable

The inability to forecast future demand, combined with the economies of longer production runs or bulk purchases, means that items are going to be built or bought that are either unsalable or in such oversupply that no reasonable need can be foreseen for them.

In theory managers are supposed to review inventory levels periodically, either getting rid of the surplus inventory or at a minimum setting up a financial reserve. The former approach, getting rid of the physical inventory, is permanent. The latter approach, setting up the reserve, is an accounting transaction and can always be reversed with a stroke of the pen. The reason this is "supposed" to happen ties into the need for firms to prepare a balance sheet that is in compliance with Generally Accepted Accounting Principles (GAAP). Under GAAP, inventories have to be reported at a value that is the "lower of cost or market." This is accounting shorthand that says you continue to carry inventory at the amount you paid for it; you cannot report a profit just by holding inventory. Suppose a contractor bought enough lumber to build six houses over the next year and had paid $100,000, in the expectation that lumber prices would increase over the next 12 months. If in fact lumber did go up 10 percent, there would be an economic gain. The contractor saved $10,000 by this astute purchase. But her balance sheet would have to show the lumber at $100,000, not $110,000. The accounting principle, which may clash with common sense, says you do not recognize a gain or a profit until you sell the items.

This is a one-way street. If the lumber market "went South" and the lumber could be purchased today at $92,000, then GAAP requires that the balance sheet recognize the reduced value, and an $8,000 loss would be reported on the P&L. Now the meaning of "lower of cost or market" should be clear. As the owner or manager, trying to put the best look on things, it is a "heads you win, tails I lose" proposition. Gains cannot be recognized, but losses must be reflected in the statements.

That is the theory. In practice—it is true—gains are never realized. However, in the real world, few items of inventory can be priced as accurately as agricultural and mineral commodities. An auditor can go to the newspaper and look up the price of wheat, gasoline, copper, or lumber. But there is no published market price for 99 percent of all inventories.

Take an inventory of spare parts carried by a manufacturer of refrigerators. Literally hundreds of models have been produced and sold over the last 40 years, and consumers continue to need and order parts for even the oldest models. At a balance sheet date who can tell what the demand for compressor #X73P will be, since this fits only a 1978 model refrigerator, which was in production for just one year? The poor auditor faces an impossible task. He knows the cost, which is the same as last year. Assuming there were 40 on hand last year and now there are 37 (three were sold during the year), the existing supply will be gone in 12 years.

What is their value? It is unlikely the manufacturer will ever make any more compressors, once the existing supply is depleted. So they are, practically speaking, irreplaceable. On the other hand, if the compressors are not sold for that model, there is no alternate use for them, and they have either no value or, at best, scrap value. The cost of the compressor on the books is $100, and this one-line item on a 150-page inventory listing has a value of $3700. If three compressors were sold in the last 12 months, for a model that is almost 20 years old, is it reasonable to assume that three a year will continue to be sold for each of the next 12 years?

A hard-nosed auditor could make a convincing case that there is excess inventory on hand and that at least some of the items should be written off and perhaps disposed of. On the other hand, if you do that and an unexpected demand arises, some customers are going to be mighty unhappy to find that *no* compressors are available at any price. Keeping slow moving spare parts inventories can always be justified on the ground of meeting customer needs.

Compounding this problem was a Supreme Court decision that affected taxes. Some companies were taking an inventory write-down, in accordance with the lower of cost or market theory, admitting that the market value was nil and that future sales probably would not materialize. But just to be on the safe side, the companies continued to keep the physical items, because of concern for possible customer demand and the practical impossibility of going back and manufacturing the item(s) in question.

The IRS complained that the companies were trying to have the best of both worlds—getting a tax write-off and keeping the items. This was perceived to have the potential for abuse, and the case went as far as the Supreme Court. In the *Thor* case the court ruled that, if you wrote down inventories (and you could any time), you then had to physically dispose of the items in question. You could no longer have it both ways.

What is good tax policy, however, puts companies in a bind. They may know that a substantial portion of an inventory may never be sold, but they do not know which specific items. So it may be better to keep everything. Further, any write-down of inventory is going to hit the financial statements immediately. There are relatively few "good" times to take a loss, since most managers want to maximize reported income each and every quarter.

So a direct conflict exists between maximizing cash flow and reporting maximum income reported to banks and shareholders. For profitable tax-paying firms, writing off (and disposing of) excess and obsolete inventory actually generates cash through a reduction in tax payments otherwise due. But because the inventory until this point was carried as an asset, almost always at original cost, a write-down for book purposes is impossible to avoid.

Inventory Valuation Reserves.   These reserves should be set up on a regular basis, just as we do with reserves for uncollectible accounts receivable. We know that a small percentage of receivables will not turn into cash, so we also know that some items in inventory will never be sold. Most firms have reserves for receivables on a generalized basis, that is, without specifying which account(s) are not likely to be paid. A comparable approach, charging a small amount off each month, perhaps as a percentage of cost of goods sold, will then allow firms to clean out the shelves periodically without taking a large one-time hit to the P&L. The inventory reserve would not be deductible for taxes until the items were disposed of and the reserve charged. There likewise is no impact on cash flow by setting up the reserve. But any action that will encourage sound management behavior is good.

As we will see, there is a real cash cost for carrying unneeded inventory. So providing an incentive to review the items and then physically getting them out the door makes good business sense. Book publishers do this with their unsold inventories of books, disposing of them as "remainders," often well below production cost. But getting some cash in from the remainder firms, plus the savings in taxes and the reduction of out-of-pocket expenses associated with lower inventory on hand, makes a periodic house cleaning worthwhile.

Customer Service.   This, along with reduced operating costs, are the primary reasons for having an inventory, whether it be raw materials, work in process, or finished goods. Cutting inventories—all other things staying the same—*will* affect customers, production, or both. Whether the benefits of lower investment in inventory will or will not outweigh the costs is hard to predict in advance. Yet experience suggests that, absent any fundamental changes in the way business is carried on, inventory reductions, like personal weight loss programs, are doomed to failure.

The question can be asked, "Will sales to customers *really* be affected if lower inventories are carried?" To answer this question, look at personal purchases at retail, say by mail order. If you place an order for five items and four of them are in stock, you will receive two shipments. The vendor will probably pay the postage charge for the second shipment because that was not your fault. (By the way, the extra shipping charge is one of the costs to the seller of lower inventory levels.) On that order, sales volume did not change. The seller's records would not show a dissatisfied customer just because one item was shipped late.

But when faced with a desire to buy something else, you may think, "Maybe I should try someone else and see if they can do better." How does seller number 1 know now that a sale was lost? Nothing is harder to track than lost sales. Even a TQM questionnaire, from seller number 1, asking you if you were satisfied, may not elicit your unhappiness with two shipments, one of which was later than you expected.

The same principle holds true for business-to-business transactions, except that, if you are relying on your vendor's product to keep your own production line going, *any* delay is going to be unacceptable. The lead time for production of some complex weapons systems, like an M1 tank, may be upwards of 18 to 20 months. Why? If there are 3000 purchased items in a tank and 2968 of them have been delivered, the Army does not have 98.93 percent of a tank. The manufacturer has a giant bushel basket of parts! Lead times have to be based on the longest procurement item. But once the schedule has been built up, and an assembly program developed, if even one vendor slips up, the entire project is at risk. The old theme that "for want of a nail the kingdom was lost" is very relevant in any sort of complex manufacturing or production operation.

Cutting your inventories to reduce your own cash investment *must* be balanced against the risks of poorer customer service. "There is no free lunch" still applies, particularly in the relationship between inventory levels and what those inventories are supposed to accomplish.

What Is the Real Cost of Holding Inventory?

Let's say you were to query ten accountants and ask them, "What is the *real* cost of holding inventories?" You would receive at least ten different answers. At least one of them would answer, "It depends," and she would be correct: No single cost figure can be applied by all firms. However, common elements should be understood so that you can develop a figure for your own organization.

Cost of Money.   Of course, this is the first thing to come to mind. At an absolute minimum the dollars tied up in inventory, if freed up to cash, could be invested in the money market or used to pay off bank borrowing. For companies with no debt, the most conservative figure to use for the cost of funds would be the current rate on Treasury bills or commercial paper for investment. This is often a relatively low figure, but represents the real opportunity cost. Many a sophisticated financial analyst would argue that a firm's cost of capital, taking into account the cost or value of shareholder's equity, is more appropriate.

The trouble with using the cost of capital is two-fold. First, few people can agree on the absolute number for any particular firm at a point in time. Second, if through some management reengineering you free up $100,000 currently tied up in inventory, you will not see anything like the cost of capital rate, applied to that amount, show up on the bottom line of your P&L. If the cost of capital is 10 to 13 percent after tax and you use this figure for short-term inventory decisions, you may make the wrong decision. On the other hand, for true long-term decisions, as in capital budgeting, the cost of capital figure is the only one to use. Inventory requirements associated with capital budgeting must be priced at the cost of capital. In short, there is no good single answer, except that, for short-term decisions, use the short-term cost of money, the borrowing rate, or the money market rate.

Taxes.   A real cost of holding inventories, taxes are not often taken into consideration. These are applied at the state and local municipality level, not by the federal government. Property taxes have become a favorite means of raising revenue, because politicians know that companies do not vote, and most employees, and managers for that matter, are not cognizant of the impact of property taxes on their employers. As an example, however, look at Nevada and California. Nevada does not impose a tax on inventories, and California does. Because of the size of the California market, many firms feel that they need inventories of finished goods to serve the West Coast market. A number of firms have, very deliberately, opened warehouse locations in Nevada to serve the

California market. The primary consideration for choosing that location was the saving on taxes.

Filing of state and local property tax returns is usually done at corporate headquarters, and the amounts are usually not shown on a separate line of the income statement. Contrast this with federal income taxes, which are highlighted and carefully analyzed. Property taxes must be paid whether you are making a profit or not, whereas income taxes, by definition, are not payable if you are running in the red. The absolute amount of property taxes at any one location may be relatively small, but in total they add up and must not be neglected.

Insurance.   Premiums are paid by most firms to guard against a variety of perils, including the loss of inventories due to fire or other catastrophe. Again, the absolute dollars applicable to inventories may not appear large. But the premiums fluctuate more or less directly with inventory levels, and the premium rate per thousand dollars of inventory is easily ascertainable.

Soft Costs

In addition to the preceeding "hard" costs, the out-of-pocket charges that represent direct savings if cutting inventory balances, many companies make an internal charge to plants or divisions for the total working capital used by the operation. Inventories are often the prime component, along with receivables, of the base for calculating such a charge. Virtually all companies that make such an internal working capital or inventory charge, however, use a rate substantially higher than that just discussed. In addition to the cost of bank borrowing, taxes, and insurance, recognition is usually made for what are sometimes called the "soft" costs. These would include warehousing, recordkeeping, and ultimate obsolescence, requiring disposal at a large write-down.

Warehousing and Other Storage Costs.   These expenses do not go up or down directly with the number of SKUs, the number of in and out shipments, or the dollar volume or physical volume of shipments. Each of these impacts the total costs individually. There are also interactions among the factors: that is, if you have more SKUs, it is likely you will have more inbound shipments, and the dollar volume of sales to customers will probably expand.

No matter how you analyze the situation, however, it is extremely unlikely that warehouse and other logistics costs will decrease with larger inventories. While there are some modest economies of scale at times, there are also discontinuities going the other way. Once the physical capacity of a warehouse has been reached, additional inventory will require capital investment in (or the rental of) more space at that location. Or a decision would be made to decentralize distribution and open a brand new warehouse closer to customers.

As a general rule there is a tradeoff between minimizing inventory levels (with concomitant warehousing) and service levels to customers. More warehouse locations (more retail stores) makes serving customers faster. It also probably reduces outbound transportation and freight expense, which the customer has to pay for, although perhaps *increasing* your own freight expense placing items in numerous locations.

The tradeoffs involved in deciding specific warehouse locations are outside the scope of this book, and numerous consultants provide this type of specialized service. The cost *factors* involved, however, are clear and understandable. The generalization that increased inventories will affect warehousing costs is not likely to be disputed.

Recordkeeping. In this era of computers, recordkeeping would not at first sight appear to be particularly expensive, much less a significant out-of-pocket cash drain as inventories increased. With regard to absolute cost, an activity-based costing (ABC) analysis of resources devoted to inventory control would show for most organizations far greater cost than appears on the surface. Computers (mainframe or PC), software, software support, and personnel in purchasing, receiving, quality control, and accounting are all involved.

It is true that, if the present system is working effectively and *one* additional SKU is added, there probably will be *no* increase in out-of-pocket costs. This argument, that today's costs are fixed on the upside, is dangerous. Reducing inventory levels by *one* item will not *save* any resources. But you are kidding yourself if you act on this argument. Accountants will perform an ABC analysis and report that the cost of the inventory control *system* is $400,000, that there are 20,000 items in the system, and that therefore the cost per item is $20. Arithmetically this is correct.

In terms of cash, it is also correct to look at it and say that, in either direction, up or down, there will be no change in cash outflow to manage the system for a change of one item. The computer rent is fixed. We own the software. The clerks perform many other functions. And so on. We have all heard the arguments. But where do we draw the line? When is it time to replace the computer, get new software, or add an accounts payable clerk to process all the new disbursements? Can those individual increases be related to any *one* item? Of course not. Increases in out-of-pocket expenses do not happen immediately after decisions are made that affect the volume of work performed. To argue that there is *no* connection is equally ridiculous.

For management decision making, the following rule should be used:

Every time you add an item to inventory, operating expenses increase.

Whether or not you, or even your most aggressive cost accountant, can identify to the penny exactly where costs will change in this specific instance is irrelevant. *Costs follow volume.* Period.

Disposal of Obsolete Inventory.   This will increase proportionately or more than proportionately, as inventory levels go up. This is true whether the increase involves more of the same items in one location, new items being added for the first time, or locations added for the same items. Inventory does not improve with age, and most analyses show that the Pareto 80/20 rule applies. That is, 80 percent of current turnover comes from 20 percent of the items. Looked at the other way, 80 percent of the items in most inventories are, to put it charitably, "inactive." We have discussed the desirability of disposing of excess and obsolete inventory, as well as the difficulty this causes in the form of a hit to the P&L. The point is that a truly honest evaluation of any inventory will find that a substantial amount is not an *asset*, if the term is meant to convey the idea of a future economic benefit. Instead, slow moving or nonmoving inventory is truly a liability; it consumes current resources.

Total Cost of Carrying Inventory.   This expense will range, per year, from 8–10 percent on the low side to 18–20 percent on the high side. Some companies will use a 25-percent or even 30-percent rate for internal decision making. It is just as bad, however, to overstate the case as it is to understate it. Saying that it "costs" 30 percent a year to hold inventory, and then setting up decision rules on that basis, may lead to some very poor decisions.

Some companies make an internal "charge" for the cost of inventories being carried, to focus management attention on this important item. There is no question that a monthly charge for inventories on the plant or divisional P&L will get management attention, particularly if performances are evaluated, and bonuses paid, on the basis of results reported after the internal charge for inventory. Since there is always room to reduce inventory levels, putting a very high premium on these actions undoubtedly will cause such actions to be taken. Inventories will be reduced.

We have seen, however, that inventories perform a very useful function. If arbitrary edicts, or their equivalent in terms of abnormally high charges, are a part of top management's approach, lower-level managers will respond. What usually happens first, though, is that fast moving items are cut back. Arrangements are worked out with two or three key suppliers to make more frequent shipments, or safety stocks of high-demand items are reduced. It is easier in the short run to reduce inventory items that are turning over than to take the hit to the P&L of disposing of slow moving items.

If internal charges for inventory are too high, all that will happen, in terms of real cash flow, is that dumb decisions will be made, suboptimization will occur, and customer service will suffer. That is not what was intended.

On the other side, if operating managers are charged *nothing* for the funds invested in (or tied up in) inventory, then equally bad decisions will be made. Perhaps levels of customer service will appear to improve, or purchase costs on a unit basis will appear to be lower. But too much inventory will be on hand. Ultimately the excess inventories generated by disregarding the true costs of inventory holding will come home to roost, and future write-downs are inevitable.

Balance is necessary. If it is felt that calculating the true cost of inventories is too hard, or if there is disagreement on the proper level, then the arbitrary use of a figure such as 15 percent is justified. This means that the internal P&L statements of individual operating units should show a charge of 1.25 percent per month for each dollar in ending inventory. Obviously on a consolidated, company-wide basis, these charges get eliminated, since you cannot make a profit for shareholders from internal charges. But a *reasonable* charge for dollars tied up in inventory will lead to better inventory decisions. This is indisputable.

Accounting and Tax Issues Affecting Cash Flows

In relatively simple accounting systems, the amount of Cost of Goods Sold, which directly impacts the profit reported for the year, is calculated by starting with beginning inventory, adding purchases (including wages and salaries), and *subtracting* the amount of ending inventory. What this means is that the larger the dollar amount assigned to year-end inventory, the greater will be the reported profits. Conversely, the lower the dollar amount of ending inventory balances, the lower will be reported profits.

Strangely enough, the business world splits into two camps when it comes to the trade-off between reported profits and cash flows. Obviously cash flows will be highest when taxes paid on income are lowest, and the lowest when tax payments are made on reduced taxable income. So some companies want low reported profits, to save on taxes, while others want high reported profits to *look* good, even if it means higher out-of-pocket payments in cash to the IRS.

Generally, profitable privately held firms usually choose to do anything to minimize taxes. As long as the principals are drawing a comfortable living from the business, it makes sense to reinvest as much as possible. Deferring taxes always helps, and, depending on the current state of tax laws, capital gains paid in the future may well be taxed at a lower rate than ordinary income.

Both publicly held firms, whose executives look to stock prices for increases in their net worth, and some closely held firms, whose owners depend on bank or other creditor financing, usually want to *maximize* reported earnings. The key point is that there is often a substantial *difference between earnings and cash flow.* As discussed in Chap. 6 dealing with banks, most bankers give lip service to looking at cash flows. In reality, audited reports of *earnings* often seem to carry more weight.

The purpose of this discussion is that the valuation of inventories, for purposes of computing reported income, is subject to very substantial management judgment. Conventional wisdom to the contrary, accounting is far from an exact science. If five accountants are asked to calculate the value of year-end inventories, you should get at least five answers. There is an old joke to the effect that the smartest of them will ask, "How high or low do you want it?"

This is *not* a cynical statement—that accountants can manipulate an answer depending on management's wishes or objectives. It is a simple statement of fact. Go back to our discussion of surplus and obsolete inventory. If you want a high year-end figure, you cast a blind eye at slow moving inventory. If you want to maximize year-end cash flow, you scrutinize every item and take an aggressive posture toward evaluating future salability. By setting up a large reserve, and actually disposing of slow moving inventory, your tax bill will be reduced, albeit at the cost of lower reported earnings.

This discussion has assumed that the only variable is a subjective evaluation of future salability. In fact there is another variable: the calculation of the actual unit cost of any specific item in inventory. Again, contrary to conventional wisdom, absolutely first-class accountants can develop and support quite different answers as to the "value" of any item at a point in time.

For items purchased for resale (either by a wholesaler from a manufacturer, or by a retailer from a wholesaler), the actual cost is readily determinable from the vendor's invoice. About the only judgment to be applied is an estimate as to whether cost is above market, that is, whether the item(s) will have to be marked down to sell.

Manufacturers, on the other hand, have a lot more discretion in valuing inventory. Usually, three elements of cost are considered: labor, material, and overhead. *Labor* is considered to be the number of work hours required to make the piece, priced out at today's labor rates. The labor content is usually not controversial, except for technical questions as to exactly *which* labor rate to use—with or without overtime, last year's vs. this year's union wages, and so on. Similarly, with an exception as to estimates for scrap loss and purchase price discounts, the *material* cost of items in a manufacturer's inventory is straightforward.

When we get to the famous category of *overhead*, accountants part company, judgment reigns, and a determined manager can obtain almost any answer she wants. We cannot go into all the ways that accountants can manipulate the amount of overhead costs chargeable to products, but the basic principle is simple. To avoid distorting costs as volume fluctuates, accountants agree that, if you are operating significantly below capacity, the costs of that excess capacity should be charged off to the current period as an expense of that period, not allocated to items currently in production or in inventory. How to define and calculate *capacity* provides a lot of scope for judgment.

The second area of potential dispute revolves around just what are the overhead costs related to manufacturing and what are Selling, General, and Administrative costs? Everyone agrees that the so-called SG&A costs do not go into inventory values. Is the Accounting Department part of manufacturing or SG&A? What about Human Resources? Calling them manufacturing overhead will increase the value of current items on hand, while denominating them as SG&A obviously lowers inventory values.

Keep in mind that, while there is a vast disparity of opinion at any one point in time, it is very difficult to switch from one approach to the other and then back again. Consistency in definition is required by outside auditors. So if you are having a good year and want to reduce reported earnings this year, it is not quite so easy to suddenly decide to take Accounting and Human Resources costs out of overhead and call them SG&A just for this year. It has been done and will continue to be done. What is very difficult is to switch this year and then next year, when you've had less than a sterling performance, decide that the original method was pretty good after all. That approach is just a short step from fraudulent reporting and cannot be recommended or approved. The first switch can always be justified; the second cannot.

Management must decide on its own objectives (cash flow or reported earnings), and then instruct accountants and outside auditors to meet those objectives. The entire thrust of this book has been to maximize cash flows, because only cash will meet a payroll or let you buy new assets. Reported earnings, actually tied up in unrealizable inventory values, cannot be used to expand a business. However, as discussed in Chap. 6, if your firm is totally dependent on the continuation of bank financing, then reported earnings, while maybe only a *perception*, nonetheless become *reality* in the minds of many bank lending officers.

Inventoriable Costs for Tax Purposes. These have been rather clearly defined by Congress and the IRS. Needless to say, the criterion used was whatever would maximize taxable income and hence income tax collections. Therefore, in light of the preceding discussion, it should be no surprise that the IRS defines inventoriable costs *very* broadly, including a number of items that reasonable accountants and taxpayers might think of as more properly being classified as SG&A. But nobody ever accused Congress or writers of tax regulations of being good accountants. Raising revenue is what they are paid for, and so the definition of taxable inventory is far broader than that used for GAAP financial statements.

In 1986 a new law redefined inventoriable costs and broadened them for tax purposes. Many companies decided that what was good enough for taxes was also good enough for their own books. Companies trying to maximize reported incomes saw this as an excellent opportunity. Even though the rules of Generally Accepted Accounting Principles actually precluded inventorying some of the costs now required by the IRS, many companies adopted the IRS's position. Basically they argued that the amounts were "immaterial" in terms of total net income, or they just went ahead and raised their inventory values so as to keep the same definition for books and taxes. Frankly, it *is* an accounting headache to keep two separate sets of records, and the fact that the IRS's approach just happened to raise balance sheet values and reported income as well was considered the breaks of the game.

To sum up this section, while the IRS spells out what cost elements must be carried in inventory, a lot of judgment can still be applied. Cash flow vs. reported income is a continuing choice.

LIFO and FIFO Inventory Accounting

LIFO stands for *last-in/first-out*. It is an accounting method by which the calculation of Cost of Goods Sold will be based on a convention that the most recently purchased items are sold first, and that the items in inventory are to be priced working backwards. The practical effect usually is to *raise* Cost of Goods Sold, which reduces taxable income and hence taxes paid. During periods of high inflation, LIFO effectively means that you are not paying taxes on so-called phantom profits arising solely from increases in the replacement cost of inventories.

Most important, companies that adopt LIFO for tax purposes *must* conform their book reporting. To get the tax and cash flow benefits, which LIFO undoubtedly provides during periods of rising prices, companies have to be willing to display the same figures on their P&L. Since LIFO charges new, higher-cost inventory to Cost of Sales, this reduces profits. By the same token, since the old lower-cost inventory is shown on the

Balance Sheet, the firm's working capital is understated; net worth is reduced. So, in effect, adopting LIFO has a double-barreled effect on the financial statements. Income is down, and assets and net worth are reduced. The only gain—but a very real one—is more cash.

LIFO has been in effect for many years and, with the steady rise in prices over the decades, it has meant very substantial tax savings for many large companies. In the footnotes to financial statements, companies are supposed to disclose how much lower their inventories are because of LIFO, and for many firms it is easily hundreds of millions of dollars or more. For example, in its 1992 Annual Report, FMC Corporation had the following footnote:

> Inventories are recorded at the lower of cost or market value. The current replacement cost of inventories exceeded their recorded values by approximately $228.0 million at December 31, 1992 and $242.1 million at December 31, 1991. During 1992, 1991, and 1990, the company reduced LIFO inventories that were carried at lower than prevailing costs. These reductions increased pre-tax income by $25.5 million in 1992, $19.1 million in 1991, and $6.3 million in 1990.

What is interesting about this footnote is the impact of *reducing* LIFO inventories. Without going into the technicalities, just accept the statement that, if such LIFO inventories are reduced, reported income will increase. Of course, if the company is paying taxes, taxes will increase also. One strategy for a company with net operating losses (NOL), therefore, is to deliberately reduce year-end LIFO inventories and generate taxable income. If you have an NOL, you may be able to obtain a tax refund, which is positive cash flow.

If a company that previously adopted LIFO continues to have taxable income, then a reduction in such inventories, which is good *business* strategy and fully supported here, is going to have the perverse impact of raising taxes! As you might imagine, more than one company has deliberately dipped into its LIFO inventory layers solely for the purpose of increasing reported income. Such firms have, at least on the surface, been willing to pay higher taxes just for the privilege of reporting more income that period.

Conversely, companies that really do try to maximize cash flow find themselves in a bind if they want to reduce inventories permanently, usually as a result of a reengineering approach to the production or distribution process. All other things being equal, it is probably better to pay the taxes and obtain the operating benefits of lower inventories. However, the worst of all worlds under LIFO, is to inadvertently eat into a LIFO layer, pay the taxes due, and then increase the inventory again the next year through poor management control.

A final word about LIFO. The concept is simple. Calculate cost of goods sold by reference to the most recent purchase price, and value the inventory on the basis of the oldest (lower) purchase price. Of course, if the items in your inventory are trending down in price or are subject to rapid price fluctuations, such as copper or wheat, LIFO is not for you.

Also, while the concept is straightforward, its application is anything but simple. There are full-time specialists in accounting and taxation whose entire expertise is in LIFO. In major cases the IRS will bring in its own LIFO specialists. The tax savings potential is enormous, but there are going to be some substantial accounting, tax, and legal expenses over the years to develop the numbers and preserve the savings. Since the IRS hates to lose tax revenue, and LIFO costs it a lot, it is worth the Service's time to undermine a company's LIFO calculations.

The subject is extremely complex in practice. One firm, for example, assigned the year-end LIFO calculation to three different accountants three years in a row. Each individual, competent in his own right, ended up silently cursing his predecessor because he could not figure out the methodology from the working papers—and, even worse, disagreed with the prior year's approach! There is still no free lunch.

A word about taking a *physical inventory* is in order. At one time nearly every company took a complete inventory at least once a year. This meant counting every item on hand, pricing it out, and reconciling the answer to the books. If the physical count revealed there was more on hand than had been estimated, the company *wrote up* the books, that is, showed a gain or profit. More usual was for the physical count to show a loss, and, as can be imagined, this negative result was not welcome.

The inventory adjustment, making the books reflect what was physically there, is a noncash charge. It is a reflection of previous errors in the accounting system, or, as in the case of retailers, recognition of theft by customers and employees, euphemistically referred to as *shrinkage*. Even though it is a noncash charge, it is still important. Any loss is bad.

An inventory loss is worse, for two reasons. First, previous profits have been overstated; management has been fooling itself as to how well the business has been doing. Second, it reveals a possibly fatal flaw in the accounting or physical control systems. Suppose the books show that the inventory should be $8 million, but upon checking there is actually only $7 million on hand. This loss of $1 million *may* be due to errors in cost accounting, it *may* be a result of factory scrap that was never reported because workers did not want to admit their mistakes, or it *may* be due to undiscovered theft.

A moment's thought suggests that it is impossible to tell the cause just by looking. The shortfall is the same, irrespective of the cause. But if you do not uncover the cause, it will just continue. Unreported scrap is a true out-of-pocket cost, a waste of material and labor, and must be corrected through process engineering and better management in the factory. Theft is equally serious, if not more so, if employees are involved. And poor cost accounting techniques, if not corrected, will lead directly to poor management decisions based on the presumption that the company really knows its costs. It is beyond the scope of this book to suggest specific solutions. What is important is the understanding that taking a physical inventory is a necessary, although not sufficient step, to getting on top of whatever inventory problems there may be.

With the advent of computers and automated inventory keeping systems, many firms have turned to *cycle counting* as an alternative to the across-the-board, once-a-year total physical inventory. The concept is that every week you check 2 percent of the items in the inventory records against the physical quantities actually on hand. For certain types of inventory, such as discrete finished parts, this approach can work. But unlike the once-a-year overall inventory, where close attention is given to such refinements as accurate cutoffs on receiving, processing of vendor invoices, and shipments to customers, cycle counting attempts to capture a stop-motion view of an ongoing ever-changing process.

Frankly, the decision as to which approach to use may not make all that much difference, because the costs involved in performing the once-a-year inventory may not provide sufficient additional accuracy to be worthwhile. Many companies have used cycle counting for years and are satisfied with the results. Perhaps the best answer, for those using cycle counting, is once every three or four years to perform the complete inventory and verify that the total does in fact equal the sum of the parts.

JIT, MRP, and Other Management Control Techniques

Starting in about 1985 or maybe a little earlier, a number of U.S. firms in industries like autos and consumer electronics tried to understand why the Japanese were beating us. Visits to Japanese auto factories showed a vastly different approach to traditional U.S. practice. One of the most obvious differences was in the extremely small inventories of purchased parts on hand at any point in time. Referred to as just-in-time, the concept appeared to be simplicity itself and a solution to our problems here. The syllogism went something like this. The Japanese, using JIT, have small inventories. The Japanese are winning. Therefore we should adopt JIT and have small inventories.

This tied in very closely with the desire of U.S. management to increase its return on investment (ROI). Any approach that promised to reduce the investment *base*, such as running with significantly less funds tied up in raw material and work in process inventory, would automatically increase ROI, even if nothing else changed. American management adopted JIT with a vengeance, hoping if inventory levels were reduced that cash would be freed up and a return on investment improved.

On the surface JIT seems simple to accomplish. Refine the accuracy of the production schedule. Make sure your vendors ship on time. Presto—less inventory, no production disruptions. What's so hard about that? It seems like truly a win/win situation, since our customers won't be hurt and our costs come down.

There were just a few problems with this scenario. In addition to the fact that the Japanese themselves did not stop improving, so that they always provided a moving target for catching up, American management soon found there was much more to JIT than simply smaller inventory levels through speedier vendor deliveries. In practice, what was referred to in a type of shorthand as JIT really represented an entirely new approach to management, involving:

1. Statistical Process Control.
2. Continuous Improvement.
3. Total Quality Management.
4. Reduced Cycle Time.

These were combined with a philosophy that vendors were partners, not the enemy, that there were other things in a vendor/customer relationship besides low price.

A look at these management tools and concepts from the perspective of Total Cash Management reveals both the power of the new approach and the severe difficulties of implementing it.

Statistical Process Control (SPC). This idea was first developed and publicized 70 years ago and adopted by the Japanese after World War II. The idea is that if variability is reduced or eliminated scrap and rework will be reduced. American firms budgeted for, say, 3 percent scrap and rework, and then were happy if such expenses were only 2 percent because they had beat the budget. The Japanese said that *any* scrap or rework was a waste to be rooted out. This, in turn, led to Zero Defects, and the idea popularized by Philip Crosby that "Quality is free."

To get Zero Defects through SPC, then, required involvement of the production workers themselves. The idea that quality had to be built in, not inspected into, a product took a long time to sink in and become operational. Just-in-time will not work if 5 percent or even 2 percent of the items are defective. If you need 100 castings today, and receive exactly 100 castings, what do you do if two or three of them are defective? On the other hand, ordering 102 or 103, in the hope that you will have enough good ones, both builds unnecessary inventory and flies in the face of the

JIT philosophy. Reducing scrap and rework—producing or buying with Zero Defects—has tremendous consequences, all favorable to cash flows. The only difficulty is that developing, installing, and managing a manufacturing philosophy that relies on SPC and worker involvement is a radical change in approach for most companies.

Continuous Improvement.   For JIT to really work requires the Continuous Improvement approach. Business is not static. Competitors are constantly moving ahead. What happened in the automobile industry in the 1980s can happen in any industry at any time. Resting on your laurels or "believing your own press releases" is a recipe for disaster. In terms of Total Cash Management, Continuous Improvement means always asking the question, "How can we do this better, with less investment?" The assumption that there *is* a better way is critical.

Total Quality Management (TQM).   With its emphasis on meeting customer needs, whether the "customer" is an internal user or the external purchaser, TQM may turn out to be a true addition to management technique, not just the flavor of the month. Do we remember Strategic Planning and Zero-Based Budgeting, each of which had its day in the sun and then vanished? Some observers argue that TQM will suffer the same fate. The benefits of a total customer orientation are so powerful, however, that it takes only one or two firms in an industry to adopt TQM, and every one else *has* to follow. Many financial journalists, as well as management consultants, have observed that the benefits from TQM take literally years to show up. Once the initial enthusiasm has worn off, and expectations of instant improvement have been dashed, it takes real perseverance on the part of management to keep TQM moving. Fortunately, the payoff is so great, and the results so visible among successful practitioners, that faith can be sustained.

Keep in mind that the process improvements, which TQM teams come up with, are absolutely critical for a JIT system to work. JIT involves changes in every aspect of production. Unless changes are made, we cannot expect the old ways of doing business to produce new results. Changes in business processes, which both reduce costs and shorten production cycles, require employee involvement, plus the requisite training in the TQM techniques that work.

A TQM approach, applied comprehensively, will ultimately affect cash requirements. Companies that have been successful have reduced not only inventories, but floor space in the factory and, of course, warehouse requirements. This, in turn, frees up the space for increased production volume with no increase in overhead costs.

In the early 1990s, during the recession, many commentators observed that the recovery was delayed, as contrasted with earlier economic slowdowns, because inventory levels were *not* being built up during the recovery period. Computerized recordkeeping, plus process improvements, meant that the JIT approach was being implemented. The only unhappy observers were economists whose forecasts of an imminent inventory increase—and hence production increase—were proven wrong.

Reduced Cycle Time.   A final requirement for JIT is *vendor partnering,* which is a key ingredient of *reduced cycle time.* In the bad old days, before these new management concepts and techniques demonstrated their value, there was always an adversarial relationship between major manufacturers and their vendors. Purchasing agents were measured on how much they were able to force down vendor prices, and this was typically done by a combination of putting items out for bid and hard-nosed negotiations. The attitude of the buyer was, "If you don't lower your price, we'll find someone else who will." For industries like automobiles, with annual model changes and redesign, a vendor could be sure of only one year's firm orders. It was a brand new ball game next year.

Needless to say, this did not encourage vendors to invest cash in facilities, when there was no assurance of subsequent business. Excess capacity only put further downward pressure on selling prices. Also, customers would give vendors a blueprint and say, "Quote me on this," even if the vendor knew more about the product and the production process than the customer. The customer displayed a degree of arrogance that, "I know all I need to know about your business, and, by the way, I know you can knock another 3 percent off the price if you really try." Incidentally, this approach to doing business did not totally disappear, as General Motors' suppliers found out in 1992 and 1993 when a new hotshot purchasing VP was brought in and tore up all existing contracts, with orders to vendors to cut their prices x percent—or else. Of course, the "or else" really meant, "We'll find someone else." Since there is always someone out there who can make it cheaper, at least in the short run, this was a credible threat.

However, as many other companies have found out, closer vendor relationships offer many long-term advantages other than price. In terms of Total Cash Management, the tradeoff for not constantly emphasizing price is closer integration of design and manufacturing. Shorter cycle times, derived from closer working relationships between both firms' design and manufacturing engineers, and more cost-effective designs are both benefits. Shorter cycle time (the elapsed time between start of a new design and first sale to a customer) is always preferable.

Expenses for product design and development, followed by expenditures for new productive machinery and tooling, represent an investment—whether charged to expense in the P&L or capitalized as an asset on the Balance Sheet. The shorter the cycle time, the more quickly the return on that investment will be seen. Put it this way. If you start an investment process for, say, a new pharmaceutical that will cost $2 million, would you rather get approval to start selling it in 1996 or 1999? The same holds true even when there is no governmental involvement. Faster is better.

Close vendor relationships also benefit a customer because of the ability to tap the supplier's knowledge base. Somewhat of an opposite philosophy pervades the Defense Department, which feels compelled to micromanage not only the design process for a new weapons system, rather than let a prime contractor assume that responsibility, but also the production and testing of each production step. If the attitude towards a supplier is, "I know best, so do it my way, or I will find someone else," this puts little premium on that company's expertise in an area.

The Japanese approach to close working relationships between large customers and their numerous suppliers has been adopted by some, but not all, U.S. firms. Closely analyzing the pluses and minuses in terms of the impact on cash flows may help settle the argument as to which approach is better. Keeping suppliers at arm's length, putting everything out to bid, and choosing the low bidder, the way most governmental units do, usually will achieve lower unit costs in the short run. So the cash savings are on the side of a price orientation, but only in the short run. As an individual you might be uncomfortable committing $1500 for tree removal after receiving only one quote. Two more quotes could be very worthwhile.

But when an ongoing relationship is involved, when products are going to be shipped on a recurring basis, schedules must be met, and quality must be maintained, then a different approach will actually save money in the long run. Trust on both sides is needed, of course. Trust has to be earned over time. Sooner or later the trust built up with a favorite supplier may well be shaken. No team plays 1000 ball and, when a long-term relationship is abused, there can be some hard feelings. But you don't throw the baby out with the bath. One or two unsatisfactory experiences should not dissuade you from adopting the concept of cooperative rather than adversarial vendor relations.

As a general rule, therefore, you should strive to have the *fewest* number of vendors. Whether it is office supplies, castings, or banks, it is far better to concentrate your activity. Maximize your resources by dealing with the fewest number of suppliers, but then demand, and expect to receive, outstanding service from each. Dealing with fewer vendors, by the way, also has some direct cash savings in your Purchasing and Accounting functions. Fewer requests for quotes, fewer purchase orders, and fewer vendor invoices to be processed by Accounts Payable can all be expected. No one will ever see a cash effect from processing one more or one less accounts payable voucher. One more and Sam has to work five more minutes; so he takes it out of his coffee break. One less and Sam's coffee break today is going to be 12 minutes instead of 7.

The attitude, however, that one more or one less piece of paper to be processed is immaterial—is deadly. How did bureaucracies ever get established? At some point one more control was added, and then somebody was assigned to see that the new control was being adhered to. Each step is small and seemingly innocuous; taken together, they can constipate an organization. Similarly, removing them has to be undertaken one step at a time. It *does* make a difference if you process two invoices from two different office supply houses or one larger invoice from a single supplier. Not being able to touch or feel the savings is irrelevant. The savings are there.

The Benefits of JIT

The lower inventory that will be needed, the assurance of higher quality, and the benefits of being able to tap into someone else's knowledge base are all long-term benefits of going to a JIT approach. The final benefit, when JIT is fully up and running, is a massive saving in warehouse space, and often significant reductions in space requirements on the factory floor. While this excess space probably cannot be sold or rented out, it either allows less use of outside warehousing or provides expansion capacity at no further cost.

JIT does not come quickly or easily. The Japanese took literally 20 years to develop JIT, and U.S. firms—knowing it works—take upwards of five years now. Regardless of how long it takes, the bottom line results, in both earnings and cash flow, are well worthwhile.

Nonvalue-Added Activities. Often identified during the course of implementing TQM and JIT, nonvalue added (NVA) activities are defined as work effort that does not accomplish anything in terms of meeting customer requirements. Examples are material handling on the shop floor or inspection of incoming material from vendors. At any point in time, given the shop floor layout, does material handling have to be done? Yes. Does the customer see the benefit? No. The solution is to rearrange the factory, into cells perhaps, so that the raw steel is completely machined with no material handling required. With regard to incoming inspection, if you have vendors who are qualified under ISO 9000, as an example, or considered certified in some other way, you can eliminate the incoming inspection, knowing that the items meet your requirements.

The term *nonvalue-added* has taken on an emotional overtone, perhaps for good reason. First, managers hate to think, or admit, that they are responsible for utilizing scarce resources wastefully. Second, workers will *never* admit to performing nonvalue-added work. "Of course, my job is important. If I didn't do it, the following would go wrong ..." It is hard to step back and relate any one task or series of tasks to the ultimate objective of meeting customer requirements.

The Total Quality Management advocates, despite occasionally overselling their message, are absolutely correct that NVA represents a waste of organizational resources. In terms of Total Cash Management, any NVA is a waste of cash. Identifying NVA, and then changing the process so that the activity is no longer needed, are two entirely separate things. Take material handling. Obviously, if three different machining operations are in separate departments, the material must be moved from department A to department B to department C or the piece will not be completed. So, as of today, while the material handling is, by definition, NVA, it does not mean material handling can be eliminated. First the basic plant layout has to change, and this will not take place by itself.

The same is true of incoming inspection. If you are dealing with a foundry that has had a history of supplying poor castings, common sense tells you to inspect them before investing further resources in machining operations. Again, the inspection is NVA. But it can only be eliminated when the vendor's performance improves. What will it take to make that happen? It certainly will not take place by itself.

Reengineering. This current term in vogue describes what has to happen, as well as the process of making improvements, to eliminate NVA. In the old days management would call in the efficiency experts (remember that term?), who would proceed to rearrange a factory layout, recommend new tooling, or try out a new welding process. Today the efficiency expert is gone, and the TQM consultant is called in to train the workers to perform the reengineering themselves. Nobody knows the work better than those who do it.

Continuous Improvement consists of learning the analytical *techniques* of process mapping, and then developing new and simpler ways of accomplishing the ultimate objective of customer satisfaction. Continuous improvement is nothing more or less than the identification and subsequent elimination of nonvalue-added activities.

From the perspective of cash flow, the most important idea is to recognize that every improvement adopted is going to require change of some sort. Many of the changes, in turn, will require up-front investments, that is, cash outlays, before the particular NVA can be eliminated. (Once again, there is no free lunch.) It may not require the formal capital budgeting techniques of DCF in every case, but at least a payback calculation should be made. In some cases it may be better to keep seemingly inefficient activities.

Spare Parts Inventories

Anyone who has ever had to buy a part to repair an old model consumer product—a refrigerator or automobile—has probably suffered sticker shock. The selling prices on spare parts for older models appear totally out of line, particularly in comparison to the cost of a total brand new product today. But your second thought probably is, "Well, yes, $1000 for a new fender is awfully high, but without it my $8000 used car is not drivable. And anyhow I bet it costs a lot to store an inventory of spare fenders for every make and model of car made in the last 10 years. In fact, how do they do it?" So you pay the $1000, plus labor, and the old clunker is back on the road again, hopefully good for another couple of years. It certainly was cheaper to get the part than buy a new car.

When you look at the economics of spare parts from the manufacturer's perspective, this analysis holds up quite well. On a gross profit basis, selling price less cost of goods sold, most manufacturers have far higher gross margins on parts than on new equipment. Why shouldn't they? There is a lot of competition for new car sales, and while a Cadillac de Ville is not identical to a Lincoln Town Car, most individuals would settle for either one. Selling prices, as well as features, are very similar. But what competition is there for a right front fender for a 1992 Chevrolet Corsica? Certainly very little. The dies to make the fender were very expensive then, and nobody would invest today to make new fenders for 1992 Corsicas. So you either buy from the sole source, GM, or you go to a junkyard. That's about it.

That explains high prices and high profit margins. In total there is good demand for automobile and refrigerator spare parts. But at any point in time, at one retail location, there is both very little demand for a specific part, and no way to forecast what demand there will be for any one of the millions of potential purchases.

Someone has to order, store, maintain, and ship replacement parts. It is a huge business, with good profit margins. But in terms of Total Cash Management, it is a tremendous consumer of cash. Spare parts inventories turn over once or maybe twice a year. For a normal manufacturer all other inventories turn over four or five times a year, while companies well along in JIT can have way more than 12 turns. In addition to slow turnover, there is high handling cost associated with spare parts. If you think about it, the demand from maintenance and repair shops is going to come in literally one at a time. What are the chances that one auto body shop will be working at the same time on two different 1992 Corsicas, each of which needs a right front fender. It could happen. But you would not want to build a business on the chances of it happening very often.

Slow demand and high handling costs are, however, only part of the story. The final problem relates to forecasting demand. If you were the parts manager at GM, how many right front fenders would you order for your inventory in July 1992 (when the production line is being shut down). Keep in mind that, if you run out, you cannot order any more, and you will have very unhappy customers who may never buy another Chevrolet, perhaps not even a GM car. The first thought is to be safe and order more than enough.

The other side of that coin is that at some point demand for right front 1992 Corsica fenders is going to go to zero. First of all, as companies get ever more involved in the Total Quality movement, products are lasting longer, and there are fewer warranty claims. The longer but better service life may increase the demand—or decrease it. Which is it? When will the demand end? At that point, what do you do with your on-hand inventory? It cannot be reworked to be a left rear fender. It won't fit any other models. It's scrap. It has to be written off. It has to be physically disposed. Meanwhile you have had the privilege of storing it, insuring it, paying property taxes on it, maintaining records, and so on. All those expenses have to be covered by the gross profit on the items that do sell.

On balance, taking into consideration the total life cycle costs involved, the spare parts business is probably as profitable as anything else, but not abnormally so. Margins are higher, but so is the investment base. ROI, the net of both variables, is going to be about average.

Who Is Responsible for Controlling Inventory?

As already mentioned, in an effort to control inventories, which seem to have a life of their own, some firms are reduced to edicts from the top. "Cut inventories 15 percent in the next four months!" The real question to ask is why such edicts are necessary. Why hasn't everyone done their job? Why do we have a problem that requires stringent measures?

"Why hasn't *everyone* done their job?" The clue is right there in the word *everyone*. There is an old saying, "What's everybody's job is nobody's job." If you think about inventories in terms of cash flows, and in light of the discussion in this chapter so far, it is easy to see that inventories are truly pervasive. The activity of *every* functional area affects inventories and inventory levels, and in turn is affected by those inventories.

In the final analysis the CEO and COO are the only people in a manufacturing organization with overall responsibility for managing and controlling inventory. Even in distribution organizations, retailing and wholesaling, sales levels and gross profits are a function of inventory *policies*, which must be set at the top. Certainly the availability of cash and borrowing power to finance the inventories is important in any company.

So Finance is involved. Marketing and Sales, all other things being equal, feel more comfortable with larger inventories; they have sufficient quantities of any particular item and the benefits of a broader line.

Production is involved in inventory levels both in terms of the amount of work in progress and in the choice of lot sizes. Mass production in the United States brought us ever increasing gains in productivity, with lower and lower costs of production. The essence of mass production is long production runs. Set-up costs are reduced, and worker efficiencies are improved. Disregarding the pressure of accounting reports to encourage excess production, engineering efficiency pushes manufacturing to maximize production. "OK, we've made it, Marketing. Now it's up to you guys to sell it." Not only is a real spirit of cooperation needed among functional areas, but a real understanding of how and why inventories grow is required if inventories are ever to be kept under control.

Engineering managers usually do not think of themselves as affecting inventory levels, but they do in two ways. There is nothing an engineer likes better than a challenge. Suppose, for example, that a marketing product manager says to a design engineer, "Customer X would like the following (small!) modification. Can we do it?" The answer invariably is yes. What neither of them thinks about is the inventory costs involved in any new item(s). The sales rep wants the sales credit, and the engineer wants to meet the challenge. Nobody is looking at the big picture.

Engineering also affects inventory every time an engineering change notice is issued. Almost by definition, an engineering change affects one or more parts now in production. More often than not, one or more existing parts is no longer useful or even usable. Guess what happens to the old part? Step 1: Put it back on the shelf. ("Who knows, maybe we'll need it.") Step 2: At some point the wishful thinking is superseded by reality, and a write-off is taken. The cause and effect are separated in time, but the engineering change *caused* the write-off.

Finally, in terms of the cast of characters who affect inventory levels, we have Production and Inventory Control. In some companies this is part of Manufacturing, and in others there is a separate organization for materials management, which would include purchasing, warehousing, and related operations. In theory production control is supposed to schedule both purchased and manufactured items to meet either customer orders or the production schedule based on forecast sales.

With the complexity in the modern factory, this task appears to lend itself well to computerization. Many firms have adopted Materials Requirements Planning (MRP) in one of its many versions. If all goes according to plan, then inventories will indeed be minimized, lot sizes will be correct, purchased items will indeed arrive just in time, and each manufacturing operation on every part will be scheduled in such a way as to maximize productivity.

There are only two problems with MRP. First, it usually does not work as planned because production schedules are themselves changed frequently, even daily. Second, as with any computerized system, the output is no better than the input: garbage in, garbage out.

Production Schedules.   The fact that production schedules change should surprise no one. Customer orders and shipments can never be forecast accurately. Hot items have to be expedited, putting them ahead of others already scheduled, thus throwing out of kilter previous smooth plans. Despite the best concepts of JIT, some vendors are late. Machine tools break down and so forth. If everything ran perfectly smoothly, there would be no need for management, but somehow every production operation known still requires hands-on control. Production schedules can never be cast in concrete, except perhaps in a command economy where performance is measured by meeting the schedule, irrespective of whether the schedule itself meets any known customer requirements.

Any time you try to be responsive to real customers, there are bound to be uncertainties. All you can do is organize for maximum flexibility to meet whatever demands are placed on the system. The point, however, is that flexibility comes at the cost of having excess inventories at times as customers change their mind half way through your production cycle. It cannot be helped, and therefore "excess" inventories are always going to be a fact of life. No Production Control Department will ever be able to get ahead of the curve on a permanent basis.

Inaccurate Input Data.   Production control departments will also never meet their goals because the basic input data is invariably inaccurate. Every worker has to report accurately good production, operation by operation, as well as *all* scrap and rework. Every part number must be identified with 100-percent accuracy. Bills of material and routings must be absolutely up-to-date, as must be all receipts and shipments. Clerical errors, deliberate underreporting of scrap, a lack of coordination between Engineering and Production on engineering change notices, and so forth all conspire to tear down the best MRP system. Ninety-five-percent accuracy, it turns out, is not good enough. Human intervention becomes necessary, but the very act of human intervention says that the computer system is giving the "wrong" answer, and, worse, the human intervention itself must now be accommodated by the computer.

In short, inventory control personnel, at best, are at the mercy of numerous variables over which they do not exercise total control. If they do a superb job, they can prevent inventories from increasing alarmingly. In the normal course of events, production and inventory control personnel often end up as part of the problem. It may be unkind, but the best and brightest manufacturing managers do not often choose to make a career in production and inventory control.

This section has shown just how many different organizational units affect inventory levels, each one trying to do its own job. Again, no one department, no single executive, is looking at inventories from the perspective of minimizing *company* resources. Any change initiated in any part of the company to reduce inventories is going to impact someone else. Inventory levels of work in process, usually the responsibility of manufacturing, can possibly be reduced by increasing lot sizes, which smooths out production, but which also creates larger finished goods inventories. Reducing the number of engineering changes may help inventories, but means that the product sold to the customer may not be "correct." A competitor's product may then have a performance advantage. Buying raw materials in smaller quantities and more frequently may reduce inventory levels, but raise purchase costs because of the loss of quantity discounts. Such tradeoffs can be continued.

The point to keep in mind is that there probably is *no good solution*. Everything cannot be optimized at once. What has to be done is to look at inventories as part of several systems. Only by changing each system through process analysis, eliminating nonvalue-added activities, can any firm hope to improve its inventory performance. But looking at systems that cut across department lines cannot be undertaken by any one department operating in a vacuum. It requires top management involvement and support. That is why we said that only the CEO or COO can control inventories. Everyone else only has a piece of the jigsaw puzzle.

Broad vs. Narrow Product Lines

"You cannot sell from an empty wagon" is a piece of old folklore often used by marketing people to justify greater inventories. A second bit of wisdom is that, "Our customers expect us to have a broad line or they won't buy from us." Since sales and sales levels are paramount in every for-profit firm, it is often easier to agree with their Marketing Department arguments than fight it and take the responsibility for losing sales.

Any smart marketing manager, at least at first blush, would be expected to argue strongly for a broad line of products with plenty of depth to meet any conceivable customer need. It would be great to go to any customer or to prospect, and say, "You want it, we've got it." Certainly that is better than having to make excuses for a certain item not being available now. It is hard to tell which is worse, from the salesperson's perspective: "We're temporarily out of stock and are back ordering that item." Or, "Sorry, we don't carry that item in our line." In both cases there is a fear, perhaps justified, that the customer will go to a competitor. And the unspoken assumption is that, once customers go to a competitor, we may never see them again.

The problem is that it is impossible for any one store, any one wholesaler, or any one manufacturer to be "all things to all people." Intellectually this is known and accepted by everyone, up to the moment the salesperson is in the customer's office, having had a hard time getting an appointment, and the first item asked for is not available.

The pressures to meet sales goals are immense and sales departments rightfully expect that their own company will be behind them 100 percent of the way in terms of having available what customers want. The economic realities are that customer wants are infinite and that the supplier's resources are always limited. One of the country's leading marketing firms, Procter & Gamble, for years had a strategy of providing virtually every size of every product, in addition to a broad range of brands within any product group. The business press reported that at one time P&G had 11 different detergent and soap brands, presumably responding to any conceivable consumer preference. However, even P&G, with all its resources, was forced to consolidate two brands of detergent (Solo and Bold). According to the same newspaper report, it had to "streamline its huge portfolio of detergents, diapers, tissues, and other household items, culling 25 percent of the types and sizes of P&G products sold through retailers."

The original P&G strategy was that, the more brands they offered, the more sizes available, the more shelf space they would have in any store and hence the larger would be P&G sales. This approach worked for years, but finally became unsustainable. The incremental profits from the eleventh brand of detergent, or the fourth size package of toothpaste became less than the inventory and distribution costs of maintaining such a broad line.

It made sense for P&G to slim down, freeing up the cash invested in separate inventories of four sizes of one brand of toothpaste or in separate inventories of 11 different detergents. But the key point is that, in cutting its lines to increase overall profitability, some sales were going to be lost. Put it a different way. Since there is no free lunch, some salespeople and some product managers were facing reduced sales volumes. Those customers who demanded only, say, the 4.0-oz size of Crest, or who would buy only Solo detergent, now gone, undoubtedly would shift to a competitor's offering. But as the same article pointed out, Colgate "saved nearly $20 million when it cut product sizes and types of toothpastes, detergents, and other products." The whole system ultimately had to shrink, providing customers with less choice. But the remaining items would cost less as the economies of lower inventories and fewer production runs worked their way through distribution channels.

It is hard to generalize, but an analysis of the country's most successful firms would probably show that firms that *specialized*–that had narrower product lines–did better financially. The curse of the American requirement for "growth," however, often forces even the most focused firm to "broaden" its product line. Levi Strauss jeans are a tremendous success story. Does the average jeans buyer really need Levi Strauss T Shirts, or does the regular Jockey underwear buyer really need Jockey socks?

At some point company management may have to face the tradeoff between good profit levels and a reasonable return on investment at current levels, as compared to the real risks and possible rewards of expansion into new product lines and new services. The history of diversification shows mixed results, with some successes and some failures. What it certainly shows is that any diversification strategy requires significant cash investments in additional inventories, inventories that cost real money to maintain.

5
Day-to-Day Cash Management

Total Cash Management (TCM) is a continuous process. Maximizing the availability of cash allows a firm both to capture growth opportunities and to achieve operating efficiencies. Cash becomes available from profits, generated by customer sales, and can also come from owners and investors. In the short run it can also be provided by bank borrowing. Bank borrowing, in turn, requires a good working relationship with your bank, as well as sufficient balances maintained to make your account profitable. Anything you can do to bring cash into the bank more quickly, or slow down its disbursement, will help build up available balances.

While the mechanics of day-to-day cash management are usually thought of as strictly the responsibility of the Controller or Treasurer, in reality everyone is affected by the way cash flows are handled. A few examples:

- Delaying payments to vendors can lead to poor relationships that in turn impacts on purchasing and production control responsibilities.

- A poorly designed expense reimbursement system can drive your best salesperson to despair.

- Too tight control over needed capital expenditures, say turning down a CAD system for engineering, breeds internal resentment.

- An overly aggressive collection effort can lose customer good will.

- Late or irrelevant accounting reports cause operating managers to question all aspects of Finance.

If any of these occur, among many others, you risk losing in advance the benefits of TCM. Total Cash Management means just that, in total, and every employee and every manager has to become cash conscious. Different parts of the organization cannot go off each in their own direction. "Suboptimization" is a multisyllable term describing how employees look only at their own operations and do not pay attention to the impact of their actions on others.

In this chapter we look at some common areas of day-to-day cash management and evaluate the *real* tradeoffs. While many of the suggestions are prescriptive, even more important is for the reader to evaluate the situation in the light of your own organization's objectives, strengths, and weaknesses. You might make a very rational decision not to follow some of the ideas. But as long as you think it through—how any cash decision affects other parts of the organization—you will be well on the way to TCM.

Disbursing Accounts Payable

It is hard to overvalue a good credit rating, whereas a reputation for slow payment will be damaging in the long run. It is amazing how even the largest, totally sound financially firms jeopardize their standing in the business community by playing games with their accounts payable policies and practices. In much of business the Golden Rule operates, defined cynically as, "He who has the gold makes the rules." Maybe it would be more appropriate to go back to the original Biblical saying.

There is no question that a large firm, buying a significant portion of a vendor's output, has substantial economic leverage and can dictate payment terms. Irrespective of a vendor's stated terms, discounts can be taken even when not earned or net payments can be stretched way beyond the normal 30-day terms. Some companies do this as a matter of course, programming their computers to take *all* discounts offered or scheduling *all* net-30 payments for 60 or even 75 days. The fact that they get away with it seems in turn to justify the practice. But vendors talk to each other, and a reputation for sharp practices, once earned, is going to be hard to shrug off. Sooner or later there will be shortages. The vendor will have to make a choice among customers for an item in short supply, and the likelihood of slow receipt of cash will tip the decision.

The other side of this is the relatively rare firm that is adamant about meeting all supplier and vendor terms precisely. There are even tales, perhaps apocryphal, that one major firm had its Accounts Payable Department work overtime to avoid paying even one day beyond stated terms. Incurring extra out-of-pocket expense to meet arbitrary deadlines is not a sign of good management; it is a sign of rigidity.

A company should set up a disbursement policy that minimizes operating expenses and that comes as close as possible to meeting vendor due dates. At one extreme, checks would be written every day of the month, 30 days from invoice date, or, if one believes in starting the calculation from the date of *receipt* of the invoice, say 35 days after invoice date for net bills. For discount invoices, offering a significant discount in 10 days, this may well require cutting the check before the receiving report is matched to the purchase order and invoice. (A few companies—and Ford is always used as the example—have totally reengineered the purchasing/receiving/invoice/payment process. Such process redesign, while highly desirable, is difficult to achieve and is the subject for a different book.)

Preparing checks every day, with the related significant clerical costs to meet arbitrary due dates set by vendors, is not conducive to TCM. Part of TCM is minimizing operating expenses; the staffing required for the daily processing of payables checks itself costs money. A company should attempt to process payables no more than twice a month. One firm commits to paying invoices from vendors whose names begin A to L on the tenth of each month, while those with M to Z are paid on the twenty-fifth. This means that every vendor will receive one check a month, and can count on when it will be received. Even if the payments are, on balance, more than 30 days after invoice, the *certainty* is well worth any possible delay.

Operating on the old saying that people can take bad news but they can't take surprises, most firms would prefer the bad news of an average collection period of 40 days, compared with the surprises of random payments—some early and some late. The alternative—having some invoices paid quickly while others are seemingly lost in a black hole—can drive a receivables clerk up the wall. Setting what may be considered a rather long disbursement period and then adhering to it is a very sound approach.

The next policy decision is how to treat invoices that offer a cash discount for prompt payment. Because the effective interest rate on almost any cash discount in excess of $\frac{1}{2}$ percent is higher than current borrowing rates, a company really cannot afford to miss any discounts. But trying to adhere strictly to stated terms is going to be costly in terms of clerical effort. Some firms have adopted a policy of deducting all cash discounts offered, irrespective of when the invoice is paid. This approach cannot be recommended. The offer of a reduced payment in exchange for speeding up the availability of cash appears to be a reasonable deal. It may not have the force of a legal contract, but certainly in the business world today there is no misunderstanding about what is being offered. Paying invoices on a net basis but still deducting a discount for prompt payment at best is unethical.

Something in between has to be found—balancing administrative efficiency with the spirit of the vendor's offer—and a workable solution is to pay invoices offering a cash discount at the next scheduled disbursement date. Taking the preceding example, if the General Service Co. sends a 2/10, n/30 invoice that you receive on the eleventh of the month, you should pay it on the twenty-fifth, which is when the M to Z firms normally are paid, and take the discount even though technically it is more than 10 days. If you waited until the tenth of next month, when the G firms are normally paid, you really should treat this as a lost discount and pay net.

Some firms put their payment terms right on their own *purchase order*. If a vendor ships according to your purchase order, they are considered to have agreed to the terms you offered and they accepted. As long as you have told the vendor what your policy is and adhere to it, it is irrelevant what they print on *their* invoice. One company printed on its purchase orders, "We deduct a 2-percent discount for payments within 30 days." Whether vendors in turn raised their prices to this customer could not easily be determined.

Frankly, if offered, vendors can live with customers taking cash discounts somewhat past the due date. What they don't like is the games that certain customers play in finding ever more creative reasons for charging back amounts and then deducting them from the next payment. Large retailers are notorious for these actions.

Another aspect of accounts payable processing deals with the bank account on which the checks are drawn. For large companies that are dedicated to squeezing out every last penny of potential interest income, one approach is to set up remote disbursement points. Imagine a company whose major offices are in Atlanta and that has a small plant in Fresno. Using computers, it could set up its accounts payable files so that all vendors east of the Mississippi would be paid with a check drawn on a Fresno bank. The more remote the location, the longer it takes for the check to be processed through the banking system and presented to the bank, in this example in Fresno, for payment. Using this approach, the Atlanta firm would keep essentially no balances in the Fresno account. Each day it would wire transfer to Fresno only an amount sufficient to reimburse the bank for the checks that actually cleared that day. If it wanted to stretch the concept even further, it could print and mail the check from Fresno, thus picking up another one or two days while the U.S. Post Office delivered the mail to East Coast vendors.

This concept of remote disbursing and zero balance accounts works. If you are prepared to monitor the balances and invest or sell securities on a day-to-day basis, you can pick up significant additional interest income. Since there is no free lunch, who loses if you adopt this system? Essentially two parties bear the cost. Your vendors are actually paid—that is, *receive* good funds—later than if the check had been mailed from Atlanta. So they lose interest for at least one or two days on the amount of your payment. The banking system also incurs a cost because the check on the Fresno bank, deposited by your vendor, takes longer to clear but the Federal Reserve gives the vendor's bank availability of the funds in a maximum of two days. Very few readers of this book are going to feel sorry for the Federal Reserve System, or for banks with which they do business. So the real issue is whether vendors measure payment from receipt of the check, basing their analysis on the postmark when it was *mailed,* or actually determine when the cash from your check is available for investment.

In theory you have fulfilled your obligation when a good check is deposited in the mail. In practice, if the Post Office is slow, your vendor suffers. But the way most accounts receivable systems are set up, if payment for a 30-day net invoice dated September 10 is received on October 10, 12, or even 16, nobody will ever know or even try to measure the impact of mail delays. Most companies have payments sent to a bank lock box (to be discussed), and nobody at your vendor's office will even know on what bank your payment check was drawn. Realistically, if you receive payment from one of your customers, have you ever looked to see what bank he was using? Do you care whether it is a local bank or one in Bozeman, Montana (a favorite location at one time for really remote disbursing)? Even if you do care, what can you do about it? It is inconceivable you would go to one of your customers and say, "By the way, I'd appreciate it if you paid me from a New York bank rather than one in Bozeman." What holds for your customers and you is equally valid for you and your vendors.

For professionals in the cash management business (and they have their own trade association and monthly magazine), life consists of trying to squeeze out every advantage that the paper-based check clearing system offers. What these professionals overlook is the even greater importance of good working relationships between you and your customers and between you and your vendors. Better to receive payment from your customers within ±30 days and disregard what bank the check was drawn on, than insist on an electronics fund transfer on the thirty-sixth day from date of invoice. Similarly, rather than trying to make a game of the payments system with your vendors, it is better to take those management resources and develop a closer working relationship that will minimize inventory levels or involve the vendor earlier in the product design stage.

Too many cash managers lose sight of the forest (good relationships with customers and vendors) for the trees (daily available cash balances). Top management has to set policies and allocate resources. While it is not conventional wisdom, most companies would be better served by devoting more resources to vendor and customer relationships rather than trying to beat either group in the zero-sum cash game.

Note: The preceding comments may well preclude the cash managers group from ever inviting the author to be a guest at one of their parties.

In terms of Total Cash Management, however, it is vital to set priorities. No company can accomplish everything. With limited management resources, is it more or less appropriate to devote them to the technicalities of the cash management game? Readers can draw their own conclusions.

Using Lock Boxes

The basic concept of using a Post Office box at a remote location, to speed up the collection of checks sent by customers, has been around for years. As postal service has deteriorated, the desire to get your hands on checks that are in the mail has, if anything, increased. By asking West Coast customers to send their payments to Los Angeles, Southeast customers to Atlanta, and Midwest customers to Chicago, a Boston company will undoubtedly get its cash two or possibly even three days sooner. Of course, as we saw, if you have the cash two days sooner, then your customer will have had the check returned to the drawee bank two days sooner also. It's still a zero-sum game.

There are two aspects of using a Post Office lock box system that should be noted. First, when the checks are mailed to you in Los Angeles, they are being sent directly to the Los Angeles bank you have selected to perform this service. The box is really rented by the bank as an extension of its check processing function. Banks charge a fee, often a significant one, for processing your lock box deposits, and, as you can imagine, there is substantial competition among banks to perform this service for you.

Selecting a bank (or banks if you are going nationwide) is either very easy or quite difficult. If you are not trying to squeeze out the last penny of funds availability, it probably makes no difference which Los Angeles bank you choose. Failing everything else, ask your main bank for a recommendation and they will put you in touch with their primary Los Angeles correspondent. Keep in mind the advice about selecting other banks in Chap. 6 and at least bring up the subject of possible credit needs in the future.

For the vast majority of customers, lock box service is basically a commodity in today's environment, and for plain vanilla service any bank will do. However, a few banks truly specialize in lock box services. If you have unique requirements for processing receivables, such as applying cash to customer accounts the same day, some banks have computerized the operation. They can send you electronically the data that was included in your customers' remittance advice. There will be an extra charge for this service but it may be worth it.

We stated that choosing banks for lock boxes is either very easy or very complex. Arbitrarily deciding where to have your boxes, based on your own understanding of where your customers are, may be sufficient. On the other hand if you are receiving either a relatively few very large checks each month or a large number (many thousands) of smaller remittances, it is not intuitively obvious in which cities, or even how many cities, to have lock boxes. As you can imagine, where there is a need there is a solution.

Some banks and a couple of independent consultants stand ready, for a fee, to analyze the pattern of your receipts and optimize a nationwide lock box system. The key variables are the postal service in the cities where your customers are located and how sophisticated a bank is in quickly processing checks once they hit the local Post Office. Since many banks process checks 24 hours a day and have developed special relationships that allow them to collect checks even faster than the Federal Reserve, there are subtle differences among banks, even among direct competitors in the same city.

For the average reader, the second aspect of lock boxes is important in terms of TCM. How will your customers react to a request that they change their remittance to you to a lock box in a remote city? They know what you are doing and that they will lose some float. Some firms refuse to mail to a lock box and send their check directly to you. Are you going to refuse to accept payment?

On a personal basis, as you pay your bills once a month, have you ever noticed where companies are asking you to send them their money, and have you always complied? For example, the author lives in a New York suburb, and the charge account payments for three different department stores go respectively to Birmingham, Alabama, to Macon, Georgia (although just recently they had been directed to Louisville, Kentucky), and to Cleveland, Ohio, while American Express wants the payment to go virtually next door to Newark, New Jersey. Occasionally, if the bank balance is low, the author's Amex payment might be mailed to Arizona, knowing it will take longer to get there than to Newark. On the other hand there is little likelihood that a New Jersey resident would mail a check to New York City rather than Macon, Georgia.

Customers are not dumb, and, if enough money is involved, they are going to short-circuit the best laid lock box system. By the way, it is hard to figure out how *each* of the three similar department store chains has optimized their payment systems when they have chosen such diverse locations as Cleveland, Macon, and Birmingham. They cannot all be correct, and this goes to show that trying to analyze this topic of lock box locations too closely may be self-defeating.

As a general rule you probably are better off with fewer rather than more locations, and a prime consideration is the cost of dealing with too many banks, each of which has its own system and reports. One exception is if you have a very large customer, such as one company that sold primarily to a very large consumer goods company in Cincinnati. It opened a lock box at a Cincinnati bank just to get that one check a month a couple of days early, and it worked. But what was a large sum to the vendor probably was considered relatively small by the customer; that is why it worked. If the positions had been reversed, you can draw your own conclusion as to who should do what.

A final word on lock boxes. The author strongly recommends that *every* organization, no matter how small, have at least a single lock box at its head office location. Even if there is *no* speedup in the availability of cash receipts—whether the checks come to your office in Albany or to your bank in Albany makes no difference in mail time from the customer—it is good internal control to have all cash go directly into the bank without being touched by your own employees. If you have your customers now send their check to a lock box in your city instead of directly to your office, you will probably lose a day in being able to apply customer payments. This means that your receivable records will always be one day out of date. If you had always posted Tuesday receipts on Tuesday, now you will be receiving the remittance advice from the bank on Wednesday.

More than offsetting this is the benefit in controlling cash. If one or more bookkeeping personnel at your office are sick or on vacation at the same time, cash receipts will still be processed every day. Having payments go to the bank and receiving only the remittance advice will not prevent all types of fraud, but it will make it much harder for an employee to engage in certain well-known types of cheating. Direct deposit to the bank would have saved one firm at least one day's interest on $1 million. It seems that a new employee was so enthralled to be handling a check of that magnitude that she took it home that evening to show her parents how important her job was! Trust me: All customer remittances should go directly to a bank, not first to your office.

Payroll Processing

It may be hard to believe, but not too many years ago payrolls were literally paid in cash—dollar bills and coins. In fact, there were laws on the books in several states that precluded companies from paying by check if employees did not want it. Today the choice for firms and for their employees is whether to pay by check or by direct deposit to the employee's checking account.

Paying by check is going to save the employer cash, if the process is handled correctly, but for employees with checking accounts, direct deposit may be more desirable. It is probably hard for many readers to believe, but a tremendous number of people in this country do not have checking accounts, as well as a number who do not have any type of bank relationship at all. This may be a carryover from the Great Depression, when many banks closed and depositors lost everything (this was before the FDIC) or these individuals believe they can control their financial destinies better by dealing only in cash.

While the trend is definitely to direct deposit of payroll into each employee's account, in terms of TCM we should examine this closely and see the real cost. The way the banking system processes electronic transfers, which is what a direct payroll deposit is, requires that collected funds be available in your firm's checking account one full day before pay day. In other words it takes one day for a transfer to be made from a Boston employer's account to an employee anywhere in the country, whether Portland, Oregon or Portland, Maine. Assuming that 100 percent of employees have been persuaded to accept direct deposit, the company must be willing to have the total net payroll withdrawn from its checking account one business day *prior* to payday for employee accounts to be credited on payday.

One day's interest, times 24 or 26 payrolls a year, may well be a significant sum to give up, depending on the size of the payroll. In reality, the interest forgone is going to be substantially higher than that. Many people have a hangup about drawing a check on an account that has insufficient funds in it the day the check is written or mailed. If you think about it, however, as the maker of the check your real responsibility is to have good funds in the account the day the check is presented to your bank for payment. Neither your employee, receiving the payroll check, nor one of your vendors receiving an accounts payable check, really cares how much money is in the account or how long it has been there, as long as the check is paid when presented.

Recall our discussion of remote disbursement programs for accounts payable. Companies will pick the most obscure and distant bank they can find, draw checks on that institution, and then only wire good funds to the remote bank on the day checks are presented. The *float* (the time between when the check is mailed to the vendor and when it arrives back at the drawee bank) will produce interest income, if the funds are invested, or delay the need to borrow. The basic principle is to maximize the float.

With respect to payroll accounts, a large number of employees, if they work at the local facility, will go to the bank and cash their checks on payday. Others will deposit their checks on payday in another local bank, and they will be presented for payment the following day. So something like 60 to 70 percent of the payroll will be withdrawn from your payroll account almost immediately. This leaves 30 to 40 percent of your payroll that will *not* be withdrawn right away. Hard as it is to believe, some employees stick paychecks in their desk drawer for weeks and sometimes months. Others are traveling on vacation.

Whatever the reason, if you set up a separate payroll checking account and put the entire net pay in on payday, the bank statement will show that the declining daily balances (and eventually it does get to zero) reflects a significant *average* daily balance. Does that average daily balance, representing potentially available interest earnings, belong to the employer or to the bank? If you have put in the total payroll on payday, then the money belongs to the bank. They can and will invest it, and they will give you credit only in terms of adding to your firm's overall average deposit level. If you need to boost your deposit to meet a compensating balance level, this may be a good way to do it. On the other hand, if balances are already high enough, you should invest the fund for the firm's account.

This means arranging to put only enough money each day into the payroll account to meet checks as they clear that day. You can do it on the basis of averages, analyzing past experience, or you can explicitly make arrangements with your bank to debit your main account and credit the payroll account each day for the exact amount of checks presented for payment. This way you get to earn interest on the funds that were paid to employees who have chosen not to cash it or deposit it in their own account.

Note the assumption that there will be a *separate* checking account, probably at your main bank. In theory all payroll checks could be written against your main account. In practice it will be much simpler to reconcile two separate accounts at the end of each month than to have one large account with both payroll and payables intermingled.

Now, going back to the comparison of direct deposit vs. payroll checks, it is obvious that, in terms of lost interest income, direct deposit can be fairly costly. The author still favors direct deposits because of other issues, which can demonstrate the ramifications of a truly Total Cash Management approach. While a company's cash manager might argue strongly for paying by check on the grounds that the interest lost by going to a direct deposit system was substantial, two other groups *must* be heard from.

Where does the *Human Resources* (HR) Department come out on this debate? It may not be feasible to conduct a survey of employees, and there is a real question in the minds of many managers as to whether management prerogatives should be held on to. Certainly how employees are paid would usually be considered a management decision. So in most organizations the HR group is considered as representing the voice of employees, assuming no union contract on how employees are to be paid. So, before deciding whether to change a payroll system, it would be totally appropriate, if not mandatory, to request feedback from HR. Such issues as how to deal with employees that have no checking or bank account, and those who do not want their spouses to know how much they make, may seem like trivial issues, but that is why you have HR professionals.

The second group to be consulted is the Controllers Department, where the *payroll* is usually located. What are the operational pluses and minuses to a direct deposit system? It is quite possible that the savings in processing payrolls will pay for much of, if not all, the cost of the lost float and related interest income. It would take a detailed cost study to refine the answer, but on the surface at least three sources of savings would be:

1. The fact that special paychecks would not have to be made up in advance for individuals going on vacation.

2. In the case of out-of-town employees, most firms try to have paychecks available on payday; so if there are remote locations, this means the checks have to be sent by Federal Express or in some other equally costly method.

3. Lost paychecks and stop payments are a thing of the past, as is the need ever to reconcile a separate payroll account each month.

While the author personally favors direct deposit (experience suggesting that the benefits in total are greater than the costs), the point is that what seems like a relatively simple decision can have far-reaching consequences in several areas. A change in the Payroll Department has ramifications in the treasury/cash management area, in human resources, and among employees in total. Nobody ever said that a Total Cash Management system was easy, just that it is important.

Expense Reimbursement

It is likely that most readers of this book do a fair amount of travel on company business. At least for those who have to do it frequently, the glamour and romance of travel usually disappears quickly (that is, if it ever existed). Most companies understand this and try to make company-sponsored travel as hassle-free as possible, within the confines of prudent financial and fiscal controls.

Total Cash Management, as we have seen, involves all aspects of a business, with the goal to optimize among tradeoffs. In travel expense reimbursement what may be good for the company can hurt employees, with a consequent effect on morale. Over the years, the way companies handle travel expenses has changed, and a review can show how no one functional department can call the tune.

Companies used to give a cash advance to an employee prior to the trip. Upon completion, the employee filled out an expense form, had it approved, and then settled up with the company. If the expenses were greater than the advance, the company would write a check; if less, the employee had to return the excess travel advance. To the extent expense forms were filled out promptly, there was a minimum cash flow from the company before it was needed, in the form of the advance, and a quick repayment at the end of the trip. The employee neither gained nor lost, and, except for the bookkeeping and the cashiering function in handing out cash or a check, the company had minimal operating costs.

This system, which works for occasional trips, is unwieldy for employees who spend a significant amount of their time on the road. Week one's expense report would not have been sent in, approved, and processed before the employee was starting the second trip. Another cash advance has to be made, the system has to be repeated, and eventually one reaches an equilibrium state, maybe three weeks' worth of advances and expenses. A travel advance is made in an amount equal to estimated expenses. So for a Chicago company, a four-day trip to Santa Fe would cost more than a two-day trip to Milwaukee, and the travel advance would be greater. Trying to estimate trip costs beforehand and minimize cash advances soon becomes a hassle.

The next step is to give employees who travel frequently a permanent travel advance, in an amount equal to approximately three week's expenses. This way if a travel expense report is processed late, or if the employee is out of town and cannot receive cash or a check, the employee still is not out of pocket. The company's goal is to preclude the employee from financing company business. Permanent travel advances have two disadvantages, however. From the employee's point of view, the money so advanced quickly loses its identity. Upon receiving the permanent advance, some people undoubtedly mean to set up a separate account and never mix the company's funds with their own. But over a two-, three-, or five-year period inevitably the employee forgets that he or she owes the company a fairly significant amount of money. Upon termination, retirement, or changing employers, many if not most employees have a hard time reimbursing the company for the permanent travel advance, made five years ago, that now suddenly is not so permanent. Employers often end up writing off such advances as uncollectible.

The second disadvantage of permanent travel advances is that, for any medium-sized company or larger, there simply is a lot of cash tied up in employee receivables. These receivables do not earn interest and, while they originally engender employee goodwill, even that disappears. Unlike customer receivables, which turn over as new sales are made and old receivables are paid down, employee receivables stay almost forever.

Where there is a business need, a solution will be found. American Express, followed by Diner's Club and Visa/MasterCard, have sold companies on the idea of providing travelers with a company credit card. There is no need for permanent or even temporary travel advances; so cash is saved that way. In addition, because it takes up to 35 or 40 days for hotel or restaurant charges to appear on the monthly credit card statement, the company actually ends up paying for travel expenses in out-of-pocket cash later than the previous method. This sales approach used by American Express accurately identified a solution to a real business problem and a substantial portion of corporate America has now gone to company credit cards. In terms of TCM, the promises of the credit card companies have been kept, but with one unintended consequence.

Processing of travel expense reports is now far more complex. The savings in cash flow—as hotel and restaurant charges now come in on a statement *after* the trip has been reported—are counterbalanced by the Accounting Department's having to do a lot more bookkeeping. The charge to department expense is made from the approved travel expense form, but cash is not disbursed simultaneously, as it was with cash advances and weekly settlement. Now a payable has to be set up to American Express for travel expenses reported by the employee but not yet received from Amex. But it is worse. There are going to be charges shown on the Amex statement for employee trips where there has not yet been an approved expense report received. Now there is an employee receivable.

Finally, although no reader would ever be guilty, some employees have been known to charge personal expenses on a company credit card! A *true* story:

> A somewhat unstable employee left a company and immediately thereafter the company received very substantial charges for two trips involving overseas flights. The former employee was contacted. He admitted he had taken the trips, and explained that he "didn't have enough cash for food so he took the overnight flight(s) to Europe so he could get a couple of meals on the plane." The company was unsuccessful in recovering from the former employee.

With company-related travel expenses charged on a company credit card, there is no cash incentive for employees to be prompt about submitting expense reimbursement statements. For some reason a lot of people dislike intensely filling them out, and someone who figures out a foolproof way of getting expense receipts in promptly (threatening to withhold the next paycheck does *not* work with some employees) should be able to turn this into a financial windfall. Meanwhile, back in the Accounting Department, a clerk is desperately trying to match up employee reported expenses with charges appearing on the credit card statement. As so often is the case, what provides a win one place has a loss elsewhere, here in the form of substantial additional clerical effort and hence cost.

There is a solution that may be almost ideal. Let employees use a credit card for company-related travel, but have it be an employee's *own* card. The company would pay any annual fee. Then the firm writes one check each week, to each employee who travels, for the total approved expenses. Since the vast majority of expenses on a trip, other than tips and tolls and inexpensive meals, can be charged, the employee is actually going to be slightly ahead in cash flow. The reimbursement check is going to arrive, on balance, before the credit card statement, more than offsetting any employee cash outlay.

There is one minor problem with this system, either with new employees who have poor or no credit or with present employees who fail to honor their commitments to the credit card firm and are cut off. Does the firm guarantee payment, risking abuse by the employee, or does the firm decide the individual perhaps should not be traveling and representing the organization? Or do you go back to individual cash travel advances, one trip at a time? Unfortunately, for some problems there is no good solution, and this is such a problem.

On balance, then, the tradeoff for any business is whether to provide company credit cards and optimize actual cash flow, as compared to the clerical time and expense involved in maintaining the credit card receivables and payables that inevitably go with the system. In the long run, one should choose the system that minimizes employee time. Cash flows ultimately will follow. To incur additional clerical expense to pick up, say, two weeks' float on overall employee travel expense does not appear to be a sound long-term strategy.

Credit Cards

This is a good point to discuss credit cards from the perspective of offering customers the option of paying with credit cards. The trend over the last 15 years has been for more and more types of business organizations to offer retail customers the convenience of paying by credit card. Consumers today can pay for a day's stay at a parking garage, subscriptions to their daily newspaper, a visit to their dentist or doctor, automobile insurance premiums, and groceries at the A&P. At one time all these goods and services had to be paid for in cash, by check, or by invoice with payment expected later.

What are the TCM implications to a business of offering credit via credit card? First, and most obvious, the credit card firms deduct a discount in the amount of $1\frac{1}{2}$ percent to, say, 4 percent. Part of this goes to reimburse the credit card company for their not receiving cash from their customer, the cardholder who bought from you, for up to 55 days. (This is the total of 30 days between billing periods, plus a 25-day grace period. On average this should work out to about 40 days.) So the interest cost would be approximately 1 percent. The remainder is for the credit card company's costs, such as physical processing of the transaction, credit losses, advertising, and, of course, profit.

Two points should be made with respect to the merchant charge made by the credit card organization. First, it is somewhat negotiable. There are no price controls, and in fact a number of competing organizations process credit card transactions for a fee. In the long run the discount charged is going to be a function of both the absolute dollar volume and the average size of transactions. Larger customers will get a better deal from the credit card firm. One ticket for $500 is going to be one-tenth as expensive to handle as ten $50 tickets, which is why some establishments say, "No charges under $15." The smaller the average ticket, the more the credit card company will have to charge you.

Second, the credit card firm, such as Visa, assumes the credit risk. Since a 1-percent bad debt loss is really pretty good for consumer receivables, if you add that to ±1 percent for the cost of money, then paying a 3-percent total discount to Visa can be more than offset by a small increase in volume of sales. Have you ever made a spur-of-the-moment decision to buy something and did it because, although you had no cash with you, you could charge it? Enough people do this to bring into question why it took so long for grocery chains to offer credit or for Sears to offer anything other than their own Discover card.

This is not the place to get into a discussion about the ethics of offering credit—whether people will buy things they cannot afford or whether the extension of credit today is in some way borrowing from the future. People buy more when credit is offered, and, in terms of Total Cash Management, maximizing sales by any legal method seems fully justified.

The real issue seems to be whether credit cards can be used when business firms are typically dealing with each other. For example, a nonprofit organization offers continuing education programs to professionals. Previously, to register for a course, one called an 800 number, provided billing information, and the employer was billed. The billing, plus waiting for payment, added both costs and uncertainty as to the final registration count. Offering phone registration by credit card increased enrollments and reduced total costs, even after the merchant fee was deducted. It was hard to tell whether the charges were on personal credit cards (with the individual putting the amount on an expense report for reimbursement) or whether they were put directly on a company credit card. Does it make any difference? No, a sale is a sale.

As American Express found out when restaurants in Boston threatened to stop accepting Amex cards, the only downside to corporate offering of sales by credit card is the fee charged. This is, to say it again, negotiable depending on volume. In fact, some trade associations have arranged to let members get purchases processed at a much lower fee utilizing the economic strength of the whole association.

Observation: If you do not offer credit card sales to your customers/clients, we strongly recommend exploring this opportunity. The real cost, after allowing for the costs of money and bad debts, is usually reasonable.

Electronic Funds Transfers

Every organization wants what some have called the rabbit and the tortoise approach to cash management. You want money to come in like a rabbit and go out like a tortoise. But since one company's inflow is another company's outflow, both parties to any business transaction can never simultaneously be able to meet these mutually inconsistent objectives—unless the world goes electronic.

For the last 25 years, pundits have been forecasting that the demise of the paper check would come within five years, that electronic funds transfers were the wave of the future. There is a substantial cost in handling billions of paper checks 10 or 15 times each, until they end up at the end of the month in the envelope with your checking account statement. If only we could get rid of all that paper! And *today's* technology permits this. So we have both a need and the means to accomplish it. No wonder change is forecast to be just around the corner.

Many people think of wire fund transfers as dealing with huge sums of money, perhaps in international transactions or in major financings. In the latter, if stock is sold to the public, the funds are wired to the seller's bank so that interest can be earned on the sums right away. When you are dealing with individual transactions in the $10-million range and above, even one day's interest is significant. (At 6 percent one day's interest on $10 million is almost $1650.) The cost of a wire transfer, plus the additional clerical work required on both sides (sender and receiver), makes wire transfers far more costly than simple paper checks—although certainly much faster in moving the funds.

Because of the cost, only large sums are usually involved, but, in terms of total *dollars*, the vast majority of funds movement probably is by wire. One $50-million transaction between bond dealers equals an awful lot of paper checks with an average amount of $60 each. So the banking system can handle wire transfers easily, but not as inexpensively as paper. You might then ask how the direct deposit of payroll into employee checking accounts all over the country can be handled so cheaply, since it is a form of electronic funds transfer. The answer is that the employer in this case provides the bank with computer information showing all the bank locations, account numbers, and amounts of net pay. In regular wire transfers, the transactions are handled one at a time, and can be done either manually, with telephone instruction, or, for firms with a high volume, by means of a personal computer. The difference remains between doing them one at a time as compared to a batch.

Some banks have attempted to introduce banking by phone, in which you as an individual can pay your bills each month. By tapping in account numbers, either on a touch-tone phone or a PC, the bank will withdraw the money from your account and wire it to the bank of your creditor, whether the electric company or a gasoline credit card charge. The beauty of the system for the banking system is the elimination of processing a lot of paper checks. It is being sold to individuals on the grounds of saving postage and the cost of checks. The fact that relatively few individuals have taken advantage of this system suggests it does not yet meet the perceived needs of consumers.

Other firms, such as insurance companies, have set up a system whereby monthly amounts for policy premiums are charged or debited directly against your personal checking account, thus again eliminating the need for you to take the trouble of writing and mailing a check. This, too, has not caught on because the individual has lost *control* over the timing of the disbursement. Suppose you are low on funds. The electronic charge from John Hancock or Prudential will still come in, and might even cause you to be overdrawn. The insurance company loves this approach because they get their money each and every month, at a known time and a known amount. Wouldn't you too like to have access to someone else's checking account?

Few individuals are willing to give someone else the right to go into their checking account and withdraw money, although these same individuals are perfectly happy to have their employer *send* money in without their own intervention. That's just human nature, to want the best of both worlds and not pay a price for it. The reason electronic funds transfer has worked in payroll and not in individual consumer bill paying is that employers were willing to give up the float from the payroll bank account in exchange for the real savings from not processing a lot of checks. Individuals have not been willing to give up the float in order to save a first-class postage stamp, particularly when a bank charges them $6 a month for the privilege.

In short, automatic payments on a recurring basis have not captured the hearts and minds of consumers. Even permitting such payments, under the control of the sender, as contrasted with having them automatic under the control of the receiver, has a hard time justifying itself on a cost-benefit basis. That is why electronic funds transfer is always going to happen within the next five years but, so far, in the past 25 years it still has not happened. Paper checks are simply too convenient and give the sender total control.

Now let's look at electronic funds transfers among businesses. Human nature seems to apply there too. We all would like to receive funds electronically. We would even send them electronically, as long as we control the timing and amount, and the cost is not prohibitive. It is the automatic nature of the payment that troubles people. What if the date could be negotiated between the parties and, if necessary, modified? The thought of any individual reader, however, *negotiating* with Sears about how to handle a monthly payment on a Discover credit card is laughable.

When two businesses are dealing with each other, however, on a more or less level playing field of economic strength, then negotiating payment terms makes a lot more sense. Ford, as well as a few other major manufacturers that have gone to just-in-time production with favored vendors, has arranged for electronic payment to those vendors. Ford, in fact, has eliminated invoices, shipping documents, receiving reports, and the like. Suppose one steering wheel (at $2 each) is used per car, and all steering wheels are ordered from one vendor. As long as quality is 100 percent so that there is no scrap, Ford figures it can pay the vendor $2 for every car that comes off the assembly line. Ford is willing to make the electronic payment automatically because of the savings in its internal purchasing, receiving inspection, and payment processes, and it is actually easier for them to wire the money than it is to write a paper check.

Because the wire transfer puts good funds in the vendor's bank the same day, the parties negotiate what that day will be relative to daily, weekly, or monthly shipments. For example, if the auto company had been paying by check on March 10 for all receipts between January 25 and February 25, then the parties would negotiate for a wire transfer anywhere between March 13 and March 16. The first date would split the difference between the mailing date (March 10) and the date good funds would be available in the vendor's account (March 16), using paper checks and the U.S. mail, while the later date would leave the two parties essentially where they were before.

While the banking system's electronic highways can handle both debit and credit transactions, very few individuals or organizations are ever going to willingly give up control over the timing of debits or charges. The basic concept flies in the face of Total Cash Management, in which you attempt to control your own destiny and make constant adjustments as circumstances change. The theory sounds good, but just because something is feasible from a technological sense does not make it worthwhile in a business sense.

It will be at least five years (from *whenever* you read this) before electronic payments supplant paper checks. Giving up control over the timing of disbursements and forgoing the float—between your mailing the check and its getting back to your bank—are not popular now and are unlikely to be in the future.

Playing the Float

The basic principle of TCM—to maximize the availability of cash resources, so that they can be invested in productive assets for the business—obviously argues in favor of playing the float. As we discuss in Chap. 9 on investing surplus cash balances, unless the sums are significant, it may not pay to invest and then sell securities on a daily basis. On balance, the longer the money stays in your bank account, the better off you are. At a minimum you are building up the average balance levels necessary to support the line of credit that provides the real financial flexibility every organization needs.

Tricks of the trade, like remote disbursement on one side and setting up lock boxes on the other, should be used so that you don't lose out in what we have discussed as a zero-sum game. Some people think some or even all of these techniques are ethically questionable, and this author respects such beliefs. It is hard to generalize about ethical behavior in cash management, because one person's unethical approach is someone else's sound business strategy. Most people would agree that deliberately sending an unsigned check and then pretending ignorance is unethical if you are trying to maintain a good credit rating. But by the same token who hasn't done this at some point inadvertently? Is the motive or the action unethical? Once we start discussing motives, we are looking down a bottomless pit, totally outside the scope of the author's competence.

All we can discuss here are actions. As long as payment terms, for both buyers and sellers, are measured from the date something is *mailed*, then doing everything possible to optimize the system for your own benefit appears worth doing. If you have economic strength and use it to negotiate favorable terms with suppliers, this appears justified. What is not defensible is changing the terms half way through. For example if the buyer agrees to pay in 30 days but deliberately withholds payment for 45 days, in our judgment that is wrong. If the buyer and seller agree in advance to 45-day terms and the check is mailed in 45 days, that should be all right.

Economic strength varies between buyer and seller, and it varies over time. Usually buyers have the upper hand but occasionally in times of shortage the seller can call the tune. Most successful business firms understand this, using their strength when they have to and roll with the punches when it goes against them.

Playing the float, therefore, in all its manifestations, is part of the American business scene. You need never apologize for utilizing the system for what is best for you. A healthy perspective is that what you do today may be done to you tomorrow, and it is probably the best way to respond to specific situations and/or opportunities. Always remember that cash management among firms is a zero-sum game. You can never really win, but you should try hard not to lose.

Daily Cash Report

Before ending this chapter, a word about recordkeeping is in order. It is a good idea to get the entire management team focused on cash by reporting what the present position is, as contrasted to the budget. Just as managers are motivated by a comparison between actual and budget on the monthly P&L, so too should they be alerted to the organization's current cash position.

As will be stated in Chap. 6, it is less important to forecast cash balances than it is to have an available line of credit. But a cash forecast, even if accurate, is of less interest to operating managers than it is to financial managers.

Operating managers want to be measured on performance, and an organization's budget for the year is the basis on which performance is measured. Therefore it is logical to report, at least weekly, and in some cases daily, how actual cash balances are doing in comparison with the *budget for the year, and possibly against last year's actual if additional information is needed. The construction of the actual work sheet format can be modified to meet individual organization needs, but it should show both cash (and marketable securities) balances on the firm's books and on the bank's books. Invariably the bank totals should exceed the company figures, because the company figures show a reduction when a check is mailed, while the bank does not show the reduction for another week or so until the check clears.*

The major budget comparison should be to the actual figure on the firm's books, but the excess of the bank figures over the company's should be displayed to highlight the importance of speeding up incoming cash, which raises both totals and, even more important, disbursement policies. Because of the ever present tension between being a good customer, paying vendors on schedule, and maximizing interest income (minimizing interest expense) by delaying or slowing down payment, operating managers can tell at a glance whether payments are being processed promptly.

Only by monitoring all components of cash flow and by seeing the actual results day to day can operating managers tell if they are doing a good job. Total Cash Management takes hard work and constant attention to detail. Measuring progress, knowing that what you are doing is having an effect, is absolutely vital to any organization.

"What you measure is what you get" is still true. Measuring cash, reporting progress against budget, will definitely help any organization implement TCM.

6
Choosing and Using a Bank

There are two primary, yet complementary, objectives in dealing with your bank(s). The first is to ensure that necessary *banking services* are performed as efficiently and effectively as possible. As with any supplier/customer relationship, price and quality are important. You are the customer and you have to insist that whatever bank or banks you choose are responsive to *your* needs. Those banks that have really adopted a true TQM approach, in practice and not just by lip service, can be of immeasurable help in smoothing out the day-to-day problems involved in moving cash around the system.

There is a second objective in dealing with your bank, and that is to be absolutely certain that *short-term bank credit* is *always* available. The standard joke that banks are always willing to lend you money—except when you really need it—has more than a shred of truth to it. The fact is that there will be times when your financial picture is bleak—perhaps you are running at a loss for the first time—and you need to borrow. Certainly banks would, all other things being equal, prefer to lend money only to profitable growing firms. A currently unprofitable business is going to have *lots* of trouble borrowing, unless arrangements have been made well in advance.

Understanding how banks really work—what their objectives are—means that you can position yourself to obtain credit when you need it most. A hard-nosed approach, recognizing that there have to be benefits to both parties for a relationship to work, requires discipline in the use of bank services and the price that should be paid. It may be redundant to say that both sides to a transaction have to benefit, but too often one party or the other may take advantage of temporary strength to work out a deal that is really unfair to the other. There is still truth in the old saying, "What goes around, comes around." If you underpay a bank for its day-to-day services at a time when you do not appear to need credit, you may become bitterly unhappy during an economic downturn to find the bank no longer wants your business if you suddenly need credit. On the other hand, a bank that squeezes you because you have no viable alternative should not be surprised if you take your business to a competitor.

Despite the seemingly inexorable trend to bank consolidation, with the rise of large local, regional, and soon national banking behemoths, there are still a large number of banks, all of whom offer more or less the same services. In short, competition still reigns. If you talk to any bank officer about competition, you will get a small chuckle, and with only the slightest prodding he or she will welcome the opportunity to tell you about the bank's competitive problems.

Individuals starting a new small business and trying to obtain credit for the first time become very frustrated when banks do not fall all over themselves offering lines of credit. Even well established and profitable smaller businesses, those that have not properly anticipated future needs, become unhappy at a perceived lack of responsiveness when they go in for the first time to borrow money. These problems of obtaining credit are not totally susceptible of solution, but understanding how the mind of a banker works will, at a minimum, reduce the frustration level.

What Do Bankers Want?

Answering this question is pretty simple. Bankers have three objectives. They want customers who (1) maintain good deposit balances, (2) use a variety of bank services, for many of which fees are charged, and (3) borrow occasionally (or even frequently) and repay the loans on schedule. A long-term loyal customer relationship, which equates to stability both in deposits and demand for services, means that the individual banker or the bank itself does not have to expend resources chasing after new accounts to replace customers who left because of dissatisfaction. A brief look at each of these three sources of bank *profit* will pull into perspective what bankers want and why they want it.

Deposits. These are the lifeblood of a bank. Banking is simple: Accept deposits, pay as little interest as possible on the funds, and then lend those same funds out to borrowers at a sufficiently high interest charge to cover both the cost of funds (interest expense) and operating costs (salaries, rent, etc.). Absent major credit losses on loans that are not collectible, and assuming even a modicum of quality service to depositors, it is almost impossible for a bank to do anything other than make a profit. Only when banks pursue unrealistic growth rate goals and let service deteriorate, or when they make large loans to known marginal borrowers for the sake of inflating short-term earnings, do banks get into trouble. Even if they get into trouble, the Federal Reserve and bank deposit insurance are there to bail them out.

But the only way a bank can survive and prosper is if it continues to receive deposits from customers. A bank can go into the money market and borrow deposits on a short-term basis, but these funds are so expensive that it provides little gross margin for a bank to cover its costs. Banks must develop their own deposit base from customers, which means providing the basic banking services of accepting deposits, providing currency, and processing checks.

If you look closely at the checks you use to withdraw funds from a mutual fund money market account or credit union, you will see that they are in fact payable through a "real bank." Effectively, *only* banks are members of the check clearing system. So if you are going to write checks in payment of your accounts, you, or the organization whose checks you are using (such as the credit union or money market account) must have a bank account. If you have a bank account, you must have "good funds" on deposit before the bank will honor your check. You know this already, but the key point is that the day-to-day balances you keep in your account just to meet the needs of your business are the very basis of the bank's profitability. Even if you think your balances are low, even if the bank officer says your balances are too low to support all your activity, whatever funds you do have, as long as the balance is positive (we talk about overdrafts later), can be lent by the bank to a borrower.

The conclusion to be drawn from this analysis is simple. Your banker *needs* you. Really she needs your cash, but the two go together. Remember this:

> The balances in your checking account are worth real money to any bank. You are the customer. Your banker needs you (your cash) more than you need her. There are always other banks that can use your deposits profitably. She has to work hard (or pay high interest) to obtain funds from *new* customers. If she ever forgets, you can remind her that it is better to retain old customers than to have to get new ones.

The conclusion to be drawn and the actions based on it are simple. You are doing the bank a real favor by letting them have your business. In exchange—and your leverage is never greater than in the beginning—you should be prepared to discuss future credit needs. This does not necessarily mean establishing a line of credit immediately. It does mean having a very frank and open discussion regarding the bank's philosophy on lending money. What type of credits are they looking for? Are they oriented to consumers, to small businesses, or to large multinational firms?

Every bank in the country *says* they are looking for good relationships with small and middle market businesses, and some of them actually mean it. Actions speak louder than words. You should put the burden of proof on them at the *start* of a relationship, if you are going to be a borrower. Since this book is written on the assumption that every firm either is a borrower or will have to be one at some time, the lending philosophy of the bank you are going to favor with your business is critical. (How to choose a bank is discussed later in the chapter.)

Services.   If deposits are the lifeblood of a bank, then services are the skeleton. Think of your own personal checking account. Has your bank recently raised its service charges for such things as stop payments or overdrafts? How much do you pay if you go below the month's minimum balance? At one time withdrawals from an ATM were free, because they saved the time of a living teller, but banks have started charging per ATM transaction. The list goes on.

What has been happening is relatively simple. When depositors were relatively unsophisticated, many individuals and organizations kept excessive balances in checking accounts and in low-paying savings accounts. This source of funds, lent out to customers, provided enough income to cover expenses and generate a profit. Over time depositors became more sophisticated, drew down balances, and kept their cash reserves in money market accounts, on which interest was earned, in commercial paper, or in certificates of deposit for which the bank had to pay market rates of interest. The low-cost deposits, which had been the basis of bank earnings, disappeared just at the time that losses from real estate, less developed country, and LBO loans all put severe pressure on earnings from the other direction.

Bank management said to themselves, although not out loud to customers, that new sources of revenue had to be developed. In the best salami-slicing tradition, fees were imposed and charges made for every conceivable service the bank offered. At least at first customers did not appear to notice, or at least not complain about, these nickel and dime charges. And the fees went straight to the bottom line, since the bank's cost structure really did not change: the same clerk who processed stop payments still did her job, but now the bank received $15 or even $20 for every entry. The clerk did not get a pay raise, and suddenly a new profit center had been created.

Like drugs, these service fees have become addictive. Many banks no longer simply bill customers for what they used to do as a routine part of their service. Now they are actively soliciting fee-type business, whether it be corporate trust work like handling corporate bond interest payments, or managing customers' pension fund assets. For a number of banks, fee income has become the *major* source of revenue and profit, while almost every bank monitors progress in this area.

What this means to companies choosing a bank is that an analysis of its pricing schedule becomes critical. We discuss this later in more detail, because we are not talking about trivial sums. Strangely enough there are very wide disparities in bank charges for the same service or activity. Most gasoline dealers in a neighborhood will charge within 8 to 10 percent of each other for the same grade of gasoline, and to the extent gasolines are virtually identical it is sometimes hard to understand even a 10-percent premium over the price leader for truly identical services. Is bank A's stop payment any different from bank B's? But in bank services there can be price differences of 100 percent or more. This is attributable to a lack of price sensitivity among bank customers, human inertia, and a feeling that the consumer is helpless in the face of their present bank's actions. In one sense banks have hypnotized customers into being afraid to challenge fees or in most cases even ask questions.

The fact is that banks now rely on service charges for a significant part of their profit, and banks also have the capability of measuring customer profitability. That is, using computer technology they are able to pull together all the services that each customer uses and measure the profit or loss. In negotiating with a bank, the degree to which specific services will be utilized, the charges for those services, and the profit generated by the charges should be an important part of the equation.

Loans.   Without carrying the analogy too far, if deposits are the lifeblood and services the skeleton, then loans are a bank's cardiovascular system. Loans and the related interest income are what keep a bank going and what separate banks as institutions from service organizations like a travel agency or a payroll processing firm. (Of course, some banks even try to provide these and many other services.) The combination of deposits and loans distinguishes banks. Most individual bank officers and certainly most of the top management of banks have earned their positions as loan officers. Finding good borrowers, lending them money at a sufficiently high rate of interest to cover costs, and then making sure the loans are repaid are, in simple terms, what a loan officer does.

Every prospective borrower presents a good case, shows how he expects to generate lots of profit, and how that will be sufficient to repay the loan on time. Experience, however, suggests that a number of those projections do not work out as planned. Distinguishing the good loan proposals from the bad, working with the promising firms and dropping the losers, is what separates successful bankers from former bankers. No bank or no loan officer bats 1000, and some level of losses is expected. A bank that never experiences any losses is being run too conservatively and a lot of profit is being left on the table. Most bankers, therefore, are prepared to live with some risk. Since the future is uncertain, in one sense *every* loan is risky to some degree.

Your objective in establishing a bank relationship, therefore, is to get your banker to understand the real risks inherent in your industry and in your particular firm. The more he or she knows, the greater the mutual understanding, the higher the probability that the bank will grant you credit when the time comes.

While a bank would like a certain portion of its customer base not to borrow, it would be disastrous if none of them did. So going to a bank and indicating that you are a potential borrower, and that in the meantime you will both provide deposits and use services that they charge for makes a very enticing package. If you can throw on top of that your growth plans, and combine it with a more or less profitable history of operating results, you should have banks beating down the doors for your business.

Concentrate Your Activity

Most successful companies are going to be approached sooner or later by bank calling officers, seeking business for their institution. Businesses rarely switch banks in total, moving all activity from bank A to bank B. The usual sales pitch, therefore, is to get a foot in the door by offering a new service or by promising to provide an existing service at lower cost. While there are often significant differences in how well different banks *perform* the same service, the range of services actually offered is usually quite similar. In an effort to reduce costs, or improve efficiency, the bank representative's sales pitch could well be very attractive. All that is required is to open a checking account with the new bank and get started with the savings right away.

Before leaping at the opportunity to save a few dollars a month, stand back and ask whether your organization *needs* another bank relationship. Too many firms have drifted over the years, saying yes to each attractive offer as it comes along. A total review of bank relationships then reveals numerous relatively inactive bank accounts, with banking services being provided by a wide variety of vendors.

The use of the word *vendors* is deliberate. In terms of providing day-to-day bank services, currency, deposit of customer checks, and payroll processing, for example, every organization should approach the choice of suppliers or vendors (in this case banks) just as it would any other supplier relationship. Does it make sense to contract with two different maintenance firms to clean two office buildings located in the same town? Would you buy standard office supplies from three or four different wholesalers, as long as each carried a complete line? Would you take a fleet of company cars to three different garages for repair?

In each case there may be special reasons to spread business around. All other things being equal, however, concentrating purchases provides much better leverage. Being a large fish in a small pond gets a lot more attention. Think of your own organization's customers. You undoubtedly have a few major or key accounts. They always receive prompt attention, and any problems are immediately brought to top management for resolution. Nobody wants to be known as the employee who lost the XYZ account! Everyone treats XYZ with kid gloves.

The same principle holds true with the purchase of banking services. If you are dissatisfied with how your bank handles a particular activity, rather than opening a new account elsewhere, it is better to discuss your problem with the existing supplier. Give them a chance to resolve the issues.

It may well be that you have outgrown your bank or that your main bank cannot or will not improve in some area. Perhaps a local bank has specialized in payroll processing and offers an unbeatable package. In either case you have to make a tough call. Or there will be times when you want to start dealing with a larger bank, perhaps one with international capabilities. In either case it should be a thought-through decision, not a spur-of-the-moment response to the latest sales representative to visit your office.

There are really two reasons for concentrating banking activity as much as possible. First, it costs time and money to have numerous bank accounts. Resources required to reconcile them each month, audit them at year-end, and control the total balances all go up proportionately—or even more than proportionately—with the number of separate accounts. Often surprising is the total amount of cash tied up in inactive bank accounts. Since cash in most checking accounts does not earn interest, that is a direct opportunity cost.

Second, the real point of having a strong relationship with banks is the provision of credit, whether needed now or not. Even if you are not borrowing now and have no foreseeable need for credit in the future, the author strongly recommends asking for a line of credit (as discussed in the next section). Banks are willing to do this because, as we saw, they must have loans to make a profit. Bankers know from experience that the unexpected does happen—perhaps a merger opportunity or a need to buy a piece of capital equipment at a favorable price—and that such loan opportunities will develop for almost every customer.

Banks are willing to provide lines of credit, even to organizations that have no foreseeable credit needs. As bank profits have been squeezed, the general principle now is for banks to *charge* for making a line of credit available. As will be discussed, you can pay for bank services in one of two ways. You can pay a fee or you can maintain balances. You can pay, say, $\frac{1}{2}$ or $\frac{1}{4}$ percent of the line of credit as an out-of-pocket charge. Or you may pay for it with the level of balances you are presently carrying or are required to increase to.

Now it is easier to see the benefits of concentrating banking activities. Having five accounts, each with, say, $5000 in it, at five different banks means $25,000 of idle balances. Except for the very smallest firms, $5000 is not going to support much of a line of credit. But $25,000, on top of your existing average daily balances at your main bank, may well support a line of credit of $200,000. Multiply the numbers by 2 or 5 or 10, and the principle is the same. Put small idle balances to work supporting a line of credit. Remember, it is easier to get the line of credit when you do not need it. As we shall see in Chap. 8, no banker likes to get a call on Wednesday that you suddenly need to borrow to meet Friday's payroll. Following this recommendation, *concentrating your banking activities and obtaining the line of credit before you need it* may well be the best single piece of advice in this book.

In addition to the arithmetic of avoiding small idle balances, there is absolutely no doubt that if you are doing all your banking business with one bank, and have established relationships with many of that bank's officers and employees, you are going to get better service across the board.

This advice regarding the concentration of banking at one bank applies to all but the very largest business firms. It is fairly obvious that a billion-dollar multinational firm will need more than one bank unless that bank is one of the country's half-dozen largest. Unless you are located in New York or Los Angeles, it is hard to do all your banking with Bank of America or Citicorp. How would Chemical Bank handle your local payroll if you are located in Decatur, Illinois? On the other hand, the community bank in Decatur certainly does not have branches in 50 different countries. So the advice about concentrating activity still holds, it's just that you truly may need more than one bank.

We discussed payroll processing in Chap. 5 but a word here is in order. Employees like to be able to cash their paycheck on payday. It is infinitely easier for an employee to cash that check at the bank on which it is drawn. Thus if you have a branch or a plant in a different city, you probably are going to want to have a bank account in that city. This does not violate the suggestion we previously made.

What it suggests is arranging for credit at the time you open up the payroll account. Maybe the account is too small, the average balances not large enough, to support a corporate line of credit. Sooner or later one of the executives at that location is going to need a home mortgage or a personal loan. You may not be able to obtain formal commitments for this type of activity in advance. It is prudent to discuss this with the prospective banks as you are deciding which bank to use in the community where the new plant will be located. Perhaps a letter of confirmation for your files and theirs is all it would take. On the other hand if one of the banks you are talking to does not typically handle home mortgages that may be a reason to choose some other competitor.

Observation: You have the greatest leverage when you are opening a new account. Bank officers are measured on the new business they bring in. Take advantage of this!

Someone once advised, regarding stock market investments, putting all your eggs in one basket and then keeping a close eye on the basket. The same holds true for banking. Put all your accounts in one bank, and keep a close eye on the bank. They should then be very responsive to your day-to-day problems. Even more important, that bank should be prepared to meet your credit needs, no matter how remote such needs might seem today.

Minimize Bank Service Charges

As individual customers, many of us are sensitive to the amounts that banks charge. At one time you could stop payment on a check just by signing a form. Now it costs at least $15. When you realize that most banks process your checks by computer and that a stop payment merely requires insertion of the check number into the program (a step already performed hundreds or thousands of times), the amount charged appears excessive in relation to the cost to perform the service. On the other hand, maybe the bank wants to discourage you from stop payment requests, and if so a high fee certainly gets your attention. The same approach—trying to prevent it from happening—probably holds true for returned checks due to insufficient funds. A charge of $20 per check, however, is adding insult to injury, particularly if the errors are the result of a cumulative chain of circumstances over which you had little control. And to get charged when one of your customer's checks bounces hurts doubly. The customer still owes you, plus you have absorbed the expense of the service charge.

In other cases banks are definitely trying to make a profit on service charges. An example is printing checks. The convenience of ordering at the bank involves a fee of perhaps $15, whereas some new mail order firms are offering a wider variety of checks at $6. Or a charge of $12.50 each month in which your balance falls below $1000 certainly encourages you to keep a higher balance, but on an annual basis this could work out to an effective interest rate in excess of 50 percent.

Given that banks can nickel and dime their customers, the truth is that the total cost to an individual of bank services for a year is relatively small.

If you follow the bank's rules and do not ask for extra services, the total relationship is well worth the charges, if any. What holds true for you as an individual, however, is not necessarily applicable to a business. Individuals do not get charged for making each deposit, withdrawing any cash, or, in most cases, writing every check. Commercial accounts do get charged, item by item, activity by activity.

Many businesses are passive about these charges, perhaps due to ignorance of the existing choices or a feeling that nothing can be done about it. Most likely is the terrific advantage the bank has in never sending you an invoice. Remember, they simply deduct the amount of their monthly charge directly from your account. A line on your bank statement shows "service charge" and that is it. If you do not reconcile your bank account that month you will never even know you have been charged. If the bank reconciliation is done by an accounting clerk, a journal entry will be made and *nobody* will ever see the charge, except in the Treasurer's budget report. But since the bank charges will already have been budgeted for the current year based on last year, there will be virtually no variance and thus still no visibility.

One solution would be to budget zero for bank charges. Then whatever is charged would show up as a negative variance and at least get some attention. But, as discussed in Chap. 12 on budgeting, the only way to get a handle on cash is to do the best job you can in forecasting what is likely to happen. If you are going to pay bank charges, they should be budgeted— but not then forgotten. Bank charges *can* be controlled.

There are essentially two ways to minimize bank charges: through keeping bank balances sufficiently high or by negotiation. Keep in mind our earlier discussion that there are two ways a bank makes money (by lending out deposits and earning interest, or through fees). Banks understand this tradeoff very well and are willing to let you choose. It is hard to generalize as to whether it is better to pay for bank services by fees or deposits.

To make the choice, some aspects of deposits have to be understood to put the problem into perspective. If someone asked you how much money is in your checking account today, you would undoubtedly pull out your checkbook, look at the balance (assuming you post every check right away) and state that was how much you had. If you called the bank and asked how much was in the account you would get a *different* amount. Obviously checks you had written and mailed, but had not yet cleared, would not appear on the bank's records. They don't know what you have done until your check shows up for payment.

Further, as anyone who has opened a bank account knows, the bank is not willing to let you withdraw money on uncollected balances. Just how a bank defines what is collected and what is not collected has literally been a subject of regulations and legal interpretation. For purposes of this book there are really only two points worth covering. First, when you deposit a check drawn on an out-of-town bank, your bank will receive good funds from the Federal Reserve system, which handles check clearings nationwide, in no more than two business days. This means that the bank cannot invest the funds in your Monday deposit until Wednesday or Thursday. If they cannot invest the funds, it is only reasonable that you cannot have access to the funds. If you make a deposit on Monday and take cash out on Tuesday (from the same deposit), the bank is essentially making you an unsecured interest-free loan! Needless to say, since they do not like to do this, they make you wait.

Even though the Federal Reserve gives your bank credit in two days, the bank does not know whether the check you deposited on Monday is going to bounce. It may take literally eight to ten days for a bad check to come back. So if the bank, not knowing you, accepts a deposit on Monday and you withdraw the funds on Friday, what happens when the check you deposited comes back unpaid the next Wednesday? If you are still around and have money in the account, it will be charged. If you have skipped town, the bank is out of luck. Guess what? This has been known to happen. So, particularly on new accounts, banks set up internal rules about when you can have access to your own money. This can be quite frustrating when you are new in town and need cash, but once your account is established with a reasonable balance, banks do not usually pay too much attention to collected balances on personal accounts—although some banks do!

From the perspective of corporate bank activity the key point is the maximum two-day availability in the Fed system (as the Federal Reserve System is called). The bank cannot invest your deposits for two days; so in analyzing your account they subtract out two days for each deposit. This does not mean that the occasional check you deposit won't come back "NSF" but that for ease of computation the bank disregards them. Since the bank cannot invest your deposit for two days, it quite properly makes that adjustment in calculating the average deposit level.

Banks will then calculate an earnings *rate*, and apply that rate to your available balances. The earnings rate should represent what the bank is able to do with your funds, but determination of the rate could range anywhere from a low of the Fed funds rate (the price paid by banks for overnight borrowing from each other) up through Treasury bill rates, and in theory could go up to or above the prime rate. Needless to say, most banks choose an earnings rate near the bottom of the scale when evaluating the profitability of your account.

No matter how calculated, then, the bank shows an earnings credit on your analysis statement, from which is then charged all the activities recorded during the month, ranging from checks deposited and checks written, to costs for lock box services and wire transfers. Notice the term *cost*. Purportedly the analysis statement represents the banks costs of servicing your account, and they then see if the costs are equal to or less than the earnings credit.

In theory, if your earnings credit is less than the bank's costs, then you have to pay the bank or increase your average balances. If the costs are less, however, the bank does *not* pay you cash; it may carry forward the balance to subsequent months to offset any future deficits.

Several points of interest should be noted. First, if you have not received an analysis statement from your bank, it is prima facie evidence that your balances are too high. The principle is simple. If the bank were losing money on your account, because of high activity relative to your average balances, you would have heard from them. In this case, no news is bad news.

Observation: Run, don't walk, to your bank and demand to see the analysis statement. In this age of the computer, the information is available. Study it. Ask questions if there is anything you do not understand. It is your money.

Several points about the analysis statement and how it is prepared warrant consideration. To get the maximum benefit from your bank relationship at minimum cost, you have to understand the bank's approach. Whether you agree with it or not, as well as what steps you can take, are covered later.

When the bank says it "costs" them 6¢ for each check you write, and then applies that amount to the analysis statement to see if your balances are large enough, is that really their cost? Or is it their selling price? Banks are notorious for having poor cost accounting systems. With high fixed costs for personnel, equipment, and rent—and low variable costs for incremental increases or decreases in volume—any assignment of costs to an operation or service can tend to be arbitrary. To verify this point, it is only necessary to look at the cost schedules of several competing banks in the same area.

Presumably these institutions should have comparable costs since their labor rates would be comparable, the equipment is almost identical, and space rent also tends to average out. Yet three banks, with equally competent cost accountants, will show costs varying by 25 percent or more. Imagine what would happen to a steel company if its real costs of producing a ton of steel were 25 percent higher than a competitor. It would be out of business. So would a bank.

The truth is that banks' operating costs are reasonably close, and what they are showing you is *not* their cost but their selling price. It might be reasonable to ask how two competitors can sell essentially the same item at prices 25 percent or more apart. In virtually no other industry is this true. But it gets back to uninformed consumers, a lack of price sensitivity on the part of buyers—you. If two grocery supermarkets competed for your business and one sold milk for 25 percent less per gallon, who would end up with the greater market share? Yet in banking there is virtually no correlation between market share and the prices charged for basic banking services.

What conclusion can we reach? Perhaps the answer is that bank officers do not really believe their own analysis statements. If the figures they produce and send to customers elicit no real response—customers pay the charges shown and do not shop elsewhere—there is no motivation to change. If customers continue to maintain large deposits to pay for bank services, instead of having their account charged on a fee basis, there is no reason for the bank to modify its behavior. Are banks taking advantage of customer ignorance or indifference? You be the judge.

In terms of the analysis statement, there is a second variable besides the unit prices charged for bank services utilized. Recall that the bank provided an earnings credit for the net funds you had on deposit, after subtracting uncollected funds and the percentage of required deposits the bank has to hold at the Federal Reserve and on which it earns no interest. The calculation of the available balance is pretty straightforward. But the choice of rate, to be applied to those balances, is critical. Banks naturally put their best foot forward and without discussion utilize the lowest practical rate they can justify in their own mind. They certainly would not credit you with the prime rate, for example; nor would they, to be ridiculous, credit you with the rate they charge on credit card balances, say 15 percent.

Any bank would be out of business if it earned only the Fed funds rate; so to credit *all* accounts with that rate grossly understates the value of deposits to the bank. Do not to try to refine the calculation. Frankly, over the years, what is the most appropriate earnings rate will probably fluctuate. What is important is to know that whatever rate the bank utilizes in the calculations they show you significantly understates the real value of those deposits to the bank.

It is hard to know whether the cost figures for each bank service are too high, too low, or about right. The bank itself probably does not know. But two wrongs do not make one right. Whether the bank's fee schedule is accurate or not has no bearing on the validity of the credit they give you for having your deposits available to them to lend out.

Now let's get realistic. In theory the bank could develop a fee schedule and earnings credit for you that differed from that offered to other customers. In practice nobody is going to reprogram a computer just for you. You can make back of the envelope calculations on what the right answer should be by comparing the fee schedules for services from several banks and developing a feel for what it should be. You can then estimate what your funds are really worth to the bank by looking at the gross interest income of the bank as a percentage of deposits. This is the upper limit and the bank's use of a Fed funds rate is the lower limit. Somewhere between is the right answer. At that point you are ready to sit down and negotiate.

What this previous discussion suggests is that there really is room for *negotiation*. Bank officers are both highly intelligent and highly motivated. They are motivated to keep your business, and they know that their real selling prices, if challenged, have to be competitive. There are plenty of books and seminars on the techniques and strategies of negotiation. What is important is that the selling prices the bank charges, the costs to you the customer, are negotiable.

You, the customer, are in the driver's seat. Every bank would like your business or, to be more specific, your deposits. Think of yourself as the seller and the bank as the buyer! What will the bank pay you, in services, in exchange for your deposits. Therefore the nominal price charged by the bank for each service, such as the charge per check deposited or per check written, *is* an important part of the equation. So is the earnings credit.

Since the bank will not change their internal system just for one customer (you), do the next best thing. You can agree that the bank, irrespective of what the computer-driven analysis statement shows, will not charge your account unless the net loss to the bank exceeds x. This solves two problems. You neither carry excess balances nor pay unnecessary monthly charges. They recognize the value of your business for what it is and do not have to change any of their internal systems. This might be described as a win/win situation, except that the poor bank officer who had to make the concession to keep your account may not think of it as a win. But it is a win for the bank if the alternative is losing your business.

To recap: Banks rightfully charge for their services in processing checks, currency, wire transfers, and the like. They also benefit from the balances you carry by being able to invest those funds and earn a return. The bank both earns income and incurs expenses as a result of your being a customer. The bank's objective is to keep you as a customer, albeit a profitable one. Your objective is to obtain the maximum bank services at the lowest out-of-pocket cost. That cost can be either in terms of fees paid in cash each month or in balance levels maintained. When two parties each have objectives that are not mutually exclusive, there obviously is room for serious negotiation.

Obtaining Your Line of Credit

In terms of Total Cash Management (TCM), having a sufficiently large line of credit *available when you need it* may be your single most important objective in dealing with any bank. As we will see in the section in this chapter on forecasting cash balances, sooner or later an unpleasant surprise is going to come up. At some time your need or demand for cash will be greater than what you have available, and at that point your choices are limited. For a short period you can stop paying invoices from your vendors. Your payroll and taxes *must* be met. You can put out a panic call to your customers and *hope* they respond with an early remittance. In the short run, however, it is hard to increase sales or decrease expenses in a meaningful way.

The only practical solution is borrowing. Remembering once again that bankers hate to lend money to those who are truly desperate, you must prepare for such emergencies in advance, that is, *before* you need the cash to meet the payroll. Of course, a line of credit, the availability of short-term borrowing power, can and will be used for other than emergencies, say to buy a needed piece of equipment or to expand seasonal inventories. Profitable companies can usually obtain credit for such purposes, and in those circumstances you will have sufficient time to prepare a loan application, explain it to the bank's loan officer, answer questions from the bank's credit department after they complete their analysis, and wait for the dreaded loan committee to approve the loan. In the best of circumstances this could easily take a month or more. To be fair, some banks have delegated to individual loan officers the authority to approve loans up to a certain level on their own signatures. Prudence suggests not relying on that. Suppose your bank officer is off to Europe for three weeks!

The bank's answer has been the line of credit, which is no more than a commitment, usually in writing, that, barring any adverse occurrences, the bank stands ready to lend your organization up to $x thousand or million. The line of credit will be for a specific time, perhaps one year, and will require you to keep the bank informed with quarterly or even monthly financial statements. There may be requirements for minimum levels of profitability or of working capital. These are all negotiable, and depend in part on how much the bank wants your business.

The two things the bank will ask for are a *commitment fee* and *compensating balances*. These are both negotiable, really depending on the current level of loan demand, as well as the bank's own growth strategy. The concept of a commitment fee is a relatively new development and arose from a shortage of loan capacity during the economic boom of the 1980s, combined with the pressure to boost fee income. In effect, the loan commitment fee really provides nothing today that bank's were not offering before. They used to offer lines of credit that totaled, for all their customers, far more than they ever expected to loan at one time. Just as with depositors, a bank knows that all customers will not simultaneously want their money at the same time. So all potential borrowers who have lines of credit won't suddenly come up to the loan window simultaneously.

But if banks used to be willing to make firm commitments to lend money, without a fee, what more are they offering with the fee? The answer is probably very little. No banker would unconditionally guarantee to lend money at some point in the future without protecting herself against unforeseen adverse circumstances. Paying a fee today really does nothing to take away the banker's safety net.

There is not much use spending a lot of time on this subject, because bankers have become hooked on the fee income. After all, in exchange for a promise that they might do something in the future, they get paid today. And then, when they do that in the future—lend you money—they charge you full market rate at the time. It is sort of like paying a surgeon today for a promise that, if you get a bad pain in the stomach over the next year, he will do his best to operate and take out your appendix or gall bladder. Then when he does operate, the previous fee is not credited against his charges for the operation! You just get an invoice at the surgeon's current rate. But that is the world of banking in the 1990s. Since the purpose of the exercise is to get the loan commitment, the line of credit, all you can really negotiate with the bank is "how much" not whether there is a fee. Rates of $1/4$ to $1/2$ percent on the unused line are not uncommon. In the final analysis it is an insurance premium and is a cost of doing business.

Double Counting Balances

The second thing the banker will want to talk about is the compensating balance. For example, if you need $100,000, you must borrow and pay interest on a full $125,000—and then leave $25,000 of the loan on deposit, unavailable for spending. This effectively raises the cost to borrow money by 20 percent. Far simpler would be to charge a higher rate and then let you use all the cash balances in the account.

The British banking system uses an overdraft approach. You are allowed to go into the red and the bank still honors your checks. But they charge you interest on the daily outstanding balance. As you receive deposits your loan is paid down, and your checks clear the bank, the loan is increased. With interest calculated on the exact daily balance, no more and no less, this is the most efficient and lowest-cost way to borrow. Too bad the overdraft system is not commonly available on this side of the Atlantic.

In the United States, the compensating balance system goes back many years and is firmly entrenched in the minds of loan officers. One reason it continues may be that banks like to show the largest deposit base possible. The implicit assumption is that a larger bank is a better bank—or at least more prestigious. Compensating balance requirements, therefore, force borrowers, taken in total, to keep substantial idle amounts that swell the bottom line of the bank's balance sheet.

While it is useless to try to change the compensating balance *system*, you can negotiate the way the required balances are computed. Balance requirements are sometimes stated like 10 percent of the line and an additional 10 percent of the amounts borrowed. For a $1-million line, this would require $100,000 of balances at all times and, say, $150,000 if and when $500,000 of the line were utilized. Other banks might request a flat 15 percent of the line irrespective of whether it were used or not. In this latter case you would be expected to keep at least $150,000 in your account at all times.

The question now arises whether you can utilize your normal everyday working balances as part or all of the compensating balance. Let's look at three scenarios.

1. You have average balances of $250,000 at the bank and have never heard from them about service charges based on activity. There is little or no reason not to keep things as they are; you should not raise your average balance level at all just to meet an arbitrary bank-requested 15-percent level.

2. You do keep at least $150,000, but the activity level is great enough that you have low to moderate service charges each month. In other words, your deposits are basically paying for the use of bank services. In this case the bank will ask for more, and you can compromise somewhere at, say, $200,000. However the new higher level should totally offset the monthly charges.

3. You have maintained low balances, such as $50-75,000, and have been paying significant service charges. You will probably be asked to raise the balances to the $200,000 level and this might mean "permanently" borrowing up to $150,000. Unfortunately that is the price you will pay for the comfort of having an additional $850,000 of borrowing power in reserve.

Two further points. First, it is critical that the compensating balance arrangements be measured on *average* levels, not treated as a *minimum*. There are normal day-to-day and month-to-month variations in every bank account. By calculating the requirements over a period of time—and at least a full year is ideal—you take advantage of months when balances run higher than expected and are not immediately penalized for being short one month. The worst of all worlds would be for the measurement to be daily. Effectively this would mean you could never go *below* the agreed-upon amount, and because normal fluctuations will always occur, your average balance would inevitably run much higher than the required minimum.

The second point deals with bank accounts at other than your main or principal bank relationship. Going back to the concept of preparing now for possible future needs, it makes sense, whenever you establish a new bank account, to at least bring up the idea of a line of credit. A medium-sized Philadelphia firm might open an account at a bank in Denver simply to process a lock box. Over the course of a year, very low average balances will be maintained (because deposited funds are transferred back to Philadelphia each day). Thus no working balances can be used to meet compensating balance requirements. Of course, a periodic discussion about your company and its prospects with the Denver bank's officers would be appropriate. It might even make sense to send them periodic financial statements even if they do not ask for them, so at least the bank will have built up a credit file. Bankers tend to take seriously long-term relationships. If you have done your part for several years voluntarily, you might get a favorable response to a future loan request even though you have not had a formal line of credit.

Where it does make sense to establish a more formal relationship is with a bank in a distant community where you have an operation, such as a plant or warehouse. You will want to have a small checking account to pay local bills, petty cash, and so forth, and to enable employees to cash their paychecks. It will most likely be a relatively small and inactive account, if you concentrate your accounts payable activity in a main disbursement account. But the loan officer opening your account is still measured on the basis of new business. And the average balance levels help grow the bank's asset and liability totals on the balance sheet.

Since you plan to be located in the town for a while and the bank account will be relatively stable, in selecting a bank in that town (there are relatively few significant locations with no competitive banking institutions) one of the criteria should be a willingness to consider a line of credit. To the extent feasible the average balances you will end up carrying should support the line. For a medium-sized firm this may mean only a relatively small line of credit, say $50–100,000. It is better to dip your toe in the water; if things go well and you really need the money, you can always ask for more. It is easier to raise a $100,000 line of credit to $250,000 than to go in one day, unannounced, and ask for that same $250,000.

A note on *personal guarantees* is in order. For closely held private firms, many banks ask for a personal guarantee of the principal(s). The individual net worth of the owners is required as security, particularly in start-up situations. Many banks have lost a lot of money lending to corporate entities, and if a corporation declares bankruptcy there is nothing for the bank to collect on, unless it has received a prior personal guarantee. All other things being equal, the owners of a company do *not* want to provide the guarantee, and in the final analysis how this negotiation comes out is a function of relative economic strength. If the company needs the funds and there is no other alternative, then the guarantee must be provided. After a certain number of successful profitable years, it makes sense to at least ask for a reduction or even elimination of those guarantees.

It would not make sense to establish credit at remote banks, where you really do not know the bank's officers, if they insist on a guarantee just for extending a line of credit that you have no immediate plans to use. Even if you decline to provide the guarantee, it still would represent good planning to send them monthly or quarterly statements and keep them informed about your organization's progress.

To summarize this section, we saw that banks provide two essential services: one related to processing checks and payments, what you might call a logistics service, and the other the provision of credit. The major thesis of this book is that the availability of cash represents an asset, one that is absolutely needed. It may be cynical to attribute attitudes and motives to well-meaning bank officers, but the fact remains that it is easier to get credit when you do not need it currently. Using your normal bank balances, wherever located, as the basis for maintaining a line of credit means that you are minimizing the cost. Banks are like any other vendor; there is always room for negotiation. It just makes sense to ask the most when you are in the strongest position. Waiting until you need the funds has to put you at a real disadvantage. Banking is highly competitive and the best time to extract significant concessions is when you are in a strong position.

Choosing a Bank

As already noted, banking is highly competitive. Every successful business is going to be approached by bank officers seeking their business. At times in the business cycle, banks are looking actively for loans: so you will be offered credit as an inducement to shift banking allegiances. At other times, if credit is tight or banks have recently gone through a period of significant loan losses, the hook is going to be services, either new ones or existing ones at lower prices.

How do you respond to these offers? The first principle is not to be tempted to split your business. The temptation is to be a nice guy and give a persistent loan officer something, maybe as a reward for persistence. Or a bank has developed a nifty new service, not offered by your present institution, and it would fit in nicely with your operation.

Further, you will be told—or maybe even think it for yourself—that it is better to have relationships at several banks. The theory is, "You never know." Perhaps the loan officer handling your account at the main bank may leave or management may change. Worst of all, the bank may be bought out by a multinational giant and the fear then is that you may become just a number when you need the bank the most. With all these things that can go wrong, many argue it is far better to have had some other lines out, to use a fishing analogy, so that you won't go hungry.

While it is hard to argue with this line of reasoning, the author still feels that it is better to concentrate activity, be a truly important account, and expect that no matter what happens to an individual officer or to the bank as a whole, you will still be taken care of. If you have handled your account properly, in terms of balances and ultimately total profitability to the bank, you should find that any other local bank will welcome your business as that of a desirable customer.

Whether you have had a small and inactive dividend payment account at that second bank, for example, is not going to influence the second bank if at some point you decide to switch over everything. In fact, if you do switch, you will be asked what caused you to change. The last thing the new bank wants is an in-and-out relationship. But if you are changing because the old loan officer left, management changed, or the bank had been bought out, the new bank will understand your reason, accept it, and welcome you. By the same token, if your account is marginal to your existing bank, you may not quickly get credit at a new institution, even if you have carried a small balance there for a number of years.

Most companies have too many bank relationships, not too few. It is all too easy over a number of years to "do something" for Charlie who belongs to your club or for Sam who is your neighbor. If they are both bank officers, they would each love to get a piece of your business, and it may be hard to say no to neighbors or fellow club members. Just remember that what they love getting, your present bank will hate losing. You cannot make everyone happy. If it is a choice between one happy banker or three moderately pleased banks, you have to make a choice. The author recommends having one happy banker, but since many have continued to use the latter approach it cannot be all wrong.

A word is in order about the *size* of bank you choose. Should you be a relatively large customer of a local bank or a small customer of a much larger institution? The latter has only two advantages. Large banks offer a much wider variety of services. Second, there is some degree of prestige in being associated with or having a relationship with a large New York or Chicago bank. One corporate financial officer, who was also a principal in his Midwestern firm, kept a fair-sized corporate balance at a large New York bank. The company had no real international activities, and the local Midwest bank seemed to meet its current needs. Someone finally asked him, "Why the New York account?" The response was as candid as could be, "Well, I like to go to the city a couple of times a year, and this way I always know someone [the bank officer] will invite me out to dinner and a show." In a closely held, profitable company, who is to say that is wrong? For most other organizations, Total Cash Management might suggest there were less expensive ways to go out to dinner and a show.

The real issue comes down to being a large fish in a small pond or a small fish in a large pond. Banking is ultimately a matter of personal relationships. Someone has to say yes on your behalf, to offset the normal banker's conservative knee-jerk reaction of no. Where are you more likely to develop and be able to maintain that close relationship?

It may be an unfair generalization to talk about excessive turnover at the local branch level of large banks, but every such generalization usually has some basis in fact. The average tenure of young loan officers in any one location tends to be short. Even if your account is just as meaningful to a $100-million *branch* of a national giant as it is to a local $100-million *bank,* just ask yourself if you can get in to see the president, or even the executive vice president, if you really have to. In many large banks the branch manager has no real authority on credit decisions, and fulfills little more than the role of administrative supervisor of the tellers.

This may be somewhat unfair, but there is no doubt that the president and CEO of the $100-million local bank makes the credit decisions right there; she does not, and in fact cannot, refer your account to head office. This is the basic reason for the strength of the U.S. banking system with its 10,000 or more local banks, in comparison with the dozen or so in Canada. Local decision making just has to be more responsive to local conditions. Local bank officers, who know their career is tied into that one community, are going to have different priorities than someone who really is in town only to "get some local experience" before he or she moves onwards and upwards.

As we indicated, one of the supposed advantages of dealing with a large bank is the wider range of services offered, and, of course, a larger lending limit to any one customer. Both of these points have to be acknowledged as correct. The answer is, "So what?" In today's environment even the smallest banks have access, through their correspondent banking relationships, to every product and service.

Your firm does not have to maintain an account at Chase Manhattan to obtain specialized foreign exchange service, such as hedging against currency risk in an obscure country. Instead let your local bank maintain that account in its own name for the benefit of all its customers, including you. Then simply "buy" the service you need. You would have to pay your own bank, were it to offer the service directly, and there should be at worst only a negligible markup, if in practice there is any, by working through an intermediary. In one sense, banks *like* offering services through large correspondents; it establishes more closely their own relationship with "big brother." Since banks swap favors (such as loan participations) back and forth they absolutely do not mind helping you, their own customer, obtain service from someone else. Their only real fear is that the larger bank will at some point try to steal you away as a customer.

The second argument in favor of having your primary account with a very large banking institution is that you can obtain a much larger loan from a single source. Banks are limited in the size of any loan to one customer by the amount of their capital. Obviously Citicorp's maximum loan is far larger than that offered by a local neighborhood bank in Racine,

Wisconsin. But does that really make a difference? Cash is fungible. One bank's loan proceeds is identical with another. If your own bank's loan limit is $1.5 million, and you need a $2.5-million loan, your bank will get one of its correspondents to participate. That is its responsibility, not yours. Let your bank argue on your behalf. If it is a good loan, they will be successful and you will have your $2.5 million. If the loan is marginal you would expend just as much, if not more, effort with the larger bank as a direct customer and with no better results.

Observation: Prestige in dealing with a large, well-known bank, and enjoying the opportunity to socialize in the Big City, should not be totally discounted—unless you are truly interested in Total Cash Management in *all* its aspects. A very good relationship with a local bank, where you are truly a meaningful account, is far better in all business respects than simply being an account number at Bank of America.

Forecasting Cash Balances

In planning this book and laying out the subjects to be covered, the author procrastinated the longest on the topic of forecasting cash balances. The reason is simple. The conventional wisdom is that every company, to achieve Total Cash Management, *must* forecast cash. *Every* book and article on the subject of cash management advises the reader to forecast cash balances; both short-term and long-term forecasting techniques are provided. If you follow the suggestions of these authors, your cash management problems should be a thing of the past.

There are two problems with the conventional wisdom. One is that nobody has yet figured out how to predict the future. Second, even if you have a perfect prediction, you probably cannot do much about it. Hopefully, you, the reader, will become a believer and save yourself a lot of guilt, particularly if in the past you never seem to have gotten the hang of how to forecast accurately.

Many organizations can forecast cash receipts with reasonable accuracy, while many others seem to have little trouble predicting cash outflows. Very few can do both, at least on a consistent basis. The reason is obvious. In the final analysis, cash receipts depend on the actions of others, primarily customers. In a market economy there is competition among suppliers of the same type of goods and services. Customers and consumers also face a wide variety of choices of how and where to spend their limited resources. Can you really predict how customers will spend their money and where it will be spent?

There are very few monopolies left. Even the electric and telephone utilities face real competition. Only a true monopolist, providing a totally needed product or service, can count on a given volume of business at a given price. The greater the monopoly the more incentives others have to try and reduce it. In short, nobody can count on customers being forced to buy at your price. The amounts and prices you will receive for next year's business are a function of what you do, what your competitors (both direct and indirect) do, and overall economic conditions. Are interest rates going up or down? Will Europe be in a boom or a bust? Who will win the next election? What changes in taxes will affect me and my customers? If professional economists cannot even agree on the *direction* of change in the economy as a whole—and often they cannot—what does this say about the potential accuracy of any one firm's sales projections?

A fun thing to do is to take out the corporate projections, the famous five-year plan that is almost *de rigueur* in most firms, from four years ago and see where you were supposed to be today. At a minimum you will smile and more likely you will break out in a guffaw. "What were those idiots thinking back then?" If even 10 percent of five-year plans come close to being accurate it would be revolutionary. Wishful thinking about your own successes is combined with a total lack of knowledge about both the economy and the actions of your competitors and your customers.

How can any forecast be accurate? The federal government, for practical purposes, has unlimited resources to apply to a problem. The economic forecasts of every administration for the past 40 years have fallen flat on their face. You might argue that the government's projections always have a favorable bias built in for political reasons, and you would probably be right. But doesn't the same phenomenon hold true in the corporate political environment? Assume five separate divisions all compete for funds, and all of their managers are competing for promotions. Which one of them is going to submit a five-year plan that shows a *drop* in revenues and profits? But is it really likely, or even possible, that all five are going to shine?

The truth is that nobody, no institution, can foretell the future. Predictions are going to be wrong. That does not mean that the exercise of looking ahead is wasted effort. Budgeting and planning are vital to the success of any well run organization. It does mean that errors (significant misses from plan) are more likely than not. Go ahead and forecast cash, short-term or long-term. Just don't count on the forecasts coming to pass.

If forecasts are going to be wrong, although you may not know when or where, what are the implications for TCM? Assume for a minute that on June 1 you make a forecast that shows on August 20, a payday, you are not going to have sufficient cash. What would you do? After trying to (1) increase sales, (2) put more effort into collections, and (3) slowing down disbursements, you would probably arrange for a loan to carry you over.

Now assume that you have made *no* forecasts, that you have put all your energies over the previous three months into (1) increasing sales, (2) collecting receivables, and (3) slowing down disbursements (all of these being worthwhile TCM activities irrespective of anything else). Comes August 20 and you do not have sufficient balances in the checking account to meet the payroll. What do you do? If you had paid attention and followed the recommendations in the previous section of this chapter, you would simply draw on your existing line of credit. That's what it is there for!

Now compare the two scenarios. In the first we had a perfect forecast but had to borrow. Forecasting is not the same as controlling cash. A forecast simply tells you where you will be if certain things happen. To the extent you are already doing the best you can in all aspects of TCM, the forecast alerts you so that you can take appropriate action. If you have already taken that action—in this case set up a sufficiently large line of credit—what does the forecast tell you (whether it is 100-percent accurate or even totally inaccurate)? Suppose the forecast said that on August 20 you would have plenty of cash to meet the payroll, but the forecast was wrong and you are short. With the line of credit there is no worry. Without the line of credit, the forecast would actually have been the worst thing, because you would have been lulled into thinking you did not have a problem.

The choices are mutually reinforcing. You can both forecast cash requirements and arrange a line of credit. We cannot emphasize too much, however, that the line of credit effectively precludes the *need* to prepare accurate forecasts. This should be considered good news, since forecasts are hard to do in the best of circumstances. The best weather forecast in the world, if it tells you it is going to rain on August 20, does no more than let you buy an umbrella in advance. If you already have the umbrella and your plans are set irrespective of the weather, such as a birthday party for the kids at McDonald's, how soon you learn it is going to rain really is immaterial.

To carry the analogy one step further, think of the line of credit as an umbrella. Think of a bank's credit line as though it is a financial umbrella that you always have with you—like Travelers Insurance's red umbrella, a powerful image for a financial firm. If you always have it, you can just repeat the line from that old song, "Let it rain, let it rain." At least you will be protected and not get wet. The businessperson who trusts the weather forecast and carries the umbrella only when told to by Willard Scott on the Today Show, sooner or later is going to get soaked. You can count on any weather forecaster, even Willard, to be wrong sooner or later.

Having suggested that a solid line of credit reduces or even eliminates the need for forecasting, the author nonetheless strongly recommends *monitoring* cash *receipts*, cash *disbursements*, and cash *balances* on a daily basis. A good solid statistical base, going back several years, is an invaluable tool, in case you ever need to do short-term cash forecasting. Even more important, it will allow you to evaluate macro trends. Are there fundamental changes in receipts relative to sales, or in disbursements relative to purchases? Measuring cash balances on your books and comparing them with those on the bank's books (the monthly bank statement) gives you a feel for how fast the checks you write are clearing your bank. This, of course, is the famous float, and over the years, as the Federal Reserve check clearing system gets more efficient, the float tends to be steadily reduced.

To the extent that you have positive cash balances in excess of the amount you have committed to keep at the bank, and to the extent that you are investing them in the short-term money market, these investments should be added on the daily worksheet and treated as cash. Most companies do this and report in their annual financials, as part of the cash flow statement, that such short-term marketable securities are included in cash. On the other hand, if you are a net short-term borrower on a line of credit, then this too should show, although obviously as a negative number when added to cash.

Figure 6.1 shows a suggested worksheet. The specific column headings can be adjusted to unique aspects of your business, such as, a nonprofit would show a column for contributions received or a restaurant could distinguish between cash and credit card sales. What is important is to have an easily accessible record of all the key cash flow statistics for your organization. If you ever want to forecast cash (or need to), use the same format. The previous daily, monthly, and annual totals will form the starting point for the projections.

Probably few readers at one time or another, and for whatever reason, have not had an *overdraft* on their personal checking account. In today's fee-driven banking environment, the bank adds insult to injury by charging you after they have bounced your check. Not only does the person or company whom you paid get upset by having your check returned, you end up paying for the action. Even worse, if you deposit someone else's check in good faith and it is returned, you may get hit with a charge by your own bank even though there was nothing you could have done differently.

Looking at it from the bank's point of view, if they pay a check that is drawn against uncollected funds or, even worse, against no funds, they are making an unsecured interest free loan to the maker. In one sense the bank

Date	Opening balance	+	Cash receipts	–	Checks written	=	Closing balance		(Memo) balance per bank's books

Figure 6.1 Daily cash balance.

is protecting its interests by actively discouraging overdrafts through fees. On the other hand, from your perspective as a customer, you do not want to aggravate your suppliers, much less bring your credit rating into disrepute, through having a series of bounced checks.

What you need is a clear understanding with the bank, and particularly with the officer responsible for your account, that they will *not* bounce any of your checks. Instead they should call you up immediately so that you can determine the cause and take steps to resolve the problem. Any number of reasons could cause you to show an overdraft on the bank's books. Perhaps it was a clerical error such as counting a deposit twice, or the bookkeeper forgot to take the deposit to the bank on the way home, or a large customer check was returned for an incorrect endorsement. It will happen! What you do not want, and must protect against, is an automatic return of your checks by a computer, a machine that does not know or care who you are. Banks are not required to return checks that would cause an overdraft in your account, even though they are within their rights to do so. This is one of the places where a solid, mutually profitable relationship really pays off.

Reconciling the Bank Accounts

Whether to make a choice between going to the dentist or reconciling a bank account at month-end for many might be a tough decision. Some individuals despise reconciling their account so much they just glance at the statement each month, to make sure their ending checkbook balance is approximately right, and then go on to other things. The assumption is that the bank is correct; it doesn't make mistakes. If you are lucky enough to be able to afford to maintain comfortable balances in your checking account, maybe it is irrelevant whether or not you do a full reconciliation each month on your own personal account.

This *laissez faire* attitude has no place in the business environment. If you have never reconciled a corporate bank statement, with stop payments, reissued checks, service charges, wire transfers in and out, checks that never cleared, old checks that suddenly showed up, and so forth, then ask someone who has. It is a miserable frustrating task, one that will get postponed if at all possible. Banks have attempted to make this job easier, particularly for accounts with thousands of checks a month, like a major payroll account. By submitting a computer tape of the checks you wrote, with date, check number, and amount, the bank then compares the checks that cleared and gives you a printout of all the open items. Many problems will still have to be resolved, but the great clerical task of sorting the checks in numerical order and matching them off against the check register is eliminated.

Bank statements must be reconciled promptly every month for two reasons. First, because mistakes can be made and are made both by banks and by your own organization, reconciliation is the only way to know your real balance. In terms of investing surplus cash, or prepaying a loan and saving interest, it is vital to know the exact balance at least once a month. In the interim you will be adding and subtracting receipts and disbursements each day, and carrying forward a running total. But any error in the system will continue to be carried forward, and you will not know about it, unless, of course, the bank gives you that fateful call that you are overdrawn. But if the error goes the other way, and your balance is really larger than you think, there will be no phone calls. In short, having the facts and being sure of them, are vital to *Total* Cash Management.

A second reason for monthly bank reconciliations by someone who does not have access to the actual cash accounts is theft. The incidence of theft (misappropriation of funds) is low. *Low*, however, is not the same as *never*. Think about how much crime there is in a town of 5000 people. Now, if there are 5000 employees in an organization, why shouldn't there be the same incidence of crime? Are corporate employees more honest than the populace at large? Perhaps not. And having just 500 employees only means that the frequency will be one-tenth as often as in the larger organization. To put this in perspective, one large Fortune 50 company only reported to its Audit Committee employee defalcations that exceeded $100,000; yet in the course of a year they averaged a dozen or more of that size.

Employee fraud is a real problem, but one nobody talks about. When it comes out, it is always caused by someone who had been trusted, an individual with many friends in the organization. Before the fact, you never want to believe that someone at the next desk or in the next office *might* have larceny in his heart. This book is not the place to talk about internal controls and fraud prevention. Others are far more competent in this area, and you can always go to your outside audit firm for help in this area.

Sooner or later, however, most fraud involves cash. "Cash" means bank accounts because it is really hard to get rich from the true petty cash. Unfortunately, many auditors spend more time worrying about the petty cash than they do about the firm's primary bank account. Unauthorized transactions in one means pennies and in the other dollars. As Willie Sutton, or perhaps John Dillinger, said when asked why he robbed banks, "That's where the money is." Control the bank account, not the petty cash. Reconciling the bank accounts promptly will never prevent fraud from occurring. It will catch a substantial portion of all fraud much sooner. It will definitely minimize losses.

7
Collecting Accounts Receivable

Few jobs are more important—and less fun—than collecting what your customers owe you. There are two reasons for this. *Asking* for money is considered impolite by many. Second, there is *fear*, usually ungrounded, that customers will resent a request for money owed and therefore will not buy again. In this era when Total Quality Management requires our meeting customers' requirements, there is too often a feeling that Quality firms should not ask for cash.

A few years ago, when interest rates were in double digits, almost everyone, companies as well as individuals, could earn substantial interest income in the short-term money market. Delaying the payment of amounts owed (accounts payable) meant that the cash management operation of a firm could become a profit center. For a brief period, when rates were as high as +20 percent, stretching out accounts payable even for two weeks could generate significant income. Companies became experienced in stretching out their cash disbursements. In fact, one observer has even referred to this phenomenon as the rise of the experienced debtor, who takes advantage of the system to the maximum extent possible and then starts to think about paying bills.

How can you bring in the cash owed to you without hurting your customers' feelings, while protecting against the tricks and traps of the experienced debtor? The answer is, "Only with difficulty." What is difficult and takes effort is not, however, impossible. Many firms successfully implement a strong collection effort as part of Total Cash Management.

A disciplined approach to the problem, with top management attention, is the key to success.

Why Companies Don't Pay Their Bills

To collect receivables, you first have to understand why you have not been paid. There are three basic reasons, and, until you understand which category applies, no progress can be made. People do not pay because:

1. They are dissatisfied in some way with your product or service, and withholding payment is the best way to get your attention.
2. The buyer has sufficient cash, but simply has a different payment schedule than you expected, or even contracted for, at the time of sale.
3. The buyer is short of cash—does not have enough to meet all his obligations. Your objective has to be to move to the top of his list.

As in any self-help system, the first step is to acknowledge that you have a collection problem. In turn, this means a disciplined system for keeping track of current receivable balances on an aging schedule. In this era of accounting programs on personal computers, *every* organization should maintain a computerized receivable record. Every receivable program will segregate receivable balances into past-due categories, that is, those that are current, 0-20 days past due, 21-40 days, and so forth. In point of fact, the programs are usually so flexible that you can define your own past due categories, even assigning different due dates to invoices issued on the same day. Total flexibility of information, in a format designed specifically for your use, is now a given. Later in this chapter we will discuss how to organize and staff for collection. But first, assuming you have good current information available, let's look more closely at why people do not pay.

Customer Dissatisfaction

Have you ever bought something on a trip and found, when you got home, that it did not work as promised? Assuming you had paid for the item with Visa or Master Card, what did you do? Given today's consumer protection laws, you tell the credit card compant not to pay, and then have plenty of time to fight it out with your supplier. You are permitted, by law in this instance, to show your displeasure by not paying until the dispute is resolved.

In a commercial, business-to-business environment, the same principle holds true. The only difference is that most purchases are on open account. As a seller you normally would expect payment from your customers in, say, 30 days. But if one of your customers is dissatisfied (such as with late delivery or substandard goods), it is highly unlikely you are not going to be paid.

If you have not received payment in 35 days, assuming you have the requisite information from the computerized accounts receivable schedule, the natural tendency for anyone with the job responsibility for collections is to assume, "They are just late this month. I've plenty of other receivables to chase down and they are not very late. In fact, they always pay their bills so I will give them another three weeks until I really follow up." Now it will be two months since the goods were shipped, and, as the seller, you still do not know you have a customer problem!

In short, what appears on your aged accounts receivable as a collection problem, isn't. The solution involves customer service, selling, engineering, quality control, or whatever. It is not a Finance Department problem, other than the fact that the cash is not available. But the cash will *never* become available until the basic business problem is solved. Further, you have now lost 30 additional days before you start to find a solution, by which time the customer will have forgotten the specifics, and your own people won't care too much because today's problems will appear to have a higher priority. This is how you end up providing a sales adjustment to write off what is now an uncollectible receivable.

Now turn back the clock and go to the aged receivable list on day 35. The customer has not paid. Place a brief phone call right then, asking, "We notice you have not yet paid our invoice. Is there any problem? If not, when can we expect payment?" This is totally nonthreatening. No customer's Accounts Payable Department is going to resent this. The payables clerk may not like answering the phone but as they say, "It goes with the territory." What you will learn from the call is that the Payables Department has not even processed your invoice; it is not in the system! Why? Because someone in Purchasing, Receiving, or Production Control said, "Hold up that invoice until we get this straightened out." Holding up the invoice is the quick and easy way to get the process of reconciliation started, but the process also probably stops there because it will take scarce management time to resolve.

In practice the seller has to take the initiative, first to find out that there is a problem and then to move things forward to resolution. Only if the good or service is truly critical to the purchaser's operation will the buyer's staff communicate with the seller. It is much easier just to sit on the invoice and wait. The lesson is clear. If they are going to wait for you to make the first move, the quicker the better.

Moral: Any invoice even slightly past due has the potential to be a customer service or quality problem. The quicker you take action, the easier the solution will be. Unlike fine wine, old receivables do not improve with age.

Experienced Debtors.   Business is carried out on the basis of trust. Selling on open account and granting credit for 30 or more days are acts of faith that the buyer will pay. Even with backsliding (discussed in the next section), most companies pay their bills. A good credit rating and, even more important, a good *reputation* are important to most business firms and to the executives who run them.

Unfortunately, one category of businesses has a very poor reputation for business ethics. Large *retailers*, for reasons that are not totally clear, have developed to a fine art the practice of *chargebacks*. Put simply, this is a debit memo. It corresponds to the credit memo, which you as a seller might issue to cancel an invoice for goods returned by the customer. In effect the purchaser debits, or charges, the supplier for the unsatisfactory merchandise. As originally contemplated, the items would be shipped back; the buyer then uses the debit memo to offset the supplier's invoice for the goods. That way, the buyer's check, plus the debit memos, would equal the outstanding invoices prepared and sent by the seller. If the seller prepares a monthly statement, showing new purchases and cash payments received, it is then up to the seller to prepare a corresponding credit memo if the books of both parties are to balance.

What started out as a relatively simple way for both buyer and seller to keep their payment records synchronized has turned into a monster. Reasonable outsiders would agree that if a buyer orders 100 of an item and receives only 96, that she should not have to pay in full an invoice for the 100. Charging back the missing four items is equitable and certainly a lot more efficient than sending back the invoice for 100 and requesting a new invoice for 96. Efficiency and equity join to make a system both sides can live with—if, in fact, the shipment did only contain 96 items.

Starting out with missing goods or with items damaged in transit, many department stores began charging back to vendors amounts for "damages" caused by "late" deliveries. Certainly if seasonal or high-fashion goods arrive late, the merchant can suffer lost sales, and perhaps it is fair to ask the vendor to share in the ultimate write-down. But the chargeback system shoots first and answers questions later. The customer issues the debit memo for the late delivery, deducts the amount from the next remittance and expects the vendor to simply accept his word that the items were late, and the amount calculated as damages is fair and reasonable. By the time the remittance, with its accompanying debit memo(s), is processed, it is hard for the vendor to get the facts, much less negotiate in good faith.

Perhaps because of internal pressures on store buyers to increase margins, or merely because it has become an accepted way of doing business in this industry, department stores have become extremely creative in developing ever new reasons for charging back amounts to vendors. One vendor was startled to receive a notice that he was contributing a $10,000 share to a store's special mail circular advertising a seasonal sale. Another vendor was first told he had contributed to a customer's sales meeting when he received a chargeback. The current prize, however, might be awarded to the country's largest retailer who charged a small vendor, right at year-end, for an amount that was to cover future damages to merchandise not yet received!

> Here's a true story: A manufacturer of children's clothing had a large retail customer. In the words of the controller, "This store, in its entire history, had *never* received a complete shipment from a vendor!" In short, it invariably charged back for missing items. The controller one day personally packed, sealed, and shipped a large order. Sure enough, the customer charged them back for a shortage. When asked what he did then, there was no answer, only a smile. A reasonable question might be, if you are going to be charged back for a partial shipment, why make a full shipment?

Ethics aside, what are the cash implications of this chargeback system? For the buyer's side, they are pretty good. If the vendor accepts all your chargebacks, then in effect you are getting $1000 of merchandise and paying out only, say, $925. Cash is saved and gross profit margins are raised, as the "free" merchandise and/or reduction in selling and marketing expenses flows through to the bottom line. From the seller's point of view (since this chapter deals with creditors and with collecting accounts receivable), it is obvious that there is a problem. Cash receipts will be less than expected and total revenues reduced, raising the cost of doing business. Put another way, profit margins will be adversely affected.

What can be done? This question is easier to ask than to answer. Put simply, the major retailers who engage in this type of behavior are exercising economic leverage, and in effect telling those suppliers, "Take it or leave it." Actual responses include taking it, that is, accepting the anticipated level of chargebacks as a normal cost of doing business with these customers and building such costs into the selling price. Others ultimately decide to stop selling into such an environment, arguing that the total costs, both the cash discounts and the administrative effort, are not worthwhile. Still others have taken the position that the Robinson-Patman Act prohibits selling to like customers at unlike prices, and that the discounts or chargebacks extracted by the customers are in fact illegal.

This latter approach would be ideal, if the courts were to sustain such allegations, but at this time we are unaware of any successful suits.

In the next section we discuss the famous Golden Rule variation that states, "Whoever has the gold makes the rules." For better or worse, if there is a disparity in economic strength between the buyer and seller and if the stronger party chooses to exercise that power without restraint, few good choices are open to the other. Sooner or later the pendulum will swing, perhaps through changes in either the legal or economic environment, but in the meantime someone is going to be hurt. Cash flow *is* going to be adversely affected. Former President Kennedy was correct, although not necessarily thinking about Total Cash Management, when he said, "Life is unfair at times."

This section has dealt with dissatisfied customers. There is every advantage in finding out about problems as early as possible, and that is why immediate follow-up on even slightly past due balances is critical. Total Quality Management, with its emphasis on meeting customer expectations, ties in directly and immediately with Total Cash Management. When your customer arbitrarily questions your quality, simply to extract a better price, you have a business problem that requires business decisions, none of which may be attractive. But at least knowing you are on top of your receivables, providing quality service to all your other customers, lets you pinpoint the real issues.

Your Customers Set Their Own Payment Terms

The second reason that receivables become past due, as shown on your aging schedule, is that your customer does not process your invoice as promptly as you expect. You think you have sold on terms of 30 days net, and the customer consistently pays in 45 days. *Should* you take action? If so, what can be done?

Technically, when a customer orders something and you ship it, you have entered into a legally enforceable contract. The terms offered by the purchaser may be spelled out on his purchase order, and, in the absence of any further negotiation on your part, you are agreeing to those terms by shipping. Check the purchase order before complaining. Assuming that proposed payment terms are not spelled out on the purchase order, then your credit terms, presumably shown on your invoice, should govern the transaction. (In any specific case, please check with your own attorney.) So if the invoice says 30 days, theoretically that should control.

Why might a customer not pay in accordance with your terms, assuming there is nothing wrong with the product and the availability of funds is not in doubt? At least three reasons may explain the situation:

1. The customer's payables system, including approvals, takes a long time.

2. Individual managers are trying to influence when the expense (or inventory) hits their financial statements.

3. The customer has a cash management policy that calls for no disbursements earlier than 45 days or for some other arbitrary period.

Customer's Payables System. Because of numerous complaints from the small business community that the federal government did not pay its bills on time, Congress responded by enacting a Prompt Payments Act. This law requires the government to pay interest on any disbursement more than 30-days old. On the surface this should have solved the problem. No government managers want to have unbudgeted interest charges on their report, and it was hoped that this would truly energize the system.

Numerous government contractors report that the Prompt Payment Act actually slowed down cash disbursements! How could that be? To avoid paying interest, individual federal employees began scrutinizing invoices under a microscope. They looked for *any* discrepancies that meant the 30-day clock would not start ticking, and interest would not be paid no matter how minor the discrepancy or how long it took to get the paperwork redone and into the system. What started out to be a way to help government contractors once again demonstrated that the Law of Unintended Consequences had not been repealed, and small business ended up receiving a very unpleasant surprise.

The key point is that companies, as well as the government, have formal procedures for processing vendor invoices. These systems can range from requiring only the initials of an authorized executive or manager to an extremely formal matching of purchase orders, receiving reports, and vendor invoices. The business press has had numerous reports as to how Ford reengineered its payables system and went from something like 500 employees down to 200. To do this it had to change the way it issued purchase orders, monitored product receipts, processed all the intermediate paperwork, and disbursed the cash. The reengineering itself took several years. The point is that large organizations for the most part have very tight controls on accounts payable.

To prevent employee theft, which will show up ultimately as an accounts payable check issued, control systems are installed, with tight approvals, and monitored by internal and external auditors, to make sure that *all* internal procedures are followed. If the key step in this process is the matching, by computer, of all key information from each of three documents—purchase order, receiving report, and vendor invoice—think of the possibilities for mismatches to occur. Each of the three documents is prepared by a different department. Quantities, part numbers, purchase order number, and unit prices must all agree precisely. Even then there can be questions about freight, taxes, packing charges, and the like. Depending on the parameters of the payables system and how tightly the program is both written and administered, it is a wonder that some large firms ever pay their bills.

So, as a supplier looking for prompt payment, you need a solution. You must understand in detail the payables system, as well as get to know the specific employees in some cases, of major customers. Just as good salespersons have to understand their customers, so do we have to understand customer payables systems, and then make sure we comply. In theory we can ask our customers to comply with *our* invoicing system and to adjust their payables systems. Common sense suggests that we adapt, if necessary, because in TQM we want to be responsive to our customers and, even more importantly, because we want our cash as quickly as possible.

If the remittances from one or a few large customers are truly significant for you, you might consider sending either your billing or accounts receivable supervisor to visit them. The purpose is to determine exactly how your invoices are processed, so that the two firms' systems can be integrated. The success rate is very high for those who take the trouble. The bottom line is to treat collections like any other business problem: Search for a workable solution and then implement it. To show how this can be done, major defense contractors have been known literally to walk through an invoice to speed up payment from the government. The time value of money permits this expenditure if we are dealing with a single $50-million invoice. For smaller amounts there is need only to make sure that your invoice and shipping documents are all in the proper format and are 100-percent accurate.

Manager Holding the Invoice.   This situation is more difficult to deal with, but fortunately is not usually part of a recurring pattern. If a department manager needs a good or service but is already over budget for the month or year to date, a very human desire is to postpone the bad budget news until next month, when "things will get better." Whether this is good accounting and financial reporting and whether a company's auditors would approve sticking an invoice in a desk drawer until next month are not the issues. It is wrong, but it happens. (Of course, the opposite happens. Once in a while you will receive a call asking to send an invoice *early*, because there is a favorable budget variance to be offset.)

Frankly, there is not much that can, or probably even should, be done if a good customer has a valid (at least in her mind) reason for not beginning to process your invoice until next month. Meeting your customer's requirements, according to TQM, should include an occasional request for an exception. As long as this is not a recurring pattern, you will actually develop a stronger relationship with your customer by doing her a favor. Postponing the processing of an invoice, which invariably triggers its showing up in budget reports (whether or not the cash has been disbursed), is a reasonable accommodation for one month. More than one month, however, and you have a different problem. Either something was wrong with what you delivered, or the buyer really did not have the authority to make the purchase. We've already covered the former case, and selling to an unauthorized buyer ultimately becomes a legal issue beyond the scope of this book.

At the risk of seeming repetitive, the sooner you find out why an invoice is not being paid on time, the easier it is to determine the appropriate action. In this case the most appropriate action may be to do nothing, but at least that invoice can be taken off the problem list and your time can be spent elsewhere.

Late Payment Policy.   The most troubling late payments ("late" being defined as beyond your stated terms) arise with customers who have plenty of money but whose stringent cash management programs are a matter of corporate policy. Cash management taken as a whole, within the total business community, is actually a zero-sum game: That is, for every winner there is a loser. If I pay you slower, and invest the retained cash in the money market, you do not have it for investment. Conversely, if I pay you earlier, then *you* can invest it. When I pay affects only who gets to invest, not how much.

Understanding this concept is vital in dealing with firms that have established their own payments policy, one that they carry out irrespective of their suppliers' wishes. Supposing a buyer always pays invoices 25 days after the due date, thus stretching 30-day terms to 55-day terms. Whether formally stated or not on purchase orders, this practice is how they manage their payables. Every vendor who does business knows this. If a new supplier calls up and asks for payment on day 31, the answer comes back quickly and unequivocally, "You won't get paid until 55 days after your invoice. Period."

Now what? In the face of what might be called intransigence, you as a seller have, in practice, two choices: You can accept those terms, or you can stop selling. Trying to negotiate in that situation, getting payment in 45 days as an example, is going to be a waste of time. After all, why should they make an exception for you? If their policy works for them—and it apparently does—your leverage is not going to be very high.

Unfortunately for many small and medium-sized businesses, a substantial number of household-name Fortune 500 firms take advantage of their economic strength and impose late payments on all their suppliers. It may be a psychological consolation to know that you are not alone, that they treat everyone shabbily. There is no need to feel paranoid. The customer is not out to get just *you*. But understanding the situation does not improve it.

Realistically, unless the product or service you offer is both unique and needed, large firms are unlikely to change basic corporate policies only for you. The hope—and it may be a slim one—is to throw yourself on the mercy of either the purchasing agent or ultimate user of your product (service) within the organization, telling them that without payment in 30 days the very continuity of your business is threatened. If this is credible, you *may* get paid promptly as an exception, depending on how stringently the customer monitors and controls its payables policy. In other words, an accounts payable supervisor or an individual buyer may have the authority to temporarily grant an exception. If so, you have to ask for it explicitly, and do it up front. The danger is that, in throwing yourself on their mercy, you are disclosing yourself as a weak supplier, which does not bode well for a long-term relationship. In the final analysis you may be better off accepting economic reality, then trying to raise your selling prices slightly to compensate for the late payments, a strategy that sometimes works.

Here is still another application of the modified version of the Golden Rule: "He who has the gold makes the rules." If someone with power chooses to exercise it, you can counter only with equivalent economic power, which a small vendor does not have.

It is totally unrealistic to think that all or a majority of any firm's vendors could get together as a group and tell the company, "Unless you pay promptly, all of us are going to cut you off." But when credit managers get together they do compare notes, and it is surprising how quickly one can identify chronic abusers. Letting others know about a reputation for "sharp practices" is the only real defense against a firm that takes advantage of its clout, and no one supplier is going to influence that. The hope is that, perhaps in a social situation, the top management or members of the Board of Directors can be persuaded that the firm's reputation as a chronically late payer is hindering it in some way. If the Board and CEO either developed or know about the policy and condone it, then nothing will change in the short run.

The power changes hands, however, in times of shortage, when suppliers are rationing or allocating production. Now the policy of late payments backfires. If you have only 100 units of output, and two customers are demanding immediate delivery of 75 units each, you will be in a position to call the tune. At that point you have the gold and can make the rules.

Until then, however, rather than brooding about things, take your management time and put it to better use collecting receivable balances from others who are neither as strong financially nor as stubborn. Fortunately, the overall "system" has relatively few true abusers.

There is one favorable aspect of dealing with firms that have a consistent policy of paying late. As long as they are consistent (in this example, always pay in 55 days), you do not have to worry about whether you have a potential bad debt or other collection efforts are needed. That is the advantage of certainty of payment: It may be annoying to be paid late, but it is still far better than not being paid at all. Put yourself in the place of the individual staring at a long computer printout of past due receivables. When you come to Company G, you can skip that firm if it is in the 30- to 60-day column because you know that, at the end of 60 days, you will have your money. It is the people who used to pay promptly, and who are now late, that are the real cause for concern.

Dealing with the Government. The best advice when dealing with the government is to get to know your customer's payables process. Just as good salespersons are instructed to learn as much as they can about their customers, so should your billing/receivables/collection staff learn about how your customers process their payments. As already discussed, in relation to normal commercial practice, a number of companies sell directly or through prime contractors indirectly to the federal government. The same principles apply conceptually. In practice, every *i* must be dotted and every *t* crossed.

Contracting officers are now making sure that every invoice submitted is 100-percent accurate. Rather than putting up with minor clerical errors, many government disbursing personnel are examining every invoice microscopically and bouncing it back to the vendor. The 30-day clock, under the law, does not start running until an acceptable invoice is received. Therefore, because they think they are doing the taxpayers a favor by delaying payment to vendors (saving cash for the government in terms of the time value of money), the government now has a reputation for extremely persnickety scrutiny of vendor invoices.

The corollary, for vendors, is clear. Check, double-check, and, if necessary, triple-check government invoices for *full* compliance with all requirements called for on the contract. This may involve a special process for government invoices, but the alternative is even worse. Doing business with the federal government truly has zero *credit risk*. By definition they cannot run out of money, because the government can always print more. But there may be more than the normal amount of *business risk*. Unless you are dealing with literally millions of dollars, it is not necessary to physically walk your invoice through the approval process, although some large defense contractors have occasionally found this necessary. It does mean learning exactly who has to approve your invoices, just what they expect, and what they are looking for.

Your Customer Is Short of Cash

This third category of customer who does not pay bills on time is certainly the most worrisome. Customer dissatisfaction can be cured or adjusted. Customers with good cash resources will pay sooner or later. The adage,

"Better late than never," fortunately is true when dealing with receivables. But what do you do about the customer to whom you have sold in good faith, expecting payment, and who now does not pay because there simply is not enough cash to go around? These customers give credit managers a chance to earn their pay.

With the exception of a very few "bust-out" con artists—individuals who deliberately plan to declare bankruptcy and order as much as they can as quickly as they can—almost every businessperson *wants to pay.* Just as a car cannot run on an empty gas tank, a business cannot run on an empty bank account. If your customer is temporarily short of cash, perhaps because one of *her* large customers is late, this is quite different from a business that has a negative cash flow.

Dealing with a Temporary Shortage.   Very few businesses are willing to acknowledge that they are experiencing a negative cash flow. At least at the beginning there is always a hope that things will improve and that the excess of accounts payable over current cash balances is temporary. The businessperson in this situation feels that all he needs is a little time and things will get better. Therefore the first thing that happens is that only the most critical invoices are settled; everyone else hears nothing and receives nothing. Those who call—and it is strongly recommended that you call immediately when an invoice is past due—are given one of the standard excuses. "I did not get the invoice, please send me another." Or, "I thought I paid that, let me check." Sometimes you are treated to slightly more creative ones involving fictitious problems (either with your merchandise or their internal operations). Any of these excuses is only an attempt to buy time.

Anyone involved in collection efforts will very quickly be able to determine (from the tone of voice if nothing else) whether or not there is a cash problem. You can afford to give them one chance, that is, believe the excuse for nonpayment, it makes sense to go ahead and send a duplicate invoice—by fax and if they are sure it was paid, wait two more days and call again. The message you must communicate is that *you* are tough on receivables and that really it will be easier for the customer to pay than be hassled. If the problem is really temporary, and the customer is juggling trying to keep everyone happy, then in practice the squeaky wheel will be paid first. Creditors who do not follow up promptly and continuously will be at the end of the line. Your objective is to go to the head of your customer's line.

Do you jeopardize a good business relationship by following up closely? No. Remember that you and the customer had a contract: merchandise or services in exchange for payment. You fulfilled your half of the bargain, and it is totally reasonable to expect the other party to complete the transaction.

In fact you may increase your business. People are reluctant to order additional goods from firms to which they owe money, fearing that they will be cut off. So if you can get your customer to pay, and they now are not past due, they will more than likely stick with you as a supplier. Also keep in mind that, to start doing business with any new supplier, that firm is going to perform a credit check. Thus if your customer has cash problems, it is not likely they will be *able* to switch suppliers. Some of the strongest mutual relationships in business have been forged when, in a time of trouble, a supplier or customer stuck with the firm. The ideal solution therefore is to be firm, demand and expect payment, but then continue to ship.

Measuring the Real Cost of Bad Debts.   Most businesses overestimate the cost of bad debts! Here is a situation where accounting reports, seemingly so precise, give absolutely incorrect information. Let's look at what really happens, and contrast that with what accountants tell us.

In the short run, almost all costs are fixed; that is, they will not decrease if the volume of our sales diminishes. By the same token, a small increase in sales does not raise our costs of doing business. The implication of this well-known phenomenon is that there is a *substantial* contribution to profit from these last incremental sales. Put another way, if we decide *not* to ship to a seemingly poor credit risk, what will be saved in terms of out-of-pocket cash? The answer is that we will save, not disburse, only amounts directly related to manufacturing the item. This might include purchased material and a small amount of electric power. But salaries, rent, depreciation, and the rest of overhead is unaffected based on shipping and selling the last marginal item. For a printing firm, as an example, in the short run the only cost avoided would be paper. The presses and press operators are there whether we print one last order or not.

Now let's look at our accounting report. Using the generally accepted accrual method of accounting, we report sales as being generated when we ship to the customer. That is hard to argue with. But then we allocate a portion of the labor, overhead, depreciation, and other expenses to that sale *before we have been paid for it.* In effect we are recognizing future profit not when we collect cash from the customer, but when we shipped the product, *hoping* the profit will be earned.

If our accounting recognized the profit only when we were fully paid in cash, how would we act differently? Right now, when we ship the goods we recognize all the revenue, including the portion associated with recovering fixed costs and overhead. Then when we have a write-off we show a *loss* equal to the entire selling price. The economic facts are quite different. We paid out in cash amounts for the variable costs (material and energy) and perhaps a small amount for direct labor to manufacture the

product. In terms of cash, you cannot lose more than you spent. By
recognizing recovery of overhead, plus profit upon sale—and *not* when
our customer pays us—we just fool ourselves. Worse, we make bad
business decisions.

We should measure potential losses from bad debts only in terms of the
out-of-pocket cash costs expended to make those specific goods. That
means customers who do pay must cover all our overhead, but, in the final
analysis, they have to anyhow. Realistically, most firms have bad debts of
significantly less than 2 percent of sales. If direct or variable costs are 45
to 50 percent of sales prices, that means we can increase total contribution
by accepting orders from marginal customers and, if we experience no
more than a 10-percent loss on those marginal orders, we will make more
profit. Certainly bad debts are going to run higher if we sell to marginal
customers, but even a five-fold increase, from 2 to 10 percent of sales on
those risky transactions, will not be bad news.

Is it likely that Generally Accepted Accounting Principles will be changed
to reflect the economic reality of cash flow? No. We can, however,
accomplish virtually the same thing.

Tip: If you consciously decide to sell to risky accounts, accepting the
chance that some turn out to be bad debt write-offs, you can have your
monthly financial statements reflect the real results of your decision
making. Each month set up a bad debt reserve equal to the difference
between selling price and out-of-pocket costs. Then, when the so-called
marginal accounts do pay, you can reverse the bad debt reserve and
recognize the profit. For those accounts that end up being a write-off, who
do not pay, the reported bad debt loss will then only be the amount of your
previous cash outlay to produce the goods.

Your Customer Really Can't Pay!   We have taken a chance on a marginal
account and it turns out to have been a mistake. The customer is in real
financial difficulty, cannot pay you and, after some back and forth discussions, you believe it. The customer really does not have the money. What
to do now is actually pretty simple. You have little leverage as an unsecured
creditor, and, unless your product is truly critical to the customer's
business, you may not get many future orders. In short, the prognosis is
bankruptcy, if not now, then quite soon.

Step 1: Make sure that no more sales are made on open account. This
sounds like common sense, but it is amazing how often a communications failure can occur within an organization. Somebody doesn't get
the word and additional shipment(s) are made. Wrong. A clear line of
communication to the Order Entry and Shipping Departments is
needed to prevent this from happening. Once a customer has been cut
off, make sure *everyone* knows about it.

Step 2: Any additional orders must be accepted on a cash with order basis. Some organizations are willing to ship on a COD (cash on delivery) basis, but, while this protects against bad debts, if you do not hand over the merchandise until you are paid, how is your driver actually going to be paid? Accepting a check is unwise, and actual cash, in greenbacks, is not likely for any significant purchase. "Cash with order," which really means a check with order, allows you to deposit the check and make sure it clears before releasing the merchandise.

Step 3: Try to collect the outstanding balance, which by this time may be 60 to 90 days old. The first decision to be made is whether to pursue this with your own staff or turn it over to a collection agency. If the latter, choosing the right agency is next. Finally, you must make sure that all the paperwork is in order and that your file on that customer is complete.

When to Turn to Collection Agencies

Unless your staff is fairly large, and has time available, it probably is better to deal with a specialized collection agency. There is a better use for your organization's time than dealing with creditors who are in real financial trouble. Better to pursue good customers who are a little late and get them to speed up payment than wasting time on difficult cases. There must be a reason for firms to specialize in collections. They have certain skills that you can use.

Companies are reluctant to use a professional collection agency for two main reasons—and both are usually emotional in nature and stem from a lack of understanding. The first argument is that they cost too much. "Why pay them 25 to 35 percent for collecting what is owed us? What can they do that we can't?" The second argument is, "If we turn the account over to an agency, they will so antagonize the customer so much that he will never buy from us again!" Let's look at each of these objectively.

Cost.   Frankly, one of the big pluses of a collection agency is that they only charge for successful efforts. It costs nothing to send accounts to an agency. If you only send them accounts that are no longer worth your while, then you have to take the position that something is better than nothing. A fear of giving up 25 percent of collections made often leads to waiting too long before contacting the agency. The sooner they have an account, the higher their success rate, but the worse is the psychology. "Gee, if they can collect it quickly, and skim their 25 percent off the top, maybe I should put in a couple of extra weeks and see what I can do."

Results.   Just why is a good collection agency going to get better results than you can? Understanding this is key to their use. Basically a collection agency is *organized* for just one purpose: collections. They have internal *systems* that work and *trained staff* who understand collections. Their staff is focused on getting cash from firms in financial difficulty. Finally, there is the psychological factor: Debtors know that collection agencies mean business.

Every professional in the collection business agrees that, the sooner they receive the account and can begin their processing, the higher the success rate. Older accounts are harder to collect because the debtor has had time to run up more debts with others.

Also, to the extent that there is any excuse for not paying, related to delivery, quality, or other issue the person or firm has had more time to dig in and set up defenses. When a debtor does not have the funds and cannot pay right away, any excuse seems better than none. "The check is in the mail" will no longer work. Now it is, "What you sent me was defective in the following ways...." Collection agencies know how to handle those excuses, and the debtor knows that, since the collection agency does not have a direct seller/buyer relationship, it is going to "focus like a laser beam," to quote President Clinton, on the one important thing: payment.

Assuming the debtor has sufficient cash, how does a good agency go about getting some? First, there is the threat, implicit or explicit, of legal action, with the ultimate course of action being involuntary bankruptcy. Assuming the debtor wants to stay in business, then the creditor who makes the most credible threat (promise *not* to take action if the amount owed is paid) will suddenly go to the top of the list.

Remember, even a struggling business is receiving some cash inflow from new sales and collection of its receivables. You may not get all of it, but a good collection agency will work out delayed payment terms (so much a week or a month), and then follow up religiously to make sure that the previous commitments are fulfilled by the debtor. As with almost any trade, once you know how it is done, it seems relatively easy. The same is true of collections. There is no magic, just persistence and an under-standing of the psychology of the debtor.

When your sales to a marginal customer represent a significant business risk, either for you or relative to the customer's business volume, you may want to use the terms of the Uniform Commercial Code (UCC) and obtain a security interest. All this does for you is put you in a much better position if your customer files for bankruptcy; before any filing you are not going to speed up cash receipts. The legal aspects of filing under UCC are outside the scope of this book, but, if you have a large sale and are at all worried, contact your attorney for advice.

Lawyers or Agencies?   In addition to commercial collection agencies—and a lot of them are available—certain attorneys specialize in collection work. Since only lawyers can go to court, when an account is turned over to an attorney the debtor is likely to take this seriously. The thought is, "If I don't pay a *lawyer*, I'll probably be sued." Since nobody likes to be sued—the time, expense, and publicity are all unfavorable aspects—the credibility of having a collection effort spearheaded by an attorney is enhanced.

The very strength of attorneys—their ability to go to court—is also their greatest weakness. If your business is in Tulsa and you are selling locally, then any competent Tulsa attorney can do the job. But what about an account located in Sacramento? How can a Tulsa attorney present a credible threat of taking a California firm to court in Oklahoma? Answer, she cannot. So your Tulsa attorney will have to contact a collection lawyer resident in California and turn the account over to him.

If your business is nationwide, there may be little difference between funneling everything through a local attorney or through a commercial agency. The only difference is that in many instances the agency is going to be better organized for the day-to-day routine of telephoning and following up on past promises. If attorneys' skill and stock in trade is going to court, or at least letting debtors think they are going to court, then their strength is not likely to be in the clerical and routine efforts that usually work in 60 to 75 percent of the cases.

Good collection agencies have attorneys throughout the country with whom they work when it is finally determined that legal action is the only solution. In fact, it could well be the same expert who acts as the correspondent for your local attorney. So if a case is going to court it may make little difference whether your first point of contact is an agency or an attorney. But the key point is that most collection efforts do *not* end up in front of a judge.

Recommendation: Try a collection agency once or twice on difficult accounts, letting them know that there is more to come if they do a good job. Let the agency decide if legal action is necessary. If you are not satisfied with your first choice agency, try another, noting the area where you are looking for improvement. Within a short time you will have a good idea of the strengths and weaknesses of various firms. One well-known credit rating firm, Dun and Bradstreet, also has a division that specializes in collections. Their selling point is that debtors will want to pay D&B to avoid affecting their credit report adversely. This may or may not be true. As with any other large national firm, the local D&B office may be excellent, but it could be managed by a somewhat less than top-flight professional. All other things being equal, if you can find a smaller local firm (one run by a real collection professional), you may get better service.

Fees.   In wrapping up this discussion about the use of collection agencies, a word about fees is in order. Most agencies charge a standard percentage for successful actions, and there is no charge if they fail. Lawyers will take a case either on a contingency or on an hourly basis. This choice has to be made on the basis of the size of the account and your guess as to the likelihood of success if you end up in court. Keep in mind that a successful suit only gives you a legal judgment, not the cash. You still have to extract the cash, although with the judgment you then have legal power to seize the debtor's assets—if you can find any. For most normal debts, the contingency method is preferable, although the lawyer invariably will want cash from you up front to pay for the filing fees demanded by the court. Strange as it seems, you have to pay out additional cash just for the privilege of trying to collect the cash already owed to you.

The percentage charge for successful collections is subject to negotiation. The factors considered by the agency are the average size of the accounts you turn over to them (obviously large is better than small), the total volume of business you do, and the actual or expected success rate. Since more recent accounts (60 days past due as contrasted with, say, 150 days) are easier for them to collect, you should be able to negotiate a lower percentage if you regularly turn accounts over to them in 60 rather than 150 days. In the final analysis, what you pay the agency is going to have some correlation with the time they spend, since it is skilled time they are selling. On any one account they may have what seems like a windfall, or they may completely waste their time. Over large numbers of accounts, with many clients, a good agency will cover its costs fairly.

One Final Word.   The federal government and most states have laws on consumer harassment. This chapter has been written on the assumption that your customers are other businesses, so that it is unlikely that threats of physical violence, or nuisance phone calls at 1:00 AM, are going to be tried either by you or your employees. Again, legal advice is outside the scope of this book, but in dealing with individual consumers, be extremely careful about going too far. If you have an occasional local consumer debt that is not being paid, look in the *Yellow Pages* for a lawyer under the heading Debt Collection. Otherwise you may receive a call from another attorney who advertised in the same phone book, "Call now for *immediate help with creditor harassment!*" In today's litigious environment, where consumers are fighting fire with fire, get a good lawyer on your side as soon as possible when dealing with recalcitrant consumers.

So Your Customer Declared Bankruptcy

About 15 years ago Congress passed a law reforming the bankruptcy system. Many feel that now the pendulum has swung too far. Up to then, the bankruptcy system was unduly favorable to creditors, and few debtors were able to work out their problems and start over. As so often happens, today's cure may now be worse than the disease.

Today we live under a system totally favoring the debtor, as the creditors of Eastern Airlines learned. In that situation the bankruptcy judge allowed the airline to continue operating, draining all its cash resources. It continued to lose money until finally all assets had been dissipated. At the start of the bankruptcy process, creditors might have received 60¢ on the dollar, but at the end they ended up receiving almost nothing.

A new technique has been developed by lawyers specializing in bankruptcy (one of the great growth professions of the 1990s), familiarly referred to as the *cram-down*. It does not take much imagination to understand that the legal system is being twisted so that legitimate creditors have fewer rights—and often end up with even fewer assets.

If you are a major creditor of a bankrupt firm, you may be invited to sit on a creditor's committee. While the attorneys and accountants get paid in cash, as priority claimants, out of the bankrupt firm's limited assets, as a member of the committee itself you end up contributing your time and knowledge, in exchange for a seat at the table where some key decisions will be reached. In short, you get to be a participant in the process, but whether you will end up recovering more than a nonmember of the committee is problematic. Secured creditors and experienced organizations like banks really have an inside advantage. Since you are probably going to lose most of what is owed to you no matter whether you serve on the committee or not, this is one honor you may choose to forgo.

One sign of maturity, according to psychologists and psychiatrists, is accepting reality and moving on. Applied to bankruptcy, this means full recognition of the fact that you probably will see very little cash from outstanding receivable balances, and, when it does come, it will be many months or even years delayed. Two things should be done. One is to pay close attention to all communications from the court regarding filing of claims—no point in losing out because of poor or late processing of paperwork. The second point is to decide whether to continue shipping new goods to the now bankrupt firm.

Bankruptcy Communications.   Paying close attention to communications from the bankruptcy court is essential. In the final settlement, only creditors whose claims have been accepted by the court will receive cash. This means that you must persuade the bankruptcy referee or trustee that you have a legitimate claim. For the most part copies of your invoices, possibly supported by shipping documents, will suffice. Of course, on the other side, there could be an attempt to show that what you shipped, just prior to the filing, was in some way damaged or delayed and thus they don't really owe you as much. If you get into this kind of dispute, and substantial sums of money are involved, get a lawyer. But this adds to your cash outflow immediately, and does not guarantee any corresponding cash inflow later.

Without getting technical, if you had very recently shipped to the bankrupt firm, it may be possible to have them physically return the items to you. If the items are of a standard nature, this will help. But if the parts are unique to that customer, and really have no value elsewhere (such as a casting made to the customer's blueprint), retrieving them is of little help. Check with your attorney *immediately* if you want to recover the physical items, since time is critical.

Another good reason to pay attention to communications from the bankruptcy court is that they can make clerical mistakes. A recent example shows this.

> A small manufacturer had several large retail firms as customers. One day in the early morning mail they received a notice that a very well-known retailer, Company X, had filed for bankruptcy. Attached was a listing by the court of the 20 largest creditors, "as shown by X's records." Imagine their surprise to find that their small firm was alleged to be the third largest creditor, owed literally several million dollars, a sum at least 10 times what was really owed. It seemed hilarious at first. But at about 11:00 in the morning other customers, suppliers, and competitors, all of whom had received or seen the same list from the bankruptcy court—and took it to be true—started calling. The key question asked, some outright and some quite subtly, was whether this firm would also have to file right away. Of course, if correct, a several million dollar receivable that was now effectively a bad debt would have put the firm under, considering its size and the reputed magnitude of the debt. Fortunately it was only a clerical error, and was explained as such. But there were a few tense hours while they gathered the facts. *Moral:* Pay attention to mail from the bankruptcy court.

Continued Shipments after Bankruptcy.   At first glance it might appear madness to continue to ship to a bankrupt customer. After all, if the company could not pay for the previous merchandise and was losing so much money that it had to file, what is going to change for the better? How could a bad credit risk ever become a good one? For once, the bankruptcy rules, designed to help the debtor, can help you the creditor. Once having filed, all previous debts effectively are frozen or suspended. This means that current cash flows will be applied solely to debts incurred *after* the filing, including payments for merchandise you ship afterwards. If you believe that the customer has at least a break-even cash flow on a continuing basis, then there is reasonable hope that new shipments will be paid for on time. Since no business can survive without suppliers and the drafters of the bankruptcy code understood this, the system is set up to protect those suppliers who choose to hang in.

You cannot, by law, attempt to recover part of your prebankruptcy debt through adding onto current billings for new merchandise. If everyone tried this, failure would be guaranteed; so again the drafters anticipated correctly. But you can generate a profit on current sales, and this is the motivation for not cutting off the customer. On the other hand, whoever is in charge of the bankrupt company, even if they do not have to worry about prefiling debts, still must balance current cash inflows with new requirements, including substantial legal and accounting fees not present before. Guess who is going to get paid first: the trustee for his or her own time or you?

About the only practical advice that can be given is to set new payment terms that are as short as possible, make sure those are absolutely adhered to, and not to ship further goods until all *current* amounts are paid on time. Ultimately this is going to get back to the two factors discussed earlier: How much does the customer need you? How profitable is the customer's business on your books? Careful monitoring and management are essential. But a knee-jerk reaction against doing further business with someone who pulled the rug out from under you by suddenly filing for bankruptcy is not warranted.

One final word of advice: The history of unsecured creditors receiving significant cash receipts from prebankruptcy debts, as a percentage of the amounts owed, is singularly limited. As soon as any creditor files for bankruptcy, quickly review your reserve for bad debts and increase it to 100 percent of the amount owed. At least you can obtain a current tax benefit for your loss.

Do Cash Discounts Speed Up Payment?

Everyone is familiar with the terms "2 percent 10 days—net 30." Taken literally, the invoice would have to be received, approved, and paid within 10 days for the customer to earn the discount. Given the present speed and timeliness of mail deliveries, it is highly unlikely that most business organizations can, in practice, process vendor invoices within this short time span. Yet many companies take such discounts, even though the vendor does not actually get the check for 20 or even 25 days after it was sent to the customer. As a seller, how should you respond to late payments where the discount for prompt payment has not been earned? In practice many firms truly abuse cash discounts. A second issue, therefore, is what should you do to *really* ensure prompt payment. Some companies have found innovative solutions but they tend to be costly. Finally, there is the issue of charging interest on past due accounts.

Dealing with Abuse.　　Realistically, you cannot expect to receive payment in your office 10 days after mailing out an invoice. If the mail takes five days each way, no one can pay promptly enough for you to *receive* the check 10 days after you mailed the invoice. If this is so, then what instructions do you give your Accounting Department? If you have *no* internal rules, some customers will soon start to take advantage of your system, as soon as they learn you are not policing the discounts. On the other hand if rules are literally programmed into a computer, so that no judgment can be applied, you risk real ill will from conscientious customers who are trying to comply with your terms.

The first step is to set an outer limit. Allowing five days for the mail each way, 10 days for actual processing, and a safety hatch of five days, it is absolutely realistic to say that discounts will not be allowed if the check is received 26 days after you mailed the invoice. This, of course, implies that charging back an unearned discount will in fact allow you to collect it. Most companies do not spend much effort trying to collect an occasional chargeback of an unearned discount. They bill the customer and if it is paid, fine. If it is not paid within, say, 60 days, an internal credit memo is quietly issued but not sent to the customer. The absence of a follow-up from you is not the same thing as open admission, via credit memo, that you have forgiven them.

The chronic abuser, on the other hand, requires serious management attention. The first thing you have to establish in your mind is whether your 2-percent (some industries have only a 1-percent discount as standard) discount for prompt payment is in fact a normal part of the selling price (that is, everyone in the industry offers it), whether you are truly offering it not as a price reduction but as an incentive to pay early. Many books have tables that show the effective interest rate implicit in a cash discount; a 2 percent 10—net 30 works out to a 36-percent annual rate of interest. The conclusion of these writers is that every customer should borrow money, if necessary, at a lower rate than 36 percent and therefore will be motivated by financial self-interest to take the discount. But in the real world, if the 2-percent discount is an industry standard, the customer tends to think of this as part of the selling price, and does not really relate it to prompt processing of the check in exchange for the 36-percent return on his money. In short, many firms think they deserve the 2 percent and then set up your invoice for a normal 30- to 45-day disbursement.

Suppose, in your own mind, the 2 percent is strictly related to your prompt receipt of cash, and a good customer chooses to take the good part (the 2 percent) and ignore the bad part (prompt payment within, say, 15 days). You really have no choice but to change the terms to that customer and eliminate the offer of the discount altogether. You or your sales manager may say that that sounds good in theory, but the customer expects the discount or it is standard in the industry. OK, then simply cut your prices 2 percent, but eliminate the offer of the cash discount. At this moment you are no worse off. But over time, as your selling prices go up with competition and/or new product introductions, that customer will soon stop making the mental adjustment. If the customer ever says, "Where is my 2-percent discount," you are in a perfect position to point out that he did not keep his half of the bargain when it was offered. At that point you are in a better negotiating position.

If, however, the 2 percent is truly standard and the customer thinks of it as part of the selling price, then you have to crank that into your gross profit analysis and pricing strategy. You cannot view the 2-percent discount as part of your Total Cash Management approach.

What about a 3-percent or even a 4-percent, discount? Some firms have taken what may be considered an innovative approach and offered a really significant discount for truly prompt payment. The highest we have heard of is 6 percent and that is extremely rare. But in industries where 2 percent is the norm, a 3-percent or 4-percent discount will get the attention of your customers. It can be introduced with a modest amount of marketing hoop-la, as your sales representatives can tell their customers that it is a price reduction and that, of course, they are going to be financially able to make prompt payment. They have to emphasize that this big a discount—which is meaningful to them, the customers—is also meaningful to you in terms of your profits, and that the only way it can work is if they pay promptly. Rather than rely on outmoded nominal commercial terms, it would be better to redesign the invoice so that it clearly says that, if payment is *received* by you no later than a firm date (not just an indefinite "10 days" from some time), they need pay only $x,xxx.xx, but that payments received after the specified date must be $y,yyy.yy. This really puts the burden on customers, giving them the incentive to process your invoice promptly, and will probably encourage them to wire transfer the funds, if necessary, to meet your schedule. A further advantage is that, by printing a certain date, not just "10 days," you no longer have to set up decision rules or expect judgment calls by the Accounting Department staff. This system works. It is easy to police. Also, it is not as expensive as it sounds.

Customers with good credit ratings really cannot afford to pass up a 4-percent or even a 3-percent discount. The ROI is too high. So they will take it. You will have your cash promptly and, most importantly, your resources devoted to monitoring and collecting past due payments will be drastically reduced. The management as well as the clerical time can certainly be better applied. But the real beauty of this system is that it spotlights companies with credit problems.

A customer who consistently does not take a 3- or 4-percent discount has very poor judgment, has poor internal controls, or is in a real financial bind. The sooner you know this and understand the implications, the lower your risk of ultimate loss. One of the first signs of financial distress is failing to take cash discounts for prompt payment. When the dollar amounts are meaningful—and at 3 or 4 percent they are—you will be alerted in time to monitor that account closely.

Charging interest on past due accounts is the reverse of offering a cash discount for prompt payment. You are attempting to penalize one of your customers for not following agreed-upon terms. Opinion is split about the wisdom of charging commercial customers who are late in payment. We are not dealing with *consumer* credit, which is an entirely different issue and not covered in this book.

The major argument in favor of charging interest is that it encourages more timely payment. The author has discussed this issue with many corporate financial managers. Almost unanimously they agree that the interest penalty is not designed to be a money maker. No company producing goods or services *wants* to be in the banking business, providing credit for a fee (interest). Firms that charge customers for past due balances find that the revenues received (that is, actually *paid* by customers) are often meaningful but never large enough to be budgeted for as an expected generator of profit. However, it is also hard to measure what impact, if any, the practice has in actually reducing Days Sales Outstanding.

If receivable balances do not really go down, and if not much net revenue is actually collected, companies would be well advised to think carefully about the full implications of this practice before employing it. There are two major problem areas: customer response and clerical or management time. Customers who have been regular payers, but consistently on a delayed schedule, will argue that their own payables system cranks out checks on a particular schedule, from which they are unwilling to change. If the vendor wants their business—which appeared to be satisfactory in the past—then no change is appropriate. Do you really want to antagonize good customers, with good credit ratings that have their own Total Cash Management system? Remember that, in total, payables/receivables is a zero-sum game. If you get your money sooner they pay it out more quickly, and vice versa. Disturbing a good business relationship, with an imposed interest charge may be a poor marketing strategy. Better to sit down and (re)negotiate directly a new mutual agreement on payment terms, if the current one is unsatisfactory. Don't try to accomplish this with what will be perceived as a clumsy and arbitrary across-the-board new policy.

The real danger of imposing an interest charge on past due accounts is that it will give legitimacy to nonpayment of amounts owed. The reaction of a businessperson who is struggling to balance demands on cash is likely to be, "Well, I don't have to pay company X for a while. I'll just let the interest accrue. After all, Visa and Master Card don't want their customers to pay off their balance every month, so I am sure this vendor of mine must feel the same way." Wrong. You as the seller *do* want the customer to pay. Do not send a signal saying that nonpayment (really delayed payment) is OK with you.

Is your real objective to collect interest, or is it to turn over your receivable balances? With the question put that way, the answer is pretty straightforward. Do not provide your customers with an excuse to delay payments even further.

For many companies that have tried adding on an interest penalty, the real disadvantage has been the clerical cost. With computerized billing and receivable systems, the accurate calculation of a charge, at any interest rate and based on any nominal formula, is very simple. But how do you communicate this to the customer. Many years ago, businesses would ship merchandise throughout the month, invoicing each separate shipment, but then recapping the month's activity on a month-end statement. Customers were expected to pay from the month end statement, corresponding more or less to the department store or American Express statements you receive once a month.

But in today's business environment only the very smallest mom and pop stores pay from statements. It is general practice to pay directly from invoices. In fact, most firms throw out any vendor monthly statements. Good internal control systems will preclude any disbursement from a statement and insist on paying only from an invoice. Given this situation, you can only let your customers know they owe you interest by generating a new, separate interest-only invoice. This now requires a corresponding entry into your own receivable system, plus recognition of the interest charge as interest income in that month's financial statements. So far, so good, if the new interest invoice is paid; it will have been worth the clerical effort at least.

But what if the customer disregards your new interest invoice? How much effort are you going to put into collecting it? Reality suggests that for good ongoing customers this is going to be written off sooner or later, probably at the insistence of your own Sales Department. "Why antagonize good old Joe?" Then you will have to reverse the invoice by issuing a credit memo, which will clear out the receivable balance and charge (reduce) interest income. Assume that the customer is a one-shot and that you do not expect to sell to the company again. What will you do when the original amount owed on the merchandise has been paid and the only open item is the lonely interest charge sitting on your aged receivable balance getting older by the day? Obviously you are not going to court to collect it, you have no further leverage with the customer from holding up future shipments, and once again the solution is to write it off.

As a generalization, any firm that expects an interest charge to do the hard work required to collect outstanding receivable balances is fooling itself. Management effort is required, and, while it might seem tempting, you are only kidding yourself if you think an invoice for interest, which most customers know you will not collect, is a good substitute. You could think at this point, "but we *will* collect the interest." That's fine if you mean it and do it, but please check with your marketing and salespeople first. Is customer ill will worth a few dollars of interest income?

Should Sales or Accounting Have Responsibility for Collections?

Unless a single individual or department in larger organizations has primary responsibility for collection efforts, the job is not going to get done. Relatively few individuals truly *enjoy* making phone calls to collect receivables. One manager, for example, enjoyed this aspect of the job, devoted one hour every afternoon to it, and invariably came out of his office in a great mood, laughing most of the time at the arguments and excuses his customers were trying to employ. Taking a positive attitude like that is desirable, but not necessarily easy to replicate. Most people treat collection efforts as part of the job, something to be endured, and at bottom seeing that they do it in exchange for getting paid.

This leads directly to a technique that some companies have found to be successful. Give the responsibility to the Sales Department, specifically to the salesperson who brought in the order. Nobody knows the customer better. Nobody is, or at least should be, more knowledgeable about the customer's economic picture and cash flow. Nobody is in a better position to relate the acceptance of future orders to payments on current balances owing. In short, the sales rep is the perfect solution.

There are two arguments against this assignment of responsibility. First is that salespersons are hired to sell, not collect. Working on collections is perceived to be a waste of a very valuable resource. Second, having the sales representative hound the customer for cash may affect the customer's willingness to buy more.

Quite a few businesses have resolved these conflicts constructively. Compensation based on sales volume (commission income) is paid only when the customer pays. No cash is paid to the salesperson until our company receives its cash. Switching over to this system from one that pays based on orders entered or on shipment may present a timing problem, but that is resolvable, as will be discussed. Payment *to* the salesperson based on payment *from* the customer immediately makes identical the interests of our company and the sales reps' own self-interest. At this point the salesperson is at least motivated (a reasonable assumption being that sales representatives are motivated by money!) to try to collect outstanding balances. Is it going to be a waste of time?

Let's put this in perspective. No time need be spent on current receivables. That is, if normal payment terms are 30 days, everything in the under-30 column can be disregarded. This will make up 50 to 70 percent of the total line items in a typical aging schedule. The first call to the customer as soon as the item becomes even slightly past due, as discussed, is to find out if there is a quality problem. Who better to make this determination than the individual personally responsible for the ongoing relationship? Who better to start resolving any customer service issue than the sales representative?

Assuming that the nonpayment stems from cash flow or customer timing issues, the sales representative should turn the account back to the Accounting Department for the normal follow-ups. Noting the customer's promises and then seeing they meet their commitments is actually quite routine and does not require the salesperson's time—although, if significant dollars are involved, it is surprising how much interest an individual may display in monitoring current progress.

A decision to turn the account over to a professional collection agency should definitely be made only with the agreement, or at least the knowledge, of the sales rep. The potential adverse consequences on future sales is obvious. Offsetting this is the potential for receiving some cash now as a result of the agency's efforts, as contrasted with a total write-off later.

The second argument against giving the Sales Department primary responsibility for collections is that a customer purchasing agent, the salesperson's primary contact with the customer, may be reluctant to place additional orders with a sales rep who just got off the phone asking for payment. True, but nobody said that the salesperson has to work through the Purchasing Department on collections. Dealing with the customer's Accounts Payable Department, which is the normal route for an Accounting Department's collection effort, should be the salesperson's method also. We have already recommended getting to know the customer's payables system and personnel. Aren't salespeople, with their particular personality traits and selling skills, more likely to accomplish this than accountants sitting in their offices? (Since the author is an accountant, implied criticisms of the personality or skills of his professional peers must be considered fair comment.) With the myriad demands on any company's cash resources, it really takes selling skills to convince a customer to put *us* ahead of others. Put another way, perhaps someone in the Accounting Department who is good at collections could be earning more, both for herself and the firm, by going into sales.

Switching over to a "cash received," from an "orders placed," basis for both calculating and paying sales commissions can be a very simple and straightforward process. Do not switch over on specific orders placed after a point in time. There will be a two- to four-month lag, and it is unfair to the salespeople to wait or have a gap in compensation.

Switch over all at once. If you have been paying commissions on orders received through March, then start paying April 1 on cash receipts. A big objection is going to be raised by someone that, "We are paying twice for the *same* order." This is absolutely correct. The cash received on April 1 relates to an order shipped in March, and commissions were already paid.

Look at it the other way, however, and the logic follows. In March we paid for one month's orders (or billings as the case may be). In April we will be paying for one month's cash receipts. At the end of the year we will have paid for 12 months of business. True, on one specific set of orders there will two payments, but total compensation is not affected. In a firm with a number of sales representatives there may be some inequities resulting from the timing of specific large orders. Do not be afraid of a small overpayment to one or two people, since the benefits of getting wholehearted cooperation from the sales staff is critical, and a little extra money now is a good investment. Similarly, if a large cash payment was received on March 30, hurting someone else's pay when starting over with the new system, an individual adjustment will be worthwhile in the long run.

Paying sales representatives based on cash received is a win-win situation. Since the switchover can be made smoothly and without cost, it truly is a good way of installing the concepts of Total Cash Management in the marketing organization.

8

Dealing with a
Cash Shortfall

*Even the weakest foreboding of what is to come
is better than a costly surprise.*
ROBERT METZ AND GEORGE STASEN
It's a Sure Thing [p. 64]

If your organization is blessed with an abundance of cash—for example, you have surplus cash to invest—if the business is profitable, and if growth opportunities are limited, feel free to skip this chapter. Most smaller firms, and even a few larger ones, however, suffer from occasional periods where cash balances may not be sufficient to meet all pressing needs. In Chap. 7, in our discussion of collecting Accounts Receivable, we looked at techniques for convincing firms to pay us. The point made was that if the demands for cash are greater than the supply, the debtors have to make choices—and in that case we want them to choose *us*. In this chapter we put ourselves in that unfortunate position. How can we prepare for a cash squeeze? How do we allocate a limited supply of cash? Can we obtain more cash from some other source?

Using the IRS as a Source of Funds

First, a warning. Almost without exception a company will try to meet its payroll obligations. Employees usually live pretty much hand to mouth, and *must* get paid. Put another way, being late with a payroll, with the possible one-day excuse of a computer breakdown, sends a message to all workers that their job is in jeopardy. Of course this will not truly be a surprise, since the rumor mill will undoubtedly have been going full tilt and employees will have discussed among themselves all sorts of scenarios. Nonetheless, cold reality will hit with a vengeance if the organization misses even a single payroll. The good employees will jump ship immediately, the remaining ones will be hard to motivate, and the organization is poised for a quick jump into Chapter 11 proceedings.

So we must assume that the entire cash gathering resources are focused on one goal—getting enough cash to meet the payroll. Before going any further, you should get out your most recent payroll stub. Look at the net pay, the amount of the check or the amount deposited in your personal banking account. Then look at the *gross* pay and calculate the total amount of deductions. This will vary widely, depending on federal tax brackets, state and local taxes, voluntary withholding [401(k)], and employee contributions to benefit plans (life insurance and health coverage). In many circumstances net pay will be no more than 60 to 70 percent of gross pay.

From the perspective of the company this means that if Friday the 12 is payday, only 60 to 70 percent of the total payroll must actually be available in cash in the bank. Assuming everyone is paid by direct deposit to their individual checking account, the money will be taken out of the company's account on Thursday so employees will have it Friday. That means to meet a Friday payroll the company has to have collected funds a day early. As was discussed in Chap. 5 on payroll, if you are still paying by check, it is unlikely that all paychecks will be cashed on payday, and if deposited by employees in their own checking account, they will not clear your bank until Monday or Tuesday. This gives the hard-pressed company another weekend to obtain enough cash to cover the payroll checks.

But irrespective of whether the payroll goes out of your bank on Thursday, or you have until the following Tuesday if you paid by check, there is no question about an absolute need for cash equal to 60 to 70 percent of the gross payroll. But what about the 30 to 40 percent of gross payroll that is *not* paid out in cash on payday? It is still a liability of the company, owed to someone.

For convenience we can look at this 30 to 40 percent in three parts. First, there are voluntary withholdings from employees for things like insurance and savings plans. Second, are legally required deductions for state and local income (and other) taxes. Third—and most important—are the Federal income tax and social security tax deductions we are all too familiar with.

Over the years, in an attempt to balance the budget, Congress has mandated that companies turn over withheld Federal taxes (*plus* the companies' own share of social security taxes) very soon after employees are paid. In years past, depending on the dollar amount of Federal taxes withheld, companies often had a week or more to remit to the government, but the tax laws have gradually been tightened to the point where there is—if one is going to comply with the law—no effective delay possible.

But if you simply do not have the cash what can you do? Can you give Uncle Sam a rubber check? No. The easiest solution is to do nothing, hoping that sufficient cash will come in to allow you to pay the Federal taxes. After all, with possibly 10 million employers depositing withheld taxes, how closely can the IRS keep track of just one small firm? Obviously, no matter how good their computer system, the service does not have enough resources to monitor every deposit every payday. What's more, how do they even know *when* my payroll was paid? They cannot possibly know that money was due, much less just how much. Thus if you are really short of cash it is easy to put the IRS on hold, to let them wait their turn, possibly even to meet your next payroll (net of taxes, of course) before paying the taxes from the previous payroll.

Wrong! Do not do this, ever. The IRS can be very tough on you *as an individual* if you screw up your personal income tax, and if you fail to file at all. If a former Mayor of New York City can fail to file for three consecutive years and get no more than a slap on the wrist (after paying the taxes and penalties), it is obvious to anyone else that, serious as it may be, the world does not come to an end. And, if you really are short of money, say, like the famous boxer Joe Louis was at one point, the IRS can and will work out terms with you, possibly even settling for 50¢ or less on the dollar. Not a good situation, but certainly not critical.

For reasons that are not totally clear, the IRS treats unpaid (even underpaid) withholding taxes very seriously. A dollar of unpaid withholding taxes is a bright red flag to every revenue agent, and is treated far *more* seriously than failing to file your own personal annual income tax return. The IRS has available to it penalties for not paying withheld taxes when due that are truly Draconian. Would you believe *personal* liability on the part of corporate officers, or even the office manager or bookkeeper? Would you believe actual physical seizure of corporate assets and padlocking of business doors? The correct answer to both questions is yes.

> *Note:* This is not a joking matter. The IRS really does go after individuals responsible for filing and paying withheld taxes. They really do seize business assets. It is hard to accept that withheld taxes have the same or a higher priority than meeting your payroll, but they do. You do not go to jail if you go bankrupt without having paid your employees; people have gone to jail for not paying the IRS the firm's withheld taxes.

Hoping for sufficient cash to come in in the next few days to meet your withheld tax obligations is unwise. The odds are against you, and if you lose, you as an individual lose "big time."

Having said all that, what should a company do if it is so short of cash that there is not enough to meet both the net payroll and the withheld taxes?

Short-Term Solutions

Some problems have no good solution, and nearly running out of cash just before payday is one of them. Realistically, going to your bank and asking for an emergency loan is going to raise a lot of questions by the bank officer. Holding off paying other suppliers will already have been done, but, as an option, it is possible that your major supplier, assuming you are a good and profitable customer, will have an interest in maintaining your company's existence. Personal funds are a possibility as is borrowing money from relatives or friends. A fourth choice, maybe the best of all, is to phone customers with outstanding receivable balances and straight out ask them to pay. Finally, what seems the hardest may in fact be the easiest, and that is to tell the truth, be up front with employees and ask them to share the problem temporarily! Let's look at each of these in detail.

Bank Loan

Working closely with your bank is an essential part of Total Cash Management. Over the last 20 years, banks have lost a significant market for their services—large Fortune 500 companies. These large firms can actually borrow at lower cost directly in the money market rather than using intermediaries such as banks. As banks lost Fortune 500 companies, they proclaimed that they were going after the *middle market*, a term never clearly defined. What they really meant was that if the bank could not obtain profitable business today from General Electric or General Mills or General Motors, they would go down one or two notches, but always with the hope that the Generals would somehow, some day, come back. In short, relatively few banks have been truly committed to small and medium-sized businesses.

The real test of commitment, of a long-term relationship, is a willingness to roll with the punches. A banker should not be expected to correct the mistakes of a business owner. A banker, who by definition, does not have an equity position, never shares in the upside profits and therefore must protect himself from unnecessary downside risk. Nonetheless, nobody is perfect. Sooner or later everyone makes a mistake and/or has a run of bad luck—in the worst of all cases, both can happen at once.

That is the point at which a bank's real level of commitment is tested. Despite advertising claims to the contrary, and more in line with the old saw that, "Bankers only lend money to those who don't need it," no banker wants to "Throw good money after bad." It is easier to say no than to risk an even bigger loss. Contrary to public opinion, banks do expect losses, they just don't like them. Risk is the name of the game in banking, but unnecessary risk makes no sense.

So, what is unnecessary risk? In the context of a real cash shortage, granting a request to a last minute caller on Wednesday whose payroll is due on Friday, and therefore would like to increase the line of credit temporarily, looks like unnecessary risk. Unless the borrower can convince the banker that the need is truly temporary, and there was an excellent reason for *not* anticipating the need earlier, the bank officer is very likely to come to the conclusion that saying no, possibly putting the customer out of business right now, may be preferable to getting in deeper and having an even bigger loss later.

Adding to this natural tendency is the changing mindset of bankers vis à vis their regulators. Following the savings and loan crisis, banks are not only more sensitive to actual losses, but they are also reluctant to have a loan on their books that a bank examiner would classify as substandard. There is a direct correlation between a bank's capital and its ability to grow. Most banks want to grow (if, for no other reason, larger banks must pay bigger salaries to their staff) and the principal constraint on growth is the availability of capital. After the massive writeoffs from loans made to both real estate and leveraged buyouts, bank capital was severely eroded. At the same time new regulations were introduced increasing the amount of capital banks had to have. To top off what bankers themselves thought was excessive punishment for their sins, bank examiners started scrutinizing loans more closely than ever.

Every time a bank examiner found a loan that appeared risky, the bank had to set up a bad-debt reserve for part or all of the loan. Every dollar of increase in the bad-debt reserve came directly out of capital. If capital ratios got too low, the banking authorities could take over the bank. At a minimum they would insist the Board of Directors get new management.

In summary, the penalties for taking on risky loans were Draconian. It was easier, not to say healthier, for the continuity of employment of the individual banker, to just say no. Risk truly became a four-letter word.

How do you evaluate risk if you are a banker? Put yourself in the banker's shoes. What do you think of the business management skills of someone who is not on top of their cash flows, who does not know until Wednesday that there will not be enough cash on Friday to meet the payroll? If a company does not have enough cash to meet its payroll, what is implied about the firm's basic profitability? Does it have a positive or a negative cash flow? Undoubtedly, a negative cash flow means that without some fundamental changes in operations things will only get worse!

This brief discussion is not meant to be pessimistic, only realistic. One of the key lessons of Total Cash Management is anticipation—knowing what will happen before decisions are made. It is easy to feel sorry for an entrepreneur with an immediate cash flow problem—after all, almost everyone individually in private life has had the experience. The point is that banks, and bank loans, are not likely to be a solution.

About the only way out is to demonstrate to the bank that they will be worse off if they do not make the loan. That is, the bank will suffer an immediate loss if the company goes out of business, but there is hope of recovery if things are allowed to continue. That hope, then, can only be obtained with the additional funds for this Friday's payroll. This is a really tough sell. If a businessperson can make this sale to a banker, selling more of the firm's basic product or services to existing and new customers should be a snap!

Supplier Credit

Some business firms have raised the use of supplier credit to an art form. They are believers in the Golden Rule. This particular version, contrary to what might have been taught in Sunday School, goes like this, "Whoever has the gold, makes the rules." Translated, it means that in any transaction between two parties, things are negotiable, but the party with greater economic strength is likely to set the ground rules.

All other things being equal, sellers need buyers. In a market economy, with numerous suppliers, the person with the money (the buyer) can call the shots. Does this mean that you as an individual can go into a Walgreen's drugstore and start negotiating the price of a bottle of aspirin? Of course not. If you ran a nursing home could you negotiate a discount on purchases from that same drugstore? You probably could. Volume makes a difference.

Perhaps the greatest asset any business has is its customer base. The familiar business term "goodwill" is based on this concept. The implications are clear, customers are in the driver's seat as long as there is some significant size relationship. Walgreen's, as a chain, can't afford to negotiate with each individual customer. But the local store manager can afford to negotiate with a nursing home manager who represents a potentially substantial sales volume for that store. Office supply stores have certainly adopted this philosophy. The price you pay for a ballpoint pen, walking in off the street, is going to be 20 to 30 percent higher than your office manager pays; of course, the office manager buys a lot more than one pen at a time.

What this is leading up to is a recognition that with your two or three largest suppliers you are probably an important factor in their profit picture. For the individual salesperson your volume is certainly significant. Who better to get on your side than the salesperson whose commissions depend on your continuing to buy? As we saw in much more detail in Chaps. 3 and 5, payment terms are highly negotiable. This means that, if anticipated in advance, normal 30-day terms can easily be extended to 60 or even 75 days. Clear communication is needed. There may be some downside risk in becoming too closely involved with one supplier. Other problems have to be analyzed, but the message should be clear. Vendors have a strong self-motivation for making sure your business is viable. They can and will help, but not at the last minute. Anticipating the need for additional credit terms, and then negotiating with vendors on the basis of *their* self-interest, may be a very sound strategy.

Add Personal Funds

Of all the options this is the least desirable, but often the only real alternative. You should ask yourself the same questions the bank will ask. Is this truly temporary, and if so why wasn't it anticipated? If it is not just a temporary blip, what is the long-term prognosis? Throwing good money after bad only prolongs the agony of admitting defeat.

The history of many entrepreneurs, is that they had to put in their own money not just at the start but later. Most business plans underestimate both the amount and the timing of start-up expenses, and overestimate the speed with which customers pay for the sales. Subsequent cash shortages, therefore, may be no more than a reflection of poor original planning. A new revised business plan, based on experience, is more realistic, but also demands more capital.

Supplying more capital can be justified if (1) the original business idea was good, (2) things are more or less on schedule, and (3) the only trouble was that there was an unanticipated learning curve for budgeting and forecasting. It is part of the price of learning about any business. The next time, if there is one, you will be less optimistic and more realistic.

If the cash shortage is, however, due to continued operating losses (a negative cash flow), very serious consideration should be given to reevaluating the original business plan. Statistics show that the vast majority of business ventures fail within the first few years. This is no consolation, financially, but it is also a reason to face the realities of life. If your business goes under this in no way diminishes you as an individual. Bad timing or bad luck may be the key factor. The point here is not to cheer you up—there are plenty of self-help books that can do that—but to cut your losses as early as possible.

Look at it this way. If you quit now, saving your remaining resources, perhaps you will be able to start over again, either in the same business or a different one. You will be like a general who retreats in the face of overwhelming enemy odds. Don't repeat the mistake of General Haig in World War I who kept sending Allied troops over the top to a certain death, in the mistaken belief that he would overpower the Germans with the massive resources he was prepared to invest. Resources, in this case, that were human lives.

The only time to put more of your own money into the business is when you are absolutely sure you know what went wrong, and have a certainty that the problems have been solved. Otherwise you are just prolonging the agony, and will still fail. What we have said here applies just as much, if not more so, to getting additional money from friends and relatives. Not only do you risk their money, but you risk their friendship as well.

If you have a truly great business idea, and if the *only* problem is a long-term shortage of capital, then professional *venture capitalists*, sometimes referred to as angels, may be tempted to commit their funds. But this will truly be on an arm's-length basis. The amount of equity they will want will be staggering. You may well end up as a minority investor in your own business. Further, this type of investor has less than no interest in bailing out a business on a short-term basis.

There are a number of books dealing with outside investor funds. Just remember that they are looking for a 3- to 10-fold return on their money—and will want control of your firm if they invest. Further, they look at 100 or more opportunities before making a single investment. For a company in trouble to start looking for funds from an outside venture capitalist is roughly equivalent to buying a ticket in the Irish Sweepstakes: It *could* work, but I would not want to bet my life on it.

Finally, with regard to Small Business Administration (SBA) loans, the theory is to help small businesses obtain badly needed capital. In practice it rarely seems to work out well. Whether it is politics, or bureaucracy, or both, SBA loans have rarely been the salvation of any business with a cash problem. And even under the best of circumstances they will probably want the firm's principals to provide personal guarantees. It is a great disappointment for many people to hear, but the SBA is not part of the solution.

Call Customers and Ask for Payment

The last section was deliberately written in a pessimistic tone—primarily because the real options facing a cash-short firm are quite few. The good news is that occasionally customers can be urged to pay early. This is not a recommended technique day-in and day-out, but as discussed in Chap. 7, many businesses (and individuals) will try to help out in case of need by paying early, at least on a one-shot basis.

> A small business was going to go public, and for reasons having to do with a rather sophisticated tax strategy, would benefit greatly by reducing accounts receivable to a minimum within a six-week time frame. A letter was sent out early in May to *every* creditor explaining that there was a very valid business reason, that it would be considered as a great favor if the balance could be paid by June 30. Some 60 percent of all creditors complied with the request, the tax strategy worked and the firm went public. None of the creditors benefited directly. In practice, they simply sent in money earlier than they would have in exchange for helping another business with its plans.

The lesson here is valid across the board. Asking people to pay what they owe you may be difficult in the sense that very few individuals *like* to ask for money. But irrespective of the reason, a surprisingly large number of us do not mind going out of our way to help someone else out, particularly if all that is required is to do something today that would have to be done very soon anyway.

In short, if you really are facing a cash shortage, get on the phone and call the people who owe you money. You can tell them, and it is the truth, "One of my customers did not pay when I expected and I really need the money. Can you help me out?" Or, "I am a cash-basis taxpayer and I really need the money by the end of the month." This is actually true of public accounting firms which are partnerships and often want to maximize cash flow in a particular year. More than once the author has cut a check early to help another business out. Each of these techniques is guaranteed to work—once! Repeated more than once a year, however, you will very quickly wear out your welcome, particularly if you are dealing month-in and month-out with the same customers. Your customers will resent hearing any story from you two times in a row.

Talk Openly with Employees, Vendors, and Creditors

In the author's experience, one of the biggest mistakes businesses make in relationship to cash shortages is to keep things quiet, hoping that nobody will notice. After all, in almost all cases a cash deficit is a sign of a business that is having trouble. The next most common thought is that if others find out your organization is in trouble bad things will happen, such as suppliers not selling to you, customers not buying from you, employees quitting, and banks calling their loans and forcing you into bankruptcy. This short list is enough.

If all these fears were to be translated into reality, then keeping quiet about your problems would make eminent sense. If even one of these fears: vendors, customers, employees, or banks, came true, your recovery could be difficult indeed. But the best antidote for panic is to look the situation straight in the eye. Reality is different from nameless fears.

Vendors do not want to cut you off. Businesses make a profit by selling goods and services to customers. Are your vendors making a profit on their sales to you? In almost all cases the answer is yes. Where vendors want assurance is that what you owe them will be paid. They don't want to throw good money after bad any more than you do.

The only reason for a vendor to stop selling you is when she cannot see how today's sales will be paid for. Painful as it is, she will even be willing to wait for payment on today's outstanding balances, as long as current sales result in cash inflow. If you were to file for Chapter 11 bankruptcy, your existing receivable balances on her books would be frozen—and the possibility of recovering 100¢ on the dollar is virtually nil. Creditors never are paid in full from bankruptcy if for no other reason than there are extremely high legal, audit, and consulting fees! Nobody *wants* you to file for bankruptcy.

Draw the logical conclusion, therefore, that owing vendors a lot of money which cannot be paid right now, when the basic business is at least breaking even on current cash flow, is actually good news. Current purchases by you will generate profits for your suppliers and will be paid for. Any sort of reasonable repayment schedule on existing debts is better than nothing.

In short, go to your vendors, taking the initiative. Offer them the following, current payment for current purchases and x dollars a month on past due balances, without any interest charges. Their alternative is for you to file for Chapter 11. Putting yourself in their position, which would you choose?

Customers represent a slightly different situation. Except for natural monopolies like public utilities, customers usually have several alternate suppliers to choose from. Therefore your customers *can* go to one of your competitors quite easily. Keep in mind that most individuals, and business organizations for that matter, suffer from inertia. Developing new buying patterns and dealing with new supplier personnel is not undertaken unless something in the existing relationship has deteriorated. In the real world your customers really "don't give a damn, my dear" about your financial health or cash flow.

Customers are interested in service and price, or to use a popular term, *Quality*. If your cash flow problems do not affect the quality of your service, such as not cutting back on the items you offer for sale, why should you lose any customers? What really happens in practice is that as a business experiences cash flow problems, quality does go down and customers respond to that change. In fact, they neither know nor care just *why* your quality has deteriorated. After one or two bad situations they say to themselves, "Let's try Jones down the street next time, the sales representatives here were slow" ... [or] ... "The choice of merchandise just isn't what it used to be" ... [or] ... "The place just isn't as bright and clean as it used to be."

The lesson is clear. In case of cash flow troubles, the emphasis on Quality, however defined, must *increase*. You should not tell customers you are having problems. Even more, however, you should not give them any reason to suspect there is a problem or any reason to go elsewhere. Of course, many profitable companies have lost sight of Quality service and lost customers. An argument could be made that a primary reason for cash flow problems was a prior lack of emphasis on providing Total Quality to customers. It is never too late to start improving quality. As U.S. automobile companies found out, it may take a long time for past perceptions to be turned around, even after real product quality and customer service has improved. That does not mean that a change in Quality, and the attitude toward Quality, should be discarded as an option—just don't expect instantaneous miracles.

Employees may be a firm's most important asset, and the one most vulnerable to the adverse effects of cash problems. Since most lower paid employees live from payday to payday, missing a payroll is a very bad symbol, not to mention a very bad symptom. As already indicated, such a short-term problem requires immediate communication.

The real problem is slightly longer-term. A company with cash flow problems is going to be cutting expenses. In practice, this means the company will have to downsize, or rightsize, that is, some employees will be laid off, dismissed, or fired. To the extent that management can choose who stays and who goes, the actual performance level may increase! Those still on the job may suddenly appreciate what they have.

What should be of concern is not current morale, but two impacts which may manifest themselves over coming months. Uncertainty about the future of the enterprise will cause every employee to reassess long-term career plans—and the best employees may decide there are greater opportunities elsewhere. In the short run the problem is straightforward. How can customer service be maintained and quality increased, with fewer employees? In the long term, how are we going to retain the key employees?

Customer Service. Total Quality ultimately means no more or no less than being responsive to customer demands or expectations, all of which comes from your employees. If employees are worried about their jobs, or whether the next payroll is going to be met, how do you motivate them to *increase* customer service? Ultimately, cash flow comes from satisfied customers who buy your product or service, and are willing to pay for it. Employees therefore hold the key to the continuity of the business and its very survival. A cash shortage is a symptom of a problem. The underlying problem can be addressed directly, but if employees do not get on board, and truly make customers or clients feel welcome, the prognosis is grim.

The solution, once again, is to treat employees as partners—which they are. If the business succeeds, they have a job. If the business fails, they are unemployed. Saying this is unpleasant, but it is the truth. Most important, the employees already know this, but are bound to be skeptical about management. Without doubt, when talking among themselves, they have been saying, and are currently saying, "Don't *they* (management) know what's going on?" As management you must communicate that, yes, you are aware of things, you want them to be aware of the real situation, and you need their help. Almost without exception, individuals are willing to help in any reasonable way when asked. Any employee who is not willing to help out in a crisis is one whose services should be dispensed with at once—both to save money immediately and to show you are serious.

Customer service can be maintained and even improved. It will not happen by itself. It takes positive management action. But at a time of cash shortage, maintaining and improving such quality service should be, to quote Ford's famous motto, "Job 1."

Retaining key employees is actually the harder job for an owner or manager. People are always willing to pull together and work harder in what is considered a crisis situation. Crises cannot go on forever. Assuming that the short-term cash problem is resolved satisfactorily, the aftereffects may be likened to post-trauma stress. Good employees, the ones you most want to build your business upon, are going to be approached by competitors. The temptation for them to jump ship is going to be enhanced by a prospective employer who will compare the future growth opportunities in the two organizations.

The term "partner" was used because at a time of crisis all employees have to share in the situation. Partnering is not something that can effectively be turned on and then turned off. If a business has survived a crisis through the actions of its employees, then at least the key personnel have to be rewarded in such a way that they truly feel an identity of interest with the future success of the enterprise. This is not the appropriate place to talk about the details of long-term stock options, bonus plans, profit sharing or any of the multitude of benefit and compensation programs that are available.

What is important is that some changes in personnel relationships, with attendant long-term cash implications, have to be made. In almost every large publicly traded company, the Chairman's message to shareholders repeats the mantra that "Our employees are our most important asset."

Trite, but true. For a smaller firm, one that has survived a cash crisis, steps have to be taken to ensure that key employees are motivated to stay.

To date, nobody has been able to find a better motivator than cash. Whether paid out in current salary, at the end of the year as a bonus, or some years down the line, is not important. What has to be recognized is that if key employees have really helped out in a time of need, some reward is due. That reward, no matter how structured, ultimately boils down to cash. Put another way, there is more than one type of cost to an organization whose cash situation has weathered a crisis. Not only must cash be found to solve the short-term problem, but additional costs in the future will present themselves, in turn requiring cash. Far better not to have had the problem in the first place.

Preparing for a Cash Squeeze

As was discussed in more detail in Chap. 6, there are two separate aspects which must be looked at independently. First is to anticipate what is likely to happen, and second, knowing what to expect, what can you do about it. An analogy would be if the company picnic were scheduled for a Saturday afternoon six weeks from now. What if it rains? If you have sufficient notice, you can reschedule the date, or move it to a different location, or hire a tent. If you wait until Friday evening, your choices are much more limited, and may include getting wet. Can we forecast the weather six weeks in advance? No. Can we make plans in case it does? Yes.

Many people have found that *preparing* for rain often brings a sunny day. Carrying an umbrella sometimes seems to have a positive effect! With cash management, the same is true. Anticipating the problem may not make it go away (it still may rain on Saturday), but the consequences will not be as severe.

This chapter started out with the hypothesis that a company did not have enough cash to meet its payroll, and warned against borrowing from the IRS by not paying out withheld taxes and employer FICA contributions. At that point options are limited, as we saw. Now let's reconstruct the situation and see what *could* have been done.

Cash is the lifeblood of any business, and like a doctor who measures every patient's blood pressure, *monitoring* cash is essential. A daily report of cash receipts and disbursements must be maintained as discussed in Chap. 6, if for no other reason than to provide the basis for forecasting. History does repeat itself. Patterns of inflows and outflows exist in every organization. Understanding, and then utilizing this information requires a simple database. The daily record of receipts and disbursements is that database.

The second step is *forecasting*, particularly if you do not have a sufficient line of credit. In the absence of any positive steps to change current behavior or actions, you simply cannot afford to find out on Wednesday that there is not enough cash to meet the payroll on Friday. As we shall see, bankers do not like surprises, but they can take bad news. If you go to your bank on July 1 and tell them that it looks like the August 20 payroll is going to be tight, what do you think the reaction will be? Whatever it is then, it is many times better than calling the same bank officer up on August 18 and delivering the same message.

The third step is *controlling* inflows and outflows to achieve desired results. Most of the rest of this book deals with how this can be done. In fact, the very essence of Total Cash Management (TCM) is developing systems to control cash, and making sure that every manager and employee understands the necessity of anticipating the cash consequences of each business decision. Given sufficient lead time, changes can be made in invoicing of customers, following-up on collection efforts, negotiating terms with vendors, and so forth.

Allocating Limited Cash Among Competing Demands

When a company is in the middle of a cash squeeze the truth is that interested parties—employees, trade creditors, and banks—already know that there is a problem of some sort. Payments to the trade will have slowed down, employees at a minimum are intimately familiar with what is happening just by keeping their eyes and ears open, while knowledgeable bankers have a sixth sense in this regard. So there really is no surprise if you talk openly with them.

What is the primary interest of those who expect to receive cash payments from you? Obviously, number one is the cash itself. But a very close second is *knowing* what is happening and what your plans are. Creditors hate uncertainty. Even the worst news is better than no news. The most typical reaction when cash is short is to hide, not answer the phone, and stall those who do get through. Most creditors are sophisticated enough to know that this is, in fact, a symptom of a deeper seated problem.

Think of this as an individual with a persistent headache who fears going to the doctor because it *may* be a brain tumor. Finally, unable to stand the pain no more, an appointment is made and the cause turns out to be only migraine. Looking back, it was the waiting and uncertainty, the fear of the unknown, that were even worse than the pain. A generalization worth pondering goes something like this:

People can take bad news; they cannot take surprises.

Telling someone you cannot pay on time is certainly bad news, but a certain amount of slow payments is par for the course in any business. Bankruptcy, a complete loss, is a surprise. Put yourself in the creditor's place and determine which of the following statements is going to be more palatable.

Plan A: "I know you granted me net 30 terms and that I am now 10 days past due, but I will have something for you in the next two weeks. (A muffled "Ha, Ha" is likely to be heard in the background.)

Plan B: "I know you granted me net 30 terms and that I am now 10 days past due. I am, in fact, having a cash squeeze and am running behind with everybody. My cash flow projection shows no payments to the trade for the next 30 days on existing balances. I can pay those balances 20 percent a month for five months. Meanwhile, since I am reorganizing the business as follows: [this assumes a *real* plan exists] ... I would appreciate it if you could continue to ship to me and I will pay within 30 days on all *current* purchases."

As a creditor, on the other side of this conversation, which would you prefer? If you chose Plan B, it suggests that from the perspective of the cash short firm a more strategic approach will get to the heart of the real problem. This means that you must have a good plan and a good forecast, a plan that is indeed workable and that you fully intend to carry it out. Credibility, once lost, is almost impossible to regain. Whatever promises you make must then be kept. *Any* reasonable plan is better than no plan from the perspective of the creditor. What he does not want to happen is to be made a fool of—extending more credit or time and then being even worse off.

When Eastern Airlines was in bankruptcy, the court believed Eastern's management that things would get better and by law was able to impose continuing delays on creditors who kept arguing that things were *not* going to get better. Unfortunately, Eastern's management and the bankruptcy court were wrong, the creditors were correct; things got worse and the creditors suffered almost a total loss. There was virtually nothing they could do because the bankruptcy laws gave total power and control to the judge.

In situations that do not involve bankruptcy, the creditors can call the shots. If they believe you and can trust your commitments almost any plan of repayment will be accepted. After all, certainty of payment, no matter how delayed, is better than a current loss. If your firm survives you will be grateful to those who went along so they have the opportunity of maintaining a very good supplier/customer relationship.

With respect to employees and the payroll due, the only solution is to tell them the facts, pay as much as you can now, and hope that they have faith in you and your new business plan. You may well have to make some promises relative to sharing in future profits if they sacrifice now. That is still preferable to having your best employees leave. (Human nature is such that the very employees you need most are most vulnerable to leaving, while the least productive people probably have no realistic alternative. The worst of all worlds, therefore, is trying to rebuild a weak business with your weakest employees. Anticipating this, by working out specific deals with the truly key staff, is probably a good idea but outside the scope of this book.)

Now assume that things are just bad, not catastrophic. You have managed to obtain sufficient funds to meet the payroll, but not enough to get current on all seriously past due amounts. Creditors are calling, making threatening demands, and the continuity of shipments is at stake. Of course, some vendors are going to talk about COD shipments, which protects them but puts you to extra expense and effort. Who wants to keep cash available to give to a delivery person? Better to send a check in advance with the order, if the items are truly critical. Saving the cash for 7 to 10 days, by waiting for a COD delivery not only affects your credit rating (vendors report to credit rating agencies that you are on COD terms) but is plain inefficient.

Now let's suppose you are just about breaking even in terms of current cash flow, but are not gaining ground very quickly. You can pay for current purchases but cannot significantly reduce your existing backlog of past due amounts. Who gets priority as cash becomes available? There are at least three strategies:

1. Pay those who scream the loudest.

2. Pay those who are most important.

3. Pay everyone a little bit, trying to be fair to all.

Human nature being as it is, the first strategy is quite common. Peace at any price may not be fair to kinder and gentler creditors, and may end up alienating those suppliers you really need. But there is something to be said to stop being hounded. And, of course, that is why some creditors are so persistent, they know that the squeaking wheel *does* get the oil. Perhaps the best way of looking at it is this: With limited cash available, you *know* that not everyone will be paid, no matter how much juggling you do. Therefore what is your next scarcest resource? The answer is time.

Allocating limited cash among creditors should be decided on the grounds of what is best for your business, not the creditors' demands. As was discussed, open communication really is best in the long run. It is no surprise if you tell creditors you can't pay right away. They already *know* that just by looking at the aging of their accounts receivable. What does any creditor really want? Can you satisfy that desire?

Any creditor's number one desire certainly is to receive cash. But a close second, and more realistic, is *knowing* when they can expect payment. Then, when a promise is made, it should be kept, which means that making unrealistic promises today to buy time ends up being totally counterproductive.

Credibility tomorrow is even more important than cash today.

You have to be the master of your own cash flow, not be tugged back and forth by competing creditors. A juggling act, the strategy of trying to keep everyone happy, is doomed to failure on day one. The more of your past due amounts you pay off the greedier the creditors will become for you to get totally caught up. It becomes a vicious circle. A vendor to whom you are past due by 90 days for $10,000, and who does not know when he will get paid may be frustrated and angry, but is essentially at your mercy. Once you start reducing the amount, however, his latent paranoia will come to the surface. "You still owe me $4000. Why aren't you paying me? Who are you *really* favoring? Should I get tougher so *I* can move to the head of the line? That sounds like a good idea!" Multiplied by 50 irate vendors, how much time are you going to spend on the phone, removing paper from the fax machine, and opening hate mail?

The solution is straightforward. Develop a plan—even if it involves a 12- to 18-month time period—communicate this to all parties and then follow the plan. To reduce the number of disbursements, recordkeeping, correspondence, and phone calls, it is a good idea to quickly clean up all of the small past due amounts. A $500 payable, to be repaid over 12 months is going to take as much administrative effort as a $6000 amount. Better to make the first $500 payment to the small vendor and get them off your back for good. That way, in this simplified example, you will be dealing with two vendors for only one month and starting another in the second through thirteenth month. The other way you'll have two creditors for the full year: 13 checks, not 24; 13 statements, not 24; and so on.

> Company A bought Company B, just before the latter would have had to declare bankruptcy. Due diligence really was not performed and B's financial statements turned out to be woefully inaccurate—substantial past due accounts payable were literally found in people's desk drawers. When asked, the individuals said about previous management, "We knew they were having trouble and did not want to bother them." The bottom line was that by the time all the past due payables were assembled there was literally a file drawer full of invoices. And on top of that, all disbursements were manual checks. No PC-based A/P system.

Given there were no constraints on cash (the buyer had sufficient cash even to meet the unexpectedly high amounts), the real limiting factor was the availability of clerical time. It did not make sense to hire additional staff just to get caught up. But at any reasonable processing rate it was going to take six to eight weeks to get current with all vendors.

The past due invoices were put in alphabetical order, so they could be accessed whenever a vendor called. Then methodically, invoices were verified, checks cut, and payments made in alphabetical order. About a third of the way through the process Xerox called up and started getting somewhat obstreperous. The system was explained and they were told that due to the luck of the alphabet they were at the end of the line, but that based on current progress they could expect to be paid in about five weeks. The vendor's receivable clerk went away sullen, but not mutinous. It was not feasible to try and change the firm's name to Gerox. They were, in fact, paid in five weeks and continued to service the copy machines in the meantime.

As a matter of interest, only two vendors said they either had to be paid immediately or the firm was going on COD. In both cases, an exception was made. Their invoices went to the top of the pile. They also ceased being a supplier from that point forward. It is easier to do business with understanding vendors.

People can take bad news (Xerox is at the end of the alphabet) but once communications had been established there were no surprises for any of the vendors. The key, of course, was that cash was available and clerical resources were the limiting factor, not necessarily a common occurrence. But the principle holds true.

Have a game plan, communicate it, and then stick to it.

9

Put Your Excess
Cash to Work—Fast!

An educated consumer is our best customer.
Advertising slogan of Sym's clothing store

Only half the readers will benefit from this chapter, assuming that 50 percent of all companies have excess funds, while the other 50 percent are borrowers. It is relatively rare, although not unheard of, for an organization to be both borrowing short-term from banks and simultaneously investing in the short-term money market. Almost invariably, interest rates charged by banks are *higher* than the interest rates paid on money market investments. If you are borrowing at the prime rate, say, 7 percent, it is likely that you will only earn in the neighborhood of 4 percent on surplus cash. Common sense suggests that if you are able to negotiate the maximum flexibility with your bank, you are better off paying down bank loans and saving the 7-percent interest being charged. Put the other way, there is a negative 3-percent spread which is usually hard to justify.

Thus this chapter is of interest only to managers in those organizations with *surplus* funds. Even the term "surplus" has to be looked at carefully, since we have been arguing that most firms are better off maximizing cash flow, and then using the resources to make further productive investments in capital facilities, inventories, and receivables—all of which are required if profitable growth is to occur. So one way of looking at it would be to say that *no* firm has surplus cash.

The short-term money market is made up of hundreds of billions of dollars, and many individuals work full time in this as a career. It is obvious, therefore, that others have chosen to define surplus in a different context or this large market would not exist. For purposes of this chapter then, *surplus cash* is that over and above the amounts needed for (a) minimum cash balance levels, as discussed in Chap. 6, and (b) forecast or scheduled short-term requirements like payroll, rent, taxes, and accounts payable.

The definition of surplus cash, or determining the exact amount available to invest, is not as critical as how you go about making the investment decisions. That is, the decision *process* is the most overlooked area, but one that is absolutely critical.

Objectives of an Investment Policy

Most people think the objective of investing extra funds can be summarized in just two words: make money. Everyone agrees it is better for you to invest truly surplus cash, and receive the interest reward, than it is to leave the cash in the bank in a checking account. Cash in a bank's commercial checking account, earning no interest for the depositor, is in fact how the bank earns its profits. Lending that money out to borrowers, say at the prime rate, provides the gross income from which the bank then has to subtract its expenses and obtain its net profit. When it comes down to a *choice* between you and the bank, the decision is easy. You owe the bank a reasonable return, but that is all.

The problem with a simple policy objective like "make money" is that it provides little operational guidance. Since there is no such thing as negative interest in the ordinary course of events, *any* money market investment is going to promise a positive return. Thus we have to be a little more specific. Do we want to get the *maximum* return possible? How much *risk* are we willing to accept? How much *time* shall we spend on our investments? If our forecast is wrong, can we *get our money back* before maturity?

The unfortunate part of these equations is that each answer, each approach to investing, has tradeoffs. Most people accept the fact that to get a higher return you may have to accept a higher risk. If you want your money back before maturity, a cost may be involved. If you call up seven dealers this morning to get the very highest quote on commercial paper, this may not be the best use of your time.

To get back to the primary tradeoff, risk vs. return, there are different philosophies in corporate money management, just as there are in personal investing. An aggressive strategy will attempt to maximize return, willingly accepting some risk; a conservative strategy emphasizes safety of principal and willingly sacrifices some return.

It is easy to overstate the differences in risk among alternative investments usually considered for temporary investment of surplus cash. The truth is that almost all types of investment have had a very good safety record. But "very good" is *not* the same as perfect. Let's take a brief look at some common investment alternatives now, although more detail will be given later.

The absolute safest investment is in securities of the U.S. government, if we define safety or lack of risk as a guarantee of the return of your principal. The risk of market fluctuations will be discussed separately. If you buy a security of the government, and hold it to maturity, you are absolutely assured of receiving 100¢ on the dollar. The reason is simple. The government can always pay off it debts by printing dollars. Corporations, banks, and municipalities do not have this privilege, so when a corporate bond or commercial paper comes due, and the issuer does not have cash available, the security *can* go into default. The federal government simply cannot default. You may ask, "If they just print money won't it be worth less in terms of purchasing power? When Russia or Brazil print money the value of the currency depreciates. If Uncle Sam follows the same course, won't the result be the same?" The answer is, of course, yes. But no matter how little it might be worth, you as the holder of government debt will at least have something denominated in dollars. Holders of any other security cannot be assured of the same thing.

This leads to the other type of risk, *market fluctuation.* If you buy a 30-year, 50-year, or one of the recently introduced 100-year bonds at, say, 8 percent, and general interest rates go up to 10 percent or even 12 percent (much less the 21 percent reached in the early 1980s) the current value of an 8-percent security, when new issues are selling at 12 percent, is going to be far less than 100. There are tables, or even Hewlett-Packard calculators, that can calculate the specific amount very quickly. The point is that the longer the maturity, the greater the impact on the principal amount is going to be for any given change in the level of general interest rates. Because of this greater market risk, bonds with a longer maturity have a higher yield than short-term securities.

Therefore if in investing surplus cash you stick to governments with maturities of no more than one year, in a worst case scenario you could always hold to maturity and get back 100¢ on the dollar. But one-year securities return less in interest than a 10-year bond held for one year, *if* general interest rates have not changed. As one observer put it, "Which do you want, to eat well, or sleep well?" High return vs. more risk!

So government securities, while they do have market interest risk, have no principal risk. But how much risk of loss of principal is there in other types of securities such as bank Certificates of Deposit? Some banks have failed, and depositors with more than $100,000 have sometimes not been paid, although in other circumstances if a forced merger is arranged, even those with amounts over the Federal Deposit Insurance level have been covered. But don't think that even the largest banks are risk-free. Over the last 10 years rumors have swirled about the ultimate safety of at least three of the five largest banks in the country. At one time it was felt that these banks were "too large to fail," that the government would *have* to step in. That bit of wishful thinking may or may not have happened. We will never know. But Continental Bank in Chicago, one of the country's largest, did get into serious trouble. It can happen.

With respect to commercial paper, actual losses have been extremely rare, but many issuers of such notes have had to stop selling the paper and redeem the entire amount of paper outstanding as it matured. Only backup lines of credit from banks which the issuers had previously arranged saved investors from massive losses. If a commercial paper issuer failed, and the backup line of credit held was provided by a bank that was under siege, the resulting picture would be pretty ugly. We all have *faith* that the Federal Reserve would step in and save the day. The essence of faith, however, as the dictionary puts it, is "Belief that does not rest on logical proof or material evidence." Commercial paper interest rates, therefore, are higher than government securities for a reason. How much risk do you want to take?

Finally, let's look at what was once considered almost the ultimate in risk-free investments—repurchase agreements. Dealers in bonds maintain inventories of hundreds of millions if not billions of dollars of debt securities. And these inventories have to be financed or funded by debt, since no dealer could make a reasonable return if the entire inventory were owned outright. Bond dealers fund their inventories with short-term borrowing. A recent book on Salomon Brothers indicated that when the firm got into trouble, they had to reduce their day-to-day borrowing by over $20 billion in just a few weeks, but it was still close to $100 billion! That's real money.

Dealers will typically borrow money for a period of a day to a month, and pledge the bonds in their inventory as collateral. This is the essence of a repurchase agreement. You, as the lender, would have the promise of the dealer to repay, based on his overall credit. In addition, in case things went wrong, you are supposed to have physical possession of the bonds as collateral, which you can then sell.

It sounds good. If you lend First Boston $5 million at 2 PM on an overnight transaction, they are supposed to notify their bank which had physical custody of the bonds to move them from the account of First Boston and transfer them to an account with your name on it. Then the next morning you receive the $5 million cash back, plus one day's interest. First Boston, in turn, receives its bonds back as the bank takes them out of your account. As you can see, there is a lot of paper moving about.

How do you as the lender *know* that the bonds were physically transferred? You are supposed to be able to send your auditor in to check. But when does the auditor go? The deal is consummated at 2 PM and the bank closes at 3 PM. Before the bank opens the next morning the deal is reversed—talk about *faith*. Some bond dealers have had financial problems, and there has been real concern that the security the lenders thought they had might just not be there when it was needed most. Few readers are going to have to worry about this particular risk. The point is that *risk* exists in virtually *every* transaction. Period. End of discussion.

Now we can get back to the original discussion. Your organization must develop a policy as to just how much risk it is willing to accept. Otherwise the individual who does the actual investing is going to find herself in an untenable situation. Right or wrong, *performance* of the portfolio manager is going to be measured. The easiest way to measure performance is to compare the absolute return received to some external benchmark.

For example if you are the portfolio manager and you have had an average of $100,000 to invest (it could be $10,000 or $10 million and the principle is the same) $4800 of interest income shows up in the year's income statement. This represents the amount you were able to generate for your firm. Someone will ask—and whether they *should* or not is irrelevant—how you did. The most logical and easiest way is to look at Treasury bills during the past year and see how they did. A second benchmark is likely to be money market funds.

Human nature being what it is, and most people in business are somewhat competitive, any portfolio manager wants to beat the benchmark, in this case Treasury bills or money market funds. It is not too hard to do this, particularly if you invest in commercial paper of companies that are barely investment grade. Lower rated companies pay a higher rate of interest, so you can always improve your yield by lowering your credit standards.

It was this striving after yield and return, in a competitive situation, that caused mutual fund managers to invest in junk bonds, or high-yield bonds as they were euphemistically called. This strategy worked for years, and the funds that adopted that policy not only showed superior returns, they attracted a lot of money from the public and greatly grew in size. In turn, the managers of those funds earned much larger compensation, and the demand for high performance encouraged the Michael Milkens of the world to encourage more firms to *issue* additional high-yield securities. Demand encouraged supply, and the demand was fueled by portfolio managers striving to beat the market. Unfortunately, with the demise of Levine, Boesky, and Milken, as well as entire firms like Drexel Burnham, the entire high-yield market came tumbling down, and investors lost *lots* of money.

This slight digression is not meant as a morality play. It is designed to bring into focus that the relationship between risk and reward, between higher returns and greater risk, still exists. It may not work itself out in any one 30-day period, maybe not even in a year. But any time you are offered two seemingly similar investment opportunities, and one offers a higher yield, ask, "*Why* is this one paying more? What does the market know that I don't?" You may still come to the conclusion that accepting slightly more risk is worthwhile, but at least it will be a highly conscious decision.

Applied to money market investments—for the portfolio manager in a manufacturing or service firm—the temptation to reach for yield, and beat the market, is almost overwhelming. Earning only average, much less below average, returns is not necessarily conducive to continued responsibility for that particular function. Accepting less risk, being more secure in knowing that the funds entrusted to your care are as close to 100-percent safe as you can make them, may be a better strategy—it may even be what the Board of Directors of your organization really wants. But it is *very hard to measure risk*, and *very easy to measure return*. What gets measured gets done, as many people have pointed out more than once.

The cure for this dilemma, therefore, is for those responsible for setting policy to recognize that their own number one responsibility is to tell the portfolio manager just what level of risk is appropriate. It is then up to the portfolio manager to demonstrate how she met that policy objective. Measuring absolute dollars of return, as compared with some overall market measure, is ultimately guaranteed to provide results diametrically opposite to the organization's best interest. A lot of great minds have tried to come up with risk adjusted measures of performance. In some senses they have been reasonably successful, but (a) there is still controversy about the methodology, and (b) most of the work deals with the stock market, not the money market. In practical terms, it is impossible to measure risk in a money market portfolio just by looking at interest income. And a detailed analysis of real risk assumed would be both time consuming and costly.

Observation: Set an investment *policy*, make sure it is being followed, and do *not* try to measure performance of the portfolio manager by comparing her yield to some overall market average. Be thankful for whatever interest return has been earned, knowing that the funds entrusted to the portfolio were not exposed to undue risk. No level of interest income will ever offset a loss of capital. If you personally are the investment manager you are responsible for other people's money. You *cannot* apply a personal philosophy toward risk—one that would be perfectly appropriate for your own money, to someone else's funds.

Written Policy Guidelines

If you have any responsibility for your organization's general management, or financial results, if you are on the Board of Directors or a portfolio manager, if you are an internal auditor or are associated with the organization's firm of independent auditors (CPA firm) you must make sure that there are *written policy guidelines for the investment of surplus cash.* It is easy to invest surplus cash—it just takes a simple phone call to your bank and you can be in Treasury bills or commercial paper or CDs in less than three minutes.

Once you have invested the first time, say for 30 days, you will get a follow-up call just before maturity asking if you want to roll over the amount or if you need the proceeds credited to your account. Really, the system is simplicity itself. In fact the students of TQM should examine how sellers have made it as easy as possible for buyers (firms with surplus cash to invest) to put their money to work. As consumers we should have Sears or Chevrolet be so easy to do business with.

But just because it is easy to get started and even easier to keep going without any formal written policy guidelines, it does not make good business practice. If the author were writing the rules, no *seller* of money market instruments would be able to complete the first transaction without receiving a copy of the buyer's written policy guidelines. The seller would then have to make sure that the product he is selling complies with those guidelines. Certainly stock brokers, subject to the rules of the New York Stock Exchange, have to know their customers. The same approach *should* be mandatory in the money market; it is, unfortunately, not required.

Every once in a while you read in the business press about some poor treasurer, often a municipal official, who was convinced to invest his employer's funds in some exotic way that promised an extraordinarily high return. Remember that in the 1920s Mr. Ponzi flourished. This was not the first time that crooks took advantage of gullible investors, and it certainly was not the last. Trying to protect fools from themselves, or from knaves, may be a hopeless undertaking. But there are a lot of portfolio managers, who often are not sophisticated, dealing with some of Wall Street's "best and brightest." It is not a fair contest. You may argue, "Let the buyer beware." In a market economy people are supposed to be allowed to fail. Nonetheless, my requirement about mandating receipt of written guidelines would prevent a lot of mistakes from happening, and perhaps a lot of people from losing their job.

Those who have tried to write policy guidelines start out with the secret expectation that it is pretty straightforward, that with just a little time and effort, such guidelines can be produced. In fact, why not go next door and get some other company's and just modify them as necessary? Stop.

No two companies are the same, therefore policy guidelines should not be the same. And it is far more difficult to write them than you may think. Originally the author was going to provide a sample. On closer consideration this would be a disservice, if only because some firms would undoubtedly copy it verbatim. Any "standard investment policy guidelines" would be inappropriate at best, and probably dead wrong at worst.

We can identify some of the areas that should be covered in guidelines, however. They include:

1. Who has the authority to invest?
2. What is the maximum maturity?
3. Is there a maximum amount in any one security or issuer?
4. What investment media can be utilized (Treasury bills, commercial paper, certificates of deposit, repurchase agreements, banker's acceptances, etc.)?
5. For any investment chosen, is there to be some minimum credit or quality rating, such as Standard & Poor's or Moody's?
6. Should trades be limited to your main bank, brokers, or dealers?
7. Should maturities be staggered so some funds become available soon?
8. Should foreign investments be permitted?
9. Who, if anyone, can grant permission to waive one or more requirements as necessary, and what is the definition of "necessary"?
10. What reports, if any, should be prepared and who should they go to?
11. How, if at all, will performance be measured?

Each of these points will be covered. In the interest of full disclosure the author admits his very conservative bias in this area. Losing part of an organizations' assets because of poor investment decisions simply reflects inappropriate policies, or good policies which were not followed. Making an above-average return on those funds, no matter how measured, will provide at best an insignificant gain.

The first decision is to decide who has the *authority* and *responsibility* to invest. At first it is fun to invest your employer's funds, undoubtedly in amounts that are much larger than any personal investments have been. Limits have to be placed on who does the investing. Further, since there will often be several investments outstanding at one time, with different maturities, it makes sense to have one person monitor and another to perform the investment function. A backup person should, of course, be designated to act in the absence of the principal investment person.

As we saw earlier, the longer the maturity of the instrument on the date of purchase the higher will be the yield, but the greater the risk of market fluctuations. A given change in overall interest rates impacts a 30-year bond significantly, whereas the market value of a 90-day Treasury bill will hardly move. The *maturity* limits must be established in advance, and adhered to. Since by definition we are talking about *temporarily* surplus funds, it is inappropriate to commit them to long-term investments. (If you have truly long-term funds available, go to the chapters on inventories, marketing, and fixed assets.)

Observation: If a company can actually earn more in the money market than it can by investing in its own business, the owners need to reevaluate their basic business strategy!

Diversification is always a good idea, and no matter how sound the credit and market analyses, there is *always* a risk that a particular company, bank, or dealer can run into unexpected trouble. Therefore it is prudent to spread investments around. Policy guidelines should specify the maximum *amount* to be invested in any one issuer's securities, as well as the maximum *percent* of the portfolio.

As will be discussed, the range of investment alternatives is wide, but every type of investment is not necessarily appropriate for a particular organization. Policy guidelines should spell out *acceptable investment alternatives*. If you cannot make a meaningful analysis, it means someone has to do more homework before stepping off the diving board and committing real cash.

Because there is an inverse relationship between credit rating and yield, paper from the best companies yields the lowest return and vice versa. A specific decision has to be made as to the *maximum credit risk*, that is, the minimum credit rating that will be allowed in the portfolio. Many people have made a lot of money by investing in so-called junk securities. Others have shunned these securities because of the perceived risk. Our advice is to make this decision rationally, in advance, rather than at the time of temptation when a dealer offers you a once in a lifetime opportunity.

Your *scarcest resource* may not be the cash available for short-term investment, but the *time available* of your financial or accounting department staff. How much time should they spend trying to improve yield? Dealing with several banks and/or brokers will expose you to more, and *possibly* better, investment opportunities, but it takes time to make the calls and evaluate the alternatives. Is this worth doing?

No matter how good your cash forecast, sooner or later you will need to disburse cash and there won't be enough in the checking account. You will have to look to the existing portfolio and convert part of it immediately into cash. Selling before maturity is usually possible, but often at a loss. If the investments had been made with *staggered maturities*, in anticipation that *unexpected* cash requirements *might* arise, this risk will be minimized. On the other hand it may mean more paperwork if, for example, one large sum would be invested in four separate transactions to mature weekly, rather than the entire sum in a single 30-day maturity.

At times there will be interest rate disparities between the U.S. market and one or more *overseas markets*. Knowledgeable investors can profit from this phenomenon, if they are willing to accept certain risks of currency fluctuations. Where do you stand?

The best prepared written policy, sooner or later, is going to be out of date, and the restrictions inappropriate for a specific situation. For example, you may have a policy of not investing in foreign paper, but two years later you start importing goods from Britain. An opportunity to invest in pounds sterling, at an attractive interest premium, might make sense at that point because you are going to have a pound obligation to pay for the merchandise. So any risk of a devaluation will naturally hedge the money market transaction. At maturity the pounds could be used to pay for the imports, rather than converted back to dollars for redeposit to your U.S. bank. This is simply an example of changed circumstances that call for a waiver in the written policy. Who has the *authority* to approve such an exception before the entire policy guidelines can be reviewed and modified?

Performance must be measured. For money market investments, what kind of *reports* will be provided, and who should review them should be decided up front. The point is that if a formal review procedure is established an organization will not drift into investments or an investment approach that is inappropriate. Some of the serious problems that have occurred can be traced to informality, rather than to clearly thought out limits and controls. Formal reports go a long way to preventing problems.

Finally, how will we know if the portfolio manager is doing a good job? What are the *performance criteria* that will be utilized. Are we interested in measuring return relative to a benchmark like 90-day Treasury bills, or do we want to look at the credit ratings of where the money went? We can *report* on both, but we cannot expect an individual to necessarily accomplish both. A conscious choice up front will make everyone's life much easier later on.

Risk and Return

The fundamental equation taught in every finance course is that to get a higher return you must accept more risk. This is a one-way street, however, since accepting more risk may not *assure* the higher return. Buying a Lotto ticket is high risk, and the odds are overwhelming that you will receive zero return. Investing in a Mexican 6-month time deposit, promising a 15-percent peso return, has a high nominal return, but exposes you to the risk of a devaluation of the Mexican peso relative to the U.S. dollar. If you are lucky, there will be no devaluation and you will earn the full 15 percent as promised. If you are unlucky, a 10-percent devaluation will more than wipe out your anticipated return. What are the odds of a devaluation in a specific 6-month period? You can find out by getting a quote for a forward peso contract in 6 months. Don't be surprised, however, if the cost of the hedge brings the net return down to, say, 5 percent, if that is the rate currently being earned on domestic bank certificates of deposits.

In Chap. 4 on inventories we quoted the well known dictum that there is no free lunch. Perhaps that phrase should have been reserved for this chapter because it is equally, if not more, true in the money market. It is a fact of life that the professionals who buy and sell in the money market, who make their living by making a market, are some of the sharpest minds in the business world. They have phenomenal communications systems, with access instantly to all business news. They have very substantial sums of capital, and one basis point, which equals 1/100 of 1 percent or .0001, on $100 million is not a trivial sum. This works out to $10,000 a year or $27.40 each and every day.

Now $27.40 for a day, on a base of $100 million may not sound like much. On an investment of $100,000, which may still be larger than what many companies invest in the money market, it works out to less than 3¢ a day. On a 30-day investment of $100,000, earning one extra basis point would provide you with a grand total of 82¢! But put yourself in the position of the trader at the other end, who has to raise $100 million that day—and such sums are being raised every day by the professionals. If she is able to obtain the required funds for only 30 days at just one basis point lower, she will have saved her employer $821.92. That would probably pay her salary for the day, as long as she earned less than $200,000 a year.

The pressures on the professionals in the money market are intense, and they will fight for every basis point. No reader of this book is ever going to be able to go up against these professionals and beat them at their own game. It cannot be done. If a single round lot of U.S. Treasury bills is $25 million, very few firms, investing surplus cash, will ever buy or sell even a single round lot. Therefore you should know, going in, that you will be buying what they want to sell, at the price they are quoting.

So in terms of risk and return, you must understand, going in, that you will never be able to maximize the return on *any* type of security. Just as when you personally by an OTC stock, there is a bid and asked price. You have to buy at the asked (high) price and sell at the bid (low) price. Buy high, sell low is not the way they teach it in Marketing 101. But this should not be a cause for concern. Remember, we are dealing with surplus funds and something is better than nothing. The fact that the person on the other side of the transaction is making a profit on your trade is a fact of life.

Market risk (relating to fluctuations in interest rates between the purchase date and the time you want your money back) differs from principal risk. It is almost impossible for anyone to effectively forecast the future course of interest rates. The stock market is hard enough, but over time earnings rise and the broad secular course of stock prices is definitely up.

With interest rates, most observers today would prefer lower to higher rates. As borrowers we want to pay less, and everyone wants to escape the ravages of inflation. Only those living on interest earnings are hurt by lower interest rates. Yet as governments seem to prefer borrowing to taxes, and inflation fears remain in people's minds, there are obviously counter-vailing forces at work affecting interest rates. Throw in the fact the United States is now but one of many players in a total world economy, and that the course of production, inflation, and economic growth abroad impacts our interest rates, it is easy to see that predicting accurately the course of interest rates is essentially impossible.

What this means for those with responsibility for investing excess corporate funds is that investing in securities with short maturities mini-mizes risk of market price fluctuations. Since the fluctuations are bound to occur—interest rates will go up and down, but we do not know in which direction—we have as much chance of making a profit from declines in interest rates as we do of suffering a loss from rising rates. Losses are always harder to explain, particularly for funds that are temporarily invested until they can be put to use in the business in inventories, receivables and PP&E. Gambling on the future course of interest rates is a bad idea, and the only way to avoid it is to stick with short maturities, no more than 90 to 180 days.

As we saw, no matter what debt instruments we might buy, they *all* are subject to market risk. A long Treasury bond or note is riskier by far than short-term commercial paper—in terms of market price fluctuations.

Liquidity and Convenience

Buying or investing in various types of instruments, in order to obtain an interest return, is itself a time consuming activity. A cost/benefit test should be made as to how much management resources can profitably be devoted to that function, say, as contrasted with putting that same time and effort on collecting outstanding receivables.

Some types of money market investments are easier to buy than others. We recommend dealing with your local bank if it is large enough to handle this function for its corporate customers. If you are dealing with a much smaller bank, then deal directly with your bank's primary correspondent in the next major city.

Yes, it is possible to search out possibly higher yielding issues from other sources, say a Wall Street brokerage firm. But dealing with a multitude of investment bankers, and commercial banks, quickly runs up both operat-ing expenses for wire transfers, and administrative effort. The latter would involve recordkeeping, confirmations and the like as well as keeping track of maturities, accrued interest, audit statements, and the like.

If you are large enough to have a portfolio requiring the full-time services of a portfolio manager, these suggestions do not apply. With $100 million, or even possibly $50 million invested at all times, the benefits of competition will outweigh the administrative costs of dealing with numerous brokers, dealers, and banks and commercial paper issuers.

But the question then has to be raised, for an organization of that size, is a more or less permanent portfolio really a wise strategic option? If availability of cash is the major limiting factor for most growth plans, what message does a permanent portfolio send to managers, much less to shareholders? If you say, "We can earn more in the money market than we can in the business," you will inevitably suggest, in this era, the dreaded words: leveraged buy out. Someone will have the idea that they can buy control of your firm with your own cash and unused borrowing power.

Ultraconservatism may appear to be a very safe and comfortable strategy, but, particularly for a publicly traded firm, it may be dangerous to the continuity of present management. Even for a closely held firm, some shareholders are going to start asking embarrassing questions and pressing for dividends. Finally, if no one else asks, the IRS can come in and tax you on undistributed profits if they can allege and prove in court that you are unreasonably accumulating cash. Being liquid is good, turning yourself into a bank is not.

U.S. Treasury Securities

Absolute *safety* of principal. Virtually complete marketability and *liquidity*. Relative *ease of purchase* and sale—three out of four is pretty good. It is the fourth factor, *yield*, where Treasury securities come up short. Because of the known benefits, and low risk, many U.S. and foreign investors are willing to settle for a lower return in exchange for absolute safety of principal. A major factor keeping yields low is investments by foreign entities, banks, insurance companies, governments, and so forth. The financial stability of the United States economy, combined with the large market (trillions of dollars) make this a perfect market for investors with huge sums to invest.

Because the market is so large, and a round lot of Treasury bills might be $25 million, smaller firms, say with *only(!)* $100,000 will find that the actual cost of buying what is considered an odd-lot may be prohibitive, at least in relative terms. It is true that you can buy Treasury securities direct from the government, through the Federal Reserve System. But for this to work you have to invest the money when they want it, not when you want to. The popular financial press periodically has articles on how you can buy, on a noncompetitive basis and at no fee, any kind of Treasury security. Realistically, for an organization that is investing frequently, and is trying to match maturities to needs, Treasury securities should only be considered when absolute safety of principal is paramount.

The author stated a conservative bias in approaching money market investments, and too many people overlook the risks inherent in most investments. But a Treasuries-only policy may be *too* conservative. Not only are yields lower, but transaction costs are higher. As we will see, the very real risks of most alternative investments can be made manageable. For those who feel undressed and uncomfortable without both a belt and suspenders, or who carry an umbrella every day no matter what the forecast, the emotional security of Treasury bills and bonds is worthwhile. For the rest of us, a little more risk is usually worth accepting.

Commercial Paper

For many organizations, investing surplus funds temporarily in commercial paper may be the best solution to balancing the risks and rewards. Essentially, for those unfamiliar with commercial paper, it represents an unsecured promise to pay by a corporation. Since the maturity is usually very short, say, less than 60 days, it is unlikely that the seller is going to have a totally unexpected deterioration in its business prospects in that short a period. Why is "totally unexpected" the relevant description?

Most of the investors in the short-term money market *are* sophisticated, and they too are risk averse. If there is even the slightest rumor that an issuer of paper is having financial difficulties, the very first symptom is going to be a rise in the interest rate that company will have to pay to sell any further debt. The second, and final step can come very quickly after that. The company cannot sell *any* paper, and must start redeeming outstanding paper as it matures.

Two lessons can be learned. First, if six major issuers are paying 4 percent and one issuer, say Company P is having to pay 4.25 percent, ask yourself just why the company would pay more than it has to. Obviously it is not willingly assuming extra interest expense unnecessarily. The real choice P faces is to pay a premium—in this case ¼ percent—or not borrow at all in the commercial paper market. Interest rates literally fluctuate daily, and sometimes even within a day, as supply and demand ebbs and flows. Lenders, purchasers of commercial paper, are very sensitive to perceived differences in risk. Some buyers are willing to assume the extra risk for that extra ¼ percent. Others are not. The lesson though is that if you are a relative neophyte you can learn from the behavior of others. Real or imagined, both the issuer and some lenders obviously believe, in this example, that P's credit rating is suddenly not as good as its peers.

Commercial paper is rated by the major rating agencies—Standard & Poor's, Moody's, and Duff and Phelps. Each has a slightly different combination of letters and numbers in ranking issuers from top quality down through highly speculative. More often than not the rating firms agree on each company's rating, but occasionally there is a difference of opinion. Such split ratings may be a warning sign, and will probably be reflected in a slightly higher rate offered by that issuer.

We mentioned that in case of trouble an issuer may no longer be able to sell any commercial paper. The usual practice is for a company that needs to borrow on average $100 million in the commercial paper market to always be willing to issue new paper. Some of it will be used to repay paper previously issued and now maturing. The company, by staggering its own maturity dates, replaces paper sold 60 days ago with new paper sold today with paper sold 60 days ago. The market is so large and rates so sensitive that a company that issues paper can exactly tailor its portfolio of borrowing. As long as it is willing to pay market rates, and its credit rating does not change, any issuer can achieve a steady state.

But what happens when the rumors start flying? Whether accurate or not, most lenders will say to themselves, "I have 10 or 20 other companies I can lend to, whose paper I can buy, so why take a risk? Maybe this Company P is going to be the next Penn Central or Chrysler, both of which had troubles and were forced to suspend selling new paper. I'll invest in Company T today." When enough lenders make that decision, P is out of the market and in big trouble.

But wait, the lenders have already anticipated that any issuer may run into unanticipated trouble. Lenders have demanded, and received, assurance that any seller or issuer of commercial paper *must* have bank lines of credit available, the amount of which is equal to or exceeds the amount of commercial paper outstanding. Then, if the worst does happen, if existing paper cannot be rolled over, the outstanding debt will be paid off as it matures by utilizing those lines of credit. Of course you may ask why, if the company is in trouble, wouldn't the banks withdraw the lines just when they were needed. Good question. In practice the issuer has been paying a fee to the banks for the unused line of credit, a so-called stand-by credit fee. In effect that fee has been an insurance premium, and the bank now has to meet its obligations, just like an insurance company has to pay on its casualty losses.

In practice, actual losses to participants in the money market, those who have invested in commercial paper and lost part or all of their principal, have been insignificant, truly infinitesimal in fact. This superb safety record may tempt investors to reach for yield by investing in lower-rated, higher-yielding paper. But since the difference in yield may be no more than ½ percent or probably even ¼ percent, you have to ask yourself if it is worthwhile. If you do lose some of your principal in exchange for having received an extra ¼ percent, the risk/reward tradeoff is 400 to 1. You will lose your job if principal is lost; you are unlikely to receive a promotion for obtaining an extra ¼-percent return. Play it safe.

As long as you stick to top-grade commercial paper, there are two other advantages. First, it is convenient to buy commercial paper. Most large banks (those that provide money management services for companies) act as agent for several commercial paper issuers. With one phone call to your own major bank you can obtain quotes on several competing issuers. After you make your investment decision the money will be transferred out of your account that day by the bank. On the maturity date, which can literally be anywhere from overnight to several months out, the money is automatically deposited back in your checking account. There are or should be no fees for this service, since the issuer of the paper is compensating the bank to act as its agent.

In addition to ease of investment commercial paper has another benefit. You can pick both the amount you want to invest, and the exact maturity. So if you have $115,000 that you want to invest for exactly 27 days (to mature, for example, to meet a specific payroll) you can do it. Even Treasury bills do not have this feature, since they mature only one day a week, and buying odd amounts is not realistic. Do not underestimate the importance of this flexibility. Again, it simplifies the daily workload of the portfolio manager.

The biggest theoretical disadvantage of commercial paper may also be its biggest advantage in practice. Commercial paper is not negotiable. It is a direct contract between you, the lender, and the issuer. In exchange for a specific sum of money the lender will return that principal amount to you, plus interest, on the maturity date. The contract is a private one. The promissory note is not *negotiable*. If your cash forecasting has gone awry, and you simply *must* have cash sooner than you expected, you cannot sell the commercial paper and the issuer has no responsibility to bail you out. Yes, in 27 days you will get your money, but on day 15, for example, if you have an unexpected need for cash you cannot spend the $115,000. Legally it is tied up. You can sell a Treasury security any business day of the year, but there is no effective market for used commercial paper.

There is good news, however. Because the issuers of commercial paper expect to use this as a more or less permanent source of funds, they plan on selling their paper for months and years ahead. In practice there develops a seller/customer relationship, and you are the customer! The issuer of the paper needs you, in one sense, more than you need him. You have a wide variety of potential investment options. He has a large number of potential investors out there, but is competing against a lot of other issuers for their cash. Now put yourself in his place. One customer comes to him and says, "Gee, I made a mistake in my forecast. True, it's my fault and you don't *have* to do anything to help me. But I sure would appreciate it if you would give me my money back, of course with only 15-days interest instead of 27 days. I cannot promise to have more money to invest in commercial paper but, when I do I'll put you right at the top of my list."

If you were the issuer would you give the money back before maturity? Chances are that just on business grounds you would be flexible. Further, if you really are selling paper every day, it only means that you are looking for an additional $115,000 that day, maybe on a total $100 million portfolio. Truly chickenfeed to you, but not to your customer. In practice, most issuers of commercial paper will work closely with investors. There would only be one exception. If interest rates have jumped dramatically, they would not let you out of your contract to let you reinvest somewhere else just to earn a higher return. If nothing else, they would have to replace your money at today's higher rate. (Believe it or not, some investors have been known to take advantage of higher yields.) As long as you are dealing with them in good faith, and do not abuse it, there is great flexibility in buying commercial paper from most issuers.

One final word. Many transactions are consummated directly through your own bank. The issuers are likely to be large local or regional firms, known in your community but not necessarily nationally. There are a relatively few large national issuers of commercial paper, such as General Motors Acceptance Corporation, that sell paper directly. That is, you can call them up and they will give you a quote over the phone. If you decide to invest with them you may have to wire transfer the funds to one of their banks, say, in New York, which can incur a bank wire transfer fee. But offsetting this, the so-called direct issuers, because they are not paying a bank to act as agent, may be able to offer a slightly higher rate. Now you again have a tradeoff, between making a couple of phone calls as contrasted with the chance of earning a greater return. In addition to the direct issuers, and banks that act as agents for issuers, some of the major Wall Street brokerage firms do a business in commercial paper, and you can call them. How much is one-stop convenience worth? It is up to you.

Certificates of Deposit

As economic conditions change so do the investment offerings. Popularity of certain instruments rises and falls, basically driven by the underlying economics. Commercial paper, which is now so popular, used to be considered somewhat daring, while bank certificates of deposit (CDs) were quite standard. Unlike a bank checking account, which is technically called a *demand deposit*, CDs are a time deposit. The difference is pretty clear.

A bank has to be ready to provide you with your funds which are in a demand deposit, you can get them on demand. A time deposit, in contrast, means the bank has made a commitment to you to keep the funds for a specified period, and at the end of that time you get them back with interest. For many years banks could not pay interest on demand deposits. As interest rates rose in the 1970s, depositors insisted on sharing some of the income their deposits were generating, and certificates of deposit became popular.

Today, deposits are fully insured by the federal government up to $100,000. In terms of safety of principal, given the banking and S&L crises of the 1980s, one would have to say that an insured bank account, up to $100,000, is about as safe as a direct Treasury obligation. To the best of our knowledge, nobody has ever lost money in an insured institution as long as the amount was less than the magic $100,000 limit. If and when a bank is in extreme financial difficulty the regulators step in and arrange a merger. Only rarely have people even had to wait to get their principal, although the new bank may not honor the old institution's typically higher interest rate.

For practical purposes, then, up to $100,000 bank CDs are completely safe. Further, they can be issued in any amount, with any maturity date mutually agreed upon between the bank and the customer. And they are easy to arrange, particularly with your main bank. A simple debit memo going out, and a credit memo coming in, processes the transaction. So on three out of four categories, bank CDs score high.

You guessed it. On the fourth category, rate of return, CDs do not appear particularly competitive. This is a function of the supply and demand for funds that banks face. Over the years, as commercial paper has proven to be a less expensive source of funds for corporations, large borrowers have looked to the money markets, not banks, for loans. As loan demand at banks for larger commercial customers went down, the banks' demand for funds in turn diminished. Supply and demand being what it is, the rate banks offered also went down and CDs simply became relatively less attractive to investors.

There is one other factor affecting the demand for bank CDs. Unlike commercial paper, where issuers usually are willing to reverse a transaction in the spirit of good customer relations, bank CDs cannot be terminated early without a substantial interest penalty. Since this penalty is imposed by law—a Congressional mandate—banks have no room to negotiate. If you buy a CD, it is yours until maturity. In theory you could use it as collateral for a loan somewhere else but that is awkward. Why go to the trouble, when you could have been in commercial paper.

So far we have been talking only about CDs of less than $100,000. There is no reason banks cannot issue CDs in larger denominations, and they do. CDs of $1 million and up are common, particularly when sold by the largest money-center banks. These CDs *are* negotiable, and certain dealers make a market for them. Thus, an unexpected need for $2 million could be met by selling one of your CDs that have not yet matured. Two things should be of concern. First, the market in jumbo CDs is driven by two factors—the credit rating of the bank issuer and the overall level of interest rates. If your CD was issued by a bank that was perceived to be experiencing credit problems, and/or interest rates have gone up since you bought the CD, you will suffer a capital loss on sale. Of course the opposite *could* happen, interest rates have come down, and the reputation of your bank improved so there was a potential *gain*. Just don't count on this happening too often.

In summary, unless you want to do your bank a favor, or their rate is particularly attractive relative to commercial paper, bank CDs are not recommended.

Money Market Funds

For many years banks were limited by law and regulation as to the maximum rate of interest they could pay depositors on time deposits. As with every other form of price control in the history of the world, this was doomed to failure. If general interest rates are 7 percent, and banks can only pay 5 percent, two things are sure to happen: (1) banks will stop receiving many funds at 5 percent, and (2) some entrepreneurs in the market will figure out a convenient way to provide investors with the 7-percent rates. This is exactly what happened.

Essentially, to get the general level of rates, investors had to buy debt securities in multiples of $100,000 or more. Small individual investors, not to mention smaller business firms, simply did not have that level of liquid resources. So someone had the bright idea of setting up a mutual fund to invest in debt securities. By pooling the funds of a lot of small investors, say, in multiples of $1000 and $2000, it was easy to amass a total portfolio of several million or even tens of millions of dollars. Purchasing a diversified portfolio of debt securities was easy. And with the influx of new money coming in, any one investor could cash out at any time without materially affecting the portfolio. Of course, if every one wanted their money at the same time, the mutual fund manager would have serious trouble.

But just as all depositors in a bank never ask for their money all at once (except in the case of a bank run) so too do investors in mutual funds have varying needs. The law of large numbers essentially protects both the banker and the mutual fund. If you get a large enough base, behavior is going to be average, and on average only a small portion of people need cash that day.

The practical effect was that the mutual fund could invest in medium-term and even long-term bonds, and yet provide virtually immediate liquidity to any one depositor. Since longer term securities typically yielded higher interest rates than short rates, the mutual fund seemed to provide the best of all worlds—instant access to your funds, and interest rates that followed the higher yields of longer term debt securities. This was better than Treasury bills in terms of rates, better than short-term commercial paper in rates, and equal if not better than both in liquidity. The ease of depositing—by wire transfer or check, and withdrawal, also by wire transfer or by check—meant that in practice the money market mutual funds had the best features of bank checking accounts, certificates of deposit, and commercial paper. No minimum amounts were required usually either for deposit or withdrawal.

It is no wonder that money market funds now have literally hundreds of billions of dollars, cash that used to be in bank demand deposit accounts earning no return, or in CDs, earning short-term money market rates. They are convenient, liquid, and earn a good return. Readers should not be surprised at this point to learn that there is at least one drawback.

Money market mutual funds are *not* insured, and the assets held are subject to market price fluctuations. There is, therefore, at least a theoretical chance of loss of principal. All mutual funds are regulated to some degree by the Securities and Exchange Commission (SEC). Money market funds are included in that category, but in reality SEC regulation is quite different from that exercised over the banking industry. Bank regulators can and do examine bank loan portfolios, investments, liabilities and overall management. With significant legal powers behind them, bank regulators can force changes, if they don't like what they see. Parenthetically, with those powers, some observers questioned just how and why the S&L and bank crises occurred. Where were the regulators? Be that as it may, the SEC essentially focuses its efforts on disclosure. That is why you receive a prospectus when you inquire about any mutual fund, including money market funds. Does anyone ever read them, other than the lawyers who draft them? Probably not.

The bottom line is, as an investor in a money market mutual fund, you are at the mercy of the investment manager. How prudent is he? How liquid is he? There was one notable case of a fund that specialized in government securities and guessed wrong on the market. Since shareholder (investor) losses would receive wide publicity and tarnish *all* mutual funds, the industry itself stepped in and provided resources so that no losses were incurred by investors. However, this was voluntary and cannot be counted on in case of a broad economic decline.

In practical terms, money market funds are probably a very good investment for most organizations, particularly since by writing checks on the fund, your account is not charged until the check clears, which may add an extra week's interest. With negligible risk of loss, high flexibility, and ease of use, the only thing really to watch is how the rate of return compares with such things as commercial paper. When interest rates are low the expense charge or load one pays to manage and administer the fund may make the net return uncompetitive. But since you can get in and out at any time, by keeping an active account, you are not tied in if rates go the other way. Most users of money market funds have had very satisfactory results and they can be recommended for small and medium-sized businesses.

Municipal Securities

As most readers know, interest earned on debt securities of state and local governmental units is free from federal income tax. State income taxes, which are growing year by year, are usually not charged on income from debt issued within that state, but are charged on income from other states. But a savings of 35 percent or more, representing federal taxes and possibly a share of state taxes, is certainly worthwhile, if all other things are equal. Given a choice between $100 subject to federal taxes, and $100 exempt from those taxes, few people would have difficulty making a decision.

But a funny thing has happened. Everyone else knows about the exemption from tax of municipal security income. The price of municipal securities therefore gets bid up to the point that the interest *rate* earned on such tax-free offerings is very close to the *after-tax* rate on corporate or bank investments. (States do not tax income earned on federal securities, but this refinement in the analysis need not be carried further at this point.)

So instead of having a choice of two income streams of $100, one taxable and one not, we really are offered a choice of one stream of $100 which *is* taxable and the other of $65 which is *not* taxable. In short, the net after-tax income to be realized by investments in municipal securities may not differ materially from that offered by taxable securities.

At one time the author used to ask participants in cash management seminars which they would prefer to invest in, securities of such blue chips as IBM and General Motors, or debt issued by New York City and California. Times change, but the principle has not. All municipal securities are not the same, just as all corporate borrowers have varying credit ratings. It is conceivable that New York City could have a higher credit rating than IBM or GM, even after the severe business problems faced by both organizations in the early 1990s. In theory municipalities and states have unlimited power to tax, and therefore *should* be good credit risks. When major cities start to run out of tax revenue, and a choice has to be made, it is usually the police and garbage collectors who get paid, not investors in the municipalities bonds. Bridgeport, Connecticut, in fact, filed for bankruptcy, the first governmental unit to do so since the 1930s.

If it is hard to analyze the credit standing of corporations, and we saw that professionals like Standard & Poor's and Moody's sometimes disagree, we submit that evaluation of municipal credit standing is even harder. Since the first principle of investing is to get your money back, and there are significant credit risks, only *above-average* after-tax returns should tempt portfolio managers to compensate for the risk. Since after-tax returns are usually *below-average* we do not recommend using municipal securities as an investment vehicle for surplus company funds, while those who do not pay taxes on income, like nonprofit organizations, or companies with a net operating loss, would never have an interest in them.

Other Exotic Investments

There are a number of other types of investment opportunities offered by Wall Street. These can be extremely complex and difficult for amateurs to understand. The old adage, "If it is too good to be true, it is," really applies. Options, swaps, hedges, and so forth (including, if you can believe it, something called a "swaption") are all representative of a broad class of assets sometimes known as financial instruments. These have been designed by professionals for sale to professionals. In theory, at least, each of these instruments is tailored to a very specific business risk or financial circumstance. Properly conceived they can limit risk, although at a cost comparable to an insurance premium (remember about free lunch).

For example, a company may have incurred a long-term debt with an interest rate that fluctuates up and down, 1 percent above the prime rate. Fearing that interest rates are about to go up, and disliking the uncertainty that a floating rate provides in terms of long-term strategic and financial planning, the company might wish to substitute a fixed rate for the debt. It is now possible to go to Wall Street and find someone who is willing to make that trade. That is, there would be someone else who is willing to take on a floating rate, perhaps anticipating a *drop* in interest rates, in exchange for a current fixed rate obligation. In such a case a swap would be negotiated. What has been described may sound complicated, but it is in fact a plain vanilla transaction, and far more complex transactions are being developed and offered every day. The legal and accounting ramifications of these exotic securities are far beyond the scope of this book.

Summary and Conclusions

The author would just like to leave this subject with one word of advice. If professionals in the securities market are advised or required to know their customer, it behooves you, as the customer, to know your advisor. Even more important, *know your product*. Once you have surplus funds to invest, there will be any number of people willing to help you. Pick someone you really can trust, and then make sure you understand all the pluses and minuses of whatever you do decide to invest in.

Investing is fun, particularly with other people's money. But it is not the primary reason for a business to exist. Funds should ideally be invested in productive assets, not the money market. Any company that has a permanent portfolio of short-term money market investments is making a mistake.

For a number of years, recent MBA graduates of one of the country's leading business schools fought hard to get jobs as managers of the money market portfolio of a major automobile company. They would be dealing, they thought, with large amounts of funds and, in addition, would have high visibility within the company. It was only after they joined the firm that they found out that the real action was not portfolio management but getting involved in the design, production, sale, and financing of the company's major product, automobiles. Those with a yen to be portfolio managers should go to work for banks, mutual funds, and pension funds, where the business is funds management. Everyone else should view investing temporarily surplus funds as a necessary evil.

10

The Road to Positive Cash Flow: Better Expense Control

Now K-Mart has to whittle down its expense structure to 1990s size. But expenses are sort of like fat: Accumulating them is easy, losing them requires a long and difficult diet.
    The New York Times, October 10, 1993

We also needed to adapt to a whole new way of setting budgets. Up until then, an area would look at what it had spent during the current year, then tack on some negotiated improvement factor and enough to offset inflation, and presto, there was next year's budget.

DAVID T. KEARNS, CEO,
Xerox Corporation
in *Prophets in the Dark:
How Xerox Reinvented Itself* [p. 223]

Individual managers invariably believe, at any point, that they have done a good job of controlling expenses if they have not exceeded their department's budget for the year to date. With payroll dollars usually accounting for a large portion of total expenses, merely having one or two less people on the payroll budget almost assures a manager of looking good. Of course, with less people all the necessary work may not get done. The solution: Have one or two more positions in the budget than you really need or expect to have.

This syndrome is perpetuated when higher levels of management evaluate subordinates on the basis of favorable departmental expense variances. If expenses are *over* budget, the question is, "Why?" Questions are rarely raised if expenses are *under* budget. Have you ever been asked, "Why didn't you spend *more* than budget on … (advertising), (travel), (training)?"

What is missing in this scenario? Neither the department head nor the higher level executive are relating cash outflows for expenses to expected *results*. Put this way, unless circumstances are the same in November as they were 14 months earlier when the budget was being prepared, it is unlikely that budgeted dollars of expense this month are at all closely related to desired operating results needed to meet *today's* business needs. Yet cash outflows, as we see, tend to track the budget much more closely than business requirements.

Ask any corporate manager whether she would rather go to the dentist, or review her department's proposed budget for next year with the accounting department's budget supervisor, and the answer may be the chair! In the next section we will review briefly the typical budget *process*, and see how it ties into cash flow projections. Then, in the following section, we will evaluate the relationship between the current year's approved budget and the inevitable changes that have taken place in the real world. We will see why managers invariably meet their expense projections, even if they miss revenue and profit commitments. In turn, this often leads top management to mandate more or less arbitrary "10-percent across-the-board reductions" in an effort once again to gain control of the budget, of expense levels, and hence cash flows. Finally, we propose a solution involving the TCM process.

The Tyranny of the Budget

Most firms adopt a bottom up approach or philosophy as the initial step in the preparation of the annual budget. That is, rather than have top management *tell* the unit what to do, an illusion is created that the people responsible for doing the work will set their own goals and objectives. A top down budget would have the CEO, the COO, and the Controller personally put together a forecast or budget, telling the troops what is expected of them. Perhaps the Army, where direct marching orders are common, can work this way. But with the emphasis on individual empowerment, the general feeling is that it is better to have active involvement from those who will be affected. As we will see, however, many problems are a direct consequence of the illusion that managers seemingly set their own goals, and hence their own budgets.

Let us go over the budget process, step by step, and identify the problem areas, how companies typically solve them, and follow through with an analysis of the cash consequences. Step 1, for almost every organization, is the sales forecast, usually built up by asking individual salesperson to forecast sales in their territory. For different kinds of analyses, sales projections are often needed by geographic region, broken down by product (often by customer or distribution channel) as well as by month throughout the year. The easiest way to get this detail, at least at first glance, is to ask *each salesperson* to forecast sales by product, by customer and by month.

Depending on the complexity of the product line, and the number of customers, a tremendous amount of detail must be collected from each salesperson. Pulling this data together represented a major clerical task for the budget department—at least B.C. (Before Personal Computers). Now, with spreadsheets, the clerical part can be automated, but the thought process has remained the same. The sheer mass of data, because it is so voluminous, appears to be accurate.

For most people, accounting or financial detail equals accuracy. The more detail, the more accurate the answers, is a very typical assumption. Thus the very first, and most important, step in the budget process, the *sales* (and cash receipts) *forecast* starts to take on a life of its own. It is precise, or at least appears that way because of the amount of detail underlying the final summary figures.

Have *you* ever tried to forecast sales? Have you ever tried to forecast anything? For most of us a typical forecast is:

1. not very accurate, because

2. it is based in large measure on very recent results.

If a salesperson has had a good month, say, August, when he is asked to prepare his budget forecast for the coming calendar year (4 to 16 months ahead), it is likely to be optimistic in total. If he had a bad August, the entire year's projection is going to be pessimistic. It is very difficult to stand back and analyze what is happening right now, and separate it from an unemotional objective view of the future. It is much easier to go with the flow, and assume that current trends will continue unabated.

Further muddying the water is the fact that no individual salesperson can possibly project by product, by customer and by month. She will be lucky if she can forecast *total dollar sales* within 10 to 15 percent for the year as a whole. Most compensation plans are based on total dollar results actually achieved, not on the accuracy of the forecast by product, by customer, or by month. The individual salesperson really has very little motivation, even assuming she has the ability, to produce truly accurate detailed sales projections. It is a mathematical certainty that the final answer (adding up all the sales projections to arrive at a divisional or company total) cannot be more accurate than the underlying detail.

If each salesperson is simply guessing, the only way the *total company* sales by product line, or by month, or by customer distribution channel is going to be reasonably accurate is by chance. Yet, as we saw, because the totals have so much supporting detail, and because so much effort went into gathering the data, it is difficult for anyone to stand back and question the final results. Thus the single most important factor affecting forecasts of future cash flows (that is, anticipated sales revenue) appears both precise and accurate but may well be no more than the sum of a number of guesses by individual sales representatives who individually and collectively have very little interest in the company's cash flow.

Compounding the problem, some, if not all, salespeople tend to be optimistic by nature. It goes with the territory. Nobody wants to turn in a budget projection lower than, or even equal to, the current year's anticipated results. If anything, there is an upward bias to most sales projections, one that management is reluctant to tamper with because the assumption is usually made that, "If we cut back Joe's sales forecast for next year, he won't work as hard or sell as much. Better to leave the high forecast in and *maybe* he will achieve it. Who knows?"

Going through the budget process, the usual next step, after the preliminary sales forecast has been approved, is to determine the *cost of sales*. This involves pricing out or costing what it will take to deliver the product or services customers are ordering. Depending on the type of business, most of the production may be performed by employees; this is particularly true of a service firm. Manufacturers, as well as retail and wholesale establishments, must also estimate the amount and price of *purchased* materials or inventory to arrive at a total cost of goods sold (CGS).

The cash flow impact of CGS is felt in three ways. First, what is the relative proportion of work effort to be performed by in-house employees, as contrasted with using outside vendors? The second concerns the amount and anticipated price level of purchased materials and supplies. Third, and most important, is the anticipated gross profit margin. How profitable are sales going to be?

Holding sales constant, and lowering CGS, raises gross profit and consequently cash flows. It is all too easy to assume that things will improve from last year, and that the gross profit *rate* will increase. Of course the total amount of gross profit is also a function of the absolute level of sales. But if sales go up 10 percent from the current year, and the gross profit percentage also rises, the impact on total profit and cash flow is highly favorable. How realistic the chances are for any such improvement is, however, often a matter for dispute between the controller and line operating managers.

In terms of cash, the final significant step in the budget process is the determination of *selling, general and administrative* (SG&A) *expenses*. These are the budget amounts against which department heads are measured. Sometimes pejoratively called overhead, the SG&A category covers everything from R&D, through Human Resources, MIS and Accounting, to Advertising and Marketing. All the mundane but important things every organization needs and spends money on—telephone, postage, rent, membership dues, travel expense, and so on, plus salaries and benefits—are included here. For budgeting purposes—but with no immediate impact on *cash*—depreciation expense must also be projected. The relation to cash flows of current expenditures on capital equipment, and the accounting related to depreciation, are covered in Chap. 12.

The only remaining steps in putting together a final budget relate to so-called financing costs, interest income, and expense (covered in Chaps. 6 and 9), and income taxes based on the projected level of net income. These are invariably calculated by the finance professionals. The more borrowing a company undertakes, the higher the outlay for interest, but in turn this becomes an iterative process requiring forecasts of production, sales and inventory levels. By the same token, if there is excess cash, interest income appears and must be calculated proportionately to investment levels throughout the year. While every aspect of Total Cash Management affects net borrowing or cash investments, line operating managers never deal with this directly.

Many firms properly consider income taxes—and strategies to minimize such payments—a key part of business strategy. The only effective way to avoid paying taxes, however, is to run a business at a loss, so before complaining too much about taxes, consider the alternative! There certainly are numerous tax strategies that tax professionals can advise a firm on, but they are outside the scope to this introduction to TCM.

The Budget Review Process

Here is where the *real* decisions impacting cash are made. To obtain a balance sheet and cash flow statement corresponding to the preliminary P&L, the controller will lay out sales, production, SG&A, and capital expenditures by month. She can then calculate the resulting levels of inventory, receivables, and PP&E and determine borrowing or excess cash as the balancing item. At that point, for the first time in the budget process, the projected ROI can be calculated. It is safe to say that the first pass results *never* meet the CEO's or the Board of Director's requirements.

The next step either has to be a repeat of the previous cycle, a bottom up *re*forecasting of sales, CGS, and SG&A—or the CEO *tells* the organization what is expected in the way of top line (sales) or bottom line (profit) results, or in some cases, both!. A shift to a top down approach to budgeting usually achieves, at least on paper, the results which are desired, such as a profit plan with the required level of profits and ROI. Such a change, to a top-down approach represents a shift that can have some very significant, although perhaps unintended, consequences in terms of cash flows.

When top management substitutes *it's judgment* for the sales representatives and operating line managers, two things are likely to happen. Whatever commitment an individual executive might have had to meet or beat a target which had been committed to, now is being measured against somebody else's goal. Since the executive had not necessarily bought in to the new (and presumably lower expense [or higher sales]) target there is less incentive to work hard to achieve the specific goal. Motivation does affect results, and a loss of motivation can be potentially serious.

Even more significant, when top management takes the budget into their own hands, the *arbitrary* reductions in allowed or budgeted expenses may be counterproductive. Top management may not be fully aware of the purpose or objective of certain proposed expenditures. Now, if they cut them back to meet overall budget goals, the line managers affected probably are going to keep quiet, and not necessarily fight for these items.

This is not to say that there was no "fat" in the first round of budget submissions. On the contrary, any experienced controller will not only tell you that fat exists, but will help you find it. This, by the way, is why financial managers are often so unpopular. Controllers who are pointing the finger, or even have the ability to point the finger, give many managers more than one or two nervous moments.

To the extent top management has to make more or less arbitrary across-the-board cuts, say, 10 percent, to achieve predetermined levels, it means that the *relationship between resources provided and activities to be performed* will have been attenuated, if not severed.

Activity-Based Management

Many readers will be familiar with activity-based costing (ABC)—a new cost accounting technique designed to relate expenditures with results. While initially used for determining product costs and measuring performance by product line or channel of distribution, the real benefit of ABC—or as some prefer to call it, activity-based management (ABM)—is to help identify so-called "nonvalue added" (NVA) activities. By definition, NVA represents work effort that does not improve the final product (or service) from the customer's perspective. To the extent that NVA can be identified, and then eliminated, costs will be reduced, cash outlays eliminated, and profits increased. These gains usually require improvements in business *processes*, and often require cross-functional *teams* to identify and then implement.

With these ideas in mind, let's look at the impact of an arbitrary 10-percent reduction in the proposed budget for SG&A. The only practical way for a manager to achieve an overall 10-percent reduction in the department's budget level is to reduce head count. Step 1 is to eliminate presently unfilled positions, or remove them from the budget. This lets you count as a savings the salaries that are *not* going to be paid to people who have *not* been hired. What is the impact of this savings on current cash outflows? Nothing!

The next step in reducing head count, from the perspective of an individual department, is to transfer *job functions,* and the individuals involved, to some other department. This again is no more than a budget game—no net cash reduction for the company as a whole is involved, but it does help the individual department head meet *the* target.

Assuming these two strategies don't work, it is then time to get down to *real* cuts. Two schools of thought exist. Politicians, in particular, are fond of making mandatory budget cuts in such highly visible activities as garbage collection or pothole filling—areas where taxpayers are directly and immediately affected. The second school says, "Let's cut clerical and support staff, because they are low paid, usually have low seniority, and the work will get done somehow." A different version says, "Let's set up an early retirement program and get rid of older staff," not recognizing that some of the organization's best workers with the most knowledge may unexpectedly choose the program.

The results of these two approaches can be predicted accurately—there will be virtually no cash savings in either case. Cutting people in visible or clerical areas rapidly lead to an outcry by those affected (taxpayers who cannot stand the smell of rotting garbage, or motorists who do not want to see their front end go out of alignment). In the corporate world, a similar savings could be achieved by proposing to fire the telephone operator or receptionist. It would not take long for employees, management, and customers to persuade the office manager to restore the cut, which then of course requires a modification of the budget.

When nonessential employees are let go for budget purposes (say, people over 55 who are near retirement, or those with little seniority at the low end of the salary scale) there are two cash costs, one visible and the other hidden. There is actual current expense for termination wages, accrued vacations, higher unemployment compensation benefit outlays, and perhaps payments for outplacement and many other related benefits.

When companies announce a significant downsizing program they set up a major accrual for these costs. In fact, under Generally Accepted Accounting Principles (GAAP), firms must accrue, at the time the decision is made, an amount equal to all anticipated outlays. A quick look at the business press suggests that in many cases this can exceed $50,000 per employee and in some instances even up to $100,000. No accounting entry, treating this as a "nonrecurring" item, helps *net* cash flows. An extraordinary expense charge may not hurt earnings per share from continuing operations, but the $50,000 or $100,000 per employee is real cash.

The second cost, although less visible, deals with the work activities performed by those now no longer employed. Does the work go away? Unless the actual work load is reduced (activities being performed are eliminated), what is going to happen? Instead of the sales manager's assistant preparing the weekly sales analysis by sales territory and by customer, the sales manager must now do it. First, he may not know just where to get the numbers, so he may actually be slower than the recently laid off assistant. Even more costly is the redirection of effort. Do you really want a sales manager performing clerical work? The company could make more profit and improve cash flow by having the sales manager sell.

You cannot have it both ways. Time spent preparing clerical reports is time *not* spent on productive activities. The answer is blindingly obvious. We would actually be better off, in terms of cash flow, by hiring a clerical assistant and letting the sales manager sell, motivate, and train the sales staff. Oops! Didn't we just lay off the assistant? Oh well, Human Resources will be able to find a replacement quickly. In fact, if we are lucky, we may even be able to rehire the same individual we just let go. So much for arbitrary, across the board reductions to save money.

If real cuts have to be made, human nature is such that lower level, recently hired employees are usually the first to go. Head count reductions are often mandated for budget purposes in terms of *number of people*, not dollars of payroll. Laying off the lowest paid 10 percent of the staff may, in practice, save less than 3 percent of the payroll dollars. For companies implementing a Total Cash Management plan, the lesson is clear—if mandated cuts are necessary, base it solely on dollars, not head count.

A manufacturing firm instructed its plants to budget for a 10-percent reduction in head count. The plant manager fired the full-time nurse. Then he turned around and hired five separate individuals each to work as the plant nurse one day a week. The company's payroll and financial reporting system distinguished between full-time and part-time employees. The latter, part-time employees, were not counted in the weekly report sent to the home office. Of course, payroll processing costs for five part-time individuals were now higher than for one full-time person, there was a lack of continuity in medical care, and so on. But the top management goal to reduce head count had been met.

Even if gamesmanship is not involved, across the board reductions of any type have a further cost, one that does not show up in the usual financial or management reports. What investment has the company previously made in *training* the existing work force? What were the hiring costs, such as advertising and interviewing, to put the people on the payroll in the first place? Current accounting requires that all such hiring and training costs be written off to expense each month. So when someone quits or is fired, or even temporarily laid off, there is no *apparent* further cost. In fact, cash had been expended in bringing these former employees on board. Not only is this cash gone, but as and when the positions are refilled, new expenditures will be required.

Accountants can argue (and they do!) as to whether there is such a thing as an asset related to the value of the current work force. Were we to have set up the initial hiring and training costs as an asset, and have a charge to expense for terminating the employees, the costs at a minimum would be highly visible. Here is another example where good accounting and TCM come to opposite conclusions.

Manage Activities, Not Costs

The *only* way to reduce a budget, to eliminate spending authority and the resultant cash flow, is to change what you are doing or the way you are doing things. If you are going to have a receptionist/telephone operator from 8:30 to 5:00, you are committed to a salary of say $17,000. How do you reduce the $17,000? Do you hire someone younger and less experienced for $14,000? If so, how will the public, which comes in contact with your organization, react? In this era of Total Quality, most of the gurus are suggesting *upgrading* points of public contact. So replacing the incumbent with a less well-trained individual is not the answer. How about changing the hours to 9:30 to 3:30. If the rate paid per hour is kept constant, this would accomplish a 25-percent reduction in cash outlay. But who would answer phone calls from customers after 3:30? This book is not a treatise on either telecommunications or office management, but here is one solution:

> Put in a new direct dial system; each employee would have his or her own direct phone number. There would be, in addition, an automated answering service with a recording saying, "Punch 1 for Customer Service, punch 2 for … "

Whether you like this particular approach or not, it would allow you to eliminate the telephone operator position. You would save the $17,000 offset by the incremental cost for the more sophisticated phone system.

Let's look for a moment at this example, because it really brings into perspective the difference between arbitrary cost reductions, and changing the way you do business—that is, managing activities. In our telephone example there will be a fundamental change in the way the firm does business. Each employee will be answering his or her own phone, and outside callers to the main number will hear a prerecorded announcement.

Public perception of the company will change—whether for the better or worse is not determinable at this point, although each of us has our own evaluation. Individual employees will have to learn new telephone etiquette. Someone will have to monitor the master recording at the organization's main number to see it is responsive to customer needs, and so on. Eliminating one position involves, in this case, changing the activities of a number of others.

Many consultants have formalized this analysis of activities, with suggestions for simplification and cost reduction, and christened it "Business Process Reengineering." A change in one employee's activities directly affects many others in an organization. To prevent chaos, as each manager redesigns or reengineers activities, someone else (the project manager or process owner) has to look at the impact of any change in one area on all others in the activity chain or process.

Business Process Improvement

> Organizing around processes, as opposed to functions, permits greater self-management and allows companies to dismantle unneeded supervisory structures. Business processes can form the link between high-performance work teams and the corporation at large. *Fortune*, May 18, 1992 [p. 95]

Two examples of a business process are the new-product development function and the order-delivery-billing cycle. Meaningful improvements in costs (genuine cash savings as opposed to budget gamesmanship) have to come from looking at the *total* process. Think of a business process as a system. Just as a physician has to look at the digestive *system* in its entirety to treat a stomach problem, so too do managers have to look at existing procedures in light of a continuous supplier-customer chain.

Let's take a closer look at the order-delivery-billing cycle to see how a process approach would allow cost reductions. If a dollar *savings* were the goal, the first thought would be "Let's cut people." Thus the sales manager would have to let one or two sales reps go, and the order entry department would fire at least one clerk. A fork lift operator in the warehouse would be redeployed, while the controller would have to make do with one less billing clerk. Each of these savings would be rationalized as follows:

1. The sales manager would argue that she was letting go the sales rep with the poorest record—the one furthest behind quota—so it would have the least impact on sales volume.

2. The manager of Order Entry, with one fewer person, would no longer be able to edit incoming orders completely, at least for part-number accuracy, but in his opinion 95-percent accuracy probably is good enough.

3. The warehouse manager knows the remaining workers will simply have to work overtime to keep up with shipments, unless there is at least a 10-percent reduction in overall sales.

4. The controller will be able to get along with one less clerk by batching up invoices and sending them out to customers only once a week.

In a word, this approach to cost reduction is all too common. Many readers may even view this as the norm! Management consultants have a term for this approach: *sub-optimization*. Each department tries to optimize its own function—at the expense of the overall system. In the example just given, what will be the impact on cash flow? This, after all, is the test we are asking every management action to pass.

Dismissing an unproductive salesperson may or may not save cash, depending on just how much sales volume the individual is responsible for. As we saw in Chap. 3 (discussing the impact of using credit as a sales tool), the appropriate test is to look at the *incremental profit* or *cash flow* from the additional sales either a sales increase or sales decrease.

In this case, letting any salesperson go will impact sales volume adversely. How much may be hard to estimate, but an informed guess is going to be better than none at all. For relatively high gross profit products and services, the lost revenues—the net cash flows—attributable to even a poor salesperson may have a greater impact than the total prospective savings in salary, benefits, and travel expenses from dismissing the individual. In short, letting go even a mediocre sales person may *not* be an effective way to cut expenses and boost cash flow. What looks good on the budget report for a particular department is not the basis for sound decision making.

Replacing the poor producer with a *new* sales representative or going out and hiring a more productive replacement, may be a truly effective action. We must consider the hiring cost, the lost sales during the recruitment and training period, the out-of-pocket expense of training the replacement, and the time needed for the new individual to build up rapport with the existing customer base. Then ask how long it will take for the new person to start developing additional or *new* volume, in addition to what the previous poor performer had accomplished, and it is easy to see that any *net* favorable impact on cash flows is going to be at least six to eight months out. Hardly an effective way to improve this year's operations.

Note: This should not suggest that a poor salesperson should be kept on irrespective of results. Sales reps get paid based on measurable results. If they do not measure up over a specified period of time a change should be made, admitting that a mistake in the previous selection process had been made. The point is that a sales manager should be reviewing performance and upgrading staff capabilities *all the time.* One does not *start* the improvement process only when current results for the organization are serious enough to call for across-the-board changes.

The second savings proposed was in Order Entry, presumably a clerical worker. Without changing the process of entering orders, say, by computerizing functions which are now manual, how will the existing work load get done? Firing the clerk saves the salary and benefits, an immediately apparent cash impact. But, who is going to do the work done by that individual? Unless the person was an absolute failure—and it should not require an economic downturn to weed out incompetence—the amount of work is going to be unchanged. The remaining order entry clerks are going to have to (1) work harder, (2) work overtime, or (3) not do as thorough a job of editing and proofreading orders. Of course, for a short period, the supervisor may pitch in and help out. Again, either the supervision effort is needed and now will not be available, or it was not really needed in the first place.

Trying to have the remaining employees work harder, when they can see the company is firing others all around them, probably will only work for a very short while. Resentment builds up quickly and most likely the best employees, thinking they see the handwriting on the wall, will seriously start looking for employment elsewhere. Company cost reductions, no matter how well intentioned, cause fear, uncertainty and doubt among *all* employees. The only variable is how long it takes any employee to react. Typically the better workers think about bailing out while there is still time, while the poorer employees, with no other place to go, hang in there. The bottom line, in terms of cash flow, is that good employees will soon have to be replaced—at a real cash cost out of pocket.

Cutting out a worker in a department without rearranging the work flow is counter-productive. This is why forced or arbitrary 10-percent across-the-board reductions never work. Unless the *work effort* is reduced there can never be true cash savings. Of course, if volume is reduced 10 percent—sales and productions declining proportionately—manpower cuts are almost mandatory. Absent such real reductions in business volume, personnel cuts will be a waste of effort. If the amount of work stays the same, and available resources are cut, *something* will change.

In practice what will change is the *quality* of work. And the change will be for the worse. In our Order Entry example, all the incoming customer orders will still be entered. They probably will be entered on time, within two business days, if that is the standard. Too many other parts of the organization would notice right away, and complain bitterly if Order Entry was perceived to have slowed down. If the volume stays the same, and the same timetable is to be met, how are fewer employees going to process a larger number of orders per person? It is simple. No matter what level of automation, no matter how sophisticated the system, people still exercise judgment. Informal rules of thumb exist. Business changes too quickly for these requirements ever to be written down and programmed. Order Entry clerks know that all orders from one important customer *must* be shipped within four days, and thus have to be expedited, while another customer does not want to be shipped and billed until the first of the month, and so on.

These examples are two aspects of Quality that are often lost sight of. From our customers' perspective—say, the first one is on a JIT production system—speedy delivery is crucial. If most other customers do not have this requirement, it makes sense to treat your one customer's requirement for quick turnaround as an exception. In the case of the customer who wants to be billed the first of next month, later than normal, there may well be cash flow implication: The customer may have to adhere to a loan covenant. An early shipment, with its consequent accounts payable liability, may throw working capital calculations out of predetermined levels.

Meeting these two customers' unique needs is what separates a good supplier from a poor one. We are trying to be a good supplier, because that is how we have built up the business—meeting customer needs. That also is the definition of Quality.

Now let's look at the impact of a cutback in the Order Entry department. Susan, the clerk terminated last Friday, handled all orders for customers A to D. If there were five clerks, and now there are four, each of her accounts will be parceled out to someone else. What are the odds that Susan had (1) written down the two customer requirements previously spelled out, and (2) communicated this to the other employees or the supervisor before she left? The answer is painfully obvious.

Following this example through, what will happen to the first order from each of the two customers? Both will be entered, processed, and shipped as normal orders. One customer's shipment will be late, with possibly catastrophic consequences for his production schedule, while the second may just have a problem with her bank because of a large early shipment.

Two unhappy customers. Two situations where there is a cost due to poor quality. Maybe we cannot measure the impact of failing to meet our customers' expectations this time. Our salespeople will hold their hands and promise that, "It will never happen again." But unless the salespeople make a conscious effort to communicate in writing the important, but previously informal customer requirements (only Susan, the former clerk *knew* them) what are the chances the *next* orders from each customer will be processed correctly? Don't forget, we also laid off one salesperson, and asked the remaining sales reps to pick up the slack.

Suppose the new sales rep does not get the word to Order Entry and the same screwup happens again. Now we have real problems. At this point the sales manager and Order Entry manager will each start pointing fingers. Questions about each other's parentage, their dedication to company interests, and their basic competence to hold their jobs will be thrown back and forth. The reader can take it from here.

Who was *really* at fault? The author submits that neither the Order Entry manager nor the sales manager can be blamed. Sure, communication, that famous scapegoat, could have been better. It can *always* be better. Sure, the specific customer instructions should have been written down. But as long as Susan was on the job the orders were *never* entered incorrectly and customer requirements were always met.

Does this mean Susan ran the company? Was she truly indispensable? Was she just lazy or remiss in not putting important customer data about in writing? None of the above! Susan did not run the company. She was not indispensable. And her behavior—not writing everything down—is shared by 99.98 percent of the population. (Have *you* made written notes about all key aspects of your job?)

Understanding this situation for what it is will go a long way in understanding why it is so difficult to save cash through cutting expenses. The truth is that people are necessary. Judgment is used much more frequently than is commonly recognized. Even the lowest level clerical worker has an important role to play. Otherwise why did we create the job in the first place? What is the job function we anticipated when the position was created?

Who Will Solve the Problem and Save Cash?

Mistakes will happen, and even companies with the most rigorous approach to Quality have more than one in a million errors. What is necessary is to determine what areas of a business are most in need of improvement, that is, where will the greatest return for the investment be. In this case the term *investment* refers not to dollars of capital expenditure but to an even scarcer resource—management time.

Before implementing cutbacks in SG&A expenses (pejoratively called *overhead* by sales reps and factory workers) management must think through the implications of changes in work force relative to work loads. Significant internal work effort has to be expended by management to accomplish some of these seemingly simple tasks. If one is going to achieve savings through computerization of a particular process, then to really solve the problems a new computer-based system has to be designed, new written forms created, and employees trained.

However, the first, and most difficult step, is simply *identifying* that a system change is needed. *Who* is going to do this? The sales manager has his hands full meeting quota. The Order Entry manager is already trying to cope with her reduced staff. Neither are system experts. Somebody has to *design* the forms, making sure that any instructions regarding customer requirements are both clear and doable. Then *training* the sales staff to actually use the new form, and fill it out every time, may not be a trivial exercise. Processing paperwork is not one of the usual criteria for selecting sales representatives.

Even after we have a good form, motivate the salespeople to fill it out accurately, and have it back in the Order Entry department, someone has to *program* the computer to add the new information to the database and devise a report that effectively utilizes the new delivery schedule information. All of these steps have to be accomplished at a time when we are trying to cut expenses.

Once again, *who* will take the lead, act as project manager, in a system redesign affecting at least three different departments, probably reporting to three different line executives? By the time most companies get their act together, nobody will remember that the impetus came from laying off Susan, with its consequent ill effects on two key customers. Maybe it is easier just to ask the Order Entry personnel to *remember* the specific requirements of important customers. But then you cannot afford much staff turnover! Like many business problems, once again we seemingly have a Catch 22 situation.

Going back to the beginning of our expense reduction case study, let's look at the reduction in warehouse staff. Here we cut one worker, and met the continuing requirements through overtime from the remaining staff. Brief bursts of overtime are far better in terms of cash flow than a full-time worker. But at time-and-a-half, plus inefficiencies as workers physically tire from the extra workload, it is counterproductive to have much more than 5 percent of work effort performed on an overtime basis.

Yes, a full-time employee costs the employer cash in terms of benefits such as health care. If benefits amount to 25 percent of payroll, at first glance it may look cheaper to reduce staff by 10 to 15 percent and just plan on permanent overtime. Given the desires for leisure time, most employees would not accept a permanent 50-hour work week. Occasional overtime will work. Permanent overtime will not.

Recall that the final element of the cost reduction case study was the reduction by the controller of one accounting clerk responsible for invoicing. We assumed the same number of invoices to be mailed out and, with fewer staff, a system change would be implemented. Instead of billing customers each day, concurrent with shipments, invoices would be accumulated in batches and processed once a week. This definitely will save in out-of-pocket administrative expense, but will certainly impact cash flow negatively and force Days Sales Outstanding to go up following delayed invoicing. Sending out invoices three days late, on average, will increase DSO by three days.

What is the overall lesson to be learned from this cost reduction case study? At first, readers may be tempted to throw up their hands in despair. Maybe expenses cannot be cut! In fact, a look at quarterly financial results, as reported in the *Wall Street Journal*, suggests that most companies do *not* control their SG&A expenses.

If SG&A expenses were fixed in practice, then they should not vary with volume. As sales volume increased, therefore, profit *margins* should go up as greater volume is spread over the same base. However, very few firms end up materially improving their margins. This means, in practice, that as sales volumes rise, so do most categories of expense. Indeed, as volume increases, many companies are lucky to keep operating profits—as a percentage of sales—constant. Put a different way, most SG&A expenses appear to be variable at least on the way up. There are very few truly fixed costs when sales volume is increasing.

But when sales decline, as we have just seen, many if not most expenses are perceived to be fixed. In the short-run it is very hard to cut expenses without affecting operating efficiencies. This phenomenon may help explain why many companies are willing to cut selling prices to maintain volume. It may be simpler to cut prices and maintain volume, than to cut expenses.

Cost-Effective Expense Control

The title of this section may be considered by some as an oxymoron, because it implies that some expense control is not cost-effective. But as we saw in our mandated expense reduction case, individual managers, meeting pre-determined targets, usually do not consider the company as a whole. They are judged on their own department's expense budget. So, following the cost reductions, if a customer order is shipped late, or early as the case may be, not one of the managers would look in the mirror and admit that *his* actions caused the problem. It is *always* somebody else's fault, if not somebody else's problem.

Two steps are needed so that cash flow can be managed positively. Step 1 is always to ask, "Who, or what, will be affected if I cut this expense?" Unless the actual amount of work is decreased there are certain to be adverse consequences somewhere in the system. Even if volume is down, and the work force reduced proportionately, work assignments are going to have to be juggled. Step 2 involves training or retraining the remaining staff. In addition, extra supervision will be required during any transition period.

Look at these in turn. Taking a true systems or business process approach is really the only answer. This in turn requires that individual line managers, those in charge of functional operating departments, really understand how their work fits into the big picture. The only way to go about this is to understand all the job functions any individual to be let go is really performing. Then one has to ask, "How are those functions going to get done without these resources available?"

This may not be as difficult as first thought. How do the job functions get done when the employee is sick, on jury duty, or on vacation? In the short run, others do pitch in. Will this (can this) work permanently? Probably not. But you will have some time to make adjustments to existing processes. You can, and must, communicate with peers in other functional areas. Proposing changes that will reduce total resources required to meet overall objectives (satisfied customers) is *your* responsibility. Since this itself involves several functional areas, and differences of opinion inevitably arise, someone at a higher level ultimately has to make some decisions.

For this reason we recommend that when costs are to be reduced, and this almost always is accomplished by reducing staff, the management team as a whole meet and plan the downsizing together. Anticipate where there will be bottlenecks and how they will be handled. Also, equally important, determine *who* will handle coordinating changes to operating procedures. Unless there is communication, coordination and advance planning, any downsizing is going to be ineffective at best, and counterproductive at worst.

Absent the front-end planning, as soon as things start to get out of control, overtime will be needed and undoubtedly will be worked. When that is no longer cost-effective, temporary help (Manpower or Olsten) must be called upon. The next step is to hire part-time employees. Finally, as business improves, full-time new employees can be justified. But guess what? The savings from the previous layoff and downsizing have vanished. We are back where we started 10 to 12 months ago—unless the total workload went down permanently or we are performing some job functions differently.

Doing work differently is the secret. There are many books, magazine articles and consultants, all of whom spell out how to accomplish these systems or business process changes. The point to be made dealing with Total Cash Management is that there is no effective way to save cash by arbitrarily cutting expenses without cutting the workload.

Cutting the work load never happens by itself. It requires positive management effort, hard work, all of which is taking place just when the organization is under pressure. Priorities must be set. Often a business process redesign appears to have low priority relative to sales. But if the business process redesign is *not* accomplished, either expenses will remain high—and cash will not be saved—or Quality, in the broadest sense of the word, will suffer. At a time of business pressure can you really afford poor quality?

Put this way, the answer is obvious. When sales are down, and margins under pressure, Quality can be and usually is a competitive advantage. The last thing you want is a decline in customer service. Yet, without advance planning, cost reductions to meet predetermined budgeted profit goals are very likely to be counterproductive. The real problem is that in practice the right questions are not asked at the right time.

Someone described this approach to business as, "Ready, Fire, Aim!" Firing an employee first, and then waiting to see how the work will get done demonstrates a lack of true cash awareness. In a Total Cash Management environment, the right questions *will* be asked.

Solving the Expense Control Problem in Advance

Many investors in the stock market, before they buy any stock, decide at what price they will sell the stock. Say, for example General Motors is at 50, with a price objective of 65; if the price goes below 44 at any point the investor will sell. This applies the theory of cutting your losses and letting your profits run.

Dealing with employees, before anyone is added to the payroll, the question is almost always asked, what is the person's work effort going to accomplish if my volume continues at present levels or even rises. Put another way, before approval is given to a new hire, someone asks that tough question, "Why?" Most managers are prepared to justify staff increases, more often than not either to keep existing customers happy, maintain or improve service at existing levels, or to handle growth. Almost everyone is willing to admit there is some correlation between volume and resources.

The concept that employee levels should fluctuate with volume is well established and generally accepted—as long as business conditions are good and rising. It is when volume *decreases* (comparable to the price decrease in the stock market) that there is great reluctance to reduce costs. The reason is clear—selling stock at a loss may be an emotional experience for the investor, but not for the shares of stock themselves. Stocks have no feelings. Getting rid of stock involves a simple phone call to the broker, and a few days later there is cash in your account.

Getting rid of employees is totally different. No manager can honestly state that he or she *likes* firing or laying off another human being. Downsizing has other costs, direct and indirect: Unemployment insurance rates will rise, negative publicity will appear in the press, and so on.

Finally, many management personnel are starting to relate the horrible labor relations in the automobile, steel, and coal industries to the very way such industries treated employees, particularly hourly production workers. It is easy to remember the days when a slight reduction in the demand for steel would immediately call for temporary layoffs. And, of course, when steel demand was soft, the need for coal went down, so the coal companies immediately responded with their own layoffs.

It is no wonder that labor union membership has great appeal to workers whose jobs are insecure. Industries with the strongest unions today are those that, in the past, treated their employees most like a commodity or a share of stock, a piece of paper to be bought and sold. The United Auto Workers, United Steel Workers, and United Mine Workers unions ultimately achieved greater economic strength than the employers in their industries. Now the number of auto companies, steel mills, and coal mines have all gone way down, as have the number of jobs for the unionized workers.

Getting back to the root cause, a very strong case could be made that when employers treat workers as a commodity, not as individuals with families to be fed, there will ultimately be a reaction. In the case of the United States, labor laws were introduced and collective bargaining enforced. The consequences included restrictive labor practices agreed to by management to buy peace, and finally wage increases granted that were totally unrelated to bottom-line productivity. The impact of restrictive labor practices—combined with too-high wages for those workers lucky enough to keep their job—has been a recipe for disaster.

Most of today's top management, particularly in other industries, is fully aware of this history and reacts accordingly. They will go to great lengths to avoid layoffs, but when the cash is about to run out, they *have* to move. And that is when the arbitrary reductions are mandated.

Now let's return to the example of the purchase of shares of stock. Good investors tell themselves, in advance, what the course of action is going to be on the downside. Shouldn't the same approach be taken in hiring an additional employee? You know why you are putting them on the payroll. You know what the cash outlay is going to be to keep the individual—things such as salary, benefits, space, travel, and so forth. You know the functions the new additional employee is to perform, and the cash flow benefits of the anticipated additional volume.

But things don't always turn out as you expected. General Motors stock can go from 50 to 44. The sales increase anticipated in the southeastern region turns into a decrease as a competitor expands distribution there. The scenarios are endless. The point is:

Whenever an employee is added to the payroll, a specific fall back position should be developed in advance. At what point are you going to take action, admitting you made a mistake, and terminate that one person? Further, if you have to let that person go, how do you plan to get that person's work done? After all, some of your projected volume increase will have been attained, even if not all of it.

If this approach is taken, if a specific game plan is developed *before* you add *any* employee, you will avoid the phenomenon, "On the way up all costs are variable and on the way down all costs are fixed." The impact of the recommended policy will be to hire much more slowly when business is increasing, because of uncertainty whether any expansion will continue. On the downside, individual employees may be terminated sooner, rather than later. But they will go off the payroll one at a time, they will be the newest hires, and there will be no headlines in the local press, "Company Y Lays Off Hundreds: Executives Admit Recession Caught Them By Surprise."

Treating an entire work force as though it is no more than a commodity or a financial portfolio is guaranteed to foster a response. It is a response that is diametrically the opposite of what almost everyone wants in the way of an employee base. Even more important, it will kill cash flow. Workers should be motivated self-starters with a genuine interest in the firm's products and its customers. It is safe to say that the managers of the Big Three automobile firms could not say 20, or even 10, years ago that they had such a work force. The implications, in terms of reported operating and cash losses of the Big Three firms in the past 15 years, suggest that a different approach to budgeting and hiring might have been an important element of their achieving the goals of Total Cash Management.

11

Proper Budgeting for Maximum Cash Flow

*I had heard that the Prudential was making
loans to a lot of retail chains .... I had my
predictions all spelled out on my yellow legal
pad, and I was sure they were going to loan us
the money. I went through my five-year plan ...
and told the loan officer how much business
we thought there was out there waiting to be
plucked. He didn't buy it at all, told us he
didn't think a company like the Prudential
could afford to gamble with us. I saved those
projections for a long time, and they were all
exceeded by 15 to 20 percent in the years to come.*
SAM WALTON, from *Sam Walton:
Made in America* [p. 95]

Not every company is going to grow as fast as Wal-Mart. In fact, very few
do. In hindsight it is easy to say what a fool the Prudential loan officer was,
turning down the country's greatest twentieth-century success story. But
as Sam Walton immediately pointed out, he was able to get his loan at
another insurance company "Only by giving them our right arm and our
left leg. We didn't just pay interest, we had to give them all sorts of stock
options in case we did go public."

What is important here is that Sam Walton presented what he thought
were very realistic sales projections, incorporating substantial growth. In
the final analysis, two sophisticated analysts simply did not believe Wal-

244

ton's growth projections as presented. Why? It is very simple. In American business nobody ever prepares a budget or forecast that does anything but go up. But, if *every* budget shows increases, then skepticism by third parties is understandable. Unquestioned acceptance of substantial growth projections would be the exception among outside analysts.

People who prepare budgets seem almost to follow certain conventions. "Maybe in the next few months we will have to get things turned around, but from there on it is straight up." Accountants have taken to calling this the "hockey stick" profile—lots of growth from here on out, with perhaps just a short-term squiggle at first. For every Sam Walton and Wal-Mart, which did grow straight up, millions of other firms have a cyclical pattern. There *are* downs as well as ups.

As shown in Chap. 2, operating decisions presented in a budget directly affect cash in numerous and often unanticipated ways. Unanticipated, that is, as usually presented in the budget process. There will always be surprises—both favorable and unfavorable—but most of them *can* be anticipated if the right questions are asked. All too often it falls to the controller to ask those tough questions. The often unstated implication of a controller asking about additional consequences of budget proposals is that the proposer was not smart enough to think through the answer. This invariably leads to an adversarial relationship, which is why a controller is almost always on the defensive in the budget process.

The truth is that accountants, and financial managers in general, are trained to ask those questions. The audit function, where most accountants get their initial training, consists of checking on the existence and functionality of controls. This involves asking lots of questions. Accounting deals with numbers—the raw material of financial analysis. And as we all know, numbers can be tricky. When financial analysts look at income and expense, assets and liabilities, cash and credit, skepticism and an analytic approach are *required*.

So by training and experience, if not by formal job description, these attributes combine to make the controller into what is often perceived as the no-sayer. Really it is not *saying* no, but asking the right questions, and following through to determine the total cash consequences of budget proposals. People realize that the proper answer perhaps should have been no. Don't shoot the messenger or, in this case, the person who just asks the tough questions.

Referring to the Chap. 2 budget cases, as employees we would all *like* to have a new 401(k) plan. But when we think through the administrative costs of both setting it up and continuing to administer it, combined with the direct expense of a $400,000 company match, we see that there may be better uses for those resources. The Human Resources manager who proposed the 401(k) plan feels like she got shot down by the controller. The real problem was that she did not look at *all* the costs, direct and indirect.

Can all managers be turned into financial analysts? Should we even try to teach them to use the tools of financial analysis? The answer to the first question is a resounding no. If anything, the world needs fewer bean-counters, not more. It would be a waste of skilled resources to retrain sales, production, and engineering managers.

Most managers today, either in college or graduate school, have at least been exposed to the tools of financial analysis. Those who have not had formal training have probably had business experience answering "what-if" questions. Understanding and using Total Cash Management in the budget process, and by extension throughout the organization at all times, does not require substantial training. It does require a willingness to think through the implications of actions and decisions. It also requires a degree of realism that, wrong as they subsequently turned out to be, the loan officers accused Sam Walton of missing. This time the loan officers were wrong and Sam was right. More often it is the other way. Those preparing budgets are too optimistic and it falls to the financial analyst, controller, or loan officer to blow the whistle.

How Growth Decisions
Affect Cash Flows

We have argued elsewhere that neither long-term strategic planning nor short-term budgeting need always show growth. A look at any historical chart of economic activity shows periods of decline. Could they have been anticipated? Should they have been anticipated? Answers to these questions are critical. An unreasoning focus on growth, a feeling that if we do not grow we will die, probably leads to more bad decisions affecting cash flow than any other single factor.

Since every forecast or budget starts with a sales projection, this is the place to start. Companies can put together a sales forecast from the bottom up—asking individual salesmen for their best guess—or it can do it from the top down, with the CEO or VP of Sales making a specific determination.

Either approach has significant built-in biases and can lead to errors. In what direction these biases will flow more often than not is a function of compensation policies. If management is paid a bonus only when they meet or beat budget targets, human nature suggests the budgets will be relatively low. If compensation is paid on some absolute basis, say, earnings per share (EPS), then management may set high targets to stretch the sales staff.

If the sales staff itself develops its own goals, the same phenomenon probably exists. Individuals like to look good. If compensation is based on absolute dollar quotas for the territory, or on a comparison with last year, the natural tendency towards optimism of individual salespeople will probably cumulate and lead to a significantly overstated sales total. Top management will hesitate to adjust the numbers for fear that cutting a sales target set by the individual will be perceived negatively. Again, there is a built-in assumption that individuals will work harder—accomplish more—depending on the goal or target. The consequence, however, is an unrealistic sales target.

If a budget is to be a useful management tool, it *must* be as accurate as possible. If you try to kill two birds with one stone you will miss both. If you try to make one budget do two things—act as a motivational device *and* guide the allocation of resources to maximize cash flow—you will obtain neither objective.

Step one in budgeting has to be a fundamental decision that the budgeted sales volume is the organization's absolute *best guess* as to what will happen, not what you *hope* will happen. Now someone will say, "Yes, the sum of all the salesperson's forecasts *is* high, but it *could* happen." The best response was one made by a marketing VP, who responded, "Yes, and if I jumped out that window I *could* go up." Would you want to bet on it? If you buy into an unrealistic sales forecast you are, in effect, betting your job if not the whole organization.

> A professional services organization one year put together a very optimistic sales budget. The executive in charge of the professional staff added up the personnel resources available to him from the existing staff and compared it with the resources required to meet the budget. He was way short. The response was clear: "If we are going to meet budget we must go out and hire immediately, so the new staff can be trained in time." This way there would be enough additional professionals to produce the budgeted volume. Unfortunately, the salespeople did not achieve *any* increase in sales from the previous year. They completely missed the "stretch" goal. The firm then had to fire all the new staff. The total cost of hiring, training, and severance was truly material. Instead of a good year, as budgeted, it was one of the worst years in the company's history.

The moral is clear:

When you start to believe your own propaganda, look out.

The watchword in real estate is "Location, location, location." The watchword in budgeting must be "Realism, realism, realism." A budget must be coherent—all parts have to fit together, all resources have to be in balance. This does not mean that if in the first month you miss sales revenue you have to throw out the budget and start over again to keep everything in balance. A budget is a roadmap showing the best way to get from here (beginning of the year) to there (end of year). Just as you may make a bad turn starting out on a trip, you don't give up and go home. You turn around and get back on track, albeit running now a little behind schedule.

If monthly financial reports are available promptly, it is quite feasible to analyze where the organization departed from budget. To use the technical term, you analyze the variances, and decide on the appropriate course of action at that point. Since everything rarely goes wrong all at once, prompt attention showing where you have departed from plan will probably indicate pretty clearly what is the most appropriate immediate new course of action. Without the budget, you might well get five different diagnoses and ten different prescriptions. With the budget, which everyone had already agreed upon was what we *wanted* to do, all we have to do is determine what is needed to get back on track.

The Curse of Growth

A few moments ago we argued for realism in budgets. Common sense suggests that if realism is truly adopted by an organization, then one year out of three (or maybe one year out of four) is *not* going to have significant volume gains. The economy, competitors, customers, suppliers, labor unions or even your own new product developments will cause a stumble. But for some reason it is un-American to show level operations, year-to-year. Heaven forbid an absolute drop.

For reasons not totally clear to the author, the growth syndrome has taken on a life of its own. A CEO's manhood will be called in question at the country club if growth objectives are not set. If they are not met, after the fact, lots of excuses are possible, and since the past cannot be undone, will have to be accepted. But because of some idiosyncrasy of the American culture, *planning* for poor results is considered unacceptable. In effect it is considered treasonous if we say, "Despite our best efforts we will not improve over last year." The fact the economy is in the tank or a competitor brought out a blockbuster product simply is not considered acceptable.

This book is not going to bring about an economy wide refocus away from growth for the sake of growth. It might be better to have a culture that stresses realism for the sake of realism. Nonetheless, the author sincerely hopes that readers take to heart the arguments made here for realism. How can you possibly control your cash resources if you don't know where you want to go? If you have an unrealistic budget going in, where will you end up? The answer is clear. You simply do not know. A realistic budget in January is no guarantee that on December 31 you will exactly meet the goals set forth a year earlier. Your chances of coming close, however, are infinitely improved as compared with an *unrealistic* budget. Both are better than no budget at all.

Responding to Pressure

You are in the following situation: Things do not appear to be going well, the outlook at best is for next year to equal this year, and there will probably be a downturn. Following the advice given here, you *want* to budget realistically. However you feel under pressure to try harder, and want to answer positively when your boss asks, "Can't you do a little better?" In short, you face a classic double bind—be true to yourself, and meet the boss's expectations.

Here is where a good controller can really help. The most practical solution is to prepare *two* separate budgets or forecasts. The first is what management, your boss, *wants* to see. The second represents what you *believe* is most likely to happen, given actual conditions. Whether the unpleasant projection is a reflection of poor conditions in the economy, specific competitive factors in your industry, or a result of internal operating problems is immaterial. Irrespective of the cause, at least you have to know what is most probable, if for no other reason than that is going to be the only way to start solving the problem.

Preparing two budgets for your area of responsibility may sound like a lot of work. Different organizations have differing philosophies about the level of detail contained in the final approved budget package. That makes no difference. Assuming short-term continuity of your employment is a high priority, obviously you must comply with your boss's request, if for no other reason than to show you are a team player. Since we have argued for budgets that are internally consistent, you have to go all the way and complete the total budget package. Presumably the bottom line of that presentation will then meet management expectations.

You, however, are still uncomfortable. You don't really want to bet your job on achieving something that in your heart you know is not likely to happen. Probably you feel, and the reaction is normal, "I'll tell them what they want to hear, but we are only postponing the inevitable bad news for a few months."

Frankly, any manager who stops right there is committing treason! The U.S. Constitution defines treason as "giving aid and comfort to enemies." Submitting a budget you know will not happen is equivalent to giving aid and comfort to your competitors—who presumably are your enemy. Adoption of a coherent integrated budget, but one that cannot be achieved, is going to waste scarce resources, both cash and skilled manpower. Unnecessarily wasting resources has to be at the top of any list of disloyal actions.

If you have to please your boss by letting him have a budget he likes, but it is disloyal to know you would be wasting resources trying to achieve it, what is the answer? Prepare a second summary of what *you* think is most likely to happen. It is not necessary to redo all the detail, line by line, department by department. What is necessary is to show what you think is *achievable*, at least in terms of gross revenues, product costs, SG&A, and related asset and liability accounts. A one or two page top-level summary will be sufficient to make your point.

To complete your package, fulfilling your total responsibilities to the organization, you should have the controller prepare a schedule showing the *difference* between the budget as submitted to comply with corporate growth objectives and what you feel is most likely to happen. Adding unnecessarily to expenses to meet growth objectives, building inventory for sales that do not materialize, and investing in capital equipment to prevent anticipated production shortages all end up wasting cash. Quantifying the difference, combined with a brief but cogent written analyis, should accomplish one of two things. You may get lucky. Someone at a higher level will read and actually pay attention to your analysis. Then your approach can be adopted, or at a minimum some compromises made to modify the unrealistic growth scenario. Assume the worst, however, that top management does *not* pay attention to your warnings, then six months or so into the budget year, when things are turning out the way you predicted, you at least have some contemporaneous support to show that the budget shortfall had been anticipated. Your explanations will not recover the wasted cash. They may well enhance your credibility (although maybe not your popularity) and people will listen to you when the following year's budget is being prepared.

Your analysis of the cash flow impact of adopting an unrealistic projection—and then acting on that projection—should not be viewed as a C-Y-A document. It definitely should not be presented that way. But if you sincerely believe that the official party line is wrong, and will lead to counter-productive actions, you owe it to your employer to present it. Errors of omission are as serious as errors of commission.

The Standards of Ethical Conduct for Management Accountants, promulgated by the Institute of Management Accountants, require its members to "disclose fully all relevant information which a reader of a report needs." Growth assumptions that you consider to be unrealistic are truly relevant. What is being called for here by the author can actually be considered a necessary step for any manager to take if he or she thinks of themselves as ethical.

Adding Staff Is the Cardinal Sin

Readers may ask at this point, whether it is really so bad to have a budget that errs on the optimistic side. If inventory is built up in anticipation of sales that do not materialize, the worst that will happen is we will have to reduce production (or purchase) levels for a while, sell off the excess inventory, and get back to normal levels. Similarly, an investment in fixed assets, to increase production capacity, may turn out to be premature, but at worst we lose the interest on the money invested, assuming the capacity will be needed at some point. If we don't achieve anticipated sales levels, accounts receivable won't go up, another place where cash can be tied up.

Returning to the scenerios in Chap. 2, what if we go out and rent more space, open a new branch office, or even start up the new warehouse, and sales projections don't materialize? In theory almost all actions can be undone, at some cost (sublet the sales office or find another tenant for the warehouse). If we undertake the sales and marketing program and find that sales do not increase as much as we hoped, we certainly should at least break even, that is, the growth in gross profit will at least equal the advertising outlay. Investing in an R&D project, figuring it will be paid for out of next year's profits, may still be a good business decision even if profits don't meet budget projections. Initiating a dating program on a seasonal product line, to smooth out production levels seems to have low downside risk. If we guessed wrong, and customers don't buy early, we may not reap the anticipated benefits, but we won't be any worse off.

The story with the 401(k) plan may be a little different. Employees, rightly, will view this as a benefit, whether individually they choose to take advantage of the plan. That is, not every employee signs up if a 401(k) plan is offered even if the company matches part of the employee savings. If earnings next year fail to meet budget levels, and the CEO calls for economies and cuts across the board, someone will suggest cutting back or eliminating the 401(k) plan.

Just as it is hard to measure the specific benefits from adopting a new benefit plan, or improving an old one, it is equally hard to quantify the negative effect of a cutback. There is no question that morale will go down. But how much does that really cost in terms of the bottom line? The answer is, in the short term, probably very little. Employees are intelligent and they know if cutbacks have to be made it is better in a fringe benefit than in layoffs. The long-term impacts, of both improvements and givebacks in benefit programs, are probably never going to be known. So maybe it is not worth worrying about putting in the new 401(k) plan if management is equally willing to cut back when necessary.

So far we have managed to make a pretty good case to go ahead and plan optimistically. If we are prepared to be flexible and adapt to changing conditions throughout the year—and if we are prepared perhaps to pay a price in terms of accelerating the timing of cash flows, if not their total amounts over time, maybe an aggressive posture in the budget is warranted. One can be unemotional and objective in dealing with inanimate assets like inventory and property, plant and equipment, or intangible assets like R&D and leases on space. Rational decisions can be made promptly and implemented quickly when no emotions are involved.

Having said that, let's turn to people. We discussed earlier the "10-percent across-the-board cut" syndrome. Why do executives order such cuts? Because it is perceived to be easier for line managers to lay people off—fire them if you will—on an impersonal basis, rather than make tough individual decisions. Why do so few performance evaluation programs work? While it is easy to counsel a high-potential employee, few like to talk to a loser and tell him or her they are going nowhere. It is hard to implement consistently a performance appraisal system. In fact, Deming makes this as one of his famous "14 points." If performance appraisals are a bad idea when nobody is losing their job, how much harder is it actually to tell someone they are no longer employed?

This writer has *never* met a manager who enjoys firing people. It may be part of the job, something that unavoidably has to be done, but show me a person who *likes* to terminate others and I will show you a potential psychopath. In the American culture a person is identified by their job. Take away the job and you temporarily destroy the person. Of course, most employees recover, ultimately find other employment and may even be the better for the experience. That still does not make it any easier to perform what is now euphemistically referred to as *outplacement.*

Termination for cause is hard, but usually occurs because of frustration in having to put up with poor performance. At some point it seems easier just to pull the plug. But having to terminate one or more employees because of economic factors, when individual performance has been good, may well be the hardest task a manager has to do. It may appear easier, or at least one's conscience may not be as bothersome, if the same arbitrary cut, in percent terms, is made company wide. Hence the frequency of 10-percent cuts.

Across-the-board cuts are perceived as an easy way out. In reality they are no more than the least painful way to escape from *previous poor planning and/or execution.* Layoffs, in short, are a sign of poor management. They are costly in terms of severance pay, poor morale, and the expenses of rebuilding the work force. The logical question to ask is, "Why do so many companies end up overstaffed?"

Hopefully, the answer is clear to readers of this chapter. In large part employment levels are too high because of the growth syndrome. Growth budgets, if they are to be internally consistent, invariably *require* adding additional staff. Pessimists, nay-sayers, are not considered team players when the budget is being put together. You can only warn about problems for so long. Then you either shut up—and ultimately see who was correct—or you leave the organization. When the top executives are committed to growth, and budgets are prepared accordingly, the inevitable result is additional employees. As we have seen, almost all expense categories (other than people) can be considered variable, or at least reduced in an unemotional manner. Cutting travel costs or membership dues or training or advertising is relatively easy. Removing employees is hard.

All right, you may say, the problem is overly optimistic growth projections, which in turn are immediately followed by adding staff. Then, if the growth does *not* occur, and the people *have* been added, something has to give. No matter how long it takes, and regardless of the interim excuses of the "things will improve, trust me" variety, cash flow requirements ultimately force a downward adjustment, that is, terminations and layoffs. To prove this point, look at IBM. For years it was committed to a no-layoff policy—as well as a growth policy. Once the growth curve flattened out, and ultimately headed south, so too did the no-layoff policy. *No organization is exempt from the inexorable laws of economics and cash flows.* Unnecessary employees must go, sooner or later, no matter how painful the process. Even Japan, with its "lifetime employment" policy, is having to reassess.

The cost to an organization of layoffs cannot be measured by the usual accounting and financial reporting tools. The impacts are subtle, but long lasting. The change in the basic contract between employees and employer has, almost all observers agree, changed for the worse over the last 30 years. The concepts of loyalty to the organization, reciprocated by career development, and benefit packages worked well as long as companies were planning for and achieving growth. But as growth stopped, cutbacks had to be made, employees in all categories stopped putting the organization first and turned instead to looking out for themselves.

In this writer's opinion almost all the operating, production, and productivity problems in "smokestack" America can be traced to the behavior pattern of corporate executives who treated hourly labor as a commodity, to be hired and laid off at will, who thought they were compensating for such an approach by agreeing to union demands for ever increasing hourly wages and benefit programs. "Yes, it is true you can be laid off (or fired) at any time, but meanwhile, you are getting $32 an hour in wages and benefits. When you are laid off not only will you be the first to be recalled (whenever that is) but between the government and our company we have put together a terrific package of benefits to tide you over. Work hard. Trust us. We know what we are doing!"

No wonder restrictive work practices grew, the focus of which was to keep as many union members getting paid for as long as possible. Labor leaders were probably smart enough to know the cost to the companies of forcing unproductive practices in labor negotiations. But they undoubtedly thought that it was no more than their members deserved, considering the employers' attitude to labor as a commodity.

The movie *Roger and Me*, about a labor union member trying to see the chairman of General Motors, was a brilliant propaganda piece. Most readers of this book probably strongly disagree with the filmmaker's basic premise, but it does accurately portray how union members regard their employers. What seems like good business to management is perceived by workers as a stab in the back every time there is a layoff. The more frequent the layoffs, and the longer they last, the greater the alienation. We would submit that the *true* costs, in terms of *total* cash flow, of high-wage levels for union employees, with at-will layoffs, and the consequent restrictive labor practices in the contract, are very, very high.

A Better Approach— Managed Growth

We cannot say, "Let's *not* project growth." That is unrealistic. Managed growth is the answer. All growth plans in a budget have to be tested. The question that must be asked is, "What are the chances that this will *really* happen?" An equally important second question is, "What will we do if the growth does *not* occur?" In other words, management must distinguish between what it would *like* to have happen, and what it *thinks* is most likely to happen.

A second line of defense is contingency planning. If asked, everyone will admit that at least some growth opportunities will not pan out. The trouble is the question is usually not asked. If cash flows, and the availability of cash resources, are critical factors, then cash should be treated as a truly valuable commodity.

Any growth opportunity has risks and we all must take risks. But forewarned is forearmed. Planning for the downside is not the same as forecasting it. It is not disloyal to ask the tough question, "What will we do with the additional staff if sales from the new warehouse do not meet expectations?" Or, "If our new marketing program does not boost sales of our old product line, how will we react?" The possible specific answers are numerous.

How much management time should be spent on this type of analysis? A common phrase, sometimes applied to management consultants—or newly minted MBAs—is that they suffer from a *paralyis of analysis*. Nothing gets done because all the time is spent on what-if scenarios.

If too much analysis is a waste of resources, then we would argue that too little is equally bad. Management must *insist* that at least some thought be given to the question, "If we plan for this growth, because it seems like a good business risk, and we add the employees you say are needed, what will you do if (1) sales growth is only half of what you predict; and (2) sales remain level?"

The most appropriate answer may be that, if things do not work out, the employees will have to be terminated. In that case, at least the new hires can be told the risks right up-front. Maybe they will even work harder, knowing their job is at risk.

More likely, ways can be worked out so that new permanent employees are not hired until the program's success is assured, or at least in sight.

Great flexibility can be obtained from overtime for existing employees, combined with utilizing temporary employees and the appropriate use of consultants. Retired employees have been effectively utilized in many cases.

The key objective is to postpone hiring permanent full-time employees until there is virtually 100-percent assurance that any growth projection will succeed. Two major benefits will flow from this approach. First, cash outflows will be controlled, as fixed costs are kept to a minimum. Second, the pain and heartbreak related to layoffs and terminations will be reduced, if not eliminated. And that in itself will help cash flow.

Flexible Budgets: Determining Appropriate Expense Levels

As has been noted before, when business is expanding, all costs are variable and when business is declining, it is often argued (at least by those affected) that most costs are fixed. "Heads I win, tails you lose" is the popular phrase equivalent to the approach used by many mid-level managers. They want to expand their domain when things are going well, but vehemently argue that any cuts, to offset a reduction in volume, will do irreparable harm to the organization.

You cannot have it both ways. What goes up has to come down. There is a way to solve this problem in advance, to avoid making seemingly ad hoc decisions every time the economy changes. Flexible budgeting is a very practical approach to the pervasive management problem of "just how much *should* we spend?" The basic concept of flexible budgeting is very easy to grasp, although in practice quite hard to implement.

If a law firm has a Word Processing department, and one typist can handle the work of three attorneys, then budgeting for the size of the department is a simple task. Divide the budgeted number of professionals by three and that is the number of typists that should be in the budget. This is the budget procedure used in most organizations and can best be called a fixed budget. In 199X we will have x attorneys and y typists.

But what if business is great and in the middle of the year an additional five professionals, not in the budget, are hired because volume exceeds expectations. Of course the argument will be made that we can afford the attorneys and any extra clerical staff because of the higher fee income. How many more typists should be added? Our formula suggests $1\frac{2}{3}$ people, an obvious impossibility, so we probably will hire two additional typists.

The monthly budget reports, in those organizations with a fixed budget will now show an *unfavorable* budget variance, that is salary expenses in Word Processing will be over budget because of the two additional personnel. But everyone who looks at the numbers will say,

"Of course we are over budget expense levels in that department, but it is all right because of the higher volume." In short, higher volume covers a multitude of sins.

If our formula is correct, and we had a flexible budget, we would *change the budget* column in the next monthly report. The budget is, in other words, not "cast in concrete" but varies with volume, both up and down. In our example, strictly applied, Word Processing's actual expense would be slightly over budget by the ⅓ person.

In a flexible budget the basic concept is to relate the budget allowance to the factor that controls it; in the example, Word Processing is related to professional employment. More often, in manufacturing firms, the budget allowances for marketing expenses are tied to sales, while production related categories (such as purchasing) are tied to production volume.

With computer spreadsheets it is easy to build in formulas calculating budget allowances. In fact each line in the budget column *could* have its own formula. In practice, for those relatively few firms that utilize flexible budgeting, most allowances are calculated on only one or two bases. In times past, the tradeoff between greater simplicity on the one hand and increased precision used to be won by simplicity. Today, with easy access to personal computers, greater precision should control.

The advantage of a flexible budget approach is two-fold. First, it focuses management attention, ahead of time, as to what *should* be the proper relationship of various overhead expense categories to the appropriate measure of volume. This means that the cash consequences of staffing levels can be managed, as contrasted with just letting nature take its own course. As we have seen, without some discipline, when business prospects are bright, employment goes up, but the reverse phenomenon never happens spontaneously.

Determining in advance that employment can increase only if certain specific quantitative goals are reached puts a damper on enthusiasm. If a manager knows that production must *increase* 10 percent before anyone is added to the payroll, and that for each additional 10 percent one more person can be hired, arbitrary staff additions made on the basis of hope will be precluded. Similarly, if for any reason production *decreases* 10 percent, someone will have to be laid off or transferred. This automatic stabilizer, however, takes both the emotion and the typical knee-jerk reaction out of the unpleasant task.

The second advantage of the flexible budget is that monthly, quarterly, and year-to-date internal reports are not distorted, which in turn leads to better decision making. In the absence of a flexible budget, actual expenses tend to be close to budget levels, even if top line sales are off. If sales are down 15 percent in a division, while a particular department's expenses are only 3 percent below budget, how good a job is the department manager doing in controlling expenses? The budget report in a typical fixed budget firm will show a *favorable* variance because actual expenses are below the predetermined budget level.

Common sense says that if volume is down by 15 percent, then expenses should go down more than 3 percent. Try telling a department manager, in a convincing manner and without appearing arbitrary, that, "Yes, your expenses *are* below budget, but not enough. They should have been cut at least 10 percent. Since you did not do this on your own, here is what you *have* to do." The department manager will likely respond, "You're the boss! Why didn't you tell me in advance that you wanted a 10-percent cut. What you did tell me, when you approved my budget, was that I should keep expenses at or under the budget amount. In fact, that is just what I did. I think I did a pretty damn good job, and *now* you tell me to cut 10 percent and are also implying I have been a poor manager. What do you guys up there really know about what is going on?" Talk about lack of communication!

A flexible budget process is not the answer to all of a company's cash flow problems. It is a powerful tool in focusing all levels of management on the relationship between volume and overhead expenses, something a fixed budget simply cannot do. The key to successful implementation is not the mechanics—any competent management accountant can set it up and run the reports. The key is a crystal clear understanding of what the relationship between different volume levels, and the corresponding expense and payroll levels *should be*. If the Word Processing supervisor at the law firm *knows*, and agrees in her heart, that only one typist is needed for every three professionals, then she will take the initiative herself to vary support staffing levels appropriately, both up and down. Absent that discipline, human nature will revert to form, and we will be back where we started. On the way up, all expenses are variable. On the way down all expenses are fixed.

Can You Control Cash if You Don't Have a Budget?

Most readers work in organizations that prepare budgets. Yet there are a large number of entrepreneurial firms, often run by the founder, that do not utilize budgets as a management control tool. In one sense, most of these firms follow many of the precepts of Total Cash Management. For such firms, cash started out, and continues, as the number one priority. It is hard to fault a company that keeps its eyes on cash. If your bank balance is growing steadily, and your bank balance continues as a focal point, something is being done right. The CEO of a growing profitable business with no formal budget process can afford to feel superior to a fellow CEO whose business has the best budget controls in the world, but whose company unfortunately is in the red.

In our example there is one key phrase—entrepreneurial firm run by the founder—that requires close attention. The number one problem of all small businesses (and every business today started out as a small business) is the availability and control of cash. Thus as a business grows, if the original management is still there, a culture of close control of cash will be in place. Further, the top management group truly knows the business. Tom Peters' *Management by Walking Around* is real-life, not a business school tool. Those who start a firm, and grow with it, understand *all* the interrelationships among orders, production, new product development, delivery, customer service, and collection of outstanding receivables. If the CEO feels that every time someone is added to the payroll, the salary is coming out of his own pocket (if he owns 100 percent of the firm, it is), budgets are never going to have to substitute for on the spot management judgment.

It is quite possible, therefore, for a good size enterprise to run effectively and profitably without formal budget procedures. Looked at differently, budgets become a necessary management tool whenever the *second generation* of management takes over. Alternatively, budgets are mandatory when the size and scope of the organization becomes large enough that the top level executives who founded the business simply do not have first hand day-to-day knowledge of every aspect of the business.

Having said that (and many medium-sized businesses are very successful without budgets), the author still recommends adoption of formal budget procedures for every business unit with more than four or five employees. The planning cycle required by the budget process, such as, anticipating sales, related production, employment levels, and product mix is a good discipline even for entrepreneurs.

For a small firm, this is a job that can be accomplished in one or two days. If business is very good, sales are expanding, decisions still have to be made as to which opportunities are worth pursuing, and which should be passed. If business is poor, where should energies and resources be concentrated? Thinking these plans through in advance is a worthwhile exercise for *every* organization. It may not be necessary, but it is still a very good idea.

One last word on the subject of budgets for nonprofit organizations.

Many readers are involved in volunteer, nonprofit organizations. All the principles of Total Cash Management apply to nonprofits. The bottom line may be break-even, not a profit. But losses are equally unacceptable for churches, civic associations, or social clubs. If cash outflows exceed inflows, then sooner or later something has to change. Installing a budget system will not automatically put an organization in the black. It will highlight what has to be done, and focus attention on required changes. It is certainly possible to budget for a loss next year. But the budget will tell you the maximum loss that *should* occur and alert the members or executive group to unanticipated problems that require corrective action.

In summary, it is hard to think of an enterprise or organization, large or small, for profit or not-for-profit, that will be worse off having a formal budget process. The only real requirement is that leaders get involved in setting the budget up front, and then pay attention to actual results during the year. If these two requirements are met, every organization can obtain the benefits of Total Cash Management. If the requirements are not met, if the leaders treat budgeting as just an exercise, sooner or later any organization is going to be in trouble. If firms like General Motors and Sears Roebuck, which were kings of the hill in the 1960s and 1970s, can have cash problems in the early 1990s, no organization is exempt from the discipline of maximizing the productivity of cash.

Total Cash Management is truly an approach to productivity *and* quality. Can any organization survive without productivity and quality? Can any organization afford to disregard where cash is supposed to come from or where it is expected to go?

12

Capital Budgeting and Cash Flows

Capital mobility and a worldwide capital shortage are the silver bullet ideas for the Nineties. Managing assets and competing for capital will be the critical abilities required of managers and investors who will be successful in the coming decade.

JOHN RUTLEDGE, from "The Silver Bullet that Won't Let You Down" *Corporate Finance*, October/November 1992

The objective of this chapter is not to discuss the methodology of capital budgeting. We are not going to argue, once again, the case for using discounted cash flow (DCF) techniques as compared with more simplistic models that do not take into consideration the time value of money. Discussions regarding the theoretical advantages of net present value (NPV) vs. internal rate of return (IRR) need not be repeated, since anyone truly interested in these techniques can go to the nearest finance textbook. Every newly minted MBA can perform all necessary present value calculations at the touch of a button on her pocket calculator. As you can see just by looking at the acronyms, the jargon alone can cause a mental blockade. What we want to look at are the *assumptions* underlying all investments in long-lived or capital assets. What are the *real* costs and *real* benefits that can be expected when cash is disbursed for property, plant and equipment (PP&E)? Are we spending too much, or too little? Who, and at what level, should make the final decisions on capital expenditures? Should we audit the results after the fact, and if so, what do we do with the information?

Expenditures by companies each year on PP&E are significant in terms of cash flows. How much do companies spend each year on capital equipment? Depending on the industry, profitability of the firm, management policy toward expansion and modernization, and several other factors, a typical industrial firm might commit anywhere between 50 percent and 150 percent of net income to investment in PP&E. Capital intensive companies, like utilities or railroads, might be well above this level, while financial service firms could thrive with smaller commitments. You will be close if you assume the same order of magnitude for capital expenditures and net income after tax.

While cash disbursements for payroll and benefits, on the one hand, and purchased materials on the other are undoubtedly larger in magnitude than PP&E outlays, the latter are still significant. Organizations have intuitively recognized this by refusing to delegate authority for capital expenditures very far down the ladder. In fact, Boards of Directors usually have to approve each capital appropriation over a certain minimum level. Relative to the size of the organization these minimum levels are often extraordinarily low. Top management, and even Board of Director, involvement in most capital proposals is the rule, not the exception. We will examine the wisdom of such micro-management later.

Whether wise or not, most proposals for capital outlays receive much closer scrutiny than virtually any other commitment involving cash. Purchase of just one 30-second advertising spot on the Super Bowl telecast can cost substantially more than a major machine tool. The latter commitment will have to go to the Board, while the other will be made on his own authority by a second or even third level marketing executive. If cash is cash, then someone's priorities are wrong.

Why Do We Need a Capital Budget?

It is an article of faith that business organizations (and not-for-profits) *must* have a capital budget. Just why this has come to pass sheds light on the process. The analysis, if understood, will allow firms to adopt a much more rational approach, not just to capital budgeting, but to the more important task of managing capital expenditures.

Underlying the concept of capital budgeting is an implicit assumption, very rarely stated explicitly, that there are a tremendous number of possible expenditure possibilities. In the absence of a formal mechanism, and unless tight controls are in place over the decision process, individual managers are presumed to run wild. Absent a capital budget, a company is presumed to run out of cash trying to fund all the possibilities; alternatively, controls are there to preclude managers from choosing poor projects while leaving high potential programs undone.

Any system put in place on the assumption that responsible executives will knowingly waste corporate assets, or deliberately choose stupid alternatives, is headed for trouble. Pile on top of that financial analysis by individuals unfamiliar with the production process or market, numerous layers of review, plus repeated audits. It is no wonder that many mid-level executives scratch their head and ask themselves, "Do those guys up there *really* know what they are doing?"

Let's take a close look at some of the common *myths* about capital budgets.

Myth 1. The company does not have enough resources to fund all possible projects.

Myth 2. Discounted cash flow techniques are the only way to analyze capital expenditures.

Myth 3. Unless a project meets a certain target ROI it should be rejected.

Myth 4. Approval of capital proposals is the responsibility of the financial staff.

Some readers at this point may feel that we have set up straw men. The facts are that many, if not most organizations, with a formal process to review capital expenditures do act in accordance with what we are calling myths—something existing only in imagination. Acting as if a myth were true, however, does not make it true.

Management, not cash, is the limiting resource.

The statement that an organization cannot pay for all possible projects is true. No company or organization, not even the federal government which can print money, has sufficient resources to do everything. We would submit that where capital expenditures are at issue, the limiting factor, more often than not, is *management* resources, not financial resources. The availability of cash is simply not the issue it is often assumed to be. If a good fairy came down one day and told every executive, "You have the cash on hand to implement *all* the projects you propose," what would happen?

Each manager would inevitably set up his own priority system and make choices from among the items on his own wish list. Even if cash were available there simply are not enough trained engineers, project managers, and purchasing agents, however, to implement each and every item that someone in the organization wants.

The best evidence that money, cash if you will, is not the limiting factor is that even companies in bankruptcy still continue to make necessary investments in PP&E. If it is competitively necessary, if the business reasons are sufficiently sound, the cash is *always* found. Over a 10-year period the author has asked hundreds of financial managers the question, "Have you *ever* turned down a really important project because the cash simply was not there?" Put that way, it should not be a surprise that the answer invariably has been that no matter how tight the financial position, all really important projects do get funded. In short, cash is *not* the limiting factor. Management time and staff resources are a far greater constraint.

This does not eliminate the need for a mechanism for identifying the truly important proposals from the "Wouldn't it be nice if ... " ideas. A formal budget process is very helpful in setting priorities, but it is not the availability of cash that sets the limits. Rather it is the demand to select, out of the background noise of many requests, those few that truly are critical to the businesses success.

If cash is not the limiting factor, then what are the consequences for the capital budgeting process? This leads to dispelling Myth 2 that states DCF techniques *must* be used.

In practice, discounted cash flow techniques produce bad decisions.

Heresy is defined by Webster as, "An opinion held in opposition to the commonly received doctrine, tending to promote division or dissension." The statement that DCF techniques produce bad decisions represents a perfect example of an heretical belief. Every business school student, every textbook author, every consultant can instantly produce examples showing how other techniques of analysis, such as payback, produce theoretically incorrect answers.

If you invest $400,000 today and the savings from the investment are $300,000 a year, but only for three years, what is wrong with such a decision? You will get your money back in a little over a year, so if you made a mistake it should be easy to recover. If an even better opportunity arises, you will soon have the cash resources to accomplish the second option.

Similarly, if you have a proposal that calls for the same $400,000 investment today, but promises savings of $80,000 a year for 20 years it will take five full years just to break even. Proponents of DCF will argue that the present value (at almost any discount rate) of an $80,000 stream of cash for 20 years is greater than a three-year stream of $300,000. Mathematically, they are absolutely correct.

The point is that nobody, repeat *nobody*, can look 20 years into the future. Are we going to be at war? Who are our world-wide competitors going to be? What about global warming? What will be the next techno-logical innovation? If it is hard to predict who will win the next election, or where the Dow Jones average will be in six months, how can any reasonable person have confidence in projections extending out 20 years? The one certain thing is that there *will be* surprises, that there will be economic, social and political changes that we did not, and could not, foresee. Anybody who invests money solely on the basis of specific 20-year projections is either a wild-eyed optimist or a fool.

The implicit assumption in all DCF techniques is that the projected cash flows are going to come to pass. At least intuitively, most observers understand that in the real world there is both uncertainty and risk. The projected cash flows may not come to pass. The analysts have an answer: Offset the uncertainties by *raising* the discount rate (for NPV analyses) or *raise* the hurdle rate (for IRR analyses). The effect is the same. To meet the new and higher analytical requirements the 20-year project now has to show more than $80,000 a year cash inflow.

One of two things will happen in this example. The proposal will be turned down, because the return is not sufficiently high. Or the analyst (perhaps at the instruction of his boss who insists the project get approved) now suddenly finds that the cash return will be $90,000 a year, not the $80,000 originally anticipated. Maybe things have suddenly improved, the 20-year outlook has indeed changed for the better. Or, more likely, instead of projecting a 5-percent compound growth in sales volume of the new product, the growth is newly estimated at $5\frac{1}{2}$ percent. The way DCF works, a small increase in one of the variables can have a dramatic effect on the overall result because of the powerful impact of compounding over 20 years. Who is to say whether sales will grow 5 percent or $5\frac{1}{2}$ percent a year?

The key point is that because of the basic uncertainties of *any* projection, and because so many assumptions go into any capital expenditure analysis, a good analyst can make a poor project look like a winner, and vice versa. This is not to say that proponents of a particular project are less than objective. It is to say that what appears to be a very objective approach to ranking capital expenditure proposals is actually a highly judgmental process.

Discounted cash flow techniques start with the presumption that a dollar today is worth more than a dollar 10 years from now. Common sense supports this assumption. Many people have pointed out, for example, that the so-called million dollar sweepstakes winners, who receive $50,000 a year for 20 years, are actually receiving significantly less in today's dollars.

By extension, therefore, a project whose earlier cash returns are higher, is far superior to one where the payoff is out in the future. What are the implications for long-term or strategic planning? Commentators have pointed to the short-termism of U.S. business. DCF methodology focuses, even encourages, short-term payoffs over longer term investments. For the economy as a whole this is certainly negative, and for an individual firm this may preclude innovation and competitive advantage. A financial technique that penalizes long-term strategic thinking should not be the basis of Finance 101 in our business schools.

Finally, a word about expected returns. Relatively few firms earn more than an 11- to 13-percent return after tax. Most individual investors would love to compound their money at a 10 percent after tax rate year after year. Modern portfolio theory suggests that individuals, by diversifying their investment portfolio, can obtain any risk profile through a combination of debt and an appropriate mix of investments in firms with different characteristics. Since the market is quite efficient, any firm with a consistently above-average ROI will be bid up in price. Such firms, in turn, find it increasingly difficult to maintain above-average returns for long periods of time. Even a Wal-Mart has to slow down its growth sometime. At one point, after several years of rapid growth, IBM was forecasting it would reach $100 billion in revenues within four or five years. A funny thing then happened—growth suddenly ceased, losses were reported, and IBM took its place in the history books as just another firm that reached a natural plateau.

Very few firms, therefore, are *consistently* able to be above-average, or earn more than 11 to 13 percent after tax. Why then do those same firms adopt a policy that says we will turn down any investment proposal that does not promise more than 15 percent? Many firms demand a 20 percent after tax return; and the author has even heard of some who permit their managers to invest only when returns of 25 percent or better can be expected! Such policies are insane.

Most companies have far more investment proposals put on the table than they can handle, although as we have argued the limiting factor usually is management time, not cash. But where there is a will, there is a way. What are the implications if a firm says it simply will not invest unless a 20 percent or better return is achieved? One of two things: Either a lot of very good proposals will be left on the table, or managers will have to fudge the numbers to meet the policy requirements.

The truth is that there are very few true 20-percent after tax investment opportunities. Any company, with more real 20-percent projects than it has cash and/or management resources to handle, will have absolutely no difficulty finding a well-heeled financial or operating partner. That is guaranteed simply because there are plenty of well financed firms, with good management, that would increase their own ROI by becoming partners with an organization that can promise 20 percent or more returns.

Any company that turns down projects with returns in the 15 to 20-percent after-tax range is limiting its own growth, profitability and, in the final analysis, management bonuses. Since few Boards of Directors are stupid, there must be a reason for adopting such high hurdle rates. There is, and it is the continuing influence of history.

The cause usually is one or more major projects, in the firms's history, that turned out to have been particularly unwise. It may be unfair to pick on General Motors, but during the 1980s they invested billions of dollars in factory automation. Undoubtedly at the time top management believed that the labor savings from robots, as an example, would be high and would provide a high ROI. But the robots did not work as expected and the anticipated returns were not realized.

Therefore, it is sometimes felt that to achieve an *average* 15-percent return, winners are needed to offset the certain percent of losers. In advance we might not know which project was going to be a loser (if we did, we obviously would not invest) but statistically nobody is ever going to bat 1000. Unless every project *promises* a 20-percent return, management may feel there is no way to actually achieve an overall 15 percent. Depending on how badly burned a company has been in the past the new hurdle rate will be raised to offset the inevitable mistakes.

The consequences of this approach are not usually thought out. This leads right into an analysis of Myth 3, that projects not meeting the minimum ROI criteria should be rejected.

Minimum ROI standards should not be required.

When discounted cash flow techniques were developed in the 1950s by leading petroleum firms, there were some unique circumstances. Integrated oil firms faced significant strategic alternatives, each involving truly enormous sums of money. Whether to invest domestically, probably with less risk and lower returns, had to be weighed against international exploration, involving potentially large returns but very high risk. Should resources be committed to petro-chemical investments or should those same resources be applied to more familiar refining and marketing opportunities? Corporate acquisitions had to be weighed against potential divestitures.

Because of the truly long-range nature of these decisions, and the impact on specific executives who would be personally affected, formal techniques had to be developed to rank the alternatives impartially and objectively. Drawing on mathematical and statistical techniques developed during the war, one or two oil companies, working with some business school professors, truly invented discounted cash flow as a methodology. And it worked. It forced discipline into the process. It forced managers to quantify the impact of the alternatives. Since some of the choices were mutually exclusive, if you picked A you could not do B, the cash flow impact of each had to be known. Also, given the nature of the types of projects involved, the length of time could vary substantially, say, between A and

B. While it seems simplistic to ask the question today, arguments were being held 40 years ago as to whether $1 million a year for 15 years was better or worse than $1.5 million for 8 years—and without DCF it is difficult to settle the argument definitively. Further, given possible personal involvement in the outcome, whatever answer was arrived at had to be understood and agreed to.

Discounted cash flow was the right solution in the right place at the right time. The professors involved in its development published books (which received little publicity) and articles in such journals as *Harvard Business Review*, which were widely read. Within a few years DCF was routinely being taught in leading MBA programs. Relatively few operating executives, however, understood the underlying logic, at least initially, and it took another 25 years for the concepts to become conventional wisdom. Now, with Hewlett-Packard calculators available for less than $75, and with Lotus spreadsheets on every PC, DCF appears to be the *only* reasonable way to evaluate capital expenditures.

There is only one small problem on the horizon. Survey after survey in the 1970s and 1980s, and even into the 1990s, showed that most business firms continued to use the now-discredited simple payback methodology. Why? Are practicing business executives stupid? Or, is there something wrong with the internal logic of DCF? The answer to both questions is no. Business executives *are* rational, and DCF remains a very rigorous and potentially valuable tool.

The key is the word tool. To cut a piece of wood in half you use a saw, not a hammer. In carpentry, even if you have only a hammer handy, everything does not look like a nail. In capital expenditures, DCF has to be treated as a powerful tool, but it is only useful in certain situations. Discounted cash flow analytical techniques are appropriate when mutually exclusive projects, with different time frames, are being looked at simultaneously. When choices must be made, *either* A *or* B, but not both, calculating the present values of each will provide useful information in arriving at a decision.

Notice that the DCF tool will not make the decision for you; it simply provides useful information. Many factors enter into strategic decisions. If all other things are truly equal, one should always pick the alternative with the highest return. That is common sense. In the real world, however, alternatives are never really equal. Competitors' response, impact of potential new technology, worker reaction and customer acceptance influence the evaluation of each alternative. None of these can really be quantified, yet each influences the final answer.

Discounted cash flow techniques provide a false sense of precision. Yes, you can attempt to quantify how competitors' responses will impact your project, or the effect of a new foreign technology. But just because a numerical weight can be applied does not make the answer correct. No chain is stronger than its weakest link. In DCF, the arithmetic is very strong. A dollar 10 years from now *is* worth less than a dollar five years from now. But how sure are we of the dollar estimates themselves? Nobody can foretell the future. The uncertainties are always there, no matter how we try to quantify them.

Thus, companies who blindly rely on a pass/fail screen—either the project meets our minimum ROI or it will be rejected—are making a serious error. Start with the assumption that those who propose a particular capital expenditure project have the firm's best interests in mind. They are not proposing to waste money. They may turn out to be wrong, but one should not doubt their sincerity when the project is put forth. If the managers submitting a proposal know, or at least feel, that the item is in the company's best interest but the numbers at first do not support it, guess what will happen. The managers will reevaluate the projections. What are the odds that, if they still believe in the project, the second proposal somehow happens to meet the stated corporate cash flow criteria?

What this corporate policy of a high hurdle rate really accomplishes is to breed cynicism, to encourage gamesmanship. Respect cannot be maintained for policies that, to produce the right answer, require bad input. And if to produce the right answer requires stretching the truth, we end up with a morally indefensible position. To accomplish the right objectives we have to break the rules. We are back to the end justifying the means—a concept no longer acceptable to most of western civilization. Respect for the integrity of the financial reporting system is going to be lost, and the entire business starts to be treated like one giant game to see who can score the most points.

Rigid rules, rigidly applied, are diametrically opposed to the precepts of TCM. We want every manager to treat the organization's cash as if it were his or her own. This means that a lot of capital expenditure projects are going to be put forth that, on the surface, may not pass some arbitrary hurdle—particularly if that hurdle is set unrealistically high. We will discuss later in this chapter the various types of capital expenditures, and the appropriate criteria for approving each. Here, we hope to have demonstrated our point that arbitrary minimum ROI standards should not be required and in practice are counterproductive.

Myth 4, stating that financial managers *must* be actively involved in each capital budgeting decision, has some far-reaching consequences, none of them good.

Financial managers should have no authority over capital expenditures.

The fourth and final myth about investments in PP&E is that it is a financial exercise—and therefore input, if not veto power, should come from the controller. But just as an operating budget is pulled together by the controller, but she does not determine (or approve) sales or staffing levels, so should financial involvement in capital budgets be limited.

Capital expenditures are, both in theory and in practice, the heart of any business. Growth in volume and increases in productivity depend directly on new capital investments. Ultimately the competitive position of a company will depend on its effectiveness, relative to others, in choosing where to put its money. Having made the proper choices, one also has to assume that such choices are going to be implemented properly. If choice and implementation are crucial, are these the responsibility of line operating managers, or financial analysts?

There are only two roles financial types should play in the capital expenditure process. The first is to ask all the tough questions they can think of. Asking questions, however, is not the same as exercising veto power. Financial analysts are trained to think through, from start to finish, all the business implications of any course of action. The second role is to make sure there is internal consistency. That is, as an example, to make sure that the labor budget shows a decrease shortly after new labor-saving equipment is installed, and to adjust depreciation expense related to the new facilities.

If a manufacturing superintendent wants to buy a new heat treat furnace, rather then sending the work out to a subcontractor, it is the financial analyst who will put pencil to paper. Questions can and should be raised about any and all alternatives. Assume though, that with realistic volume and cost projections agreed to by the controller, the proposal still promises at best a 12-percent ROI, and the company demands 15 percent. The production people continue to insist on this project because:

1. *Quality* of the end product will be held to tighter tolerances by performing heat treating in house.
2. By shortening the *cycle time*, the company will more nearly comply with JIT requirements set by customers.

Theoretically both improved quality and reduced cycle time can be quantified. In practice, this is hard to do with any degree of precision. Any attempt to put realistic dollar values on such intangibles can raise more questions than it answers. On the other hand, just because an intangible value may not be quantifiable does not make it any less important. Some management gurus argue today that improved quality and reduced cycle times are the two most significant competitive weapons a company can deploy.

What do we do now with our heat treat proposal? The financial staff says it will not meet corporate minimum ROI requirements. Production and marketing say that the numbers are not as important as meeting customer requirements and accuse the financial staff, somewhat derogatorily, of living up to their traditional role as bean counters.

Both sides are correct. Somebody has to make a decision. Who should do it and how should they make it? At first glance, it seems that since the calculated ROI is 12 percent, and the corporate minimum requirement is

15 percent, the two are close—so let's go with the idea because, "Maybe things will be better than anticipated." That argument, however, can be turned around. Things may be worse, not better. Then where are we?

A second factor arguing against pushing blindly ahead is, once lower levels of management deliberately disregard one corporate policy, internal controls of all sorts are in jeopardy. Maybe the corporate policy *is* wrong. You do not solve that problem by deliberately flouting it.

Quantifying Intangibles

The only possible solution in trying to quantify the benefits of intangibles (in this example improved quality and reduced cycle time) has very real problems. In the hands of less knowledgeable analysts, quantifying intangibles leads to a situation where almost any answer can be derived, and at least a surface plausibility given to it. That is why hard nosed financial types tend to treat with scorn such soft numbers. Can anyone *prove* what poor quality costs—or the benefits of good quality? Just what does reduced cycle time in production really accomplish?

Putting hard numbers on soft concepts is both difficult and risky. Difficult because there is no way of verifying the answer is right until much later, when the project is in, and then it is too late. Risky, because bad projects can be made to look good, and vice versa.

The first step is to argue that good quality is better than poor quality and reduced cycle time better than extended production. Everyone will buy into that argument. Now, can we try to get more precise?

A lot has been written about the cost of quality, although what is really meant is the *cost of poor quality*. Techniques have been developed recently that do allow you to put a price tag on most aspects of quality and permit you to analyze what an improvement in quality means. The one area of analysis that still eludes total quantification is asking how our customers will react if out product's quality improves. Probably the best way is to reverse the question and ask, "What will happen to sales if our quality goes down—or, the same thing, if our competitors' quality improves while ours stays the same?" A decline in sales volume can be related to gross profit; hence cash flow then is easy to project. The exact dollar amount is going to be no less precise than many of the other variables in the capital budget exercise, such as what prevailing labor rates will be over the next ten years.

Similarly, reducing cycle time, speeding up delivery and meeting customer JIT requirements may be the price of staying in business. Of course, in this case *all* our gross profits are at risk. More reasonably, good marketing staff, in touch with customers, can estimate the benefits of reduced cycle time, or the penalties of not being competitive. It is often surprising just how much the sales reps *know* needs to be done—as well as the costs if the firm does not keep up to date.

Is it better to disregard the value of intangibles in capital budgeting, because it is hard to estimate them accurately, or to estimate them as best you can? Most hard-core financial managers have the attitude that if you cannot verify the answer, if it cannot be audited, you are better off disregarding it. On the other hand, a wise observer commented:

It is better to be approximately right than precisely wrong.

By refusing to accept imprecise estimates of intangibles like quality and cycle time, you can be precise—yet wrong. In trying to estimate some values, even though you know the number you come up with is not absolutely correct, you know you will be wrong. But you will still be *closer* to whatever the real answer turns out to be than by sticking your head, ostrich-like, in the sand and saying, in effect, "All or nothing."

In many cases of proposed capital expenditure the magnitude of intangible costs and benefits may outweigh those elements that can be quantified. Rather than throwing up your hands and saying we can't cope, recognize the degree of fragility and move forward. Specifying the assumptions underlying any numerical approach to intangible values allows the reader of an authorization request to draw on his or her own judgments. Explicit recognition that the dollar amounts *are* estimates will actually lend a degree of professionalism and credibility to the proposal.

The decision process involving capital expenditures should allow for significant judgment, a strong recognition that intangible elements may affect a company's competitive position to a greater extent than the more easily quantifiable hard revenues and costs. This in turn leads to the conclusion that decisions about which capital expenditure projects to accept, and which to reject, cannot and should not be made on a straight index of profitability. If you are dealing only with hard numbers, then a project involving improved quality and delivery time, but promising only a quantitative 12-percent ROI, may be superior to an 18-percent proposal that is a straight cost reduction, but one that has no impact on customers. There is no way to judge between the two unless someone makes an effort—sticks their neck out—and puts numbers on the intangibles. To mix a metaphor, you may not have a true apples to apples comparison but you will at least not have fruit salad. A "delicious to macintosh" comparison is not all bad, and it is certainly better than going hungry. Disregarding intangibles is the financial equivalent of leaving a lot of food on the table.

If we are going to permit, even require, that intangibles be quantified, the net effect is to put even more reliance on the judgment of those making the proposals. Put a different way, it will be harder for those at higher levels to evaluate individual projects based solely on comparing the anticipated ROIs. This in turn suggests that multiple levels of review can be eliminated, or certainly greatly reduced. If qualitative judgments start to replace quantitative answers an organization will have to rely on lower level management, those individuals who are truly on, or at least close to, the firing line.

Most organizations that have a formal capital budgeting process find that at the end of the year, actual expenditures in total are always close to budgeted levels. However this often results from two countervailing effects. Individual projects that had been approved and started often tend to take longer than anticipated and end up costing more than planned—the famous cost-overrun syndrome. Offsetting this impact is the phenomenon that because management time, not financial resources, is the true constraint, many projects originally approved in the budget end up being postponed for lack of managerial time.

If this phenomenon is an accurate representation of how most companies work in practice, although not in theory, the implications are far reaching for the approval and decision process. If a division has an approved capital budget of $5 million, consisting of 10 discrete projects, but ends up only implementing seven of them (still staying within the $5 million limit), how were the decisions made as to which projects to delay?

Basically, the answer is simple. Local management sets its own priorities. It started the most important project first and so on. The end of the year came and only seven projects had been started, even though top management, or the board had approved all 10 in the final budget. Divisions do not typically go back and say, "We made a mistake, we really don't need projects 8, 9, and 10." Presumably they are still needed or wanted, just not as badly as projects one through seven. There is only so much time to devote to capital expenditures, since current production and sales goals must continue to be met. Inevitably, individual projects will slip, and some may never get done. So be it. Who can better make those decisions than those on the firing line?

But if this is the way things are really done, why set up a formal capital budgeting procedure or process (one that requires significant management time and effort) that assumes local management cannot or should not make the final decisions? As noted at the beginning of the chapter, the whole system is based on the false assumption that cash is the limiting factor, when in practice it is management time which is the constraint.

This suggests a major change in capital budgeting. Do not make each division or operating unit submit detailed capital expenditure proposals, each quantified to meet rigidly predetermined ROI minimums, and in many cases developed with unrealistic assumptions required to meet these unrealistic targets (that is, 20-percent minimum ROI). Go the other way. Give each unit an appropriate amount of funds to spend as they see fit.

Give them an overall ROI or ROA (return on assets) criterion *for the profit center*, and then trust local managers to make the correct decisions. If in point of fact they are doing that now, albeit after going through a complex budgeting exercise, why not get the same result with far less effort?

Two questions immediately come to mind. How do we determine the amount of funds to allocate to each unit and how do we know they will spend those funds wisely, that is, meet corporate goals, unless we know each project they propose to undertake?

The Purposes for Which Capital Expenditures Are Made

Many companies attempt to categorize investments in PP&E. Typical categories would be (1) cost-reduction, (2) expansion or new product, (3) replacement, (4) legally mandated and (5) a final nonquantifiable catch-all. How a proposal is categorized affects the decision process.

Cost reduction proposals should be the easiest to deal with. By spending *x* dollars now we will save 2*x* or 3*x* dollars in the future. Here is where the discounted cash flow techniques can be worthwhile, if in fact there are more good proposals than dollars readily available. Implicit in every cost reduction idea, however, is the assumption that the future demand is going to be maintained for the product whose cost we will be reducing. A suggestion in 1910 that would reduce by 20 percent the cost of tanning the leather that went into buggy whips would have passed every DCF hurdle, as long as horses were going to be the dominant form of transportation over the next 10 years.

The key variable in the exercise is the future *volume* of production, assuming that current and future operating costs can be estimated accurately. That is if we are taking an hour to do the job now, at a cost of $15 and a new machine will allow us to perform the operation in six minutes ($1.50) then the cash savings of $13.50 per unit can be related to the cost of the machine, disregarding maintenance for the moment. It may be appropriate to project that future volume will follow past trends, but also it may *not* be correct. The relative attractiveness of the idea is a direct function of *future volume*. How good is our crystal ball? The most refined analytical techniques known to financial theorists stumble on this one key variable. The bottom line is that we have to rely on someone's judgment.

Expansion or new product proposals are the ones that receive the greatest management scrutiny, for two reasons. Corporate growth can only come from expansion of capacity, which in turn usually involves new products of one sort or another. There are more *assumptions* necessary in this type of proposal, and more functional areas are involved in the decision, including engineering and marketing as well as production. Unlike the cost reduction ideas, which really do not impact marketing or customers (except to keep our costs competitive), expenditures for new products are crucial for long-run corporate success.

With the greater importance comes much less assurance about the future, since in the final analysis we are going to be dependent on how *customers* react. The history of new product introductions in the consumer packaged goods field suggests that forecasting customer tastes is risky at best. A 20-percent success ratio, which means an 80-percent failure ratio, might lead one to observe that today's techniques could be improved, but the fault is not in the DCF methodology. It is in the wishful thinking of the project team. After all, if you and your colleagues have spent the last 18 months developing a new pudding dessert, you have a vested interest in its success. Why wouldn't you put together an optimistic sales projection? The bottom line is that we have to rely on someone's judgment.

Replacement decisions, at least at one time, were considered easy. The old typewriter, as an example, wore out or broke and we *had* to buy a new one—no typewriter, no secretarial output. If a critical machine tool or special tooling could not hold tolerances, the organization really had little choice but to replace the asset. Most replacement decisions, therefore, were more or less exempt from rigorous financial analysis.

Today, however, there really are very few, if any, one-for-one replacements. The rate of technological change has meant that whenever an item wears out physically, and this is usually way longer than the period selected for financial depreciation on the books, something new has been developed. As typewriters wear out we buy a personal computer. If a machine tool can no longer hold tolerances, it truly is not worth repairing physically, then what we buy today will be new technology, not a replication of the old asset. In effect, today we have no replacement decisions, only cost reduction proposals. What kind of PC do we buy, networked or stand alone? Do we get a 5-axis N/C machine, or something simpler? Making these judgments again requires a look ahead, not just blind issuance of a purchase order just like the last one. Once again, the bottom line is that we have to rely on someone's judgment.

Legally mandated expenditures are becoming far greater in number, and in dollar amount than they used to. If replacements today are far less, because of improved technology that has lengthened useful lives, then government-mandated requirements are increasing geometrically as compared even with 10 years ago. *Required* commitments to meet EPA and OSHA regulations, or depending on your industry any other Washington agency's mandates, are capturing an ever-increasing portion of corporate capital spending. In fact, environmental costs alone are going to continue to grow for a long time before they level off, much less shrink.

Now the one characteristic of government-mandated spending is that it is mandated. You *must* do it, either to get permission to do something else, or in the worst case simply to keep doing what you are presently doing. If you don't spend the money you get shut down. It does not take a Harvard MBA to calculate the ROI. Without the expenditure there will be *no* R in the ROI calculation. So, almost irrespective of the I side of the equation— the amount of the investment, we have to do it or there is no *r*eturn on *any of our existing investment!*

That is why a separate category is usually set up in capital budgets, to recognize that items in that grouping do not have to pass the usual financial screening. Is this a "blank check"? Possibly. In some instances managers have undoubtedly managed to include a pet project in an otherwise required expenditure. There is a limit to how many controls can be set up to prevent this type of gamesmanship. The bottom line is that we have to rely on someone's judgment.

Nonquantifiable expenditures are often categorized by the example of repaving the employee parking lot, or upgrading the cafeteria. There is no direct connection between today's outlay and tomorrow's cash inflows for this type of expenditure. There is no need to analyze them further in financial terms. How does top management decide among the various proposals in the broad category? Sometimes it is on the basis of how much cash is left, either in the budget or at the end of the year. While not a theoretically neat solution, it is a practical approach. The bottom line is that we have to rely on someone's judgment.

We Have to Rely on Someone's Judgment

No, it was not an editorial error that permitted the same phrase to be used in explaining each category of capital expenditure. What we were trying to prove was that over-reliance on quantitative techniques, which most medium and large firms do, is an exercise in futility. The truly vital aspect of any and every capital expenditure proposal, irrespective of the exact financial analytic technique used, and irrespective of the discount rate or hurdle rate, is the assumption(s) about the future. These assumptions require judgment. Whose judgment will be used, and how that judgment will be reviewed, tells a lot about the management culture in an organization.

In a centralized firm, top management effectively calls all the shots. In a decentralized firm, lower level executives can approve capital expenditures up to varying limits. Just as in banking, so different levels of management have discretion; usually, however, all large projects must still go to the Board of Directors, as do large loans. Nonetheless there are widely varying approaches to setting these limits; some banks vest sole authority for large loans at relatively low levels, while other banks insist that a top-level committee approve virtually everything.

In this era of empowerment and employee involvement it is hard to understand the lack of trust implicit in a requirement that a top level committee or a senior executive approve, and sign off on, almost all loans or almost all capital expenditures. In effect, the policy in those centralized firms is saying, "We don't trust you or your judgment." To which the response has to be, "Well, then, why am *I* here and what should I be doing?"

We just saw that virtually every capital expenditure decision involves the exercise of managerial judgment. Wouldn't it be better to give managers at lower levels the flexibility, and then hold them responsible for overall results? How can you have a true profit center if you don't give the executive real authority to make capital expenditure decisions? If you really do not trust him not to go off the deep end, why not find someone you do trust?

Forecasting the Future—
What Are the Real Cash Flows?

There is an emphasis on quantification in today's capital budgeting decision process, a requirement that every approved proposal must have a positive net present value using the company's required rate of return, or have an internal rate of return in excess of an arbitrary hurdle rate (one that almost always is way above the real cost of capital). This leads very quickly to the advocate of any proposal to "cook the books," so to speak, to make the projection come out where it has to.

If you are going to do it right estimating future cash flows is, in practice, a very difficult process. Explicit projections have to be made about broad economic conditions (interest rates, exchange rates, government deficits, and taxes), customer responses to your future sales efforts, and perhaps most important of all, what your competitors are going to do. We can add nothing in this book to any analysis of future economic conditions. Similarly nobody from the outside has more insight on customer reactions than those dealing with those same customers today.

What is usually overlooked in most cash flow projections is the response of competitors. It is easy to *assume* a so-called "steady-state" environment, where competitors will keep on doing what they have in the past. For example, in this approach, putting in a new 5-axis N/C tool will cut costs 20 percent on one product. If you then assume that selling prices for that product stay the same, you can pay for the machine in a year—put the other way, it easily passes the firm's ROI tests. But what if your major competitor upgrades his factory, his costs come down 20 percent and selling prices are reduced for everyone? You still made the right decision, it's just that the expected return, the future cash flow, will not materialize.

Maybe this is why the basic profitability of most companies does not change much. Competitors prepare their own capital expenditure plans, trying to cut their costs and introduce new products. Industry suppliers are calling on your competitors as well as you. If that new 5-axis N/C tool will cut *your* costs, why shouldn't your major competitor be assumed to be acquiring the same model to reduce *his* costs?

Once you start to get realistic about the broad market place, you must take into consideration real world reactions to your actions. It is hard to project future cash flows for any single investment that will produce much above a 12 to 14-percent after-tax return, which happens to be slightly higher than the overall ROI for American business. Why does overall ROI stay remarkably constant year to year and even decade to decade if there are all those wonderful +20-percent returns? Part of the answer is in the mandated and nonfinancial investments that don't produce a good ROI. But the rest of the answer is competition that holds down selling prices, and keeps operating costs more or less comparable among firms. It is almost impossible to achieve some sort of giant breakthrough and then keep news of it from competitors and customers. If nothing else, your suppliers will spread the word, taking credit for your results.

What all this means is that today's capital budgeting systems, now almost a part of a corporate religion, are counterproductive. Far better to realize that continuing capital expenditures, usually in excess of current depreciation expense, are a necessary part of staying in business. Rather than take up a lot of valuable management time (with analysis, preparation of proposals, reviews, rework of the proposals, and finally, at long last, approval), there is a better way.

Allocate capital funds to the profit centers based on current ROI. This of course is in line with the concept of backing your winners, as contrasted with throwing good money after bad by putting dollars in low return areas. Once the funds have been allocated within broad areas, then let each profit center executive team make their own decisions. Input from the local engineering, marketing, and production staff, with questions being asked by local financial managers will lead to the right answers at least as often as today's formal rigid and hierarchical approach.

Postcompletion Audits

This section can be brief. Many companies ask their internal audit departments to review major, and sometimes even minor, capital projects, say,
one year after completion. The purpose of the exercise is to see whether
things came out as expected, whether the future cash flows materialized
as anticipated in the written project plan.

This has always seemed like an exercise in futility for three reasons.

1. The cash has been spent—if there were ever a definition of a sunk cost,
   this is it. Whether the 5-axis machine tool was a good idea or a bad idea,
   the vendor has been paid. If someone made a mistake are you going to
   receive a refund from the manufacturer? Not likely. If there were an
   overrun, what are you able to do about it? Nothing.

2. If you can't get your money back, what can you do with the audit report?
   Defenders of post-completion audits then respond, "We'll be able to tell
   who does a good job in preparing their AFEs (authorization for expenditure) so next time she submits one...." The response has to be that
   if management has to have the internal audit department determine
   who is doing a good job and who is not, there are some very serious
   performance measurement problems in that organization.

3. The final justification for post-completion audits is that it will help us
   do a better job next time. The trouble with this is that there never is a
   next time. Circumstances change and people change. One never sees a
   second AFE on the same subject with the same background facts and
   circumstances. If the people who prepared the last AFE need improvement or training in the basic methodology of investment analysis, then
   why wait a year for the audit report?

If a company had a basic approach of using management judgment to
evaluate capital expenditures at the front end, and applied an equal
amount of judgment after the fact to evaluate actual results, a lot of internal
audit staff time could be saved. Even more important, there would have to
be recognition that circumstances do change. Competitors respond in
unexpected ways. Customers don't necessarily continue buying the same
mix of products. The economy changes, and so forth.

Business is dynamic, but most formal capital budgeting systems assume,
at the point of decision, that the world is static. The world is going to
continue changing. Maybe the formal rigidity of capital budgeting should
also change.

13

How to Avoid the Traps in Leasing

*Leasing's growth as an industry is based on a
single premise: that lack of capital or some
other financial roadblock must not deter the
development or expansion of a promising
commercial enterprise.*
    Equipment Leasing Guide for Lessees
            by ALBERT R. McMEEN III,
    John Wiley & Sons, 1990 [p. 253]

For most managers, short-term leases—such as an automobile or a piece
of office equipment like a copier or fax machine—are quite common. This
chapter will be primarily devoted to this simple type of lease. Readers
should end up with a better grasp of the real pros and cons of leasing. The
fact that leasing continues to grow as a source of financing, despite many
predictions over the years that it would fade away, suggests that leasing
provides benefits. What is the true cost of these benefits? In short, when
is leasing appropriate, when should it be considered a cost-effective tool
of TCM?

Surprisingly, there are few issues in financial management that are more
controversial than leasing. Financial professionals view leasing as but one
form of financing, often appropriate for complex projects. Structuring a
major leasing transaction involves substantive tax and legal issues. In
addition, because a lease is *not* the same as a purchase or sale (depending
on the perspective of the buyer or seller), decisions have to be made as to

how long the asset will be used and what its value will be at the end of the lease. Who will gain or lose the value inherent in the asset at the lease termination? Determining the true net cost of lease financing is an extremely complex subject, one on which financial analysts often disagree.

Accounting for Leases

There may be nothing duller than the accounting issues associated with leasing—after all, what does accounting have to do with *real* cash flow? Accounting should report what happens, so whatever business decisions have been made should be reflected simply in the financial statements. This gets us very quickly to the heart of the issue. From the perspective of the purchaser/user is a lease the same as a purchase? Is an airline that borrows money and purchases its planes outright, having to pay off the borrowing in 15 years, in any different situation than a second airline that acquires the identical planes, but pays for them by signing a 15-year lease?

Ask yourself this question. How would you answer it? Assume the monthly payments are identical for each and every month of the 15 years. Disregarding taxes, there is no difference in cash flows so, irrespective of the discount rate used, the net present values of the two streams of cash —repayment of the debt vs. monthly lease payments—appear to be the same. But there *is* one key difference. At the end of the fifteenth year, airline 1 owns its planes free and clear. Airline 2 has a pile of cancelled checks but the lessor still owns the planes. Airline 2 can now go out and lease brand new planes. But to continue using the same old planes the next day, it can do one of three things:

1. Buy the planes at some previously agreed upon price.
2. Buy the planes at their then fair market value.
3. Sign a new lease.

Airline 1 could sell its fleet, using the cash receipts as a down payment on new planes. In terms of continued use of the old planes, however, the two airlines are now, at year 15, in fundamentally *different* positions. Airline 1 has no further cash payments (again disregarding taxes) while airline 2 will have both continuing cash outflows and reported expense on the P&L for operating the identical fleet.

Leasing does differ from purchase because of one simple, yet critical, aspect. The airline leasing the planes does not own them. They are committed contractually to 15 years of cash flows, and at the end of that time can either walk away or, as they say in the Army, "re-up." The airline that bought its fleet need make no decision at the start of the sixteenth year, and with the debt paid off, now has an operating cost advantage.

It is the difference in ownership that leads to differing accounting treatment. Airline 1, which own the planes outright, treats the planes as does any firm with property, plant, and equipment (PP&E). It capitalizes the original cost of acquisition, sets up an assumed life of the asset for purposes of determining depreciation expense, and then charges off as an expense $\frac{1}{15}$ of the cost each year (assuming straight line depreciation). At the end of the 15 years no further depreciation expense will be recorded, even though the planes may have significant market value and a remaining useful life of, say, seven years.

Airline 1, which sold 15-year bonds to pay for the planes, will have been recording interest expense each month. As debt is paid off throughout the life of the loan, each year's interest expense will decrease. Depending on how the debt was structured, if it were like a 15-year home mortgage, monthly cash payments would be level, but each month less would go to interest and more to debt reduction. Since interest is an expense, both for books and taxes, while repayment of principal is not, the actual P&L effect of buying will change from year to year.

So one accounting impact of leasing is to switch the timing of P&L expenses. Leasing is essentially straight line, while purchase (outright ownership) has high expense in the beginning and low expense at the end, tailing off to no expense when the asset is fully depreciated and the debt is paid off. Keep in mind that for this example we assumed that the duration of the debt, asset life for depreciation, and initial lease term were identical—here, 15 years. In the real world it need not be so, but the concepts remain identical.

If there is an accounting impact of purchase vs. leasing in terms of reported expense, even with no impact on cash flows for the first 15 years, there is another accounting consideration that often assumes greater importance. Certainly everyone would agree that for airline 1 the planes should show as an asset of the company, and the related debt as a liability, on the company's balance sheet. That is simply the way we do our accounting.

The question is, should airline 2, which leases the planes, also show them on the balance sheet as an asset, offset by the future commitments to make lease payments as a liability? This volume is neither an accounting textbook nor a history of Generally Accepted Accounting Principles (GAAP). Readers should understand, however, that the answer to the question—whether leased assets should be capitalized—has had a tremendous impact on both the growth of leasing and the structure of individual deals.

Off-Balance Sheet Financing— Something for Nothing

Under GAAP you do not show, as a liability on the balance sheet, commitments to pay property taxes in future years, even though we know they will become due and payable. We do not show a liability for future salary payments to an executive who has a five-year employment contract. We do not add up all the rent due on a 10-year commitment to rent warehouse space and show it on the balance sheet. In short, the current definition of liabilities under GAAP does not encompass all commitments to make cash payments in the future. The problem is simply stated:

Are future lease payments liabilities?
If so, they must appear on the balance sheet.

It may be easier for an accountant to say which future cash commitments should be shown on the balance sheet than it is to accurately describe just what the rule is. There is an absolute continuum of future commitments, from paying for merchandise that has been ordered but not received at one end, to principal and interest on 30-year bonds at the other end. It has proven almost impossible for the FASB to write definitive rules defining liabilities—rules that will be applied identically by everyone. No matter where the cut-off is made, there will still be grey areas over which reasonable people can disagree.

It just so happens that in the area of leasing, what started as a crack in the dike threatened to become a dam burst. Originally the people who made the accounting rules started out with the common sense approach that in a lease someone else owns the asset, and the asset appears on the lessor's balance sheet. Therefore future lease payments were no different from future property tax payments or future salary payments. This meant that from the perspective of the *lessee*, the asset being used was not on the balance sheet and consequently the future lease payments also did not have to appear as a liability.

Wow! Why don't we write a 5-year lease that calls for payments over that time (which would include interest), and then at the end of the lease let the lessee buy the asset for one dollar? That way the lessee would pay no more for the asset than if the money was borrowed from the bank for five years. We all know that bank loans have to appear on the balance sheet, but if lease payments do not have to be on the balance sheet, and the cash outflow and net expense are identical, it is not hard to guess that a certain number of firms (say +95 percent!) would choose the lease option.

The key is that the lessee can buy the asset for one dollar at the end of the lease. Most people, looking at that fact situation, would say that it was really a purchase in the form of a lease, that substance should rule over form, and there is no question the asset and liability should be on the balance sheet. So where do we draw the line? When does a lease in form become a purchase in substance? Fifteen years, and hundreds of pages of rules later, the FASB is still wrestling with this issue.

Borrowers, that is, actual or prospective lessees, love having no reported liability on the balance sheet. The assumption (and this has been borne out in numerous studies) is that bankers and credit analysts judge a company primarily by ratios derived from the reported balance sheet. If it is on the balance sheet it is a liability—period. If it is not on the balance sheet, it is *not* a liability—period. Therefore leased assets, as long as they do not appear on the balance sheet, do not affect a company's credit rating or borrowing capacity. Stated this way, many readers may raise their eyebrows.

Are bankers really that dumb? GAAP does require that all lease commitments be shown as a footnote in the financial statements. So the credit analyst or banker *can* calculate total liabilities *as if* the lease amounts were determined to be equivalent to other financial commitments that are on the balance sheet. Since the real world is not always totally rational, it is no surprise that how an accountant classifies a lease, whether it should be capitalized on the face of the balance sheet or shown as a footnote, does impact total credit availability for some borrowers.

The author's personal view is that most lease commitments are fully equivalent in terms of cash flow to a corresponding amount of secured or unsecured bank borrowing. But there is a difference in financial position because the lessee does not own the asset, does not share in the so-called risks and rewards of ownership. Put this way, leasing might be perceived as the worst of both worlds—equivalent in terms of total costs, cash flow and debt (the liability side)—not equivalent in terms of the benefits of asset ownership.

Getting back to our airline example, airline 2, which leased its planes, would not show the liability for the future lease payments, nor the corresponding aircraft, on its balance sheet at the start of the lease. At the end of the lease, in 15 years, if they do buy the used equipment outright at fair market value, the accounting is straightforward and is the same as for any asset purchase.

Which airline is better off? Airline 1 owns the equipment outright with no debt at the end of 15 years, but meanwhile has had a balance sheet that disclosed significant debt all that time. Airline 2 has had a clean balance sheet in terms of debt, although some observers might wonder how an airline can operate without airplanes as an asset! The answer of course is in the footnotes to the financial statements.

Observation: Whenever you are presented with a set of financial statements, read the footnotes first. There is more good information openly displayed there than in the balance sheet and income statement combined.

If, during the life of the lease, airline 2 were able to use its clean balance sheet to obtain more debt, and perhaps expand faster, it could gain a competitive advantage over airline 1 whose balance sheet precluded additional borrowing. Offsetting that, airline 1 might choose to expand in round 2 through leasing, if it could not persuade so-called standard borrowers to extend additional credit.

The question then comes down to a factual issue. Does leasing provide access to additional asset use? Can a firm increase its cash resources by leasing instead of relying on more traditional forms of borrowing? The growth of leasing over the past 20 years suggests the answer is yes. But there is no free lunch. Keeping the asset and related liability off the balance sheet comes at a price, and that price is the payment required by the lessor to buy the asset at the end of the lease term. In effect, you may pay twice for use of the same asset, but in exchange gain access to more assets. If growth is constrained by the availability of cash and/or credit, then leasing *may* make very good business sense. Paying a significant premium, hoping to fool credit analysts and bankers, may not be a good bet.

The Current Accounting Rules on Leasing

Before listing the actual rules, let's see why people have an incentive to beat the game. For accounting purposes, there are only two types of leases, and they provide diametrically opposite results. *Operating leases* do not show up on the financial statements of the lessee (user of the asset), while the lessor has to carry the item as an asset on its balance sheet. *Capital leases*, on the other hand, must be shown as an asset and related liability on the lessee's financial statements, while the lessor shows only a receivable for the future payments due from the lessee. If a manufacturer is the lessor, then it treats the lease as a *sale*, reporting any manufacturing and selling profit at the time the financing lease is signed. Put another way, if the requirements of an operating lease are not met, the transaction is considered a capital lease; the seller recognizes a profit, but the buyer (lessee) must show a liability on its balance sheet corresponding to the receivable on the lessor's books.

All other things being equal, the seller would like to treat any lease transaction as a capital lease, while almost all buyers would like to treat the asset acquisition as an operating lease. Believe it or not, there have been cases where the same transaction has, in practice, been treated both ways by the two independent parties. The seller, for example the airplane manufacturer selling to airline 2, tells her auditor, "This is a financing lease. I am entitled to recognize the sale and profit right now. As the buyer makes his payments I will keep reducing the receivable until he has fully paid for the equipment." That way the seller maximizes his reported earnings right in year 1, and has only a long term receivable on his books.

In this situation the buyer, for example airline 2 above, tells his auditor, "This is an operating lease. I have no investment in the asset itself, merely a contract to pay rent for 15 years. I will show the future payments I have contracted for in the footnotes but will not put any liability on my balance sheet. Of course, I cannot show the plane(s) as an asset, or take depreciation on them, but that is OK because I will deduct the total lease payments as expense."

Can the same transaction have two separate and distinct accounting treatments with diametrically opposite results? If indeed things are handled as described we have a real anomaly. The planes, as an asset, are on nobody's balance sheet! The manufacturer shows a long-term receivable, but the buyer does not show a corresponding payable! In short, there is absolutely no symmetry, yet both parties argue they are only following the rules.

There is tremendous incentive for each side to argue. After all, manufacturers like to report maximum sales and profits, and buyers (lessees) like to keep their balance sheet as clean as possible. The only flaw in this ideal solution is from the perspective of the reader of the financial statements of both parties. Where did the asset go? Is there a liability or not, and if so why doesn't it show on the lessee's books? These are very good questions, and help explain why the accounting for leases has grown so complex.

You would think it would be easy to write a rule defining an operating lease and thus distinguishing it from a capital lease. In fact the FASB did so when they issued SFAS 13, which is the basic document controlling lease accounting. What they said was, for a lease to qualify as an *operating* lease, four tests must each be met. They are:

1. The lease does not transfer ownership to the lessee at the end of the lease.

2. The lease does not contain a bargain purchase option.

3. The lease term is for less than 75 percent of the estimated economic life of the leased property.

4. The present value of the minimum lease payments is less than 90 percent of the fair market value of the asset.

Just for fun, let's look at our airplane example. The lease to airline 2 did not transfer ownership at the end of the lease, or have a bargain purchase option. In fact, the lessee would have to pay fair market value at the end of year 15. But is 15 years more or less than 75 percent of the economic life of a jet aircraft. If the life is 21 years, we pass the test. If the life is only 20 years, we fail. Who can precisely estimate exactly how long a particular model of airplane will last two decades from now? With regard to the fourth test, the present value is a function of the amount of the payments, and the discount rate. What is the appropriate discount rate?

At this point we will stop the analysis, but it is easy to see how reasonable people could differ, particularly if they have a vested interest in the outcome, as to the real economic life and the correct discount rate. Suffice it to say that over the past 15 years a lot of energy, on the part of both lessors and Wall Street investment bankers, has gone into devising lease terms that get around the rules while the FASB and SEC keep tightening the rules. The trend is clearly toward calling *all* leases capital leases, except that, as we saw, a lessee in practice is not in the same economic situation as an outright owner.

Observation: Any time you are offered a lease and one of the selling points is that you will not have to show the liability on the balance sheet, right then check with your independent auditors and see if they agree. If they will let you treat the transaction as an operating lease, prior to signing the papers, go ahead. Just do not wait until year-end, get in a fight with your auditors, and find out too late that the salesperson misled you on the accounting treatment.

It may be expensive to obtain an operating lease for an asset, rather than buy it outright or acquire it as a capital lease. Simply keeping debt off the balance sheet, in the hope that bankers and credit analysts will extend more credit, may be a costly source of cash to acquire capital assets. As we will see, there are good *operating* reasons to lease needed property for shorter periods of time. Letting accounting considerations drive business decisions is usually a mistake.

Tax Consequences— What Is a "True" Lease?

In a true lease, for tax purposes, the lessor is considered the real owner and consequently obtains the benefits of depreciation and any investment tax credit. This allows a lessor, with substantial income that would otherwise be taxable, to offer great flexibility in payment terms to lessees who cannot use the tax benefits right away.

In structuring a lease that has tax implications as one of its motivating factors, the IRS will look closely at the substance of the transaction, not its form. Who is the real owner, is the key question, because only the owner gets to claim the depreciation. Given the relatively short lives the IRS now allows for most types of assets, combined with accelerated depreciation, lessors can quickly generate substantial amounts of tax shelter.

In the effort to protect the government's revenue stream, the IRS has an incentive to challenge those leases that appear to be motivated primarily by tax considerations. Since the risk of tax disallowance falls on the lessor (unless this is spelled out somehow in the lease document) you as a lessee probably don't have to worry. But because lessors do this all the time, and you as a lessee are an infrequent participant, it pays to scrutinize the documents before signing. Just how is the lessor protected with regard to tax benefits?

As a rule of thumb, the IRS' approach to leasing is not all that different from the accountant's. A properly structured capital lease, with the real economic risks and rewards shared equitably between the parties, probably will stand up to scrutiny. Only if tax motivations are the controlling factor, and they sometimes are, should lessees be on guard.

Observation: In terms of TCM, taxes should not be a primary or even a secondary concern in most leasing decisions. The main factors should be the terms of the lease, the lessee's responsibilities, and the present value of the cash payments committed to.

Leasing Automobiles and Computers—The Cash Consequences

A major automaker's advertisement headlined, "Leasing a luxury car entitles you to certain privileges" then goes on to state those privileges as:

1. Getting into a luxurious *way of life.*

2. 24-hour roadside service.

3. Trip-interruption protection.

4. Trip routing service to map trips for you.

Getting down to the bottom line the ad text reveals that "at only $499 a month—on a 24-month lease—this life of privilege is *surprisingly afford-able.*" In a discreet box the $499/mo. payment is followed by the term "$1500 down payment."

Then if you are still interested there are several lines of text, in type that is much smaller than the rest of the ad. It says:

FIRST MONTH'S LEASE PAYMENT OF $499, PLUS $550 REFUND-ABLE SECURITY DEPOSIT AND CONSUMER DOWN PAYMENT

OF $1,500 FOR A TOTAL OF $2,549 DUE AT LEASE SIGNING. Taxes, license, title fees and insurance extra. You must take retail delivery out of dealer stock by [2/2/93]. [The financing source] must approve lease. Example based on a [1993] luxury model, $34,751 MSRP including destination charge. Monthly payment is based on a capitalized cost of $29,756 for a total of monthly payments of $11,796. Your payments may be higher or lower. Payments may be slightly higher in Alabama, Arkansas, Hawaii, Texas and Virginia. Option to purchase at lease end for $21,789. Mileage charge of $.10 per mile over 30,000 miles. Lessee pays for excessive wear and use. See your participating dealer for qualification details.

Let's look at what your cash outflow would be if you wanted to experience this life of privilege. First, you would pay $1500 as a down payment. In most leasing situations there is no down payment, but this way the manufacturer can offer monthly terms of $499, below the magic psychological level of $500. There is an implicit assumption that your existing automobile, almost irrespective of age and condition, would be worth at least $1500 and thus you need not come up with any cash for the down payment.

Making the first month's lease payment in advance is fairly standard. In over hundreds of thousands of leases, the value to the lessor of receiving payments at the *beginning* of the month instead of at the end, can have a significant impact. The interest earnings on $1/12$ of your total cash flow is going to add up to a significant amount. For any one lease, paying $500 one month early, if interest rates are 8 percent, is a net cost of less than $4. Let the lessor have that one-time gain. Of course on a lease payment of $5,000 per month this is a little more significant, while on a +$1 million-lease transaction the timing of the payments is both significant and subject to negotiation, like all terms. But only on truly large deals is this worth worrying about.

Second, the security deposit of $550 is refundable at the end of the lease. This ties into the term that states that the lessee "pays for excessive wear and tear." We will discuss the definition of "excessive" later. The point is that the lessee must come up with an interest-free loan to the lessor for two years. If all goes well the funds will be returned in total, but without interest. There is a cost in terms of foregone interest on the security deposit. Again, it may seem small, but it can add up to big numbers on thousands of deals.

Finally, the lessee has the right, but not a requirement, to buy the car in two years at a predetermined price, in this case $21,789. Because the payment would be made two years from now the present value, in today's dollars, is actually less than the stated amount.

At this point we can look at the net present value, assuming three different rates of interest.

	7%	8%	9%
Present value of 24 monthly payments of $499 each.	$11,145	$11,033	$10,922
Present value of purchase of car for $21,789 in two years.	19,934	19,570	19,217
Present value of foregone interest on $550 security deposit.	69	78	87
Nonrefundable $1500 down payment, paid at lease inception.	1500	1500	1500
Net present value today of total cash outlay.	$32,648	$32,181	$31,726

The first thing that strikes the reader is that the lowest cost for leasing, in terms of net present value, is at the *highest* interest rate. This is primarily because the major cash outlay, buying the car for $21,789, is postponed two years in this leasing proposal. The more you can earn on your money—the higher the interest rate—the less you have to put aside today to come up with the $21,789. Similarly, the present value of the 24 monthly payments is less at higher interest rates. The down payment is in today's dollars and does not change. Only the foregone interest on the security deposit increases with higher interest rates.

Before making a decision to buy or lease this luxury car, to obtain entry to the life of privilege, you would have to determine what interest rate you would pay on a 2-year (24 month) car loan. Note that this is *not* the monthly payment on a car loan, but the annual percentage rate (APR). If you can get a car loan at 7 percent from your bank, or even the auto manufacturer, the benefits of stretching out the payments are less than if your car loan costs at least 9 percent, where the time value of money is greater. Of course, you always want the lowest possible interest rate. The lower the interest rate the better off you are in absolute terms; it just shifts the balance between outright purchase and leasing.

Assuming you could get an 8-percent car loan, the next question is, how much could you buy the car for in an outright purchase transaction. The MSRP is $34,751, but nobody pays sticker price for a car. Just by walking in the front door of the dealership you will probably be able to get $1500 to $2000 off the MSRP. If the dealer were hungry that day, or you were a good negotiator, it is quite possible you could buy the car for $31,200 which would represent a 10-percent discount. If you could then finance that purchase at 8-percent, leasing would be more expensive—except for the amount of down payment the bank would insist on. On a 24-month lease would the bank want you to put up 20 percent, or $6000 or maybe even

30 percent or $9500? Cars do depreciate substantially when you leave the dealership and the bank wants to be protected against any conceivable contingency—thus the down payment requirement.

What leasing offers is the low ($1500) down payment. But at an 8-percent interest rate, and with good negotiating skills, many buyers could bring the outright purchase price down to $31,200, thus making leasing subject to a cost penalty of roughly $1000. Put a different way, if you have the down payment (say in the value of your existing car) you may still choose to lease rather than buy just to get the flexibility the lease offers. Maximizing cash flow is important, and TCM must always be kept in mind, but there are other things in life. Leasing a car may be a one stop transaction and, if your time is worth something, a small cash penalty might be justified for the benefits of simplicity.

The Operating Consequences of Leasing

As we saw in discussing the accounting aspects of the airplane case, leasing is *not* the same as ownership. There are differences and an understanding of the attributes of leasing can be helpful.

In a capital lease the lessor is really financing the entire purchase price—in exchange for turning over the asset immediately, the cash will be received (paid by the lessee) over several years. Thus a full-payout lease represents not only the extension of credit, but an extension for a long period of time. All other things being equal, a lessor is assuming more credit risk than a banker on a line of credit, primarily because of the difficulty of forecasting the creditworthiness of the borrower (lessee) for a significant number of years into the future.

Go back to the fine print in the "Life of Privilege" lease ad. The words "The financing source must approve lease," sort of stuck in there so casually, really mean that the lessor (the auto manufacturer in this case) is going to run a credit check on every prospective lessee. Given the availability of computerized credit databases, both for individuals and companies, this is neither time consuming nor intrusive. But woe to a prospective lessee if the credit check does not prove out. If you have been delinquent before, the lessor assumes you may treat him the same way.

Some people think that you can get more credit through leasing because the lessor still owns the asset. In case of nonpayment it is much easier for a lessor to reclaim his property than for a general unsecured creditor to walk away with any cash in a Chapter 11 filing. If the leased property is critical to the continued functioning of the business, say, on a vital piece of machinery or the sole factory location, monthly lease payments may continue to be made even as other creditors are standing in line with their hands out. So the lessor is in a favored position, vis à vis unsecured creditors. But the fact remains that reclaiming leased assets from a debtor is no fun—not to mention that the lessee, knowing she is in trouble, may not treat the leased asset too kindly. In the final analysis, from the lessor's perspective the extra security of owning the hard asset is offset by the requirement to extend credit for a longer than normal period of time.

In a capital lease the lessor does not expect to see the asset again—if all goes well. A full-payout lease is just that, a full payout, and at the end of the lease term the lessee will take title. But for both operating leases, less than the asset's useful life, and for true tax leases, where the lessor must retain the risks and rewards of ownership, asset condition is vital. A beat up car is worth less than a creampuff. A properly maintained machine tool will have a much higher fair market value than one run 24 hours a day with only minimum care. How does the lessor ensure the condition? In a phrase, with difficulty.

Think of the difficulty in drawing up a contract and trying to spell out, in advance, every aspect of maintenance and condition. As with other things, it is easy to know the results of good maintenance when you see it, but very hard to define it in legal terms. So the lease terms use the most general language, and both parties hope there is no dispute. If there is, look out.

Go back to the luxury car lease ad. Again, in the fine print was the phrase "lessee pays for excessive wear and use." Sounds fair. But what is "excessive?" An article in *Forbes* [2/1/93, p. 99] reported a case as follows:

> "Mr. _____ took the car back to the dealer and leased another car. The luxury car, he says, was in near mint condition when he turned it in. "My wife and I treat a car the way you would a child" he says. Several months later he got a bill from the Lessor for $1048 to cover "excess wear and tear." He called to contest the damages, but the car had already been sold. The lessor kept his security deposit of $681, charged him a $250 disposition fee and dunned him for another $367. When he called the New York City Department of Consumer Affairs he eventually settled for $200."

Forbes advice is worth repeating: "Before you sign the lease, make sure it states clearly that you can be present during the lease-end inspection. If you have a beef, contest it then, or get an independent inspection. You can also have any needed repairs made yourself—probably a lot cheaper than the leasing company will charge." After the fact, it is impossible to judge who was right in this situation. The way some people "treat their children" might not be the way I would want my car treated. The point is that the value to the lessor of the asset at lease termination is going to be a function of its then condition. Reasonable people can disagree about condition.

Unreasonable people, and that could be either party, may end up in court. This area for potential dispute should be thought about in advance, although just what can be done is not quite so clear, other than to use good judgment in maintaining the asset.

A related point in the luxury car lease, and applicable to most auto leases, is the phrase, "Mileage charge of $.10 per mile over 30,000 miles." For a two-year lease this means that if you drive more than 15,000 miles a year, there will be potentially significant extra cost. High mileage drivers cannot, therefore, shift the costs associated with excessive use to a lessor. An outside salesperson who "lives" in her car could easily put on 40,000 miles a year or 80,000 miles in two years. Such a car is worth far less than one with only 30,000 miles on the odometer. The monthly lease terms offered by the lessor were set based on an assumption as to the residual value of the car. Anything that adversely affects that value is going to impact the realized profits. The $.10/mile charge may seem excessive, and possibly could be subject to negotiation, but undoubtedly at the cost of a higher monthly lease payment.

The reader should not think that there are all negatives in leasing. If you are planning to turn in a car every two years, for whatever reason, leasing eliminates any concern about future values of used cars and from the effort of finding a buyer. Of course trading in the old car to the new car dealer is also easy, but every study of the economics of auto ownership suggests that, in practice, trading in cars every two years is the most costly way to dispose of an old vehicle. You will get more for a used car you own by selling it yourself—not to a new car dealer. That, however, incurs costs in time and effort. If ease of transaction is important, and for many people it is, leasing may be the easiest way of all. That was what we meant when we said that TCM was not everything in the world.

Leasing (Renting) Office Space vs. Purchase of a Building

Renting office space, production or warehousing facilities, is virtually identical to equipment leasing. In fact, the legal document you sign is just that—a lease. But because it is by far the most common way to obtain needed space, the similarities can be forgotten. In terms of cash flows, let's start with the simplest lease of all—an apartment for personal use.

After checking you out for credit and personal characteristics, the landlord asks you to sign a document, the lease, that calls for you to pay rent once a month at the stated rate. You will probably be asked to put up one additional month's rent as a security deposit to protect the landlord if you were to "skip" at the end of the lease. Two areas of concern to the landlord are nonpayment of the last month's rent, and abnormal physical damage to the property. The landlord is basically responsible for normal maintenance; put the other way, your obligation as a tenant does not encompass repairs to the property. Depending on the condition of the premises, you may ask the landlord to repaint the rooms, either at the beginning of the lease, or if you are going to renew and he wants to keep you. This is, in short, negotiable.

Also negotiable is who pays the utilities—gas, electricity, water, sewer, and heat. If the apartment was designed for each tenant to pay her own there may be little to negotiate. On the other hand in a small apartment there is likely to be only one heating unit, one electric meter, and so on, so some fair means of apportioning the costs must be found. But there are usually established policies in any local area so controversy may be minimal.

The only real dispute (other than pets and children which are outside the scope of a book on cash management!) is the term of the lease. In a soft market the landlord wants a long lease, and the renter a short one. Renters want to be able to move, or negotiate a lower rent. A three year lease, being a legal document, really binds both parties to the terms agreed upon, so if conditions change, one party or the other will feel unfairly put upon. This would argue for a shorter term. Except that if rents are going up in the area, the tenant then would prefer to have a fixed amount negotiated earlier when rents were lower. Absent a known intent to move, the final term of the original lease is going to be a function of each side's estimate as to the future course of inflation and/or the local housing market.

In terms of the tenant's cash flows, a three-year lease involves two month's rent up front, a commitment to make payments on the first of each subsequent month, an expectation the premises will be kept in good order, payment of agreed upon utilities and return of the security deposit at the end of three years, or its application to the last month's rent. The landlord is responsible for property taxes, insurance, and his agreed upon share of utilities. All in all a pretty straight forward transaction. Because there are so many apartment rentals, and most legal issues have long been settled, the disputes, if any, tend to be personal in nature.

Rental of commercial space follows this model very closely, but there are far more variables affecting cash flow. This is not a primer on real estate, but let's look, from the tenant's perspective, at some of the key areas needed to optimize cash flows. First a word of advice.

Observation: Commercial landlords are professionals. They negotiate leases for a living. Because the cash consequences of leasing are substantial in amount, and can last for 10 to 15 years, it behooves a prospective tenant to get the best possible professional counsel. This can be a lawyer who specializes in real estate, a tenant's broker working for you, or both. Do not try, as an amateur, to beat professionals at their own game. You will not "out negotiate" them!

Let us look at four areas affecting cash flow.

1. Length of lease and the impact on business flexibility.

2. Cost pass-throughs and inflation.

3. How much space are you getting?

4. For retailers, contingent rentals based on volume.

Length of Lease.   A large new office building was built in New York City. A prospective tenant approached the leasing agent about renting an entire floor. This was a significant, although not gigantic, transaction. After everything else was worked out, and the tenant was prepared to sign a 10-year lease, the landlord came back and said, "By the way, would you mind signing a 15-year lease instead, it certainly would help our financing." Long-term lenders are interested in how much of a building is leased out, and for what period. The larger each is, the more the building owner can borrow to pay off construction financing. So extending from 10 to 15 years certainly would help the building owner, but the tenant, satisfied with the terms and conditions, agreed without asking for anything in return.

Ten years later, the original rental rate per square foot was substantially below then current rental rates, and the tenant had another five years of below market rent. Near the end of the 15-year lease, when it came time to negotiate the renewal, the landlord conveniently forgot about his request to extend the original lease term, and only focused on the current below-market rent. The tenant moved, and shortly thereafter the New York office rental market started its long decline. So much for loyalty in real estate.

The point is that a lease on office space is a legally binding contract on both parties. Over a 10- or 15-year period conditions are going to change. Neither party knows which way. The tenant may need more or less space. The market may firm up, or get weaker. The tenant will come out all right if he needs more space in a weak market, or less space in a strong market. She will be in trouble if she needs less space in a weak market or more space in a strong market. Even in a weak market, getting additional space contiguous to the existing location may not be possible.

Do you know how large your office requirements will be 5, 7, or 10 years from now? Most organizations do not. You can consciously rent more space than you need today to allow for future growth, but this pushes up the current cash outflow relative to actual need. You can rent excess space and try to sublet it; this puts you into the real estate business. You can rent exactly what you need today, and if growth occurs simply plan on paying then market rates and hope the space will be close, if not contiguous.

Because of the fixed long-term nature of office space rentals, advance planning is essential. However, virtually no one knows what requirements are going to be in the future. Leasing space actually has less flexibility than it seems. True, on day one you can custom tailor the space to today's exact requirements, but the landlord cannot be expected to save space for you in case you need it. In a large building there is always movement in and out so some space undoubtedly will be available when you need it and this can be a real plus. Whether the additional space is desirable and whether it will be priced properly represents a more or less normal business risk.

Where things really get difficult is when a tenant wants to downsize in a weak rental market. That is when the fine print in the contract is really examined for the first time. Guess what? The tenant with excess space is not going to have a lot of options. Monthly rent is going to be due whether the space is needed or not, whether it is wanted or not. Simply stopping the sending of a rent check is not a very good alternative. The lease undoubtedly permits the landlord to sue and collect the rent in accordance with the contract. Short of filing for Chapter 11, which affects the entire company, *there is no good way out of a lease for space you do not need.* Negotiations are always possible, both with the landlord and with other tenants in the building, but experience shows that when *you* have excess space so do others. In the final analysis paying for unneeded space is the cost of poor planning at the time the lease was signed. The cash commitment inherent in a space lease is going to be very much a fixed cost just when you would like to have maximum flexibility.

Cost Pass-Through. Landlords have fixed expenses just like everyone else, such as property taxes, maintenance of elevators and HVAC, and cleaning of common areas. (Depreciation, because it is related to the landlord's tax basis, is never of concern to tenants.) Because of the long-term nature of leases, and the uncertainty of how much these costs will increase, landlords cannot realistically commit to providing maintenance and so forth for 10, 15, or even 20 years into the future based on today's rents. Base rents per square foot are usually fixed for the period of the lease term. Nobody, not even unpopular landlords, can manage cash flow in an inflationary environment if total revenues are fixed, and all or most operating expenses are variable.

The solution is for tenants to agree to compensate the landlord for all *increases* in the agreed upon expenses, over and above the base level established when the lease was signed. This seems fair in concept. If the mayor decides to increase local property taxes, tenants should bear their share. If the cost of janitorial services rises too much the landlord might choose to vacuum the carpets only once a week. Tenants want a well maintained building and have to expect to pay for it. If they owned their own space their occupancy costs would be going up.

The problem is, in practice, one of agreeing on how to pay for it, and then auditing the actual amounts passed on. The simplest approach, for both landlord and tenant is to agree to use some sort of government prepared price index, such as the CPI, applied to an agreed upon portion of the base rent. If the CPI goes up 3 percent, the common charges, as they are sometimes called, can go up 3 percent. Or, by agreement, the charge could be, say, .8 or 1.25 (or anything agreed to at lease inception) *times* the change in the CPI. In this scenario the lower the percentage of the CPI the better off is the tenant. Trying to outguess *which* index to use may well be an exercise in futility. How well will the CPI track real inflationary operating costs ten years from now? It is not worth worrying about, since most price indices tend to follow one another over longer periods of time.

The other approach to passing through increases in common costs is to provide tenants with financial statements (usually audited) showing all common costs, assessing each tenant her prorata share. Problems can arise in how much overhead the landlord includes in his costs, how he allocates common costs among more than one building, whether his cost really includes a profit allowance, and so forth. In this situation the landlord has all the advantages. It is often perceived to not be worthwhile to check the landlord's calculations, either because his figures were audited, or because as a small tenant the potential savings are not worth the effort.

Interestingly enough this situation has resulted in some entrepreneurs establishing a business that consists of auditing a landlord's cost pass-through statement. Often there is no up-front charge for this service, the tenant agreeing to compensate the auditor with a percentage of the savings. If a company does not have the resources to do this kind of checking on its own, use of such a service is worthwhile. Of course, you will kick yourself if your auditor finds $10,000 of overcharges and you receive a check for only $5500 after he takes a 45-percent cut. But any time a service is performed on a contingency basis (think of lawyers) the savings in up-front cash to the client have to be made up somewhere. On balance we would recommend use of the audit services. Unless you have a full-time internal audit department with the expertise to carry out the review, leave it to a specialist. Keep in mind that potentially there are significant dollars at stake.

How Much Space Are You Renting?   What could be easier than to determine how many square feet there are in the space you are renting? In fact, the answer is that a *lot* of things are easier. In discussing one landlord, a New York real estate broker, only half in jest, accused him of using a rubber ruler to measure space. Do you measure the outside perimeter of a building or the inside? How do you handle common areas like the elevator shafts on your floor? What about space in the ground floor lobby, who does it belong to?

In one sense it makes no real difference in terms of cash flow, since rents per square foot are themselves negotiable. Is there is a difference between paying $20 per foot for 10,000 square feet or $21.05 for 9500 square feet? If the landlord says that the area you have picked out is 10,000 square feet, and you measure it at only 9500, in terms of *usable* space, it is only a matter of semantics. Your cash outflow will still be $16,667 per month, so it is immaterial to your employees whether it is *called* 9500 or 10,000. In point of fact, do you know exactly how many square feet your organization is utilizing today. Space measurement is considered a very low priority, and rightfully so.

But wait. Remember the so-called common charges we discussed? They are prorated among all tenants in a building. If your space is exactly 3 percent of the total building, and if every tenant's space was measured the exact same way, nobody would be hurt. But, if during the course of lease negotiations with 35 tenants five different individuals had made the space calculations, what are the chances they would each handle the difficult definitional problems the same way? To be fair to all—and the common charges are often material costs to tenants—it is vital that standard definitions for measuring rentable space be applied equally to all tenants.

Observation: As part of your lease negotiation ask to see the definition of rentable or usable space that the building owner applies, and verify that all tenants' calculations use the same definition. If you have an outside auditor checking landlord charges this is one item for review.

Contingent Rentals.   Base rents are usually fixed for the term of the lease. But retailers, often in a shopping center, will be asked to pay, *in addition*, an amount based on their sales volume. The theory is that being located in a shopping center provides the tenant with sales volume over and above that which would be available in some other stand-alone location. Being located next to a Sears or Penney store brings a lot of extra traffic, which in turn leads to extra sales. The shopping center developer wants to capture some of the extra profit which she feels she brings by virtue of supplying the extra traffic.

This is typically done by having the lease call for the tenant to pay, say, 3 percent of sales volume, perhaps over and above some base level, as *extra rent*. In effect this turns out to make part of your occupancy cost a variable expense. On the upside, this may be all right. But what if sales volume is not up to expectations? Will the landlord share in the shortfall? Not too likely.

Some experienced merchants are willing to pay contingent rentals, and if they have numerous outlets in many malls, expect to have one or a few losers. Other retailers have a policy of owning or renting space near major mall locations, but not in the mall itself. Traffic may be down somewhat, but occupancy costs are also reduced. Specific advice cannot be given here for any particular business. Generally speaking, if you have high gross margins, the incremental profit from the extra traffic can justify a percentage rental. Lower margin businesses will find that too large a portion of their gross profit is being eaten up in occupancy cost. Maybe that is why there are always so many shoe stores, with high gross margins, in most malls.

Lease Terms and Business Flexibility

The alternative to leasing an asset is outright ownership. Both leasing and ownership require similar decisions. Specifically, the decision to acquire the asset in the first place should be identical, irrespective of how it is to be paid for. The *same* capital budgeting analyses should be performed. Despite the possibility, under leasing, that an asset's value can be kept off the balance sheet, in terms of *commitment* of future cash flows there is no real difference.

At one time lower level managers, perhaps frustrated with their own firm's capital budgeting systems, would go out and lease assets. The monthly payments would be charged to expense, there was no asset or corresponding liability, and the entire decision-process involving levels of review and approval would have been eliminated. Because the impact on future cash was the same, some firms instituted controls preventing lower level managers from signing operating leases. Then the accountants came along and in a series of ever tighter rules, turned many operating leases into capital leases. Flexibility of approval was dead.

But there is another type of flexibility that should be taken into consideration. What if business plans change? You have to move to provide more space in the home office, or a sales branch has to be shut. A product line is discontinued and the production equipment should be disposed of.

The question that should be asked is whether it is easier, and less expensive, to get out of a lease or to sell an asset you own. At first it might seem easier to make a change if you are leasing the asset. Since you do not own it, it is just a matter of renegotiating with the lessor. The lessor will continue to have the asset and only has to find another lessee and everyone will be happy. Except for one thing, the lessor may not want to, or even be able to, find another lessee.

Take the production equipment. Most leases of machinery and equipment are by what is called third-party leasing companies. That is, the leasing company buys the equipment from the manufacturer and leases it to you. The manufacturer is out of the picture. The equipment was bought for you, the lessor investigated *your* credit. The deal was structured for you. Why should he want to change? What incentive does he, the lessor, have to let you off the hook? Of course you can always buy out the lease, paying all the future lease payments, but that can get expensive, and is not what many people think of as flexibility. Or you can find someone to lease or buy the asset. But often the fair market value of the asset is less than the sum of the remaining lease payments, so you would have to absorb the economic loss.

Contrast that scenario with outright ownership by you of all the production equipment. In that case, if you wish to sell, you can contact competitors, suppliers, customers, and dealers and make your best deal. There are only two parties to the negotiation. Previously negotiated terms, perhaps when interest rates were higher, will not get in your way. What you own you can sell. What you lease is not yours to dispose of, but is yours to continue paying for until the lease runs out.

The bottom line is that leasing is less flexible. That is true also for real estate. Assume you lease an entire floor in a downtown office building and have four years left on a 15-year lease. You now need 50 percent less space. (This really happened in Wall Street after the 1987 crash.) If rents are currently $25 per square foot, and your lease calls for $40, how eager is the landlord to let you out of your lease? Ask the landlord, which is better, $40 or $25? The only way you are going to get out of the lease is to find your own subtenant, at something less than $25 (because you can only offer a 4-year term, the remaining period on *your* lease). Or you promise to pay the difference between what the landlord rents out the space for and the $40 you are contractually liable for.

The point here is that your lease is a contract and you are obligated to meet its terms calling for specific cash outflows, whether or not your economic situation has changed. Realistically, the only way to avoid paying the amount called for in the lease is to file for bankruptcy, or present a *credible* threat that you will file if the landlord does not do something.

Contrast this with outright ownership of a branch office (say 20,000 square feet) or a small warehouse. If your plans change you can put it on the market. Yes, if the real estate market has gone south you will take a loss, but the other side of that coin is that if values have gone up you are a winner. Nobody ever said that economic risk could be avoided. That's what business is all about. By offering an entire self-contained office or warehouse for sale, at a realistic price, you should easily be able to dispose of it in six to twelve months, with no third party looking over your shoulder. If you had financed the building with a mortgage, the bank or other lending institution does not care what you do with it. It's just that any proceeds from the sale must go first to pay off the mortgage.

In short, on almost all counts, outright ownership provides more flexibility than does leasing. Flexibility, the ability to respond quickly and prudently to changed circumstances, is a highly desirable characteristic for any asset. Signing a lease *commits* you to a definite series of cash payments, which must be met irrespective of what you do, or what you want to do, with the asset.

Leasing as a Source of Funds

Many proponents of leasing argue that a company can obtain access to *additional* funds. After exhausting extensions of credit from suppliers, banks, and other borrowing that appears on your balance sheet as a liability, the assertion is that you can obtain further assets by leasing. Implicitly the assumption is made that lessors will provide credit where others will not. If a manufacturer is doing the leasing directly, as IBM and Xerox did with office equipment, then the gross profit from the sale can be used to provide credit through leasing, comparable to what was discussed in Chap. 3.

If the lease is handled by a third party, a financial organization specializing in leasing, why should the leasing company take any more credit risk than a bank? One reason might be that the asset being leased does, in practice, have a ready market. In that case the lease is really a loan secured by the property itself. But if the asset is a so-called "special purpose" piece of property, designed and used just by the lessee, there effectively may be very little fair market value. The leasing company, in that circumstance, is looking to the *general credit of the lessee, not the asset itself* for repayment.

It is hard to figure out how a company, as a potential lessee, is going to obtain more credit from leasing company A than from bank B. In fact, many leasing companies are owned by banks, and use the same pool of depositor's funds.

The only way that you can obtain more funds, if you are near your credit limit, is to pay a higher interest rate on the additional borrowing. This compensates the lender for the greater risk he assumes in letting your debt ration climb. How can a leasing company charge a higher interest rate? Very, very easily. Calculating the true or effective interest rate implicit in a lease is difficult at best for one reason: What is the fair market value of the asset going to be at the end of the lease? Nobody knows. The leasing companies, to protect themselves, will often assume for purposes of calculating the monthly payments that they will receive a low residual. If, then, they can sell the asset for more at lease termination they will have a potentially significant profit.

In practice many leasing companies anticipate generating a significant amount of their profit from selling the leased assets, often to the lessee, at fair market value. If the original estimate of that value was low, and the lease payments calculated accordingly, then the transaction ends up being quite profitable. If, as in the case of some recent computer leases, the actual fair market value is *less* than the leasing company had estimated, there will of course be an economic loss to the lessor. In entering into a lease, do you want to bet the lessor does not know what he is doing?

The Bottom Line—
To Lease or Not to Lease

There is one aspect of leasing that we have not covered, and it is an important one. That is, the impact of *taxes* on the lease transaction. This is an extremely complex subject made only slightly simpler since the expiration of the investment tax credit.

A properly structured lease transaction, with top-flight tax and legal advice, can be written so that a true win/win situation is created. A company's tax benefits, say, net operating losses, are captured in the lease and transferred to the lessor. For example, if you have carry-forward losses, additional depreciation does not help, since you are not paying taxes anyway. In exchange for a slightly lower cost of funds to you, the lessor obtains the depreciation on your assets that he can use if *he* is paying taxes. Since the IRS allows accelerated depreciation and relatively short lives, such tax motivations drive a significant portion of actual lease deals.

The specifics of each of those transactions has to be worked out carefully, and a detailed explanation of so-called *leveraged leases* is outside the scope of this book. The quotation at the front of this chapter is from an excellent book on the entire subject of leasing, and anyone seriously thinking of entering into a tax-motivated lease should read that book.

For profitable companies, paying taxes currently, it is hard to find a lease transaction that provides real cash flow benefits to the lessee. If the basic principles of TCM have been followed, banks should be willing to provide term loans to finance significant asset acquisition programs, while truly large-scale expansions should be funded with bonds—way beyond the reach of this book.

The author recognizes that leasing, despite changes to the accounting rules, and to ever-tightening scrutiny by the IRS, continues to grow unabated. Convenience in obtaining the assets up-front, combined with good salesmanship on the part of equipment manufacturers and sellers can explain this. If you want, or even need, a piece of new equipment, and you are near what you think your credit limits might be, it is awfully tempting if the salesperson, sighting the opportunity to make profit from the sale, tells you how easy it would be to get the asset on a lease. The leasing company, of course, obliges, because of its profit potential in the implicit interest rate plus the chance for additional profit from the residual value.

If you, as the prospective lessee, do not run the numbers, do not ask the tough questions about what might happen if circumstances *do* change, then you end up paying for that convenience. We have discussed management time as a limiting factor in capital expenditure plans, and have to admit that entering into a lease may save time—but at what cost?

14

How to Cope with Inflation When It Returns

*The fastest and most effective way for a
company to realize its maximum profit is to
get its pricing right. The right price can boost
profit faster than increasing volume will; the
wrong price can shrink it just as quickly. Yet
many otherwise tough-minded managers shy
away from initiatives to improve price for fear
that they will alienate or lose customers. The
result of not managing price performance,
however, is far more damaging. Getting the
price right is one of the most fundamental
and important management functions.*
   "Managing Price, Gaining Profit"
  MICHAEL MARN AND ROBERT ROSIELLO
Harvard Business Review, September, 1992

The words quoted here are virtually a universal truth. In times of inflation,
however, they are an absolute *necessity*. It may be hard to accept, but in
many eras of U.S. history, inflation was *not* the pervasive issue it has been
for the last 25 years. In fact, the opposite of inflation, which is deflation
(defined as decreasing prices) was the norm for long periods.

So having a chapter on the impact of inflation on cash flows implicitly assumes a continuation of recent economic history, a prediction that many readers may hope turns out to have been wrong. If inflation is brought under control, even totally eliminated in this country, most of the material in this chapter will still have value for firms operating overseas. There will always be some countries that try to solve their economic problems through inflation, in some cases "managed" and in others unintentionally. Finally, as an argument for reading this chapter, many of the points made here highlight and reinforce the principles of TCM. Inflation, up to reasonably high levels, simply accelerates the *need* for TCM. Put the other way, in inflationary economic environments to be a survivor *requires* managing cash in a positive, take-charge manner. The alternative is economic death.

Inflation is no more or less than an increase in the overall price *level*. Without getting into an economic analysis of the causes (or cures) for inflation, we at least have to understand its nature. If you wake up one morning and find that the price of your local paper has gone up from 35 to 50¢, and the same day the local gas station raised gasoline 5¢ a gallon—is this inflation? In every market economy (where the government has not tried to repeal the law of supply and demand through price controls) individual items will both rise and fall, each responding in its own way to all the types of pressure affecting business.

We have been sensitized to prices that go up, because of the pervasive inflation most of us have experienced for many years. We are less sensitive to prices that decrease. Consumer electronics and personal computers, are two categories of goods where significant and continuing price declines have been common. Automobile tires are an example of a product where price has been quite constant but quality has dramatically improved, as measured by miles of usage and the reduced number of flats. In short, price increases on individual items we purchase are *not* signs of inflation.

Instead, inflation is the general rise in prices of more or less *all* items. Complicating the issue is the public's *expectations* about future price increases. The evil of inflation is that it all too easily becomes a self-fulfilling prophecy. One can experience a steady 4-percent year-in-year-out price rise. This is inflation, pure and simple. But to the extent the *rate* (4 percent) does not change, businesses and individuals can adjust relatively easily to the phenomenon. Where things get out of kilter is when the public expects the rate of inflation to increase—that while prices are actually going up just 4 percent this year they are felt, more likely than not, to go up 5 percent next year. In such a situation, whatever strategy a firm or an individual has adopted for the steady 4-percent price rise now has to be modified for the *greater* increase expected next year. And so on. It is the continuing series of modified expectations and subsequent behavior that soon becomes self-reinforcing.

In any period of inflation the value of cash, almost by definition, decreases. If $1000 today buys a bundle of goods and services that will cost $1050 very soon, one obviously does not want to hold cash. Either you buy today, before prices go up, or you invest the money and demand a return sufficiently high to compensate for the higher prices that will have to be paid when your investment matures and the cash is returned to you.

In the context of TCM, what are the implications? Buying today, before prices rise, increases inventories. This may be a smart financial move, but it is totally contradictory to what was discussed in Chap. 4. Similarly, if your company is a net borrower, interest costs paid to carry the inventory will rise, putting a burden on cash outflows. The remainder of this chapter discusses the strategies that an individual company should adopt if it feels inflation is going to continue at a constant rate. Where appropriate, suggestions for handling an expected increase in the rate of inflation will also be provided.

Some of the proposals may truly be counterproductive for the economy as a whole. That is, if everyone did the same thing, or tried to at the same time, the economy itself would be worse off. Our actions and those of others similarly motivated would, just by being carried out, increase the risk of runaway inflation—that is when governments institute price controls (and ultimately business controls) in trying to stamp out inflation. While history repeatedly shows that such governmental actions are totally counterproductive, politically they probably are a necessary first step before the real solution can be applied.

The only true solution to inflation and inflationary expectations is fiscal and monetary discipline on the part of political leaders. In turn, politicians more often than not try to please the voters. Inflation can be beaten only when the people truly believe that the pain and suffering of wringing out inflationary expectations (and it is painful) is less than the pain inflicted by inflation. Inflation continues because citizens—voters if you will—either do not believe in their hearts that inflation is bad or they are not willing to pay the price. While we said that American history has had long periods of price stability or even price decline—at the risk of advocating actions which can contribute to the very inflation itself—the author is not at all confident that the will to conquer inflation is yet present.

Pricing

Inflation is defined as an increase in the general price level, not just of certain specific goods and services. Presumably, in that environment we will generally be facing increased prices for the inputs we acquire—labor and materials—as well as interest expense on borrowed funds, higher tax *rates* on nominally higher income, and new additions to property, plant and equipment. Absent an escalator clause in our leases, items like rent that are contractually fixed may not increase month by month or even quarter by quarter. Upon expiration of any contractual obligation, however, the two parties will arrive at a new price that takes existing total inflation into account and probably provides for anticipated future inflation.

In most inflationary environments not everything moves up at the same rate or with the same frequency. Prices in free markets, such as grains or metals, may fluctuate upwards and downwards on a daily basis. Items with a strong seasonal pattern may be adjusted with much less frequency, often with larger jumps or increments when changes are made. Absent rampant inflation of the Latin American variety, or that experienced in Russia after the dissolution of the former Soviet Union, prices in the United States' economy, even at the height of our recent inflation in the late 1970s and early 1980s period, went up in fits and starts. We were never forced to the point, for example, of having to apply broad indexes to all retail items in a store on a monthly or even daily basis, as in Brazil, post World War I Germany, or the former Yugoslavia.

If you are operating in an environment where price increases are made individually—where you still have to ask yourself how your competitors and customers will respond—*the number one responsibility of management is raising prices quickly enough to offset inflation.* No other single management action can be thought of as having a higher priority. Only those individuals with profit responsibility have the will to raise prices. With the possible exception of true luxury items—where a higher price may actually increase demand and/or volume—common sense and experience both suggest that raising prices adversely affects volume. No customer likes having to pay more today than was paid yesterday. What was your own reaction the last time your gas station raised prices 5¢ a gallon or the supermarket charged 8¢ a gallon more for milk?

Put simply, customers are unhappy when suppliers raise prices. (Of course, the reverse is *not* true. If prices are lowered, customers naturally assume it *should* have happened and you get no credit for it!) Salespeople and sales managers do not like unhappy customers so there is never going to be pressure to increase selling prices coming from that direction. Manufacturing managers basically are volume oriented and, with reason, correlate in their own mind that if prices are raised their job will be that much harder because of reduced volume. Engineering, Human Resources, Legal, and other staff departments hardly ever think about unit selling prices—treating them as an "operational detail" if they do.

The only conceivable internal pressure for raising prices comes from the Financial staff. When they point out that with costs rising the only way to meet budgeted profit levels is to raise prices, the immediate answer from marketing types is highly predictable: "What do you even know about marketing? We're out in the real world, you're not, and if we raise prices just now...." This sentence is then completed with a choice from standard answers *a* through *f* taught in every first year marketing textbook as to the adverse impact of price increases. The bean counters are pooh-poohed, Marketing digs their heels in against the idea, and a company can have deep cash problems within a remarkably short time, depending solely on the current rate of inflation.

If there has been one lesson taught by *every* period of inflation, in every economic environment known, it is that the only way for an individual or firm to stay ahead is to raise its own selling prices as fast, if not faster, than its costs are going up. Put this way, everyone would agree. Unfortunately, this logic—so powerful in the abstract—usually loses its cutting edge in the ebb and flow of day-to-day decision making.

The emphasis on *volume* and the implicit assumption that almost all business problems can be solved by increases in volume, is the basic reason that managements hesitate to raise prices. Why risk a known impact, such as lower volume, in the hope of greater total profit contribution from that lower volume. Make no mistake, at any reasonable level of price inflation, buyers are still sensitive to relative prices. No competitor can afford to get too far out ahead.

But the very aspect of inflation that makes it so insidious is the fatalistic assumption that "it [inflation] is beyond our control, so let's get on with business." This also means that steady price increases, *are* accepted, no matter how grudgingly. Since in this age of Total Quality the customer comes first, if the good levels of service in all other aspects that differentiate one firm from another will continue, your price increases can be justified with the flat statement, "These simply cover *our* cost increases. We *have* to pass them on." The implication is that some greater power is controlling things. Surprisingly, inflation *is* that greater power.

As already mentioned, this approach—raising prices as quickly if not more quickly than the general rate of inflation—actually contributes to the continuation of inflation. After all, your selling price increases become cost increases to your customers. So the cycle continues unabated. However, it is absolutely ridiculous for the management of any one company to think that they have any public policy responsibility in this situation. Inflation is purely and simply a result of *government* policies. As citizens you have a responsibility to influence your legislators in Washington, while as businesspeople your primary responsibility is to your shareholders, customers, and suppliers. Each of these stakeholders will lose if you have held back on needed price increases out of some fuzzy idea you are helping society. Instead, to use a popular phrase, you yourself are more than likely to be history. Who gains then? Only your competitors who were looking out for Number 1.

Every company should develop analytical tools to measure price increases actually realized from sales to customers. Such an index may be easy to construct in those industries where output is measured in physical terms, such as x number of cases or y units per day or z tons of product. It is much harder in service industries. Retailers have to look constantly at gross margin, while labor intensive firms must compare payroll dollars as a percentage of revenue. Any measure, looked at constantly and reacted to promptly, is better than waiting to develop the perfect measure.

Similarly, it behooves a company to carefully study how fast its own costs are increasing relative to the economy as a whole. The government publishes an index called the *GNP Deflator* which is the broadest indicator of prices available. It probably will be necessary to construct more than one index of your costs. The one for labor would be in terms of cost per hour worked, or average cost per employee. To the extent wages and salaries are going up, not every employee will receive increases at the same time. Union and nonunion employees may leapfrog each other, and so forth.

Nevertheless it is necessary to see how your firm's overall wages are doing relative to the economy. If yours are rising faster, why, and what can you do about it? If your rate of increase has been slower, that's good, but maybe it is just a lull before the storm. Similarly, studying costs of purchased materials and services, for the major categories affecting your organization, will give you advance warning about what you should do with your selling prices.

Inflation means rising prices. It is a treadmill, and the belt on that exercise machine often seems to accelerate. That is truly bad news for you, your organization, and the economy. But you will not be *surprised*. Keep in mind the old adage:

I can take bad news, but I can't take surprises.

Keeping on top of inflation, both your costs and your revenues, may be a continuing source of bad news. At least it will not produce any unwanted surprises. It may sound unpatriotic to say it this way, but "*survivors raise prices.*"

Price Controls

Price controls do not work. They never have worked. They never will work. Having stated this—and the author knows of no one who seriously disagrees—one only has to go back to the early 1970s to find that hope springs eternal in the breast of politicians under pressure. Few may remember that President Nixon imposed price controls on the U.S. economy when inflation had advanced to the alarming rate of something like 5 percent. They did not work. As this is written [1994] fears are being raised about possible price controls on health care.

The reason that price controls do not work, and can *never* work, is that they are an attempt by man to suspend, if not repeal, the laws of supply and demand. A price increase means that the demand for goods and services exceeds the supply available *at that price*. In a free market, the supply will increase at higher price levels or demand will drop off. (Any additional explanation can be found in an Economics 101 textbook.) Price controls attempt to supersede the workings of the market. They try to keep prices constant at a given level of supply in hope—in an always unstated fashion—that demand will not exceed the supply. Of course the very reason for the pressure to increase price is the excess demand; the price controls do nothing to control or reduce that demand. Therefore the result is the creation of shortages and/or rationing.

What should a company do if it is facing price controls? First is to anticipate and plan for shortages of the materials it buys. Good relationships with key suppliers—always a good idea—become critical. With price controls, there will be shortages, but there will still be goods for sale and delivery. You want to be at the top of the list of favored customers of your key suppliers.

Assuming you do not want to cheat (that is, actually pay cash over and above the controlled price), are there other things you can do? Definitely, and the answer comes straight out of TCM. Your vendors, with selling prices limited by law or regulation, will be feeling a margin squeeze. You can at least help alleviate it by paying for your purchases *faster* than normal. If 30-day terms are normal in your industry, and you have been a good citizen and been paying on average in 35 days, now is the time to go to key suppliers and say, "We know you are being hurt by price controls just as we are. We're both too large to play games trying to evade the law. We must assure ourself of a continuing supply of your product. Here is what we will do: We will pay you, perhaps through electronic payments, within five days of receipt (or even shipment)."

Think of the benefit to the supplier. In an inflationary environment everyone else is going to be hanging on to their cash as long as possible, stretching out payables. Now you come along and offer just the opposite. Who is going to receive the limited output the vendor has available? You, or your competitors? One is promising immediate cash, which the vendor can invest at what will then be a relatively high interest rate. The other will, in effect, be asking the vendor to finance their operation and ship scarce product at a below-market price.

The cost of this strategy, to your firm, is only the interest on the amount of the purchase for 30 days. If short-term interest rates are running at a 12-percent annual rate, then for a vendor from whom you buy $50,000 a month you will be incurring additional interest expense of $500 a month, $6000 a year. This effectively is a 1-percent price increase paid to your vendor, a 1-percent cost increase to us. Put that way, in a time of shortages, is it worth 1 percent to keep production running smoothly? This is truly a no-brainer, when analyzed correctly. Fortunately, most other managers instinctively react to inflation by slowing down disbursements, so this strategy can be a strong competitive tool.

Cash management is essentially a zero-sum game; if you slow down your payments and invest the money, your supplier loses the identical interest income opportunity. If you pay more quickly, then you lose the interest income (or incur interest expense if you are a net borrower) and the vendor wins. The lesson to be learned from this is that in a price control environment what works with your vendor—assuring a source of supply—will work with your customers.

If the demand for your output exceeds your ability to produce, and if by law you cannot raise prices, the first thing to do is negotiate and insist on prompt payment terms. This is no time for your customers to rely on gamesmanship in holding back payments. Remember that golden rule we discussed earlier: Whoever has the gold makes the rules. In this case, you have the gold (your product) and you *can* make the rules about payment. In fact, you might ask for payment with order. This in no way should be construed by your customers as a questioning of their creditworthiness. Present it bluntly as a legal way to partly offset the impact of price controls. No more and no less. Customers are intelligent. Better for them to pay up front and get needed supplies than suffer shortages.

The one thing that creators of price controls overlook is the total creativity of buyers and sellers. Price controls are always set up as of a given point. But what if you stop producing product A, and now offer product A′ instead? Then the rule makers have to start defining what is a new product and how it should be priced relative to items on day 1. Tie ins are another way around price controls. During World War II, scotch whiskey was in short supply, but gin was available. Go to your local liquor store, ask to buy a bottle of scotch and you will also go home with the basic ingredient for a martini. If you are sitting in Washington writing the rules, how do you cope with that gambit? The total characteristics of goods and services consist of so much more than the invoice price that it is impossible to write rules for price controls that cannot and will not be evaded by "willing buyers" negotiating with "willing sellers." For purposes of this book on Total Cash Management, this is enough.

Since adequate rules can never be written, much less enforced, the only tool left to governments in inflation, after price controls have created shortages, is to impose rationing. Then the government says, not only will gasoline sell for $2 per gallon, but also since people want more $2 gasoline than is being refined, we will limit the demand for gas in physical terms.

Every driver can buy only 10 gallons a week. Ration coupons are then distributed in terms of 10 gallons per week per driver. That of course is when your 83-year-old grandmother suddenly starts driving again, or the old beater of a car sitting untouched in the garage for 6 years suddenly becomes your required means of transport to work, and so on. It may be harder to evade rationing than price controls, but a black market inevitably will develop, and we will be back to the same principles of TCM previously discussed. Inflation leads to price controls. Price controls lead to rationing. Rationing leads to economic chaos. Need we say more about the evils of inflation?

Cash Receipts and Disbursements

As discussed in the last section, inflation focuses management attention on cash flows. Interest rates rise as a result of the public's expectations about price increases for goods and services. Essentially interest rates will be 2 to 5 percent above the level at which prices are expected to increase. If you think there will be 12-percent inflation over the next year, you can afford to pay 16 percent for money. Lenders, or investors, demand such rates because the money they give you today, when paid back in a year, will buy 12 percent less. The 4-percent premium covers the risk that prices may increase more rapidly—and the so-called "basic" cost of money, sometimes estimated by economists at 2 to 3 percent.

As interest rates rise, companies with surplus cash start showing interest income that can exceed reported operating profits. In the early 1980s this phenomenon really was seen with many industrial companies, at least for a period of time, looking more like a financial firm than a manufacturing enterprise. Companies in a net borrowed position found that the single largest element of cost affecting the bottom line was turning out to be interest expense. In previous inflationary periods the U.S. government had attempted to ration the amount of credit, by limiting interest rates, in the hope of forcing a recession to cure the inflation. Then, however, the government made sure money was available at ever increasing rates, finally reaching a prime rate in excess of 20 percent. If you have a choice between no funds at 7 percent, or all you need at 21 percent, the economy is undoubtedly better off with the latter, no matter how painful.

The point is that high interest rates, for either borrowing or lending, get the attention of all levels of management. Total Cash Management becomes a daily way of life, although this author—an ardent proponent of TCM—does not wish for this state of affairs. Having said that, the natural tendency is to slow down all disbursements and simultaneously put pressure on customers to pay quickly.

If this type of cash management is no more than a zero-sum game, then the law of the jungle will prevail, the strongest players will be winners and those with little economic clout (usually small business firms) will end up as losers. Large companies will find a million and one reasons to delay payment. To the extent that the small vendor needs the volume there is probably little that can be done. Many large firms in the early 1980s told their suppliers, "Our policy is to pay in 60 days. We don't care if you have 30-day terms. You will see our check in 60 days. Period." In effect, take it or leave it. In such a situation the room for negotiation is probably quite limited and ultimately the vendor must make a decision whether to continue selling.

There is only one way to avoid the zero-sum aspect of cash management: improve internal efficiency or productivity. In this case we are talking about shortening the total cycle time from receipt of customer order to shipment to billing. These are all points discussed earlier and need not be repeated. What is critical to understand is that maximizing working capital turnover, reducing inventory and receivables through quicker order entry, speeding up billing, and doing things right the first time has an even higher payoff during rapid inflation.

To the extent that you improve your own internal operations—and there is greater pressure than ever to do so—you can beat *part* of the impact of inflation without affecting your suppliers or customers adversely. True productivity gains are always desirable. Inflation focuses the mind wonderfully on productivity.

Investing Surplus Cash

Interest rates increase during inflation. Thus funds invested in the money market earn a higher return, in nominal dollars, than they did earlier. Going back to the early 1980s, when commercial paper could be purchased at rates yielding upwards of 15 percent, many firms with excess cash found that their interest income constantly exceeded budget projections. Often the interest income, shown in the profit and loss statement as "other income," was greater than "operating profit." Talk about distortions to the economy being rampant—and accurate.

If the activities of the company Treasurer impacted the bottom line more than those of the sales manager or the production manager, what kind of signal did this send? Since the focus of everyone from top management on down is supposed to be on the bottom line, if that bottom line is impacted more by interest income than sales, who can be blamed?

As noted in the previous section, if management attention is focused on improving real productivity, there can be a net gain. But if management time is spent trying to outguess the money market, trying to anticipate changes in the yield curve for example, the basic business is going to suffer. If economic rewards are greatest for those bringing in the most profit, cash management and the treasury function start to assume an *abnormal importance* during inflation.

The point that should always be kept in mind, and it is hard to do so, is that the then current high interest rates are a reflection of underlying price increases—increases that are eroding the value of all the other company assets. In the last section of this chapter we will cover how the accounting profession has attempted to deal with this issue, but anticipating that discussion it is safe to say that most businesspeople were not happy with the accounting gyrations required at the time. Nonetheless, there is a direct connection between high money market yields and the ever decreasing value of working capital, particularly accounts receivable. The trouble is that the interest income showed up on the P&L immediately, while the true loss in value of receivables and other assets, representing the increased cost to replace them, required intellectual insight.

This is not to say that surplus cash should not be invested. It is more important than ever to keep noninterest earning bank balances to a minimum. The problem that inflation presents is *how* to invest. The normal relationships among investment media discussed in Chap. 9 may not hold. U.S. government securities will continue to have no credit risk, and thus will continue to have the lowest returns. Higher returns usually available from certificates of deposit, money market funds and commercial paper will continue.

The question is whether the underlying *risk* of these various investment media has changed. For example, investment in commercial paper represents unsecured borrowing by industrial firms. You have to ask to what extent are such firms, who by definition are net borrowers, going to be adversely affected by current and anticipated inflation. The lessons of the past, what industries and what firms have what kind of track record, no longer hold true. Over a period of time, if inflation continues, different industries will rise in relative safety simultaneously relegating previous winners to second class status.

The risk of investing increases dramatically in inflation. To the extent the market is efficient, rates among borrowers should reflect the differences in risk. But with the absolute level of interest so much higher than normal, the signals which differences in rates among borrowers are supposed to show may not be visible.

If inflation currently at 15 percent is expected to continue at that rate, a firm prepared to invest at 15 percent would only do so if rates are expected to go down. If inflation is expected to rise to 17 percent in a few months the only protection is to have invested very short term, say, for 30 days or less. (Of course, at all times, the borrower with whom you are investing your money has the opposite perspective.)

What if rates do go down because expectations of future inflation diminish? Companies with significant levels of high interest debt, sometimes referred to as junk bonds, are going to be under significant financial pressure. If rates had continued upward, the borrower's financial position would be safe and their management would look (for a period of time, at least) like geniuses for having borrowed at what turned out to be very favorable rates. But when the downturn comes and interest rates returned to "normal", investors who were chasing those high yields, trying to maximize interest income, may well face real credit problems—including loss of principal. Being committed to pay high interest expense, at a time of falling rates, and perhaps a declining economy, is an almost certain recipe for financial disaster. As a lender to such a firm you face loss of principal. As the borrower you face loss of your firm. It has happened before.

The solution, if it can be called that, is to stand back and ask some key questions. Assume that the market *is* efficient, that there are sound reasons for rates to be where they are. If rates are higher than you are used to, this is *not* a wonderful windfall the market is giving you as a gift. There are no gifts!

The new higher rates represent the overall evaluation of the market as to the then current risks. You may agree with the market or you may disagree with the market. If you disagree you are implicitly arguing that you are smarter and have greater insights and information than many individuals *who make their living studying money markets full time*. Thinking you can beat professionals at their own game may be the world's best description of the term *hubris*.

Reality tells us that high short-term money market rates do reflect overall perceptions of risk. What people so often forget is that there are many types of risk. We mentioned credit risk. There is also risk related to changing levels of interest. The longer the bond, the greater the fluctuation in price for a given change in rates. If rates go from 15 to 17 percent, then a 3-month Treasury bill will be virtually unaffected in terms of current market price. A five year note will go down moderately. A 30-year bond will suffer a real loss of principal. Trying to lock in high yields, by buying securities with longer maturities, represents a bet on the direction of interest rates. If there is one thing taught by history it is this: it is *harder* to forecast interest rates than stock market prices. Few people can consistently beat the stock market. Even fewer can consistently beat the money market. High interest rates represent high risk.

If you have excess cash during inflation, the real issue to be analyzed is whether or not to stay liquid. Irrespective of whether you invest in short-term or long-term securities the question *should* be whether now is the time to invest in *real assets* (inventory or property plant and equipment) before prices go up even further. If prices of machinery are going to be 17 percent higher next year, should we buy now and forego 15-percent interest income. Or do we invest at 15 percent and hope that prices of machinery and equipment really only go up 12 to 14 percent? Answers are not easy to get. But at least this is the right question.

It is all too easy to be seduced by the lure of interest income, particularly when it is large and growing as a percentage of net profits. If prices are really going up, and that is what the market is telling us high rates mean, it is imperative that we ask ourselves what the purpose of our business is. Is it making shoes, constructing houses, manufacturing valves, or acting like a bank? Different managements may answer differently. Either answer may be correct, as long as it is a *conscious* decision.

Inventories

At a time of increasing interest rates the short-term impact on profits of investing in the money market is great. Equally appealing is the impact on gross profit margins. Assume the prices of your purchased materials have gone up 10 percent in the last year (this rate of inflation is common throughout the world and has been experienced in our own recent history). Then, as you sell your old, lower cost inventory to your customers at today's higher prices (assuming you raise your selling prices at the same rate as your suppliers) you will report *higher* gross profit. The old lower cost inventory, bought last year at 90¢, rather than today's one dollar, is being sold at $1.40 rather than the previous $1.30. Put another way if you were used to a gross profit of 40¢ markup over cost, and you raise your selling price concurrently with vendor price increases, you will realize what is sometimes referred to as a windfall profit on your existing base inventory. For the inventory *on hand* (and only for the inventory on hand) you will report a 50-percent margin, 25 percent higher than normal.

This phenomenon can be seen in the price of retail gasoline sales. When crude oil prices go up refiners increase the wholesale price of gasoline, and this action is widely reported in the press. It seems like the very next day your local gas station raises its prices 5¢ a gallon, explaining their costs went up. But when the refinery price comes down there is a delay in reducing the retail price, since the station owner now must recover costs on the high cost product. This approach to pricing actions has also been perceived at banks—many observers feel banks are very quick to raise rates to borrowers, or lower them to depositors, depending on which way things are going but are much slower in going the other way.

The point here is not the ethics of business, but the impact of rising prices on reported profits. One of the reasons a "little touch " of inflation is so popular is that people, as well as businesspeople, *feel* richer. If the current value of your house goes up to $250,000, and you just bought it four years ago for $160,000, you have "made" $90,000, much more than most people can save from current income in four years. Similarly, the business that sells items at $1.40 for which they paid out only 90¢ very recently is suddenly a lot more profitable—on paper.

In terms of cash flow the business has to replace the inventory at its new higher price, and this requires cash. As a consumer you do not go out and buy a house very often but you do buy an automobile. Remember, your basic Chevrolet, the one you had paid $7000 for five years ago, now has a list price at the dealer of $18,000? It is the same phenomenon. Inflation increases the dollar value of inventories, assets on hand, but then exerts its influence in terms of cash flow as soon as something has to be replaced.

If you are running your business using the precepts of Total Cash Management how should you respond? If you are *sure* the prices of materials you buy are going to go up should you undertake anticipatory purchases now? The answer is far from clear. On one hand everything we have thought about suggests that keeping inventories at absolute minimum levels—full adoption of a JIT philosophy—leads to optimum cash flows, plus greater efficiency, productivity, and quality in actual operations. Less floor space, lower scrap and rework, faster delivery to customers are all benefits of lower inventory. Going in the opposite direction, deliberately adding inventory is going to send a very strange message to employees. Having changed from a culture where inventories were a way of life to the new culture where excess inventories are a liability, how do we suddenly justify stocking up before we really need the items?

Buying today what will not be needed for, say, six months, to take advantage of today's lower price, is speculation. There is nothing wrong with speculating—some call it gambling—if you do it as a conscious decision. One way of looking at advance purchases of inventory, in the hope that the savings from future price increases will more than offset any interim carrying costs, is to compare it to hedging.

In a traditional hedging operation, as an example, a cable manufacturer whose major raw material is copper, will contract to sell to a utility customer so many thousand feet of cable, containing 100,000 pounds of copper at a fixed price per foot. The cable will not be manufactured and delivered for another 60 days during which time the price of copper can rise, but the price to the utility is fixed. By buying a copper futures contract today, for delivery in 60 days, the manufacturer locks in the price of copper. In effect the manufacturer is speculating on copper prices going up. If he really knew they were going down he could save the price of the futures contract. Since he does not know, and cannot afford to lose, he pays an insurance premium which is the cost of the futures contract. If copper does rise, his raw material cost bought in the spot market will have gone up, but he will have offset it by the gain on the futures contract. If spot copper goes down in 60 days, he makes money in the spot market and loses on the futures contract.

Now look at an advance physical purchase of copper, at today's price, for a raw material that will not be used for another 60 days. The only difference is that in this scenario the cable manufacturer has not fixed the selling price of the cable to a utility. Based on past experience he knows he will have orders, and the price per foot will be a function of spot copper prices then. Buying physical copper today purely and simply is a bet on rising prices. During periods of inflation this can be a winning strategy— with two caveats.

The inventory must be financed. The copper supplier wants to be paid now, not in 60 days when the copper becomes cable. During inflationary periods we saw that interest costs rise. The bank loans, required to pay for the copper (or the lost interest income if otherwise surplus cash is not available to be invested) will be costly. Further, the cost of carrying physical inventory, including storage, taxes, and insurance (for a material like copper there is no risk of physical deterioration but for many items, e.g., flour, there is) must be factored into the equation. When the cost of money and storage are added together, what are the chances there are going to be really significant savings? If you assume the copper supplier is equally astute, isn't it likely that the price today of copper will reflect market expectations about future prices?

It is tough to beat the market. People make their living buying, selling and trading futures. Other people make their living manufacturing and selling cable. Do they require (a) the same skills or (b) different skills? The answer should be obvious. Very few people can make their living doing both because speculating and manufacturing each depend on different skills.

There is nothing wrong with hedging known transactions, even though in one sense it is placing a bet on the future. There is nothing wrong with speculating on the future prices of specific commodities or products— members of the Chicago Board of Trade or Commodity Exchange provide a service to society and are handsomely rewarded. Just do not get hedging and speculating mixed up.

Even in periods of inflation, buying before need is still speculating. If you add up all the costs—of money and carrying charges —it often turns out not to be profitable on balance. In short, the basic principles of TCM hold true during inflation. The one-time gain shown in the financial statements when old, low cost inventory is sold at today's new higher price is just that—a one-time gain. Some have called it a money illusion. Any wealth generated from rising prices, inflation, is an illusion.

If you truly can outguess the market you can make money whether prices are rising or falling. Someone will always be better than average in forecasting price movements. But for everyone who is above average someone else is below average. This writer suspects there is a strong negative correlation between forecasting skills and business management skills. Good executives do not make good speculators, but the reverse is certainly true.

Fixed Assets

Should acquisitions of fixed assets be speeded up if serious inflation is present in the economy? Since inflation has been defined as an increase in the *general* price level, this does not mean that everything goes up at once, at the same rate. Competition still exists in most industries, although shortages, in some areas, can be more prevalent. The question, therefore, with regard to productive equipment, as well as new construction of real property, boils down to analyzing each requirement closely.

While it is hard to generalize about the course of inflation, two observations can be made. First, speculation increases in all areas of the economy. Second, individual workers become restless. If they feel they are underpaid they are more likely to feel they can find a higher paying job elsewhere, so turnover increases in industries with a more mobile labor force.

Two markets where speculation about the course of future prices impacts today's actual prices are real estate and the stock market. Leaving aside the stock market from this discussion, how do speculative real estate prices impact organizations planning to buy or build new facilities?

History teaches us that while prices go up in an inflationary period, ultimately they do come down. If we knew just when they would return to normal the decision when to buy would be easy. But as someone once observed, they don't ring a bell to notify you when it is time to buy or sell. Buying at the peak of prices, only to find that prices drop immediately afterward is painful, both financially and psychologically. "*Why* did we buy *then*?" is going to be a refrain around any management group that got its timing wrong. On the other hand those who bought a building, or a plot of vacant land, early and are sitting on a nice gain are tempted to think of themselves as real estate geniuses.

In line with our previous advice about not speculating in inventory, even though at times it can show nice profits, similar advice holds true for real estate. If the growth of the business really requires expansion (additional space) it makes sense to acquire the land and put up the building as quickly as possible. Price increases are likely to be greatest in raw land, followed closely by labor and materials in building construction. The wealth effect of inflation (the feeling that our asset prices have gone up and our net worth has risen sharply) encourages a lot of individuals and businesses to put into effect long delayed building plans. So as real demand rises it adds to the price pressure already existing. One feeds on the other, which is why land and construction tend to rise faster than average.

At some point the music will stop and some buyers will have over committed themselves. As noted, trying to forecast that point accurately, in advance, is impossible. In fact, the longer prices have been going up, the more natural it seems that ever rising prices represent a new order. "The old economic rules no longer apply" is heard at its loudest just before the rules in fact assert themselves! Providing advice about timing of investments in inflationary times is difficult, but since the inflation usually does last longer than the experts think, on balance it is probably better to buy early and try to beat the price increase. Speculation is still present in any decision, no matter when you buy. But if you have bought sooner, and prices do continue upwards after you are in, then any subsequent fall will have less impact on you because of your lower basis.

Machinery and Equipment

This is the tough one. A good sign that prices of capital goods have not unduly gone up, is if shortages are not apparent, and if delivery times have not lengthened. This implies that the market is still competitive, from the perspective of sellers of capital equipment. Then, as a buyer, you retain the advantages of any buyer in a competitive market and inflation, per se, should not distort your decision. Buy when you can justify the acquisition. If it is for expansion, or a new product, the timing is going to be affected by other operating factors. You cannot buy machinery and equipment in advance; you have to wait until production or operating plans are firmed up.

If the equipment is being bought as a replacement for existing assets, or as a cost reduction project to reduce labor and other operating expenses, a different approach is needed. Here we must look not only at the cost of the equipment today, as against our best guess what it will cost six months from now, but also at the favorable benefits of the anticipated operating savings. To take a simple example, if acquisition of a new N/C tool will cost $100,000 today, or $115,000 next year, and interest rates are running +15 percent, it may appear to be a matter of indifference in cash terms. Assume that the machine will replace a worker and the total cost of salaries, benefits, and variable overhead is $40,000, representing a 2½-year payback. In other words, a reasonably good investment, whether made today or next year, but not an absolute home run. (In capital budgeting a home run would be a cash payback in less than one year—a rarity.)

Should we buy the N/C tool today? Absent any anticipated changes in technology—inflation probably has little impact on technology developments—there are two strong reasons for pushing up the decision and buying as soon as possible. First, it is likely that the cost of labor (your employee's total costs to the company) will increase at least as fast if not faster than the purchased cost of the asset. Your operating cost savings, in other words, may well be greater than projected. Further, depreciation charges will be lower for the entire economic life of the asset, so the P&L savings (cash is only affected by the impact of depreciation charges on taxes) will continue into the future.

Put another way, if two competitors have comparable physical facilities, but one was bought five years ago before inflation and the other was acquired last year, with a cash outlay 50 percent higher, who is going to have a competitive advantage? We have already seen that the useful physical and economic lives of assets is greater than the arbitrary "life" assumed for financial and tax reporting. So the operator of the facility with an average age five years older will not likely have severe operating penalties in real terms. (In rapid technology fields, like semiconductors this would not be true, but few industries move ahead that rapidly.) Having a lower cost facility is *always* an advantage, and buying replacement or cost reduction assets as soon as possible provides a real hedge against higher prices later. In short, you will obtain a competitive advantage, or prevent a competitive disadvantage, by having as modern a facility as quickly as possible.

The second reason for buying machinery and equipment early has to do with the impact of high interest rates on the standard DCF methodology used by most companies for making capital budgeting decisions. Recall how one determines the present value of future cash flows. After the cash flows are anticipated or estimated, they are discounted using a rate approximating the firm's cost of capital. Since the cost of capital is a weighted average of the cost of debt and equity—and debt costs (interest rates) rise dramatically in inflation—the future cash flows attributable to any investments will be discounted at a much higher than usual rate.

Utilizing a high discount rate *penalizes* all investments with a *longer* payback. Put another way, a high discount rate *favors* investments with a very *short* time horizon. So the higher the inflation rate the more the emphasis on quick returns. Mathematically that is the correct answer. In terms of just cash flows this is the distortion that inflation introduces into business operations.

U.S. business has, for a long time, been criticized for its short-term preoccupation with reported earnings, its unwillingness to invest with a long-term outlook. Readers may or may not agree. You can argue that it is *not* happening. You can argue that it *is* happening. What you cannot argue is that raising the discount rate, which inflation does, emphasizes the short term, at the expense of the long term. Few observers feel that this is going in the right direction.

Inflation, by raising interest rates, focuses undue attention on quick payback investments and penalizes decisions with a longer time horizon. The solution, if firms want to retain their usual pattern of growth, is to disregard the mathematics of present value discounting. Decisions on cost reduction and replacement projects then will be made the old fashioned way—using management judgment. In larger companies, those with rigid decision rules, this may be hard to accomplish. It does provide an advantage for smaller more nimble competitors who can change their way of thinking. Even large bureaucratic organizations, slow to change, will have to adjust. The logical alternative is to stop investing.

If a cost of capital figure of 30 percent or more is used—and even moderate inflation will generate such a rate—very few possible investments will pass the hurdle rate test. If potential candidates, just to enter a track meet, had to run the mile in 3:50 or demonstrate a broad jump of 29 feet, the promoters might find they had a very small field of contestants—and few spectators. If you have to discount all proposed capital projects at +30 percent, you will have at most one or two winners, but that is all.

There is no question about it—inflation distorts decision making. Managements who have the luxury of taking a long term view, who believe that "normal" times *will* return sooner or later, must step back and apply real judgment. Reliance on old formulas and blind adherence to past policies will be very costly.

Leasing

Does the leasing of assets become more attractive during inflation? As we saw in Chap. 13 there is no free lunch. The lessor and lessee are each making a bet on the future. The course of future interest rates, and the ultimate residual value of the asset, are two key elements in evaluating any lease proposal.

Taking interest rates first, it is no easier (and no harder for that matter) to guess the timing and magnitude of *changes* in interest rates whether we are analyzing short-term borrowing, long-term borrowing, or leasing. Entering into a five-year lease fixes, for the period of the lease, the interest rate implicit in the lease payments. If short-term rates were currently 20 percent and long-term rates 16 percent (rates actually experienced in the early 1980s) entering into a five-year lease represents a gamble on the part of the lessee that rates will stay the same or go up over the five-year period. Otherwise you would be better off financing the equipment with short-term borrowing, anticipating that the average short-term rate over the five-year period is less than 16 percent.

However, if it takes the government three or four more years before the inflation battle is truly won, and rates in the interim have gone above 25 percent, then the lessee will have looked pretty smart. Of course every win for a lessee is a loss for the lessor, and vice versa. Before signing a long-term lease ask yourself, "Who has a better handle on the course of future interest rate movements, the leasing company or us?" One of you is going to be right and the other wrong.

The other aspect of leasing is the residual value. If inflation continues at a high rate, the replacement cost of the asset will be, at least in nominal dollars, much higher than the original purchase price. Thus if the asset is still 40 percent useful at the end of the lease term, and inflation has been running at 20 percent a year, the real residual value will be higher (in nominal dollars) than the original cost of that asset five years earlier.

Many leases provide for the lessee to have an option to purchase the asset at its fair market value at the lease expiration date. As the lessee, to retain the asset at the lease termination, you may have to pay the leasing company an amount, at least in nominal dollars, that equals the asset's original cost! Some people refer to this phenomenon as paying for the same asset twice.

Just as you and the leasing company were making a bet on the course of future interest rates, when you sign a five-year lease during a period of inflation, you are also placing a bet on the future course of asset prices. Again, both sides cannot win that bet. For some reason, successful leasing companies seem to win more often than not. True, the history of computer leasing suggests that over optimistic estimates of residual computer values have led some lessees to getting a bargain. But many of those lessors soon went out of business.

If anything, inflation makes the leasing decision more difficult than ever. The course of future interest rates, and asset values, is never easy to predict. Inflation only makes it worse. There are a lot of valid reasons, involving both taxes and the amount of credit a company can obtain, for leasing assets. On balance, primarily because of the impact on residual values, lessees have to be extra careful in negotiating during inflationary periods.

Borrowing

Negative real interest rates: You get paid for borrowing money. The sound is music to the ears of borrowers. During the last period of significant inflation in the United States, negative real interest rates were not uncommon, in part because the government tried to hold down interest rates. If prices are rising at a faster rate than interest, such as inflation of 8 percent and interest rates of 6 percent, then borrowers will make money simply by holding assets. The greater the leverage, the more borrowing relative to existing levels of equity, the more money you can make. This is true almost irrespective of what type of assets you hold, although buying inventory and tangible property, real and personal, is probably a better bet than financial assets, such as common stocks.

If, indeed, interest rates remain below the rate of inflation, borrowers are winners and investors (lenders) are losers. Consumers with savings accounts and holders of debt instruments—everything from savings bonds and certificates of deposit to long-term bonds—are subsidizing borrowers. Of course any consumer with a mortgage is a borrower, so individuals with a large mortgage, and small savings, do well. No wonder that prices of single family residences had a startling rise. In California, at one point, home prices were going up 2 percent a month, 24 percent a year. If you could obtain a mortgage at even 14-percent annual interest, particularly with a small down payment, there was no limit to how much you could make.

The cycle became self-fulfilling. House prices continued to rise as more and more people took advantage of this perpetual money machine. As prices rose more people decided they could not afford to wait—*now* was the time to move up. Only two things stopped this wonderful phenomenon. First, like every speculative frenzy in history, right from the *tulip mania* and the *south sea bubble* on, sooner or later (and it is often later) the number of speculators starts to decline. And at that point the cycle goes into reverse. Recent home owners can't meet the monthly payments, have to sell at declining prices and lose their equity. The next round of sellers not only lose their equity, but the declining values cause losses to the lenders—the people and institutions who granted and held the mortgages. This reversal of the cycle, known as the great savings and loan mess in the late 1980s, showed that the fundamental law of economics—there is no free lunch—had not been repealed.

What is the lesson? If you are lucky or smart enough to keep ahead of the curve, to do your borrowing before the inevitable correction you are a winner. If you jump on too late, if your borrowing at high rates comes just before asset prices go down (or even when prices stop rising) you become one of history's losers.

Borrowing to the hilt, taking full advantage of leverage, is a winning strategy at the beginning of an inflationary cycle, when governments and individuals hope that price rises will be contained. The reverse is also true. Lending at high interest rates, after prices have been rising for some period of time, carries *significant* risk.

In terms of Total Cash Management it is only partly facetious to recommend that you increase your leverage—the level of borrowing relative to the size of the business—just as inflation starts to take hold. This, of course, begs the question of how do you know when inflation is going to get started. If we all knew that, we would all be rich and nobody would be a lender just when inflation is getting started.

The lesson is clear. Trying to beat inflation is, once again, essentially a zero-sum game. For every winner there is a loser. On balance, if a business firm is well financed and has conservative amounts of equity, it is probably safe to raise borrowing levels and invest in *expansion*. Not only can you gain from rising asset prices, but operating profits should increase and provide the resources to repay the debt if it becomes necessary. But there should be a real distinction between borrowing for expansion and borrowing for speculation. As we discussed in Chap. 11, most organizational units have many expansion plans for growth. They cannot all be financed and implemented.

But during periods of inflation, and incipient inflation, it makes sense to increase borrowing levels, thus reducing the cost of capital. A lower cost of capital, in turn, leads to acceptance of more expansion proposals. Not all of them will be winners, but many of them will. And that is how the company can expect to repay the debt as it becomes necessary.

There is a fundamental difference between a company borrowing for basic expansion and an individual borrowing to buy a larger home. The home does not generate any cash, the monthly mortgage payments only consume cash. When a business borrows to invest in the plant, equipment, and the related working capital, it expects to generate additional positive cash flow from those very assets. A lender may not choose to care who borrows or what they do with the funds. Shareholders in many savings and loan associations, and ultimately all of us as taxpayers, found out what prudent bankers have known for a long time: It makes a difference what a borrower does with your funds. In fact, what we have just discussed is why lenders want realistic projections from prospective borrowers and why it is so hard for small start-up businesses to borrow funds. Without the assurance of repayment from operations, from profits generated by the investment—the only way loans can be repaid is from selling assets. And even in inflationary times, the prices of *second-hand* or used assets is not very high.

A reasonable level of borrowing is a sound strategy at all times, and a very good strategy when prices are rising. There is a very real difference, however, in borrowing for expansion and borrowing simply to speculate on beating the next price increase. Professional speculators make money. Businessmen make money. Businesspeople who think they are speculators, or even worse, businesspeople who don't realize they are speculators, ultimately will regret borrowing simply to take advantage of price increases. Anticipatory borrowing and anticipatory buying fly in the face of Total Cash Management.

Accounting for Inflation

Over the years accountants, particularly accounting theorists, have worried about the distortions that inflation causes in financial statements. If it takes $15,000 today to buy an automobile that only three years ago cost $8000, most people would agree that is a symptom of inflation. If you are analyzing a firm's financial statements—where some assets like cash and receivables are represented by recent prices—the single name of "dollar" applied to all these categories represents far different concepts.

Depending on the rate of inflation and the rate of asset turnover, the impact of inflation on the understandability of financial statements will vary widely. We all agree that if hyper-inflation exists (as in post World War I Germany, or more recently in Latin America), then denominating everything in a single unit-of-measure produces answers that are useless. On the other hand, comparing the P&L of a company in 1994 with the operating results of the same firm 20 years earlier, even though the value of the dollar (in terms of purchasing power) has been cut in half, does not stretch the imagination. We are able to, and do, make mental adjustments of that magnitude.

At what point do financial statements, denominated in a currency whose value has shrunk, need to be adjusted? This is a question that has come up every time inflation has reared itself. Answers are proposed—or even implemented—and then as soon as inflation dies down the "inflation-adjustments" are dropped or forgotten.

A basic question remains unanswered. Can accountants develop a method that accurately adjusts for the impact of inflation? The same question, put another way, might be: Can the real impact of inflation be offset by accounting entries? Succinctly, the answer is no.

As we saw earlier, individual prices both rise and fall in periods of low inflation, no inflation, or even deflation. All that happens in periods of high inflation is that most prices tend to rise much more rapidly, some rise slowly, and a very few actually go down. But *relative price changes* still exist. Unlike the tide, inflation does *not* raise all boats in the harbor to the same height. This means that no simple, "one-size-fits-all" accounting solution can realistically adjust for rising price levels, because price *levels* do not go up uniformly.

The most common accounting technique to adjust for the impact of inflation is to apply a *price index* to previous year's financial statements. If the GNP Deflator has increased 15 percent from last December to this December, we multiply all the numbers in last year's financials by 1.15. This actually does reflect the change in the *purchasing power* of the currency unit—in our case the dollar. A similar approach is used in translating foreign currency into dollars. Nobody would think seriously of adding French francs to U.S. dollars to arrive at a consolidated financial statement. First you would convert francs into dollars at the appropriate exchange rate, and then add up the two sets of dollar figures.

Proponents of indexing for inflation argue that multiplying last year's numbers (19X3 dollars) to arrive at current amounts (19X4 dollars) is no different. They are correct, at least mathematically. Column A, times column B, equals column C. This is true whether column A is French francs or 19X3 dollars and column B is current exchange rates or the current GNP Deflator. The difference is how we, as readers of the statements, *use* the information presented. Looking at the consolidated financial statements of a multinational company, knowing that everything abroad has been translated into U.S. dollars, does not provide a false sense of precision. We *know* there are many conventions, assumptions, and estimates that go into any financial statement. The artificiality of foreign exchange conversion (what rate to use, how to handle current vs. fixed assets, liabilities denominated in different currencies, etc.) means we can accept the relative imprecision that exists and not make poor decisions inadvertently.

Indexing last year's dollar statements, in the hope of making them "comparable" to this year's statements, is different. When we look at last year's income statement and balance sheet and are told that they are in current year's dollars, we naturally assume that if the dollar amount for inventories is the same Production Control has done a good job. If net fixed assets have gone down we can draw a conclusion about productive capacity. If long-term bonds outstanding have increased, this has some significance for understanding changes in financial flexibility, and so forth.

The problem is that changes in the prices of the items making up inventories—fixed assets and long-term debt—may or may not track general inflation. Yet the way the financials are presented, there is an implication that they do. If the price of our major raw material inventory item has risen only 6 percent but we apply a 15-percent index, then we will be showing a drop in inventory, year-to-year, that did not occur. Similar examples abound.

Theoretically the solution is to use *different* indexes for different categories of assets. The trouble with this is (1) agreeing on which indexes to use, and (2) if we really want to know the price today of yesterday's assets we are dealing not with general inflation but with changing prices. Some have argued that what users of financial statements really want is today's prices. What would it cost today, in today's dollars, to acquire the assets owned by the firm. This could be very useful information, particularly helpful in finding the real value of the company, unaffected by all the conventions which go into a set of financial statements.

Current Value Statements

If inflation adjusted statements have problems in terms of usefulness and understandability, then so-called current value statements should be the answer. If we really knew what things were worth today, then either as shareholders or managers we could make intelligent, cash-oriented decisions. As shareholders we could determine how the market price of the

\

stock compared with the real value of the company. As managers we could decide which assets to sell because the current ROI was insufficient. If we had true current value statements we would at last be looking at economic reality, the ultimate goal of all managers, investors, and, of course, their accountants.

There is only one small problem. What is reality? Trying to develop true current value financial statements for a company is the business of professional appraisal firms and is outside the scope of this book. Suffice it to say that there is no such thing as "The Value" of a company. Depending on how the information will be used (whether we're buying or selling) the answers will differ. Again, one size does not fit all.

The point to remember is that inflation affects fair market values—prices that would be paid between a willing buyer and a willing seller. But the accounting solutions for inflation do not provide any real information about today's transaction prices. All they do is adjust, through some formula, the prices paid at the original transaction date. This may be helpful information to security analysts, although experience with the FASB's Statement 33 showed even they did not use it. What conceivably might help a security analyst, however, was of no use to management. If a transaction involving cash is *not* going to be undertaken, how in the world do you *use* value information.

The essential element of Total Cash Management is the testing of every business action by its impact on cash flows and cash availability. Obtaining theoretical information about value, when no transaction is contemplated or even possible, goes against the precepts of TCM.

Note: In the interest of full disclosure, the writer has spent 25 years in the appraisal business. Contrary to conventional wisdom, appraisers know only too well the limitations of value information. Thus appraisers and appraisal companies have never pushed for mandatory disclosure of value data by companies, even at the point of greatest inflation. For certain types of assets, with a ready market, like traded securities, *disclosure* (as contrasted with running the information through the income statement and balance sheet) makes sense and is being required by FASB. We support that. Development of across-the-board values is an idea whose time has not yet come.

15

Installing a Total Cash Management System

Still, IBM's culture continued to stifle sales of printers.... A team of marketing executives had gone around to talk to computer dealers about how to market printers, and they got all sorts of good advice.... IBM would need to work with dealers, providing higher profit margins, easier payment terms, and so forth, to entice them to recommend IBM printers.... But it's hard at IBM to do anything that hasn't been done before.... So when IBM fixed its dealer profit margins and other terms on its PC printers, they turned out to be exactly the same as the terms which dealers had said wouldn't fly. They didn't. The ProPrinter bombed.
From *Big Blues: The Unmaking of IBM*
by PAUL CARROLL [p. 133]

Perhaps it was Donald Trump, the real estate developer and casino operator, who put it best during a time when he was under financial pressure and trying to develop short-term liquidity to meet some of his current debts. With creditors knocking at his doors he appeared to be forced to sell off some of his crown jewels, perhaps at less than what he thought they were worth. After one particular transaction—when he had just raised a significant amount of cash—he uttered the magic words to explain his actions. People were wondering, if things were going so well (he had not let on to the public about the financial pressure) why he was *selling* when his whole life seemingly had been about spending cash, buying. "Cash is king," he declared.

Until you are truly short of cash, you may not fully appreciate the wisdom summed up in those three words. Every company facing bankruptcy, every turnaround situation, every recession for that matter, again brings the importance of cash to the forefront.

To stay in business you *must* meet your payroll and pay your creditors. You cannot pay them in profits. You cannot pay them with depreciation, sometimes erroneously referred to as a source of cash. You can only pay with cash, essentially amounts currently in your checking account. And cash is only deposited to your checking account from two sources—customers and bank loans.

In the real world, the easiest time to install Total Cash Management is at a time of financial distress, which "concentrates the mind wonderfully." But why wait for hard times. The sign of successful management is the ability to anticipate. Because every company can gain by having more cash resources available, successful managements will try to speed up the growth process by making available the maximum amount of cash—and then utilizing that cash in the business through profitable investments.

Total Cash Management is a *process*, and as the Total Quality movement has shown us, every process is susceptible to continuous improvement. Let's look, therefore, to the Quality movement and Business Process Reengineering and apply some of those techniques to Total Cash Management.

There are three basic areas available to increase cash in a business. First is in accounts receivable, second in inventories, and third in developing or increasing a bank line of credit. Obviously such things as processing payables and payroll, leasing vs. purchasing fixed assets, and good tax planning cannot be overlooked. Nonetheless, go where the money is. Go to receivables, to inventories and to the bank.

Step 1 in implementing TCM is to squeeze out cash currently earning low returns, by reviewing receivables and inventories. Step 2 is to work with the bank to increase the amount of credit available. Step 3 is to judiciously invest the now available additional cash resources where it will give you the maximum competitive advantage.

Review Receivable Collection Efforts

As we saw in Chap. 7, a tremendous amount can be done to minimize cash tied up in receivables. What is necessary is to determine just who is responsible for the level of receivables, and then develop programs to minimize unnecessary levels. This is a two-way street, however, because as we saw in Chap. 3, the extension of credit to customers can be a powerful sales tool. This apparent contradiction can be easily resolved.

There is a real distinction between initially offering generous credit terms, and being generous in following up on outstanding amounts owed by your customers. There is a feeling that if we call up a customer and ask for money, that in some way this will be taken as an insult. The unstated corollary is that feeling insulted there will be no reorder. In other words, collection efforts will adversely impact future sales.

When this feeling is combined with a natural reluctance among most Americans to come right out and ask for money, it is easy for individuals—whether sales representatives, accounting employees, or even credit department personnel—to procrastinate. In fact by *not* calling the customer, so the individual thinks, I am really helping my company. Be honest with yourself, would *you* like to be given a list of your firm's past due accounts and be asked to call them?

Let's go to the facts, since emotions tend to cloud the mind. When you owe someone money, are you aware of this, with or without a reminder from the creditor? The answer is obviously yes. There may be a number of reasons why you have not paid the amount, ranging from dissatisfaction with the product to a lack of cash. Absent any indications from the creditor, you are going to sit back and do nothing. If they don't care, why should you? Further, rather than waking up that sleeping dog, you probably are going to delay further orders, at least until you pay the now past-due invoice or get satisfaction on your complaint.

Newton's laws of motion have not been repealed. An object at rest will continue that way. A past due debt without follow up is never going to be paid. Calls must be made, and the sooner you call someone who owes you money the quicker you will find out the nature of the problem. In a worst case scenario, the customer has a legitimate complaint about your product or service, a complaint that requires management attention. The principles of TQM are sound—getting to the root cause of a problem so it will not recur. But as with any program, the first step is admitting you have a problem. Until you call the customer you don't even have that knowledge—you are not even in a position to start a recovery program.

Put this way, it should be clear that prompt follow-up of all past due receivables is in everyone's interest. You will not hurt anyone's feelings. You will not prevent future sales orders. You are not even asking for money. The first call is for information only. "Is there a problem, and if so what is it? Is there anything we can do about it?" It is true that those who have been procrastinating on sending you a check because they want to hold on to their cash, maybe because they are short, will start the game. You know, they did not get the invoice, please send a copy. Or the now infamous check-is-in-the-mail ploy. OK. You have learned something, there is not a business problem with your product and service, they have a cash problem. Not necessarily good news, but not all bad either.

Universal experience is that if a firm is short of cash, but not in desperate straits, the limited cash resources are going to be directed toward those vendors who ask for their money. Just to stop the phone calls the buyer is going to put your invoice near the top of the pile. While it is true that very few people like to ask for money, the typical follow up collection call does not have to ask for money; what you are doing is to ask for *information*. "What is the status of our invoice we talked about last week?"

A well organized system of follow up calls, with notes taken each time as to what the customer said, need not be threatening to your customer, nor difficult for any employee to perform. Further, sales will be enhanced, not restricted, because the customer will not be embarrassed to ask for more from you. While he still owes you money he will be reluctant to reorder. Once he has paid for the last order he will have a sense of freedom that permits further purchases.

To sum up, then, a crucial step in implementing a Total Cash Management system is to establish a formal, even rigid, system of getting in touch with customers on a strict schedule, say no more than five days after payment was due. You do not even have to think of this as a collection effort—just a part of everyday management. What *is* happening? Put this way, the information calls should probably not be made by the Sales department. It is easier for an unknown third party to ask the seemingly tough questions about past due invoices.

Granting of credit—both to whom, and for what amount—must be completely separated from collection efforts on amounts already owed. The former is a business decision, subject to management discretion. In fact, the beauty of using credit as a marketing tool is that it is so flexible. Terms can be adjusted to accomplish seasonal goals, geographic expansion goals, short-term volume goals, and so forth. Commitments can be for short or long periods of time.

But once a sale has been consummated, the customer has agreed to buy your product at a specific price with payment due at an agreed time in the future. You both have entered into a mutual contract, and you have carried out your side of the transaction. It is totally reasonable to expect the other party to do the same. Agreeing to 45-day terms, instead of normal 30-day terms, to introduce a new product is a good business decision. Letting the customer take 60 days to pay a 45-day invoice is not a good business decision. Your own sales and profits will be hurt, not helped. Your customer's cash flow may be helped by a delay in payment, but you have already done your bit by extending 45 days. You did not offer 60.

The author's experience, and that of many others, suggests that within a month of starting up a formal follow-up system, outstanding receivable balances can be reduced by at least 10 to 15 percent, or even more. A never ending source of amazement is how many firms really do not pay their bills until someone calls. The reaction essentially is, "Well, if you really want me to pay, I guess I will. Since I hadn't heard from you, I didn't think it was very important." One can argue the ethics of such an approach. But in Total Cash Management what counts is the *cash*, not a theoretical discussion of business practices. Asking for your money, while it may appear distasteful to some, really works!

Dig into Your Inventories

Most companies, when they go on an economy kick—when they want to squeeze cash out of the system—look first to inventories. In terms of TCM, the assets called inventory on the balance sheet represent an investment of cash. Whether it is raw material, work in process, or finished goods, the assets can be converted back to cash by selling the product to end users—your customers.

Finished goods are seemingly easy to convert to cash. Just keep up the same level of sales but maintain lower inventory levels. Put another way, speeding up the turnover of finished goods inventory definitely releases cash for other purposes.

Work in process inventory may be hard to reduce much. But it usually represents a relatively small portion of total inventories, with a few exceptions, such as aircraft and shipbuilding on one hand or aging whiskey on the other. If nothing else, the limiting factors on work in process are the physical space in the factory and the need to finish existing orders to make room for the next items on the schedule.

Raw materials inventories, invariably acquired from other firms, can also be reduced by working with suppliers to achieve some sort of just-in-time deliveries. Four shipments per month, once each week, instead of one large delivery will definitely increase turnover. Looked at the other way, average inventory levels, in that category, will be reduced by more than half.

While these approaches to reducing inventories and releasing cash appear very common-sense-oriented, they may not be a real panacea for the cash-starved firm. Inventories, as we saw in Chap. 4, perform a useful function. Finished goods at a distant warehouse location provide rapid customer response. Closing the warehouse and consolidating the inventory with another location will definitely free up inventory. But the question has to be answered, "What will happen to sales?"

The essence of TCM is a *total* systems approach. You cannot change inventory levels in a vacuum, but have to look at the impact on both production efficiencies and customers. Maybe in an ideal world, orders could come in for a variety of products. And products could be made to order quickly and at low cost, and shipped out with no longer lead time than any competitor. The term *mass customization* popularizes this concept. Unfortunately neither the equipment nor the technology is available today to achieve this goal. As long as we have significant investments in yesterday's production techniques, we will continue to need inventories.

We can request four shipments a month instead of one from a supplier, and this will reduce funds tied up in inventory. But what is the impact on inbound freight cost? Or on paperwork processing, including purchasing, receiving, and accounting? The truth is that inventory levels represent a tradeoff between operating efficiencies (ordering infrequently in larger amounts) and dollars invested. If you were ordering hand-to-mouth every week, someone would suggest fewer but larger orders to *save* money! Reducing inventories to save money is a great idea, but automatically focusing on just one variable in the equation has led many companies to reverse direction quickly after the full impact of the decision became clear.

Unlike receivables, where an increased level of effort on the telephone is going to bring in cash (just as a result of the effort itself), there are no corresponding easy answers when it comes to inventories. The worst of all worlds is the arbitrary top down edict: "Thou shalt reduce inventories by 10 percent within 90 days." When the goal is put that way, any competent manager can accomplish the task on a short-term basis. If the only goal is the level of inventories, and management is unaware of the collateral costs incurred in terms of customer reaction or increased operating expenses, then most managers will start to live hand-to-mouth on the high-volume items that are really in demand. Thus finished goods inventories of fast moving items will be cut, at the expense of possible stock-outs. Materials inventories will be reduced, but at the expense of increased freight costs and possibly the loss of volume discounts offered by suppliers. When it comes to arbitrary edicts, there is indeed more than one way to skin a cat.

The only way inventories can meaningfully be reduced is to apply the techniques of Total Quality Management, which involve process mapping, followed by cross-functional teams empowered to make real changes in the way the business is run. The results of redesigning the inventory system can show up fairly quickly and are usually permanent. Virtually every business firm can obtain a high return on investment for the management time invested to accomplish each meaningful change.

Doing business the same old way and expecting to permanently cut inventories is impossible. Doing business in a new way is very possible and will lead to permanent inventory reductions. Unfortunately there is no magic bullet to be shot at the problem of inventories. Anyone who finds such a solution has his or her fortune made.

Meet with Your Bank

One of the key tenets of Total Cash Management is the need for flexibility. It is impossible to forecast cash receipts or cash disbursements accurately. TCM involves not only *reducing* cash requirements, but at times *increasing* cash requirements through specific investments, either in assets or in expense items like R&D and advertising. It is poor business practice to keep large amounts of cash on hand (even if invested in money market securities). To obtain the necessary financial flexibility, some source of outside funds is essential, and in our society commercial banks perform that function.

Contrary to popular myth, banks *are* in the business of lending money, and they are prepared to take some prudent risks; otherwise they would only buy U.S. government securities. Every loan a bank has ever made had some degree of risk, so you cannot say bankers are unwilling to accept risk. It all boils down to the perceived *level* of risk they see in your business.

In the final analysis lenders do not really look to collateral for repayment; after all, they don't want to collect your receivables, sell your inventory, or dispose of your production equipment at auction. Banks make their decision based on their evaluation of the competence of your management and the realism of your business plans. You demonstrate competence by showing them realistic plans, that is, annual budgets, followed up with subsequent monthly or quarterly financial statements that track that budget.

A track record of reasonably accurate budgets, even if you occasionally miss, is all right. Nobody bats 1000. The secret is in keeping the bank informed, of both good news and bad news. Human nature is such that everyone likes to pass on good news quickly, whereas the tendency is not to tell anyone about bad things because, "Maybe it will get better soon." But what if it gets worse?

"I can take bad news, but I can't take surprises" is sound advice fo anyone, but particularly for those dealing with banks and financial institutions. Put yourself in the bank officer's shoes for a moment. Realistically, what are the chances that everything will always go well for every one of her customers? The answer, of course, is zero. What are the chances that at any point in time some of her customers are going to be having a hard time—whether it is due to bad luck, bad management, or tough competition? The answer, of course, is almost 100 percent. Therefore, the fact that *you* are having a business problem is no surprise, because if it weren't you it would be someone else. If no company ever had business problems, would there be much of a demand for bank loans?

What the banker really wants to know is if *you* are truly on top of your business. What plans do you have to solve this problem? How long will it take? What is going to happen to your cash flow in the meantime? Remember, banks make their profit by taking deposits and making loans with them. Like two blades of a scissors, they need both deposits and loans.

They will always get deposits, if only from day-to-day working cash balances. What they need and want are borrowers, but borrowers who know what they are doing and have a very high probability of repaying any loans. No problems, no loan demand.

So having a business problem and being up-front with the banker is actually good news to him. It means you are looking ahead, gauging what will happen in the future, and minimizing any surprises. If you walk in on a Wednesday asking for cash to meet a payroll on Friday, what does that tell the bank officer about your ability to manage your business? If she is surprised—which means you were surprised too—the message is one that no bank officer wants to hear. How can a management team take decisive action if they themselves are surprised at a sudden need for cash? If you don't know where you are going (and any road will take you there), that's fine. It is just that the banker does not want to be a traveling companion!

If you are just starting to implement a Total Cash Management program, the second thing to do is to communicate with your banker. The first, of course, is to develop a comprehensive plan of action. Discussing the plan with the bank, pointing out its strengths, and admitting where weaknesses might exist, will help to put the bank on your team. Bank officers are evaluated by the growth and profitability of the customer accounts assigned to them. A company that has specific growth objectives, realizes that the availability of cash is an essential ingredient of those growth plans, and is doing everything it can on its own to accomplish TCM represents a unique situation—because not many firms have adopted TCM. If you were a bank officer, wouldn't you like to have a portfolio of firms that understand the importance of cash and are taking positive steps towards a specific goal? Wouldn't you be tempted to help those firms, through an appropriate line of credit, to achieve their objectives?

To summarize this section, remember that cash flows and cash balances fluctuate, making them very hard to forecast. Flexibility is needed. Bank loans represent the cheapest and easiest form of financial flexibility. Put yourself in the bank officer's place, and provide the bank with current monthly, quarterly and annual financial statements. They can take the bad news with the good news. Whenever you develop a new business plan or budget, go over it with the banker. Make the banker a partner, with a vested interest in your success.

Focus Everyone on Cash, Not Profits

"Get top management buy-in." Every book on management, every article in *Harvard Business Review*, every speech on new techniques repeats this mantra. Installing Total Cash Management certainly requires top management involvement, because it represents a *change*, both in policy and in actions. If ever a new approach represented a paradigm shift (to use the currently popular phrase), going from a focus on reported net income (as calculated by accountants) to a focus on *cash* represents such a shift.

People perform well when they are being measured. Analyze the cash impact of proposed actions, and then measure the actual results against the plan. This is the best way of communicating the new priorities. Actions speak louder than words. So plants, divisions, or operating units that accomplish their cash objectives have to be rewarded. Managers who fail to meet cash targets must be penalized, one way or the other.

The switch in emphasis from reported income, as calculated by accountants, to cash as the measure of performance will not come naturally. At first it will appear to be an "unnatural" act, particularly the first time a plan is proposed that will improve cash flow, but will lower reported earnings. One example is a recommendation to dispose of very slow moving spare parts inventories. A small amount of cash will be raised from their sale to the scrap dealer, and some warehouse space will be freed up. But the big win comes in a major tax write-off, saving cash otherwise to be paid to the IRS. The price to be paid is the requirement that the reduction in the inventory carrying value be shown as a charge to net income this period: cash up, reported income down.

Top management approval is also required when the cash being invested is visible but the returns are hard to identify. One example is a recommendation to grant credit to marginal customers. The increase in receivables will show up right away. The gross profit from the increased sales, most of which will be positive cash flow, has to be offset against any increased credit losses. Run as an experiment, with careful monitoring, the actions can be measured. Without such a monitoring system, however, it is hard to separate sales, receivables, bad debt write-offs, and operating expenses of normal sales and the incremental sales derived from the more aggressive cash-oriented policy.

A third area requiring top management's willingness to break the rules is the requirement to spend extra cash today to achieve favorable operating results tomorrow. The accounting requirement that all advertising and all research and development expenditures be written off right away definitely inhibits many managers. They may know that an engineering project holds great hope for a breakthrough new product and resort to a skunkworks mentality. When the accounting system forces conscientious employees to work off the books, this should be a wake-up call. Total Cash Management prevents this, since the immediate cash outlays for the new project are clearly specified. Far better to budget the expenditure openly, get the total resources needed to complete the project timely, and coordinate all the firm's resources.

It is no surprise that many large well run firms are today starting to measure cash returns in operating units, often compensating managers on the basis of the cash generated, not accounting income. The thing that must be guarded against is viewing cash through a one-way mirror. As every entrepreneur knows, you have to spend money to make money. Putting total emphasis on cash inflows can be just as dangerous as focusing on maximizing next quarter's net income. *Total* Cash Management involves outflows just as surely as inflows.

Don't Just Reduce Cash Outflows—Spend to Grow

In this final chapter we must reinforce a theme that has run throughout the book. Total Cash Management it not just a series of techniques to *minimize* cash balances in bank or to take advantage of discontinuities in the banking and postal system, or to lean on vendors by delaying payment. Many writers have covered these points well, and in this book we too have gone back to the basics of what is usually thought of as cash management. *Total* Cash Management is far, far more pervasive than a mere list of tips and techniques for corporate treasurers.

Minimizing cash balances so that a firm can have more funds to invest in the money market has always seemed like a contradiction in terms or, to use the currently prominent phrase, an oxymoron. If you want to be in the investing business, start a bank, an insurance company, or a mutual fund. There you get paid for your skills as a money manager. Daily you pit your skills against thousands of others, each trying to beat the Dow Jones Average or the Treasury bill rate. The amount of money under management and your relative performance make up the basic scorecard.

But America was not built on money management. Somebody has to *produce*. Agriculture, manufacturing, and the distribution of goods and services are the only things that build real wealth. Once profits have been earned productively, it certainly makes sense to keep the wealth. But managing money does not *create* wealth.

What is paramount is to utilize productive resources for growth and expansion. Any firm that can make more for its shareholders by investing in the money market than it can in its basic business needs to rethink its mission. We submit that there are practically no product lines without growth potential. Growth requires investing resources now, in the hope of recovering the amount of the investment plus a profit in the future. The primary resources to be invested are two: financial and management.

That is why, in discussing capital investment decisions in Chap. 12, we stated that the limiting factor is often managerial, not financial. It takes time and effort to design and implement most major investment programs in property plant and equipment, and the people charged with responsibility for any one program usually have other day-to-day responsibilities. Building a new factory or even installing an N/C machine tool requires a lot of time and effort, as well as the financial resources.

While a lot of management and academic effort has gone into trying to improve the capital expenditure process for PP&E, designing and implementing a marketing program for a new product also involves cash resources and management time and effort. In this instance different individuals are involved, but exactly the same thought process *should* be used. A new marketing program is an investment. The only difference is in the accounting and budgeting.

PP&E is reported as a fixed asset and shows up on the balance sheet. Most firms strictly control who can authorize and approve the amounts to be spent. But when it comes to marketing programs, the control point is the budget. And the budget is usually limited by the impact of any program on the Profit and Loss Statement. An advertising program, for example, is always charged to expense by accountants, and the extension of credit to marginal customers may also result in a charge to expense, in this case bad debt expense.

From the perspective of Total Cash Management, there is *no difference* between buying a $200,000 machine tool or committing to a $200,000 advertising program. Investing $400,000 in additional inventory at a new warehouse location involves risk of future inventory write-offs, just as selling $400,000 of product to a new group of customers involves risks of future bad debt write-offs.

Cash is cash. How the accountants treat the way it is spent should be absolutely irrelevant to making the decision. The basic thesis of this book, and of Total Cash Management as a concept, is that every organization has growth opportunities requiring cash resources and, of course, management time. There may be no easy way to rank the relative importance of an investment in a machine tool, a new advertising program, or the inventory at a new warehouse. Conceptually, they should each be submitted to the rigors of a Discounted Cash Flow analysis.

In practice, the machine tool would be examined in excruciating detail in many firms, with calculations in some organizations carried out to the third decimal place. The inventory decision would be made on the basis of the availability of funds, perhaps with little analysis because inventory is an asset, not an expense. The advertising program, if it were in the approved profit plan for the year, would get no scrutiny, as long as the amount was comparable to previous years.

We submit two points. First, the *same* techniques can be and should be utilized in reviewing each of these operating plans. Second, if the principles of Total Cash Management have been followed, there probably are sufficient cash resources available to do all three of the projects. Cash should not be the limiting resource. Finding good ideas and having sufficient management time are the real limiting factors. Get the cash, and don't let obsolete accounting rules distort the decision process. Whether an item is capitalized or expensed has no impact on future cash inflows resulting from that investment, other than the timing of related taxes. And companies that run their business on the basis of taxes, not real operations, are headed for disaster.

Budgeting and Forecasting Cash Flows

It could be argued that many firms spend too much time on preparing the annual budget or profit plan. Some organizations start the process as early as May for the following year's January 1 budget. The cycle of presentations, reworks, approvals, consolidations, more approvals, and other activity, is often counterproductive. Of course, if the alternative is *no* budgeting (seat-of-the-pants management), a firm may be in big trouble if the founder or boss ever takes her eye off the ball. Indeed, many large and growing firms don't have a formal budget process, and many of them are quite successful. Budgeting per se is neither good nor bad. Too little and a company can get out of control quickly. Too much and the internal process can become more important to individuals than meeting and dealing with customers— those people who send us cash in exchange for our output.

This discussion, however, assumes that:

1. The reader's organization is preparing an annual budget.
2. The budget goes through a normal review process.
3. The budget is the basis of allocating overall resources to accomplish growth and profit objectives.
4. The budget is used to measure management performance in meeting those objectives.

Points 3 and 4 are vital for Total Cash Management. The annual budget or profit plan is where most of a firm's basic strategic and operating decisions are really made. As we saw in Chaps. 10 and 11, a budget must be *integrated*. That is, the sales goals must be matched by production capabilities, new product introductions must be achievable based on engineering timetables, capital expenditures and hiring plans must tie in with operating assumptions, and so forth.

Almost without exception companies prepare their top-level budgets— the plan that is approved by the CEO and the Board of Directors—using

the same format as the published monthly and quarterly financial statements. In short, the emphasis is almost always on reported profit and loss,
measured by accrual accounting. The forecast balance sheet is then usually
a residual result of the projected operating results. Rough rules of thumb
are used to estimate ending receivable and inventory balances, usually in
relationship to overall sales growth; if sales are expected to go up 5 percent
from the current year, then ending receivable balances are plugged in at
a 5 percent higher rate. The same holds true for inventory levels and
often accounts payable. The balance (the difference between begin-
ning-of-the-year asset balances plus anticipated profit for the year and
end-of-the-year balances for all assets taken together) is an assumed
level of borrowing.

This approach, so common in practice, is an effective means of controlling resource commitments that are not constrained. That is, if you are not
attempting to use the maximum amount of cash available and are assuming
that sufficient borrowing power is available to meet any required balance,
then the traditional budget will be as good as any. It certainly is easy to
measure management performance against such a budget.

What if your major competitor, however, is using the concepts of Total
Cash Management in its strategic planning and budgeting. By squeezing
out excess cash from low-priority uses and redeploying those same resources into growth and profit areas, even a smaller competitor will soon
begin to capture market share. If he is then able to finance further growth
from utilizing additional borrowing capacity—that is, he assumes a more
aggressive posture in terms of financial leverage—growth rates are going
to start to diverge sharply.

The solution has to be to adopt Total Cash Management in your own
organization, budgeting specific operating plans against the test of
whether they use or generate cash. The term *economic value added* (EVA)
has recently assumed a place in the business press. Essentially it is no more
than adopting the concepts of Total Cash Management and then paying
management on the basis of achieving those goals.

As we saw, there is really no distinction in economic terms between
investing in a marketing program and investing in fixed PP&E. The
purpose of Total Cash Management is *not* to discourage such investments. In fact, they should be encouraged, because that is the only
way growth will come about. What TCM does is focus on *cash* as one
of the two limiting resources, the other being management time and
skills. Let's assume management can be hired, given that cash is
available to pay the going compensation levels. If you had to make a
choice between good management depth and not enough cash or the
opposite (plenty of cash resources and thin management), the latter
would be a much more comfortable position. It is easier for a
$25-million firm, with a $3-million line of credit already established,

to call up a headhunter and hire two top-flight regional sales managers than it is for the same firm to suddenly raise an extra $1.5 million in cash from its bank. The latter might well take two years of planning and working with the bank to instill confidence. Hiring the sales managers could be done in six months.

So we assume that cash is the limiting resource affecting growth and profit opportunities, it makes sense then, to test *every* significant budget decision for its impact on cash, record this as part of the budgeting process, and then measure performance against that goal during the year. Traditional budgeting puts a premium on having a cushion in the budget, and then coming in under budget in expenses and over budget in sales and profits. TCM, on the contrary puts a premium on sound spending plans, and then would fault a manager for not accomplishing that task. Better to open the new warehouse on time and even have a small overrun on expenses or inventory level than to delay the investment—just to look good on a quarterly P&L.

The secret is to decide what you really want to accomplish during the budget year, plan as realistically as possible for the cash impact, plus or minus, and then monitor that the plans are carried out on schedule. This does not mean blindly following a budget if external conditions truly change. It is amazing how often excuses are found to justify not accomplishing something that was committed to. If a positive decision is made not to go forward with a planned action, and everyone concurs, so be it. Not getting it done and then apologizing doesn't cut it. The concept here was well put by Bruce Marlow, chief operating officer of Progressive Insurance: "We never punish failure. We only punish sloppy execution and the failure to recognize reality." From Michael Hammer's book, *Reengineering the Corporation* [p. 106]

Report Cash Flows

If you have established sound objectives for the Total Cash Management program, and have then developed the budget or profit plan to capture these plans, then developing a reporting mechanism for measuring progress is easy. Essentially the monthly reports should follow the same format as the budget.

TCM puts more of an emphasis on cash flows and less on income and expense as ordinarily reported. The world has not yet adopted TCM, although the accounting profession has endorsed the concept in terms of mandating a separate statement of cash flows in all published financial statements. A typical statement is shown in Fig. 15.1, taken from the Newell Company 1992 Annual Report.

CONSOLIDATED STATEMENTS OF CASH FLOWS

Year Ended December 31, (IN THOUSANDS)	1992	1991*	1990*
CASH FLOWS FROM (FOR) OPERATING ACTIVITIES:			
Net income	$ 119,137	$ 135,637	$ 125,502
Adjustments to reconcile net income to net cash provided from operating activities:			
Cumulative effect of accounting change	44,134	–	–
Depreciation and amortization	53,881	44,924	43,347
Deferred taxes	(14,914)	(4,143)	(3,750)
Net (gains) losses on:			
Marketable securities	(8,616)	(2,127)	(26,404)
Sale of businesses	(82,945)	–	6,533
Write-off of intangible assets	11,664	1,953	9,197
Other	(4,377)	(119)	(1,774)
Changes in current accounts, excluding the effects of acquisitions and sale of businesses:			
Accounts receivable	39,010	95,208	3,864
Inventories	26,715	(6,592)	13,843
Other current assets	1,043	(5,190)	(4,230)
Accounts payable, accrued liabilities and other	53,505	(23,088)	(1,593)
Net Cash Provided from Operating Activities	238,237	236,463	164,535
CASH FLOWS FROM (FOR) FINANCING ACTIVITIES:			
Proceeds from issuance of debt	181,320	145,000	–
Proceeds from exercise of stock options and other	9,038	6,452	5,043
Payments on notes payable and long-term debt	(168,513)	(85,469)	(54,168)
Cash dividends	(46,261)	(40,300)	(33,054)
Redemption of stock	(15)	(9,000)	(3,962)
	(24,431)	16,683	(86,141)
CASH FLOWS FROM (FOR) INVESTING ACTIVITIES:			
Acquisitions	(177,317)	(5,700)	–
Expenditures for property, plant and equipment	(77,613)	(59,149)	(42,054)
Purchase of marketable securities, net	–	(10,872)	(10,446)
Purchase of other investments	(11,930)	(181,116)	–
Sale of businesses	–	–	8,197
Sale of marketable securities	72,879	–	–
Disposals of noncurrent assets and other	(18,060)	(1,525)	(5,415)
	(212,041)	(258,362)	(49,718)
Increase (Decrease) in Cash and Cash Equivalents	1,765	(5,216)	28,676
Cash and cash equivalents at beginning of year	42,512	47,728	19,052
Sanford decrease in cash in December, 1991	(16,269)	–	–
Cash and Cash Equivalents at End of Year	$ 28,008	$ 42,512	$ 47,728

Restated to include the merger with Sanford Corporation, which has been accounted for as a pooling of interests (see Note 2).
See notes to consolidated financial statements.

21

NEWELL CO. AND SUBSIDIARIES

Figure 15.1 Statement of total cash management for the month.

Several points of interest should be noted. The accountants have decreed that this statement should tie out to the accrual-based statement of income, so the top line is the reported net income. To arrive at an amount called *net cash provided from operating activities* the company adds back depreciation and amortization and write-offs of intangibles, so-called "non-cash charges." Disregarding the deferred taxes—which hardly anyone understands—and the gains on sales of marketable securities and sales of businesses, we get down to the important adjustments.

Newell's heading "changes in current accounts:" shows four lines, for (1) receivables, (2) inventories, (3) other current assets, and (4) accounts payable and accrued liabilities. These are the important differences discussed in the book. A first observation is that for the year 1992 the company *added* $120,273,000 to its cash flow—more than net income since cash flow is bigger than net income.

The next point to consider is that having a positive cash flow from accounts receivable can come about either from better collection efforts, a reduction in days sales outstanding for the same level of sales, or from reduced sales. Since on a year-to-year comparable basis sales went up 5 percent, the reduction in receivables necessary to generate $39 million must be attributed totally to better receivables management.

The $26,715,000 cash generated by a reduction in inventories also must be related to production levels throughout the year, and could be analyzed in terms of raw materials, work in process, and finished goods. From data elsewhere in the annual report it appears that work in process was reduced, perhaps because of successful implementation of just-in-time production methods.

The $53,505,000 cash provided from operating activities attributed to accounts payable and accrued liabilities really reflects a slowdown in payables, perhaps negotiated with vendors and possibly associated with increased purchases near the end of the year. If accountants try to be conservative and allow for future expenses this year they accrue liabilities, which has the effect of reducing reported income but does not represent a cash outlay until the amounts are actually paid out—perhaps many years in the future in the case of environmental liabilities. Combining the payables and accrued liabilities together makes it difficult to gauge or assess management performance. Since accountants can be as aggressive as they wish in thinking up possible liabilities to accrue, each dollar accrued reduces income but has no effect on current cash outflows.

In the third and last section, cash flows from investing activities, the only important figure for our purposes is the $77,613,000 for "expenditures for property, plant, and equipment." This, of course, is a direct cash outlay, but does not appear in the statement of net income because it is capitalized as an asset. What is significant is to relate the amount spent on *new* PP&E to the depreciation expense charged on *old* PP&E, in this case the $53,881,000 shown as depreciation and amortization in the first section, cash flows from operating activities. As with most growing and profitable firms, expenditures are very likely to be greater. In fact, how is a company to grow and expand if it does not increase its investment in capital assets? That is why you have to have a positive cash flow—to provide the resources for this type of expansion.

We have illustrated the analysis with a real-life statement of cash flows for three reasons. First, to demonstrate that the recently adopted FASB standard format for this important information can be used for analysis. Second, to show that companies and their accountants are at least paying lip services to the importance of *cash*. The third reason for displaying the Newell statement—which is as good an example as you will find—is to show the *differences* between information for shareholders and that needed for management. This is not a criticism. The format of the *published* statement starts right at the top with net income and then proceeds to decompose the various elements affecting cash to get to the bottom line—defined as the change in cash and cash equivalents for the period shown. Contrast the Newell statement with our Fig. 15.1.

For true *management* purposes, TCM has to start with a budget of what you want to accomplish, and then measure progress against that objective. For example, reporting on cash collections on receivables—the top line and a very important part of TCM—will combine the effectiveness of the collection effort with changes in sales volume. If sales the previous month were higher than expected, and average days sales outstanding (DSO) is 45 days, then in the ordinary course of events one would expect more cash to come in this month. So a measure of cash receipts, compared to budget, might show a healthy trend in absolute dollars, but really reflect poorer collection *efforts*. That is why we also show the DSO.

To complicate the situation just one step further, suppose we were using the extension of credit as a sales tool to introduce a new product, as discussed in Chap. 3. Then we would *expect* DSO to increase, but correspondingly so should the billings.

It is impossible to design a single all-purpose report when dealing with cash that can accurately report on all the permutations and combinations of TCM. If we are going to use cash as a strategic tool—and we should—it will involve doing some things more efficiently to squeeze cash out of the system while at the same time investing cash elsewhere.

The secret is anticipating what the cash effect of proposed actions will be. Then the forecast column can be adjusted appropriately and actual results measured against that forecast as well as against the original budget or profit plan for the year. As discussed in Chaps. 10 and 11, it is absolutely essential that the budget or profit plan for the year be cast in concrete and not changed. It is equally important to retain operational flexibility and the best way to do this is to revise the forecast as often as necessary.

"What you measure is what you get" is never more true than when it comes to cash flows. If you measure and report cash flow information—and top management reinforces this message through promotions and by paying bonuses based on achieving cash flow goals—then TCM can become operational. Before going on to rewarding performance, one point must be put under stress again.

The goal of TCM is *not* just trying to reduce cash invested in receivables, inventories, and fixed assets, or in stretching out payables to take advantage of vendors. The goal is to utilize cash, the lifeblood of the business, as effectively and efficiently as possible. This involves wise *investments* in productive assets. There is no simple one-line measure of progress. Judgment in investing has to be matched by judgment in evaluating results.

Pay Bonuses Based on Cash Flows

Someone once observed that there are two basic emotions that motivate people: fear and greed. In the long run, managing by fear can be counterproductive. Managing by greed sounds worse than it is. Suppose we said instead that we should motivate employees by giving them a financial reward if they perform. That *sounds* better, but still is based on the very common observation that people work for money, and that many people will work harder and smarter if they earn more money in meeting your objectives. This is not the place for a recap of MBO (managing by objectives), but one of the basic criticisms of MBO has been that it is subject to gaming because people set out objectives that are meaningless and easy to meet.

If, however, one of the primary objectives for a period (one, two, or three years) is to maximize cash resources, and then invest the cash in expansion opportunities, this *can* be reported on and *can* be measured. It is hard to argue with cash. Even highly trained and creative accountants have a hard time playing games with cash. Sales can be accrued, even before shipments are made to customers. Expenses can be capitalized. Earnings can be manipulated. Cash is the one hard, tangible asset—it is either there or it isn't.

If a firm budgets on the basis of cash flows, reports performance internally on the basis of cash flows, and pays bonuses based on meeting those cash flow targets, then Total Cash Management will truly be internalized. Since the firm's interests will coincide with that of every employee, profitable self-sustaining growth can be achieved.

Get the cash. Invest it wisely. Grow the business and generate more cash flow. Instead of a vicious cycle down into bankruptcy, which faces firms that run short of cash—a virtuous cycle of cash flow, growth, and more cash flow can be developed.

In point of fact, the history of every profitable growth firm has followed this pattern. It is just that when things are going well, in practice, people tend to forget the critical role played by cash. We described in Chap. 1 that cash was the lifeblood of the business. Every successful business proves this over and over again. Companies do not split their stock and raise their dividend unless there is good cash flow, and the promise of more to come. It can be done. It has been done. Follow the suggestions in this book and you *will* do it.

Total Cash Management truly is a technique that works.

Good Luck.

Index

About the Author

Alfred M. King is senior vice president and director of Valuation Research Corporation. He was formerly managing director of the 90,000-member Institute of Management Accountants, and oversaw that association's education, publication, and research activities. He has written more than 35 articles for professional journals and holds an MBA in finance from Harvard Business School.